GERMAN SCHOLARS AND ETHNIC CLEANSING

D1598730

GERMAN SCHOLARS AND ETHNIC CLEANSING
1919–1945

✦ ✦ ✦

Edited by

Ingo Haar

and

Michael Fahlbusch

Foreword by

Georg G. Iggers

Berghahn Books
NEW YORK • OXFORD

Published in 2005 by
Berghahn Books

www.berghahnbooks.com

© 2005 Ingo Haar and Michael Fahlbusch
First paperback edition published in 2006

Library of Congress Cataloging-in-Publication Data

German scholars and ethnic cleansing (1919–1945) / edited by Ingo Haar
and Michael Fahlbusch; foreword by Georg G. Iggers.
  p. cm.
Includes bibliographical references.
ISBN 1-57181-435-3 (alk. paper)
  1. Political culture—Germany—History—20th century. 2. Germany—
Ethnic relations. 3. Germany—Race relations. 4. Racism—Germany—
History—20th century. 5. Genocide—Germany—History—20th century.
I. Haar, Ingo. II. Fahlbusch, Michael.

DD238.G39 2004

2004047674

British Library Cataloguing in Publication Data

A catalogue record for this book is available from
the British Library.

Printed in the United States on acid-free paper

CONTENTS

✦ ✦ ✦

FOREWORD

———————— ✦ ✦ ✦ ————————

Georg G. Iggers

It is striking how little has been done in West Germany to examine the role of the historians in the Nazi period and their participation in the genocide, much less so and much later than in some other academic disciplines. The leading historians in the post-1945 period emphasized that the bulk of German historians continued to be honest scholars and remained aloof from the regime. Werner Conze, one of the most important historians and mentors of the post-1945 generation of West German historians, still commented in 1983 that "a serious confrontation [*Auseinandersetzung*] with Nazi historiography was not necessary because the few Nazi historians had either died or lost their positions,"[1] overlooking his own important role in the planning of ethnic cleansing in the East and the elimination of the Jews. Two historians of an older generation who played eminent roles in the West German historical profession after 1945, namely, Gerhard Ritter, who was arrested after the 20 July 1944 attempt against Hitler, and Hans Rothfels, who was removed from his professorship under the Nazis because of his Jewish parentage and forced to emigrate and thus could lay claim to having been victims of the Nazi regime, assured the German public that with very few exceptions historians during the Nazi period had maintained their scholarly integrity.[2] This overlooked that their own ultranationalist and antidemocratic views coincided with a great deal of the Nazi outlook. Both had been outspoken opponents of the Weimar Republic, wanted an authoritarian state, and endorsed German foreign policy aims after 1933. Ritter a conservative, who did not accept many aspects of Nazi ideology, nevertheless supported the war against the Soviet Union to safeguard European Christian culture, and volunteered in 1944 to lecture to the troops in France, where he told them that the French should take Prussia as a model and learn to "starve and obey" (*großhungern und gehorchen*)[3] if France was to regain its nationhood. Although he was already aware of the early phases of the Holocaust, a memorandum, forwarded under his signature in January 1943 to the anti-Hitler opposition group around Carl Goerdeler, argued that Jews must not be permitted to regain the rights of German citizenship that they had acquired in the course of the nineteenth century.[4] Rothfels, despite his Jewish origin, was close to Nazi positions of ethnic expansion in the East and left Germany only very reluctantly after his applications for honorary Aryan status were turned down despite Joachim von Ribbentrop's support. All this points at areas of consensus between a broad spectrum of established historians and National Socialism.

Yet just as there was the image of the clean Wehrmacht innocent of war crimes, there was also the picture of an academic discipline that kept apart from the Nazi Party and pursued "objective" scholarship. Still relatively recently a dissertation written at the University of Frankfurt argued that there was an inseparable gulf between the conservatism of the broad majority of German historians and Nazi ideology, and that as a rule the historians remained faithful to their scholarly ethos.[5] Even researchers who were aware of the support given to the Nazis by historians who played an important role in the West German historical profession after 1945 had not realized the extent to which many historians were directly involved in Nazi plans for ethnic cleansing and genocide.[6]

The great contribution of this volume is that for the first time it makes available to an English reading public the results of the extensive scholarship of the last decade and a half on the role that German scholars played in the programs of ethnic cleansing. A good deal of new material became available with the opening of East German archives after 1989, but already much had been readily accessible in West German archives and simply ignored. It is also striking how little East German scholarship utilized the sources on this topic contained in its archives. A first important work on the role that scholarship played in the planning of ethnic cleansing was published in English, Michael Burleigh's *Germany Turns Eastwards: A Study of Ostforschung in the Third Reich*.[7] A first careful analysis of the politics of German historians appeared in 1992 in Karen Schönwälder's *Historiker und Politik. Geschichtswissenschaft im Nationalsozialismus*.[8] Yet the most pioneering work in this direction was Götz Aly and Susanne Heim's *Vordenker der Vernichtung* in 1992, published in English in 2002 as *Architects of Destruction: Auschwitz and the Logic of Destruction*.[9] Drawing on documentation that had been largely neglected, Aly and Heim reject interpretations that identify Nazi leaders as primarily responsible for the Holocaust and show to what extent demographers, geographers, economists, civil servants, and academics were involved in the planning. The 1990s increasingly saw studies that dealt with the role of the historians. In 1992 Karl-Heinz Roth and Angelika Ebbinghaus discovered a previously secret document in which Theodor Schieder, shortly after the fall of Poland in 1939, had prepared and edited a protocol that called for the deportation of hundreds of thousands of Poles and the "dejewification" (*Endjudung*) of Poland.[10] Writings by Werner Conze between 1936 and 1944 went in a similar direction.[11]

An important contribution of Ingo Haar's dissertation *Historiker im Nationalsozialismus*,[12] published in 2000, and also of the present collection of essays edited by him and Michael Fahlbusch, is that they do not concentrate on individual historians, although they deal with them, but examine the institutional basis of the scholarship serving Nazi policies of ethnic cleansing and the genocide of the Jews. They establish a clear continuity between this scholarship before the Nazi rise to power, during the Nazi period, and after 1945. The origins of the *Ostforschung* (research on the East) of the Nazi period are to be found when a movement of young neo-conservative intellectuals, historians, sociologists, and ethnographers outside academe began in the 1920s to create a *Volksgeschichte*[13] as an alternative and as a challenge to the established academic historiography with which, in fact, these young historians shared many political attitudes. For both, a prime task of the historian was the revision of the borders created by the Versailles Treaty. Both were passionately opposed to the parliamentary democracy of the Weimar Republic, which they sought to replace with authoritarian government, and strove to restore Germany's position as a major power, and both for the most part were outspoken anti-Semites. Yet there were fundamental differences. The historiography that had dominated the German universities since the last third of the nineteenth century saw the state as the key institution in history, specifically the German national state as it had been forged by Bismarck, with its semi-autocratic aspects distinguishing it from Western European democracies. They proclaimed an ethos of objective, impartial scholarship, although in fact their scholarship was highly ideological, nationalistic and socially conservative.[14] Clinging to a classical historical outlook (*Historismus*), they rejected any approaches that replaced the focus on leading individuals and political events, and vigorously rejected the turn to social history in the historiographies of Western countries as nonidealistic and collectivistic, even Marxist.

But on three important points the new *Volksgeschichte* differed emphatically from the established historiography that it considered outdated. For it, the center of history was the *Volk*, conceived not as a people in a democratic sense but as an ethnic community in biologistic, racial terms. In the place of the struggle between states for hegemony, the young neo-conservatives now saw an embittered conflict between ethnic communities and posited the cultural and racial superiority of the Germans over all other ethnic groups in Eastern, and for that matter also in Western, Europe. They now radicalized the political assumptions of the academic historians for whom Germany was a political unit whose natural borders were those of 1914, possibly with the addition of post-1918 Austria, and sought an expansion of German borders far to the East to include all territories where

German minorities lived as well as others that at one time or other had had German populations. Eastern Europe, they argued, was overpopulated, and room would have to be found to settle Germans by removing non-Germanic populations. Instead of a Germany ruled by conservative elites, the young neoconservative historians wanted one based on the broad masses governed by charismatic leaders. Thus, there very soon arose an affinity to the National Socialist movement, and after 1933, and in some cases already before, many joined the Nazi Party.

Like the academic establishment, the advocates of *Volksgeschichte* emphasized the role of scholarship. For them, however, its aim was not to establish the results of objective inquiry but to serve as a means for ethnic struggle, as a *"kämpfende Wissenschaft"* or a fighting science. This science was to establish the ethnic compositions of areas and communities in the East, their historical development, the conditions of life, family patterns, occupations, structures of authority, and cultural patterns. This history rested heavily on demographic, geographic, and economic studies based on statistics, thus asserting its character as an empirical science, superficially similar to the innovative *histoire totale* that the *Annales* circle was pursuing in France, but with a totally different aim. At its core was a Social Darwinian pseudo-science of race, the purpose of which was to identify German and non-German populations and to classify the latter for separation and ultimate removal. An idea that became prominent in the 1930s, as propagated by Theodor Oberländer and Werner Conze, was that the East was overpopulated and that it was necessary to remove "surplus populations" of Slavs and Jews to make room for German settlement.

As has been noted, to begin with the practitioners of *Volksgeschichte* were largely outside academic institutions. Their major, but by no means exclusive, focus was *Ostforschung*, research about Germans in Eastern Europe. True both the government of the Weimar Republic, guided by Gustav Stresemann's policy of achieving revisions of the Versailles Treaty by peaceful negotiations, and the Social Democratic-led Prussian government distanced themselves from the extremism of the neoconservative *Ostforschung*. But the position of the government toward this ultraradical movement of ethnic scholars was marked by contradictions. Officials from the Foreign Ministry and the Ministry of Interior welcomed studies that would throw light on the assimilation of German minorities in Poland, the Baltic states, and Czechoslovakia after 1918, and on their emigration from these countries, in such a way as to strengthen its arguments for border revisions. Governmental money thus began to support the research of the *Volk* historians. The Leipziger Stiftung für deutsche Volks- und Kulturbodenforschung (Leipzig Foundation for Research for Ethnicity and Land Cultivation), founded in 1926, funded the scholarship of specialists from the government as well as advocates of a radical ethnic approach. The extreme ethnicist direction of the foundation was soon brought under control, and it was dissolved in 1931. But the integration of extreme ethnicists into the academic institutions had begun. At the University of Königsberg, with Hans Rothfels and the sociologist Gunter Ipsen as mentors and Theodor Schieder and Werner Conze as their students, proponents of *Volksgeschichte* received a firm academic basis. After the Nazi accession to power in 1933, the institutionalization of racial ethnic research took off. Between 1931 and 1934 the *Volksdeutsche Forschungsgemeinschaften* (ethnic German research societies), a scientific network with up to a thousand members in at least six regional branches, were founded as an umbrella organization to finance and coordinate this research on a national scale. The most important was the Nord- und Ostdeutsche Forschungsgemeinschaft (North and East German Research Society) in Berlin. Increasingly, representatives of this racial historiography and of related social sciences entered the universities, mostly younger scholars eager to pursue career opportunities. Now large-scale projects were funded with public money and increasingly controlled by the Nazi Party. The Nazis made use of the racist scholarship, which lent its services gladly.

The essays in this book trace the path of this scholarship from its early attempts to legitimize German claims to the East through scholarship which claiming to be scientific to the role this scholarship played increasingly after 1933 and particularly after the conquest of Poland in 1939 and the invasion of the Soviet Union in 1941—in the Nazi program of ethnic cleansing and the annihilation of European Jews. Two of the main themes of these essays are the institutionalization of *Ostforschung* after 1933 and the specific tasks it carried out in the expulsion of Poles and others and the genocide of Jews and Roma. Ingo Haar outlines the main themes of the volume, the role that demographic and historical studies played in defining ethnic groups and in laying the foundations for segregation and ultimately expulsion or annihilation. By collecting demographic data on the composition of Eastern European areas, the *Ostforscher* participated directly or indirectly in the segregation of ethnic groups in the Eastern areas and in the deportation and genocide of the Jews. Haar examines the role of a number of historians, such as Theodor Schieder, Werner Conze, and Hermann Aubin, who in a scholarly capacity contributed to the Nazi program. The know-how developed in the North and East German Research Foundation found direct application after 1941 in Nazi practices. Michael Fahlbusch describes the highly organized network in which *Ostforschung* and *Volkstumsforschung* were carried out in collaboration with the SS. He thus refutes postwar accounts that maintain that *Landes-* (regional) and *Volksforschung* had been conducted in a serious, scientifically innovative way and had not been subject to Nazi infiltration and control. A multiplicity of research programs that were created after 1933 were closely coordinated during the war and after 1943 fully subordinated to the SS. An increasing number of scholars were integrated into the programs, in many cases in newly created university positions. The

North and East German Research Society, with its staff of 150 by far the largest of the research groups, active in the course of the 1930s, controlled more than 400 research projects. But there were also other large research foundations, such as the West German Research Society and the Southeast German Research Society, headed by Otto Brunner, who too was to play a major role after the war, first in Vienna and then at the University of Hamburg, and whose research group participated directly in ethnic removals in the Balkans.

The chapters that follow deal with research groups as they related to the transfer of populations with the aim of germanization and genocide in various areas surrounding Germany. Again, demographic and historical studies defined members of ethnic groups in order to carry out the program for replacing of non-German populations far beyond the borders of Germany with German settlers. In their chapter on the ethnographic research of Georg Leibbrandt and Karl Stumpp in Ukraine, Eric J. Schmalz and Samuel D. Sinner make an important point, citing Michael Burleigh on *Ostforschung:* "Deportations, resettlements, repatriations, and mass murder were not sudden visitations from on high ... but the result of the exact, modern, 'scientific' encompassing of persons with card indexes, card-sorting machines, charts, graphs, maps and diagrams."[15] For most of World War II, Leibbrandt functioned as a high official in the political department of Alfred Rosenberg's Ministry for the Occupied Territories. By late 1941 he was making top-level policy decisions concerning the liquidation of Eastern European Jews, and in January 1942 he attended the Wannsee Conference, which planned the implementation of the "Final Solution." Stumpp prepared extensive studies of villages intended for ethnic exterminations in Ukraine. Alexander Pinwinkler's chapter deals with Erich Keyser's activities in basing *Ostforschung* on a history based on the study of population along ethnic lines in specific spatial areas. As early as the 1920s he considered the history of population to be an appropriate instrument for restoring Germany's lost position as a superpower. Keyser's history, as Pinwinkler shows, rested on the invention of pure myths that envisioned a Germanic population that dated back basically unchanged to very early times. From the beginning *Volk* and *Raum* were irrevocably connected with each other. One of the basic principles of his work is the supposed social and racial opposition of Germans and Jews since the Middle Ages. The chapter by Christof Morrissey highlights the Institut für Heimatforschung (Institute for Local Research), which started as a modest center for the study of German culture in Slovakia but was soon integrated into the vast network that prepared the research groundwork for German expansion and ethnic cleansing. Michael Wedekind addresses the research intended to prepare the way for Germany's ethnic cleansing and annexation of areas in Slovenia and Northern Italy in the predominantly Italian regions of the Trentino. In his examination of Nazi occupation policy in Northern Italy,

Wedekind points at the leading role played by experts from the Southern branch of the scientific network, the Alpine Research Society. The Carinthian and Innsbruck institutes for regional research (*Landeskunde*) worked especially closely with the SS.

Viorel Achim's essay, "Romanian-German Collaboration in Ethnopolitics: The Case of Sabin Manuilă," goes in a somewhat different direction from the other essays in the volume, which all deal with Nazi-directed studies aiming at the displacement of non-German minorities in Eastern, Southeastern, and Western Europe to make room for German settlement and the physical elimination of Jews and Gypsies. Manuilă, whose main area of expertise was ethnic demography, had specifically Romanian goals in mind. Achim stresses that he was no Fascist and was perceived before and after the war as a democrat. Nevertheless, his demographic studies were intended to achieve an ethnic homogenization that would cleanse Romania of non-Romanian ethnic groups, which would be removed to the surrounding countries—to Yugoslavia, Bulgaria, Ukraine, and Hungary—with borders redrawn along ethnic lines. Germans and Turks would be repatriated and Jews and Romany deported to Ukraine, which actually happened, and where most perished. Manuilă was a close adviser to Antonescu on population questions. He conducted a study of the number of Jews in Romania on the basis of the 1930 census, which he used generally for his ethnic studies, and concluded that the Jewish population was close to 750,000, not the up to 2.5 million that far right circles claimed. At the same time he argued that the Romanian Jews constituted a threat to Romania, not because of their numbers, but because of their economic power, constituting a qualitative rather than a quantitative problem. He maintained close contact during the war with German demographic statisticians, particularly Wilfried Krallert, the director of the Publications Office (Publikationsstelle) Vienna, which focused on Romania and Hungary. Like most of his German colleagues, he did not experience any postwar consequences of his wartime activities; in fact, he became a leading member of the National Peasant Party, on which, according to Achim, Romanians pinned their hopes for a democratic future.

The chapters by Wolfgang Freund and Hans Derks turn to *Westforschung*, which worked to legitimize the removal of French populations in large areas of Walloon Belgium and Northeastern France that at one time supposedly were inhabited by Germanic Franks. Freund deals with Fritz Braun, who from 1936 to 1945 directed an institute for Saarland and Palatine local studies following racist lines. Soon he expanded his activities into occupied France and participated in the newly founded Institute for Research on Region and *Volk* in Metz while almost one hundred thousand French-speaking people and all Jews were expelled from Lorraine. Braun was then also involved in the settlement and extermination program in Poland. The Nazi regermanization policy was supported scientifically by kinship group information furnished by his institute and used for the selection of population. Hans Derks focuses primarily on Franz Petri, who in close cooperation with the military occupation in Belgium conducted racial population studies for the reorganization and germanization of populations in Belgium and Northeastern France. *Westforschung* was started at the University of Bonn directly after World War I. Petri worked closely with Hermann Aubin and Peter Steinbach, who after 1939 became important in the population studies and the ethnic relocation planning in the East. The essay by Eric Kurlander deals with Otto Scheel, of an older generation, from Schleswig Holstein, who even before World War I had supported ultranationalist, often *völkisch* policies. Although he had originally combined liberal reforms with racist exclusion, including virulent anti-Semitism, he placed himself fully into the service of the Nazis after 1933. Frank-Rutger Hausmann follows the establishment of cultural institutes in the countries occupied by, or like Bulgaria or Hungary, dominated by Nazi Germany to propagate the Nazi "scientific" doctrines as well as in a small number of neutral countries. Finally there is the essay by the Polish scholar Jan M. Piskorski, who surveys German *Ostforschung* as it emerged in the 1920s aiming to provide "scientific" proof of Germany's right to a major part of Polish territory, and the Polish response of a *Westforschung* (*myśl zachodnia*), admittedly less widespread and with less governmental support, which sought to establish historic claims to territories up to the Elbe River once inhabited by Slavs who were forcefully germanized. Karl Heinz Roth's chapter presents a biographical, political sketch of the same Hans Rothfels we have already discussed, who played an important role in the emergence of a school of ethnic, expansive historiography and who, after he had been designated as a Jew and forced into emigration while, returned to Germany to play an important role in the reconstitution of the historical profession in post–World War II Germany.

But the story does not end here. Whereas in East Germany there occurred a virtually complete exchange of elites, there was virtually none in Western Germany after 1945. The historical profession was no exception. Thus, almost all of the historians and other scholars involved in the Nazi planning and carrying out of programs of ethnic cleansing and extermination were restored to important positions in the western half of Germany soon after the end of World War II. The essays in this volume document the continuity. Theodor Schieder and Werner Conze became the two most important mentors in training a new generation of West German historians between the mid 1950s and the mid 1970s. They did in fact move away from their *völkisch* positions, especially Conze, who now advocated a history that focused on the social structures of a modern industrial society. A new generation of historians, among them Hans-Ulrich Wehler, Wolfgang Mommsen, and Hans Mommsen, who received their university education in the Federal Republic as students of Schieder and Conze, and in Hans Mommsen's case also of Rothfels, applied the concepts of modern social history to a critical examination of the German past. Winfried Schulze, in a study published in 1989 on German historiography after 1945, saw the new social history as an outgrowth of a denazified *Volksgeschichte*, a history that abandoned the dependence on race but in contrast to the old historicism preserved a broadly social perspective. But this overlooked that the new critical historians were emphatically democratic in their perspective, indebted to historians from a different tradition who while not Marxists, borrowed from Karl Marx an emphasis on social inequality and social conflict and were mindful of the close relation between economic and political power relationships as seen by Max Weber, and who had been influenced by the democratically oriented historians of the Weimar Republic such as Eckart Kehr and the exiled Hans Rosenberg, and by the Critical Theory of the Frankfurt School. Yet the ethnic demographic perspective on which both *Ostforschung* and *Westforschung* rested was by no means dead. Now Hans Rothfels, Theodor Schieder, Werner Conze, and Theodor Oberländer, in a major compilation sponsored by the West German government, documented the expulsion of the Germans from the East[16] without adequately dealing with the context of German genocidal practices that had led to it. Almost all the other scholars dealt with in this volume again took up population and *Heimat* studies and founded or refounded institutes dedicated to these studies. Petri at Bonn and Fritz Braun in Kaiserslautern took up *Westforschung* again, though they would no longer speak of the revision of borders. On the other hand, the Herder Institute in Marburg, founded in the 1950s with Erich Keyser, as director, followed the older tradition of *Ostforschung* and was committed to revising the post-1945 borders of Germany.

It is striking, as the essays in the volume point out, that from 1945 until the early 1990s there was complete silence about the criminal activities of the scholars involved in the planning for ethnic cleansing. Their colleagues honored them as committed scholars who had not misused their research to aid the Nazi cause. Theodor Oberländer served in Konrad Adenauer's cabinet as Minister for Expellees. Karl Stumpp was a close adviser to Adenauer on Russian affairs. Several of these scholars were awarded the *Bundesverdienstkreuz* (Federal Cross of Honor) for their scholarly and patriotic contributions to Germany. Still more surprising is that their students, who were committed to a democratic Germany, declined to question their mentors on their past. It took a new generation of scholars to raise these questions on the basis of new materials, some of which had been available before but not utilized. As Nicolas Berg points out in an extensive study published in 2003 on how historians in the Federal Republic dealt with the Holocaust, there was a conscious attempt to shield scholars who had been deeply involved in the Nazi regime.[17] The Holocaust was seen as a horrendous crime carried out from the top by the party but not involving the broad masses of scholars who remained dedicated to honest scholarship. The reaction of the students of Conze and Schieder, when confronted with the evidence, was to defend them. As Hans-Ulrich Wehler argued, notwithstanding their involvement in the Third Reich, his mentors were able to learn after 1945 and to make significant, innovative contributions to historical science.[18] Wehler suggested that if we cannot forgive Schieder and Conze for their involvement with the Nazis, then neither can we forgive Edward P. Thompson for his membership in the British Communist Party,[19] forgetting that Thompson was not an accomplice to ethnic cleansing and genocide and left the Communist Party in protest of the Soviet suppression of the Hungarian uprising.

Nevertheless, the involvement of German scholarship in the Third Reich has finally become a burning issue to which the German Historians' Congress (Historikertag) devoted a special session in 1998. In 1997, the American historian Charles Maier had admonished his German colleagues at the first conference in Berlin of the Center for Comparative Social History to critically confront their mentors. If they were unwilling to do so, he warned, the task would be left to non-historians. We no longer need to fear today that historians will shy away from critical examination of the past of their discipline and from the broader problem of the ways in which historians and social scientists have permitted themselves to become instruments of those in power. Yet because this question of an alliance between professional scholarship or science and those who control society and the state is not restricted to Nazi Germany but recurs in other modern societies as well, it should be a subject of serious study. The controversy about the complicity of German historians under National Socialism is by no means over. Passionate debates rage even today between those like Heinrich August Winkler, who wish to exonerate their mentors, and those like Ingo Haar and the contributors to this volume, who through a careful analysis of the sources engage in a critical examination of how historians and other social and humanistic scientists actually functioned under the Nazi dictatorship. Most frequently this debate has been reflected in the efforts of Heinrich August Winkler, a student and defender of Hans Rothfels, to discredit Ingo Haar's research on the role that the German historical profession played in the Nazi regime, and in Haar's defense of this research.[20]

Notes

1. Cited in Götz Aly, "Theodor Schieder, Werner Conze oder Die Vorstufen der physischen Vernichtung," in *Deutsche Historiker im Nationalsozialismus*, ed. Winfried Schulze and Otto Gerhard Oexle (Frankfurt am Main, 1999), 178.
2. See Gerhard Ritter, "Der deutsche Professor im Dritten Reich," *Die Gegenwart* 1, no. 1 (24 December 1945): 23–26, and Ritter, "Deutsche Geschichtswissenschaft im 20. Jahrhundert," *Geschichte in Wissenschaft und Unterricht* 1 (1950): 81–86, 129–137; Hans Rothfels, "Deutsche Geschichtswissenschaft in den 30er Jahren," in *Deutsches Geistesleben und Nationalsozialismus*, ed. Andreas Flitner (Tübingen, 1965), 90–107. Rothfels here suggests that professional historians were generally uninvolved in Nazi historiography, which had the support of only a handful of "rabid secondary teachers [*wildgewordene Studienräte*] and outsiders." See also Rothfels, *The German Opposition Against Hitler* (Chicago, 1948).
3. Werner Berthold, *"… großhungern und gehorchen" … Zur Entwicklung und politischer Funktion des westdeutschen Imperialismus untersucht am Beispiel von Gerhard Ritter und Friedrich Meinecke* (Berlin, 1960).
4. Klaus Schwabe, ed., *Gerhard Ritter, ein politischer Historiker in seinen Briefen* (Boppert am Rhein, 1984); see "Denkschriften des 'Freiburger Kreises,'" ed. Rheinhard Herd, Anhang 5 "Vorschläge für eine Lösung der Judenfrage in Deutschland," 769–774.
5. Ursula Wolf, *Litteris et Patriae. Das Janusgesicht der Historie* (Stuttgart, 1996).
6. Even if I was not aware of this, when I mentioned in my study of the German historical professions the active support that historians, whom I named, had given to the Nazi Party, but did not realize the extent to which they had contributed through their scholarship to the planning of the relocation of non-German populations and the destruction of the Jews. See Iggers, *Deutsche Geschichtswissenschaft. Eine Kritik der traditionellen Geschichtsauffassung von Herder bis zur Gegenwart* (Munich, 1971), 318–328.
7. Michael Burleigh, *Germany Turns Eastward: A Study of Ostforschung in the Third Reich* (Cambridge, 1988).
8. Karen Schönwälder, *Historiker und Politik. Geschichtswissenschaft im Nationalsozialismus* (Frankfurt am Main, 1992).
9. Götz Aly and Susanne Heim, *Vordenker der Vernichtung. Auschwitz und die deutschen Pläne für eine neue europäische Ordnuing* (Frankfurt am Main, 1992), in English, *Architects of Destruction: Auschwitz and the Logic of Destruction* (Princeton, 2002).
10. Angelika Ebbinghaus and Karl Heinz Roth, "Vorläufer des 'Generalplans Ost.' Eine Dokumentation über Theodor Schieders Polendenkschrift vom 7. Oktober 1939," 1999. *Zeitschrift für Sozialgeschichte des 20. und 21. Jahrhunderts* 7 (1992): 62–94; see also Aly, "Theodor Schieder, Werner Conze," 163.
11. See Aly, "Theodor Schieder, Werner Conze," 181, notes 34–40.
12. Ingo Haar, *Historiker im Nationalsozialismus. Deutsche Geschichtswissenschaft und der "Volkstumskampf" im Osten* (Göttingen, 2000).
13. Willi Oberkrome, *Volksgeschichte. Methodologische Innovation und völkische Ideologie* (Göttingen, 1993).
14. Georg G. Iggers, *The German Conception of History: The National Tradition of Historical Thought from Herder to the Present* (Middletown, 1968), does not contain the section on the Nazi historians cited above in note 6.
15. Burleigh, *Germany Turns Eastwards*, 10.
16. *Dokumentation der Vertreibung der Deutschen*, 7 vols., published by the Federal Expellee Ministry (Bundesvertriebenenministerium), of which Theodor Oberländer was minister. Chief editor was Theodor Schieder in "association" (*Verbindung*) with Hans Rothfels, Peter Rassow, and Rudolf Laun, and beginning with vol. 3 also Werner Conze (Berlin, 1953–1960).
17. Nicolas Berg, *Der Holocaust und die westdeutschen Historiker. Erforschung und Erinnerung* (Göttingen, 2003).

18. Hans-Ulrich Wehler, "Nationalsozialismus und Historiker," in Schulze and Oexle, *Deutsche Historiker im Nationalsozialismus*, 306–339, and Wehler, "Historiker sollten auch politisch zu den Positionen stehen, die sie in der Wissenschaft vertreten," in *Versäumte Fragen. Deutsche Historiker im Schatten des Nationalsozialismus*, ed. Rüdiger Hohls and Konrad Jarausch (Stuttgart and Munich, 2000), 240–266.

19. Wehler on Thompson and Eric Hobsbawm in *Frankfurter Allgemeine Zeitung*, 4 January 1999.

20. See Heinrich August Winkler, "Hans Rothfels—ein Lobredner Hitlers? Quellenkritische Bemerkungen zu Ingo Haars Buch 'Historiker im Nationalsozialismus,'" *Vierteljahrshefte für Zeitgeschichte* 49 (2001): 643–652; Ingo Haar, "Quellenkritik oder Kritik der Quellen," *Vierteljahrshefte für Zeitgeschichte* 50 (2002): 497–506; Winkler, "Geschichtswissenschaft oder Geschichtsklitterung. Ingo Haar und Hans Rothfels. Eine Erwiderung," *Vierteljahrshefte für Zeitgeschichte* 50 (2002): 636–652.

PREFACE

✦ ✦ ✦

In the twentieth century, border conflicts, ethnic cleansings, and genocidal policies altered the landscape of Europe. Examining Nazi population policies in occupied Europe, this volume attempts to shed light on the crimes of that century by considering them not only as barbaric acts, but also as a component of modernity.

Standing prominently in the foreground, alongside statesmen and confirmed murderers, are humanities scholars. In fact, science and politics constituted mutual resources for each other. Humanities scholars not only sanctioned state actions, but also contributed fundamentally to the process of placing border and population conflicts onto the political agenda. They constructed minority groups by using ethnic-racial classifications, supplied statistics and cards in order to delimit the groups, and employed their expertise in order to segregate whole peoples—going so far as to support genocide.

Academically certified specialists were and are a sought-after resource in politics. This volume presents the most recent research results regarding how the knowledge of experts in the pre-1945 era came to be applied to the resettlement and genocidal policies of the National Socialists, how this knowledge was organized, and which consequences followed its application. From this perspective, National Socialism is to be understood not only as a return to barbarism, but simultaneously as the most radical orientation of the European idea of the national state.

The editors sincerely thank Marion Berghahn and the many historians in the United States who supported us in this work, or who stood ready to offer advice on how to make such a volume, up to now noticeably lacking in Germany, accessible to an English-speaking public. We are grateful to Shawn Kendrick for her unlimited patience while resetting the manuscript with short notice, to Nadine Mette for preparing the index, and to the contributing authors, all of whom were committed in their collaboration to the end of the project.

— *Ingo Haar and Michael Fahlbusch*

ABBREVIATIONS

◆ ◆ ◆

AA	German Foreign Ministry (Auswärtiges Amt)
AFG	Alpine Research Society (Alpenländische Forschungs-gemeinschaft)
AHSGR	American Historical Society of Germans from Russia
ANIC	Arhiva Naţională Istorică Centrală
AWLV	Working group of West German Research on Region and People (Arbeitsgemeinschaft für westdeutsche Landes- und Volksforschung)
BArch	Bundesarchiv
BayHStA	Bayerisches Hauptstaatsarchiv, Munich
BayKM	Bavarian Ministry for Cultural Affairs
BDC	Berlin Document Center
BDO	League of the German East (Bund Deutscher Osten)
DAF	German Labor Front (Deutsche Arbeitsfront)
DAI	German Foreign Institute (Deutsches Ausland-Institut)
DDP	Democrats (Deutsche Demokratische Partei)
DeVlag	Deutsch-Flämische Arbeitsgemeinschaft
DFG	German Research Foundation (Deutsche Forschungs-gemeinschaft)
DNVP	German National People's Party (Deutsch Nationale Volkspartei)
DP	Deutsche Partei
DPO	Deutsche Post aus dem Osten
DSB	Deutscher Schutzbund
DVG	German People's Community (Deutsche Volksgemein-schaft)
DVL	German National List (Deutsche Volksliste)
DWI	German Cultural Institutes (Deutsche Wissenschaftliche Institute)
E.K.I	Iron Cross First Class
EWZ	Central Immigration Office Lodz (Einwandererzentrale Litzmannstadt)

FstR	Research Office of the Russian Germans (Forschungsstelle des Russlanddeutschtums)
Gestapo	Secret State Police (Geheime Staatspolizei)
GRHS	Germans from Russia Heritage Society
GStAPK	Geheimes Staatsarchiv Preußischer Kulturbesitz
HMP	Historisches Museum der Pfalz, Speyer
ICS	Central Institute of Statistics (Romania)
IHF	Institute for Local Historical Studies (Institut für Heimatforschung)
KE	Carpathian German Teachers Corps (Karpatendeutsche Erzieherschaft)
NAGN	Algemene Geschiedenis der Nederlanden
NL	Nachlaß (unpublished works left by an author)
NOFG	North East Ethnic German Research Society
NS	National Socialism
NSDAP	National Socialist German Workers' Party
NSDStB	National Socialist German Students League (Nationalsozialistischer Deutscher Studentenbund)
OEFG	East European Research Society
PA	Politisches Archiv des Auswärtigen Amtes
PCM	Preşedinţia Consiliului de Miniştri
P-Stelle	Publication Office (Publikationsstelle)
RFSS	Reichsführer SS
RKF	Reich Commissioner for Strengthening Germandom (Reichskommissar für die Festigung deutschen Volkstums)
RMI	Reich Ministry of Interior (Reichsministerium des Innern)
RMO	Reich Ministry for the Occupied Eastern Territories (Reichsministerium für die besetzten Ostgebiete)
RMVP	Reichs Ministry for Propaganda
RSHA	SS Reich Security Main Office (Reichssicherheitshauptamt)
SD	Security Service (Sicherheitsdienst)
SHB	Schleswig-Holsteiner Bund
SOFG	Southeast German Research Society (Südostdeutsche Forschungsgemeinschaft)
VDA	League for Germans Abroad (Volksbund für das Deutschtum im Ausland)
VDR	Association of Germans from Russia (Verband der Deutschen aus Rußland)
VoMi	SS Ethnic German Liaison Agency (Volksdeutsche Mittelstelle)
WFG	West German Research Society (Westdeutsche Forschungsgemeinschaft)

Chapter 1

GERMAN *OSTFORSCHUNG* AND ANTI-SEMITISM

◆ ◆ ◆

Ingo Haar

The subject of *Ostforschung*, German academic research on Eastern Europe in the Weimar Republic and Third Reich, would seem to have been exhausted in the historiography. Yet a closer glance brings to light a certain conceptual insecurity. On the one hand, historians have described the discipline as a "success story" that developed and applied innovative methodologies.[1] On the other hand, *Ostforschung* has come to stand for a politically compromised research agenda that disqualified itself through active participation in the National Socialist program to "germanize" East-Central Europe.[2] In order to better understand the role *Ostforschung* played in National Socialist policies, historians must transcend the conceptual boundaries of considering the subject simply as an isolated academic discipline or from a political-institutional standpoint alone. Rather, they should understand *Ostforschung* as a scholarly discipline that operated in the context of a dynamic political situation—a situation that *Ostforscher* consciously intended their discipline to help shape. One concrete aspect of *Ostforschung* on which to orient a study on the interplay between politics and scholarship is anti-Semitism.

When intellectual historians analyze the development of a "school of thought," they need to investigate complex connections between the creation of paradigms and changed patterns of thought, on the one hand, and the development of academic research agendas and their grounding in institutions, on the other.[3] Professionalized academic disciplines based in and connected to universities are products of a long historical development. Despite their reputation as breeding grounds for new scientific approaches, universities rarely promote truly innovative research. In the Weimar Republic, new research agendas could only compete with more

Notes for this chapter begin on page 21.

traditional university-based programs through the support of research foundations outside the universities.

Historians should therefore concentrate not only on *Ostforschung*'s development as an academic discipline, but above all on its origins during the Weimar Republic as a research agenda geared toward political consulting. The rise of *Ostforschung* was inseparably tied to the establishment of *völkisch* concepts, which defined the *Volk* as a "community of blood," within Weimar's secret anti-Versailles revisionist circles. Yet it was not until the National Socialist takeover that *Ostforschung* became established as an academic discipline rooted in universities. Under these auspices, German *Ostforscher*'s anti-Semitism and their role in National Socialist crimes need to be reexamined.

The German *Volks- und Kulturboden* and the Leipzig Foundation, 1922–1931

After Versailles, many former citizens of the German Reich found themselves living in the new states of East-Central Europe. Right-wing parties in Weimar Germany wanted to instrumentalize former Reich citizens' dissatisfaction with their new minority status to further their own revisionist aims. According to these revisionists, Germans had a "special mission" to resist absorption into the "successor states," regardless of whether those states relied on subtle or more brutal integration methods. As part of the Weimar Republic's clandestine revisionist policies, German minorities received political, economic, and cultural support. The continued presence of unassimilated German minorities in the states of East-Central Europe seemed the best guarantee for an eventual revision of Versailles and restoration of German hegemonic power in the region.[4] In order to evaluate the integration policies of "enemy states" and prepare possible countermeasures, the "functionary elite" of *Deutschtumspolitik* (German minority policy), situated just below the ministerial level in the Foreign and Interior Ministries, began supporting a new research agenda focused on ethnic group issues in the East in 1924. In support of their minorities policy, the Stiftung für deutsche Volks- und Kulturbodenforschung (Foundation for Research on German Ethnicity and Land Cultivation) was established in Leipzig in October 1926. Minority policy experts in the Reich ministries consulted with selected social scientists and scholars from the humanities in an effort to understand how social communities function in ethnically diverse regions and how ethnic differences could be manipulated to stabilize or destabilize international borders.[5]

The program of *Volks- und Kulturbodenforschung*[6] took advantage of established statistical and cartographical research strategies. In addition, participating scholars constructed arguments around a racial concept of the *Volk* as a "community of blood" to provide an ideological basis for border revision policies. The newly invented term *Volks- und Kulturboden* implied that an ethnic group establishes itself in a fixed zone of settlement whose peripheries dissolve into ethnically mixed zones. German *Volksboden* (the soil in which an ethnic group is anchored) in areas bordering Poland and Czechoslovakia was to be protected by "internal colonization" measures, specifically by erecting a "settlement wall" of German peasants there. The *Volks- und Kulturboden* agenda integrated racialist models for a "reordering" informed by population policy; the purportedly homogenous German *Volkskörper* (ethnic body) was to be stabilized or at least reestablished in areas where formerly German-speaking populations were considered to have already been assimilated. German *Kulturboden* referred exclusively to areas inhabited not by German but usually by Slavic ethnic majorities and whose German inhabitants had historically played an important cultural and economic role.[7]

The political ambiguity of such a doctrine is evident. Weimar foreign minister and chancellor Gustav Stresemann built his revisionist policy on a peaceful balance between the European states. He demonstrated his support for the liberal post–World War I European order by engineering Germany's entry into the League of Nations.[8] The intellectual strategists of so-called ethnopolitics, on the other hand, spoke in favor of eventually gaining a new hegemony for the German Reich in *Mitteleuropa*, and their pursuit of this goal included efforts to instrumentalize minorities policy in the near term. Max Hildebert Boehm, for example, proposed reservations for the German minorities in Eastern and Central Europe in order to prevent their integration into the new states. Through an "irredenta," Boehm argued, the German minorities had to destabilize the existing political order so that the German Reich could intervene. Boehm called for the establishment of a "Greater German Empire."[9]

In debates among the Leipzig scholars, a division across that ran straight across the various political camps became evident. One group was reconciled to the existence of the new states and wanted to pursue a legally based minority policy with the help of the League of Nations. Another group looked for chances to intervene politically in order to destabilize Germany's neighbors. Whereas the foundation's manager, geographer Wilhelm Volz, supported the view that Germany's "natural space" corresponded with the German and Austrian borders of 1914,[10] geographers Albrecht Penck and Friedrich Metz resurrected Germany's expansionist objectives of World War I.[11] For this reason they came into serious conflict with the Prussian Ministry of Interior, which had no interest in allowing an adventurous minorities policy to cause diplomatic tensions.[12]

Albrecht Penck, along with Karl Christian von Loesch, Karl Haushofer, and Max Hildebert Boehm, put no stock in diplomatic conflict resolution. Loesch assumed that both the Weimar constitution and the peaceful European order that Stresemann sought through Germany's entry into the League of Nations blocked Germany's ascent to a hegemonic position in Europe. As a proponent of the idea of the "Greater German Empire" he demanded the "reannexation" of Austria and was concerned about the ethnically "endangered areas in the North and East on both sides of the border." The creation of a continental European customs union between Austria and Germany had to be completed before a "reordering of European issues" could take place. The termination of the Versailles system should constitute a new order of nationalities in Europe under the predominance of Germany. Loesch hoped to solve the problems of "overpopulation," of the "ethnic hodgepodge" and the "primitive-brutal conceptions of the state" in the Eastern and Southeastern European states. He regarded the German minorities living in those regions as "raw material" that needed Reich support in its efforts to maintain its "Germandom."[13]

The view that occupation of foreign territories required not only colonial economic exploitation and enforcement of an internal legal order but also population policy measures was a new feature of the program developed by Penck, Loesch, Haushofer, and Boehm. They foresaw the need to exercise control down to the lowest level, including neighborhoods in villages and towns, achieved through a policy of *völkischer* border security, the precondition for which would be ethnically homogenous communities with stable social orders.[14] Before this new settlement policy could be implemented, *Ostforscher* would explore ethnic conditions on both sides of the German border. All cultural and social sciences sharing the doctrine of the *Volkstumskampf* (struggle for ethnic heritage) would contribute to this "sociography" of Germandom. The German minorities living in Central Europe would be counted with statistical methods and their settlement areas would be recorded in comprehensive mapping projects and encyclopedias.[15]

The invention of *Volkstum* as a research agenda intended to support the ethnic segregation of Europe was completed by the end of the 1920s. By contrast, the process of establishing university-based disciplines of *völkischer Wissenschaft* (*völkisch* scholarship) and new institutions of political consulting got underway only during the mid 1930s. Before 1933, *völkisch* research programs lacked academic legitimacy. In 1929, Prussia's Social Democratic Interior minister Carl Severing subjected the work of the Leipzig Foundation to greater parliamentary control because the foundation had been increasingly infiltrated with extremist right-wingers. The historian Walter Goetz, a Reichstag member, democrat, and declared League of Nations supporter,[16] became supervisor of the Leipzig Foundation.[17] The institutionalization of *Ostforschung* could not prevail against the will of these *Vernunftrepublikaner* (republicans of reason). Friedrich Meinecke and Hermann Oncken, as well as Wilhelm Volz, committed themselves to liberalism and to the borders of 1914. These "statists" loyal to Weimar managed to block *völkisch* aspirations in the leading Prussian historical institutions until the early 1930s.[18]

Although the mostly young geographers, sociologists, and historians who participated in *Volks- und Kulturbodenforschung* failed to become part of established historical or geographical publications and research councils before 1933, they received support from the Prussian Notgemeinschaft der Deutschen Wissenschaft (Emergency Community of German Science), the predecessor of the German Research Society founded in 1934 by the Reich Ministry of Interior. This official backing ensured a relatively safe position from which to wait out the removal of republican hindrances to *völkisch* scholarship that followed the Nazis' "seizure of power." In fact, a majority of academic consultants who started their careers after 1933 came directly from the Leipzig Foundation or had at least received funding through the foundation. Werner Essen, who as Karl Haushofer's student had compiled the first statistics on the ethnic makeup of the Baltic states,[19] became a specialist in the Reich Ministry of Interior's department of *Grenzziehung und Volkstum* (borders and ethnicity) in 1934. Essen worked his way up to become special assistant to State Secretary Wilhelm Stuckart, until promoted in 1941 to head the division for "settlement and race policy" in the Generalkommissariat Ostland (Office of the General Commissioner for the Eastern Territories).[20]

The geographer Emil Meynen, who as Albrecht Penck's intimate in the Leipzig Foundation edited the *Handwörterbuch für das Grenz- und Auslandsdeutschtum* (Encyclopedia of Border Area and Foreign Germandom), later coordinated the activities of the Volksdeutscher Forschungsgemeinschaften (Ethnic German Research Societies). As a leading member of Georg Leibbrandt's staff, Meynen set up the Publikationsstelle Ost (Publication Office East) in the political department of Alfred Rosenberg's Reich Ministry for the Occupied Eastern Territories (RMO). In that capacity, he served as liaison between ethnic researchers and the settlement and race policy experts of the SS agency Volksdeutsche Mittelstelle (Ethnic German Liaison Agency, charged as of 1938 with politically coordinating all ethnic German minorities in Europe) and in the Foreign Ministry.[21] Leibbrandt, who between 1928 and 1930 had visited the United States and Soviet Union to study German emigrants through the procurement of the Leipzig foundation, took over the NSDAP's "Foreign Policy Office" in 1933. Following his appointment to head the main political section of the RMO in 1941,[22] Leibbrandt represented Rosenberg at the Wannsee Conference in January 1942.[23]

"Fighting Scholarship" and the Genesis of *Ostforschung* within the North East Ethnic German Research Society

After the National Socialists assumed political power in 1933, the researchers of the Leipzig Foundation found themselves in a stronger position vis-à-vis the reigning historicist school. Their agenda, based on catch-phrases such as *Volkstum, Lebensraum* (living space), *Volk ohne Raum* (people without space), and *Volksboden*, got its first serious chance to establish itself.[24] The political radicalism of Hans Rothfels and his students in Königsberg seriously rattled the strong position of Friedrich Meinecke and Hermann Oncken in the historical profession. In 1932, one year before the National Socialist "seizure of power," Rothfels staged his first confrontation with Meinecke. Rothfels ostentatiously declined to participate in a meeting of the Historical Commission for the Reichsarchiv (the Reich's central archive) on 8 March 1932. Rothfels opposed the projects of Veit Valentin and Martin Hobohm, who sought to chronicle the emergence of the Weimar Republic. Rothfels denounced Valentin as an unqualified historian and rejected his project, a compilation of sources from the republic's early years, warning that "academic tasks that are extremely urgent today might take second place." Therefore, according to Rothfels, it would be "almost impossible" to "tackle those problems (German minorities in foreign countries, recent history of colonization in the east, etc.) relevant to today's foreign policy in terms of the defensive intellectual struggle (of the German minorities against other ethnic groups) and which have or might have a role to play in promoting national unity."[25] Rothfels complained that "all opportunities are blocked" for the "best-educated academic youth," by which he meant his own students.[26] Rothfels saw National Socialism first and foremost as a chance to institutionalize the new *Volksgeschichte* (ethnic history) on a broad basis within specially conceived research facilities.

Rothfels' students took advantage of Max Hildebert Boehm's concept of a "self-sufficient people" to appropriate new tasks for the historical profession in the National Socialist regime's Eastern policy. Boehm's catalogue of criteria that characterized the "self-sufficiency" of a people, meaning their ethnic homogeneity, was open to racist social planning techniques. These would help identify both *Volksgenossen* (ethnic comrades) and *Volksfremde*, those "alien" to the German ethnic body.[27] Young historians organized in the Verein für das Deutschtum im Ausland (League for Germans Abroad or VDA) Königsberg working group demanded a radical change of policy. They proposed steps to stop the migration of the rural population from eastern Germany to the industrialized regions of the West. Economic migration should be diverted to areas inhabited by *Grenz- und Auslandsdeutschtum* (ethnic Germans in border areas and foreign countries).[28] This political model for "reordering" the "front from Bucharest to Reval" dovetailed with the expansionist and racist programs of Leipzig Foundation geographers who supported National Socialism.[29]

Völkisch-minded historians' affinity for National Socialism was evident, even though their views diverged on the matter of anti-Semitism. In a radio address on the occasion of the Nazi takeover, Rothfels stated somewhat didactically that history should not be interpreted as the result of a "race-based original disposition."[30] Like his student Theodor Schieder, Rothfels promoted a voluntaristic conception of race.[31] Under this model, racialist categorizations depended on the preparedness of non-German ethnic groups in Eastern Europe to submit to the rule of a German "Third Reich." The Königsberg historians dreamt of a confederation of peoples under German direction. They promised protection for the Baltic ethnic groups if these chose German domination over Soviet rule.[32] Notwithstanding this subtle but important distinction in their respective interpretations of race and its meaning to society, the Königsberg historians were eager to participate in the new regime after 1933.

The price the Königsberg historians had to pay for their establishment as experts in National Socialist settlement and population policy was high. Hans Rothfels was forced to give up his position in Königsberg because of his Jewish descent, despite the interventions of Hermann Rauschning, the National Socialist president of the Danzig Senate, and of Theodor Oberländer, who directed the Bund Deutscher Osten (League of the German East or BDO), as well as the NSDAP's East Prussian intelligence service, which was concerned with questions of Germandom in border areas and foreign territories.[33] Although as a World War I veteran Rothfels could have continued his official duties up to a point, he was unable to keep his position in the political consulting institution that succeeded the Leipzig Foundation. Internally, the NSDAP leadership justified Rothfels' removal with a reference to the future function of the Königsberg historians. They were to assume a central role in National Socialist settlement and population policy. Rothfels' membership in the new political consulting institutions had to be suspended if the anti-Semitic attitude required of his students was not to be permanently tested. For their part, the *Ostforscher* considered Rothfels's forced resignation a severe blow to the discipline.[34]

Ethnographic historians tried to effect a change of paradigms by replacing the "concept of the state according to the *kleindeutsche* school (which favored a Prussian-led Germany that excluded Austria) with the idea of the *Volk* as an organic racial community."[35] Albert Brackmann played a leading role in promoting this paradigm shift. Brackmann, the general director of Prussia's state archives and member of various historical commissions, wanted to found a new research organization for the study of the *Grenz- und Auslandsdeutschtum*. In late 1933, he succeeded in forming an alliance with VDA chief Karl Haushofer, Theodor Oberländer, the leader of the BDO in Eastern Prussia, and the NSDAP's central party administration. This alliance facilitated the integration of the young Königsberg historians into the Prussian historical establishment. Political and personnel intrigues formed the basis for dissolving the Reich Historical Commission and the gradual *Gleichschaltung* of the ethnography of Eastern Europe, especially in Breslau and Berlin.[36]

Anti-Semitism and the Construction of *Volkstum* in the North East Ethnic German Research Society

The establishment of *Volkstum* as a factor in settlement policy planning did not lead directly to National Socialist "reordering" of the East. *Ostforschung* experts were by no means ardent National Socialists. Otto Hoetzsch, who was denounced in 1935 as being too accommodating of Poland and the Soviet Union, had been a member of the rival German National People's Party (DNVP, a conservative nationalist party in the Weimar Republic).[37] Schieder had been affiliated with the National Conservative Union, a right-wing splinter group of the DNVP.[38] Hans Rothfels had not been a member of any party, but did enjoy good contacts in the East Prussian "camarilla." All had exploited their connections to the highest ranks of the Prussian government long before 1933. Albert Brackmann had been a member of the German Democratic Party (DDP).[39] As a member of various historical commissions and general director of the Prussian state archives, Brackmann enjoyed access to the strongholds of state power as well as the financial resources of the Prussian administration. As head of the Nord- und Ostdeutsche Forschungsgemeinschaft (North East Ethnic German Research Society or NOFG), founded in 1933, and as special adviser to the Deutsche Forschungsgemeinschaft (German Research Foundation or DFG, the successor to the Notgemeinschaft), Brackmann had decisive influence over the distribution of 1,200,000 Reichsmarks that the DFG earmarked exclusively for organizing the newly created research fields of *Volksforschung* (ethnopolitical research on peoples). In comparison, all other fields of historical research received only 150,000 Reichsmarks from the DFG.[40]

The research alliance headed by Albert Brackmann promoted the establishment of *Volksgeschichte* (ethnic history) as a discipline at eastern German universities. In addition, the NOFG became the institutional link between ethnographic research and state policymaking. Temporarily, more than 150 experts in ethnographic and cultural studies, as well as archivists from thirteen scholarly institutions, joined the research alliance.[41] National Socialist settlement and population policy started with ethnic segregation in border regions between Germany and Poland, which was also reflected in ethnographic historians' research agenda in the form of dissertations, conferences, and publications. From the start, anti-Semitic influences figured prominently in this research agenda. On 7 December 1933 Hitler proclaimed in the Reich Chancellery to the assembled leaders of the VDA and BDO, who exercised political control over the new research societies, that he would stand up for the "freedom of *Volkstum*," by which he meant not only Germans but also other major nationalities. After 1945, *Ostforscher* who continued their careers in the Federal Republic used this proclamation as "proof" that Hitler had concealed his anti-Semitic intentions from them.[42]

In June 1934 Albert Brackmann received his first political instructions straight from the center of secret revisionist policy, the Deutsche Stiftung (German Foundation). This foundation was responsible for the secret financial and political support of German minorities in all contested border areas. The head of the Deutsche Stiftung personally referred Brackmann to a paper by Jan Skala, who had closely connected the segregation of Europe on the basis of population policy to the "Jewish question."[43] Skala's paper made clear that Hitler's December 1933 reference to "freedom of *Volkstum*" was a euphemism. What Hitler really had in mind was the forced expropriation and deportation of Europe's Jews. This "freedom," Skala argued, should be achieved through a policy of "dissimilation," which aimed to regain the particularities of a specific ethnic group that had been assimilated into a majority population. Evidently, Jews themselves would be made to pay for their expulsion from the German *Volkskörper* (ethnic body). In that way, "damage" to the German "ethnic body" supposedly caused by the emancipation of Jews in the late nineteen century could be repaired.[44] Skala's paper confirmed the general political direction of the Reich Ministry Interior, which supported the deportation of Jews and other groups from the Reich as early as April 1934. German scholars of population presented this doctrine at the International Congress for Population Policy in Berlin in 1935 in order to justify National Socialist policy toward Jews.[45] This political anti-Semitism in settlement and population policy was sanctioned by the establishment of Sippenämter (offices for racial and genealogical heritage) and Sippenbücher (registers of genealogical heritage) in the Reich's border regions,[46] which Brackmann's archivists had been informed about.[47]

The members of the NOFG were initially rather reserved in their public statements about the "Jewish question." Their research commission was geared primarily toward other political tasks. It was no coincidence that the publications of German ethnic historians focused either on the role of colonists in settling the contested border regions in West Prussia, Posen, and Upper Silesia or on the German population's participation in constructing the Polish state.[48] Polemical remarks or scholarly papers that questioned the sovereignty of the Polish state or were anti-Semitic were still considered inappropriate. From 1934, the NOFG regulated the language of its publications in coordination with the Ministry of Interior.[49] Scholars were to avoid any statements that questioned the German-Polish Friendship Treaty of 1934 or gave the League of Nations cause to assail German settlement and race policy.[50] To back up this order, the Ministry of Interior secretly decreed in August 1936 that every doctoral thesis dealing with issues of *Volkstum* and the *Grenz- und Auslandsdeutschtum* must be presented to the ministry for approval. Controversial papers were to be classified "secret" and kept unavailable to the interested public. Violations would lead to the revocation of academic titles.[51] Anyone wanting access to classified publications had to negotiate a complicated bureaucratic process at the NOFG. This invisible machinery of censorship relied upon a complicit academic community. It was no coincidence that the Königsberg historians who dominated the NOFG came from the same radical right-wing circles as the responsible functionaries in the Ministry of Interior.[52] Those who were part of this inner circle shared common values and knowingly accepted the violation of civic rights and even crimes against humanity as the price they had to pay to achieve their goals. Accepting this rationale became a prerequisite for building a career in the leading circles of German *Ostforschung*. The *Ostforscher* compensated for their external reticence through considerably greater eloquence in the arena of secret political consulting.

In March 1935, the leading lights of *Ostforschung*, including Theodor Oberländer, Werner Markert, Peter-Heinz Seraphim, Erich Maschke, and Werner Essen, exchanged ideas at the BDO Ostschulungslager (training camp for the East). They hoped to achieve "harmony between theory and practice" in their work in the border regions. A "base" (*Etappe*) that included 58 professors, lecturers, and research assistants met a "front" of political functionaries: seven training specialists of the NSDAP, the Hitler Youth, and the Königsberg academic community, in addition to three heads of the Reichsarbeitsdienst (compulsory labor service), two civil servants, and two elementary school teachers. Oberländer, the training camp's patron, introduced the 72 participants during the first "full day of the camp" to the tasks of the *Grenzkampf* (border struggle). He accused the Polish state of "denationalizing" the German minority through repressive policies. He contrasted the Polish policy with the favorable German policy toward the Poles, which he claimed was not aimed at "germanizing" the Polish minority. Oberländer interpreted the Polish-German Friendship Treaty solely as a "political commitment by the state to non-violence." He supported the "border battle" against the Polish minority in the Reich, and demanded that social relationships between Germans and Polish immigrants be prohibited.[53]

Oberländer added another hypothesis to his assumption that the "pressure of overpopulation" would affect German border zones if the Germans failed in their "border battle" against the Poles. He implied that the Polish state was incapable of agrarian and sociopolitical reforms because Poland was not a racially homogenous nation-state. Oberländer described the social and economic situation in Polish cities as hopeless because the urban population there was nothing more than "transplanted rubes." Since unskilled rural laborers were no substitute for a specialized urban workforce, an efficient industry could not emerge. In Oberländer's hypothesis, the Jewish population had assumed a special role in the social order of Poland's cities.[54] Seraphim, who headed the Polish section in the Institute for Eastern European Economy in Königsberg,[55] considered the "Jews in Eastern Europe" a kind of "intermediate layer" in the social order, who made up the middle class following the emigration or assimilation of the region's Germans.[56]

Whether or not Seraphim's assertions that the Jews exploited native Poles and avoided investing in the Polish economy constituted a model for domination that anticipated National Socialist settlement and population policy remains an open issue.[57] In any case, it was not controversial within *Ostforschung* circles to classify Jews as inferior in the political and cultural life of Eastern Europe. The *Ostforscher's* own reports from field trips, conferences, and discussions reveal a language of violence and anti-Semitism. Theodor Schieder, then head of a regional research unit under the Gauleitung of East Prussia, wrote a field trip report about Europe's "peripheral state regions" (*Randstaatengebiete*) that he sent to the Foreign Office. Schieder elaborated on the economic potential of the individual countries, listed their industrial sites, and portrayed their situations from the perspective of population policy. He emphasized the "racial type" of the Finnish worker and described his negative impressions of "Jewish German immigrants" in Leningrad.[58] In 1936 Conze, who worked in "Dr. Oberländer's office" (Brackmann's term for the espionage complex in the Königsberg Gaugrenzlandamt or "district borderland office"), turned in the first outline of his *Habilitation* thesis, which analyzed "ethnic questions" in northern and eastern Poland. Conze was convinced that, in contrast to Germany, Poland lacked a broad middle class. He argued that the region had become socially, ethnically, and economically pauperized because the German agrarian order introduced 400 years before had ended in 1864 with the emancipation of Russian serfs, which in turn spurred an increase in the region's population. Conze based his intellectual model on the assumption that the spiral of population growth could be stopped only by reintroducing a German agrarian order.[59]

Conze's statements about the relationship between Germans, Jews, and Poles should not be mistaken for a purely "academic" anti-Semitism. His recommendations for "solving the problems" of minorities in Europe's ethnically diverse regions excluded Jews as independent legal subjects. Conze considered Jews outside the law. Gunther Ipsen, Conze's academic mentor, discussed this notion with other *Ostforscher*, characterizing the basic principle of equality in international law as a concept of the Western nation-state and as an attack on German minorities abroad.[60] He advocated a dogma developed by Hermann Kier and Hermann Raschhofer in the Kaiser Wilhelm Institute for foreign, public, and international law to prevent "miscegenation" between Jews and non-Jews.[61] Within these circles, the Nuremberg Laws were discussed and accepted as normative for international law.[62] The maxim of German ethnographic researchers' political thought was to consider the Jewish population only in negative terms in any future social order in Eastern and Central Europe.

The *Ostforschers'* plans to link a new "Polish partition" with ethnic segregation of the country's peoples have not received sufficient attention from historians. Martin Broszat explicitly rejected the possibility that such plans might have existed before the German invasion of Poland. Broszat emphasized that BDO leaders who had close ties to the NOFG were not National Socialists but rather conservative nationalists. Apparently, Broszat assumed that racist and conservative nationalist dispositions were mutually exclusive.[63]

The Radicalization of Ethnopolitical Scholars and German *Ostforschung*'s Conceptions of *Lebensraum*

German *Ostforschung* had fully developed a model for organizing Poland in a "new order" through population policy by the spring of 1937. The model predicted the development of two opposing blocs: the German Reich on one side, the Soviet Union on the other. Poland, considered a site for German ethnic policy experimentation, was to be denied national sovereignty. Polish Jews were the most disadvantaged group in this model; they were to be declared stateless and deported. The destiny envisioned for non-Jewish Poles was not quite as drastic. In the summer of 1937, Oberländer advocated a "divide and conquer" strategy for Poland, first pitting the country's minorities against one another and then installing German rule.[64] Competition between National Socialism and Soviet Communism would help determine which of the two systems would shape the future European order of states and peoples. First, the Poles' own "ethnic struggle" would have to be redirected away from the German minority and toward the Russians and the Jews. Oberländer called for the elimination of "assimilated Jewry," which he considered the primary carrier of communist ideas. The Polish peasant, Oberländer argued, must be taught that he would profit more from German special property laws than from forced collectivization under Soviet rule. Polish peasants tended to be indebted to Jewish creditors. In order to gain allies in Germany's struggle for Central European predominance, Oberländer wanted the Polish population to share in the theft of Jewish property. Three and a half million Polish Jews should be deprived of all rights, including 1.5 million people who were culturally assimilated but considered to be of Jewish "descent."[65]

It would not be wholly accurate, however, to include Oberländer among the *"Vordenker* [intellectual strategists] of extermination" only because he developed the theory of the "overpopulated" Polish village and considered the "Jewish question" in his thoughts on a future occupation of Poland.[66] Oberländer, a member of the NSDAP since 1933 and of the NOFG political leadership, lost all of his positions toward the end of 1937. The reason for his dismissal had nothing to do with his position on the "Jewish question." Rather, Oberländer opposed those in the NSDAP's planning and propaganda bureaucracies who advocated a hard line toward the Polish population and whose views eventually won out. As a result, Oberländer's role in political consulting was as good as finished by 1938. Hermann Behrends, the ex-head of the Inland section of the SD (interior intelligence) and Werner Lorenz, chief of the Volksdeutsche Mittelstelle (Ethnic German Liaison Agency) together gained control over the VDA and BDO. This takeover opened the door for radical forces to gain decisive influence in the field of settlement and population policymaking. Once Oberländer's concept of "overpopulation" had been "scientifically" developed and integrated into political practice, policies based on the concept could be realized without the participation of its creator. Records of internal discussions about war objectives among the *Ostforscher* reveal that the doctrine of depriving Poland's Jewish (but not Polish) population of its rights remained in effect until the German attack on Poland.

When Ipsen wrote to tell Reich Education Minister Bernhard Rust that he planned to present the "new aspects and results of our ethnographic research" at the 14th Sociological Congress in Bucharest, planned for the fall of 1939, he immediately received the minister's support. Ipsen, who in the NOFG handled questions of population policy, wanted to assemble a small, reliable "team" that would prevent "political enemies—Jews, Popular Front alliances, liberals, Marxists"—from taking over the "field." With his team, Ipsen intended to counter the "Western European theory of society."[67] Ipsen hoped the congress would facilitate the export of German population and settlement policy to Eastern Europe. Ipsen believed German sociologists—he meant his students from Königsberg—should make the "Jewish question" an issue in upcoming agrarian reforms in Eastern Europe. Ipsen wanted Werner Conze to present the problem of rural "overpopulation in Poland."[68]

Conze envisioned a social policy based on racist principles that would regulate the populations residing in German "living space." He did not define population as the sum of individual persons, rejecting this formulation as a "colorless" definition originating in liberalism. Rather, Conze understood "population" as a dynamic process that described the "healthy" relationship between the birthrate on the one hand and "living space" on the other.[69] He demonstrated his concept using the population history of "Polish Lithuania" as an example. The German *Hufenordnung* (a system based on the medieval land unit of the *Hufe* or "hide") introduced by Sigmund II August, who in the sixteenth century had effected the union of Poland and Lithuania, had initially guaranteed that "health" of the population order. But since the Poles had revolted against the system shortly after its introduction, Sigmund's reform had ultimately failed. The Polish peasants had rejected the hide system not because they did not want to pay the German taxes, but because their "petty peasant instincts" had revolted against the German order. Conze mixed deprecating judgements almost inextricably with empirical results and transferred his racialist concept of society to agrarian conditions in East-Central Europe.

Conze argued that the Polish population had "degenerated." According to his theory of racial development, Poland's "surplus population," which resulted from uninhibited "vegetative" procreation, had not disseminated successfully into the cities. The rural population had been restricted from social progress in the cities because Jews blocked trade and the handicrafts.[70] To fight the Polish population's chronic "condition of need," Conze recommended two solutions. First, he wanted to solve the problems of the agrarian economy through traditional instruments of order, such as "parceling" the land or "separating" and "intensifying" the country's agriculture. Second, Conze proposed a social-technocratic inter-vention to change Polish society as a "population." He supported *Ent-judung* (purging the Jews) of cities and small towns. This would free Poland's rural population for social ascent, according to Conze.[71]

Conze and Ipsen's plan to offer Poles agrarian reform in exchange for relinquishing Polish national sovereignty and at the expense of the coun-try's Jews was by no means an isolated idea. Their plan was supported within the group of academic political consultants on Eastern policy, many of whom had similar ideas. Conze's plan was never implemented, however. After the German attack on Poland, the model of an "ethnic reordering" there received a complete overhaul. By September 1939, the two pillars of a future settlement and population policy in Poland were firmly in place in the NOFG's vision. The Polish state would be smashed and carved into new Gaue and administrative districts, and a small Gene-ralgouvernement established, where a core element of the Polish and Jew-ish populations would remain.[72]

Theodor Schieder summarized the profound measures of the Berlin working group of German *Ostforscher* in a memorandum on "settlement and ethnic questions in the reclaimed areas [of Poland]." He justified the planned deportations of Jewish and non-Jewish Poles with the unre-stricted rights of the victor. Schieder based his argumentation on the assumption that an "unprecedented destruction and displacement of Ger-man *Volkstum*" had taken place after the formation of the Polish state. This had resulted in a loss of 2.5 million acres previously owned by Germans. Schieder demanded "restitution" on account of the harsh *Volkstumskampf*. He legitimized his demand for a clear "differentiation" between Polish and German *Volkstum* by referencing the "dangers of racial mixing" and "ethnic infiltration." To facilitate the new settlement and population pol-icy, Schieder demanded the "detachment of Jewry from the big Polish cities" and "agricultural intensification," as well as the elimination of the Polish intelligentsia. He envisioned only one "positive" measure: the 150,000 Kashubians, a supposedly Germanic group living in West Prussia, should receive full Reich citizenship (which included compulsory military service) after a probation period.[73]

Schieder's memorandum was not the only one of its kind. Walter Kuhn, the leading scholarly consultant to the German minority in Poland, drafted a position paper on "German settlement areas beyond the old Reich bor-ders" for the German-Soviet border commission. Kuhn listed those places to be annexed by the Reich and outlined their ethnic makeup.[74] In contrast to Kuhn, however, Schieder specified in his own memorandum German *Ostforscher*'s war objectives regarding settlement and population policy. His settlement plans included ethnic Germans from the Baltic states and Soviet Union,[75] who were to be resettled in the Reich according to Ger-man-Soviet bilateral treaties. Schieder's political terminology closely matched that of a paper written a few weeks earlier by Erhard Wetzel, an expert in the NSDAP's "Office for Racial Policy."[76] Not only had Wetzel called for curbing Polish population growth through forced emigration, he also advocated a "peaceful integration" of "Kaschubians," "Masurians," "Water Poles," and *Goralen*, regional subgroups whose language and culture placed them outside the mainstream of Polish nationality, into German *Volkstum*. All of Wetzel's proposed measures aimed to extract "Nordic racial elements" from the Polish population and "germanize" them, if possible. Members of ethnic groups with a *rassenfremden Kern* (a core "alien" to the German race) should be enslaved and deported to *Kernpolen* ("core Poland"), the drastically reduced rump of the Polish state.[77] Schieder's memorandum echoed these measures first proposed by Wetzel.

The scenarios developed by *Ostforscher* did not simply continue traditional Prussian policies toward the Poles, as Martin Broszat has suggested regarding the plans of minority policy experts in the Ministry of Interior.[78] Comparing border policies between Germany and Poland before 1918 and plans for a post-occupation Poland developed by Reich agencies in 1939, as Broszat does, leads to a historically inaccurate analogy. As a result, Broszat misunderstands the role of German race and settlement policy in *Ostforschung*. The discussions held between Polish representatives and the Central Powers from 1916 to 1918 to determine the borders of a future Polish state also foresaw relocations and even deportations on a large scale. But those population transfers were subjected to the interests of German, Austrian, and Polish negotiators.[79] Furthermore, "racial hygiene" was wholly alien to Prussia's internal colonization policies. In contrast, Schieder's recommendations were based entirely upon Otto Reche's directives on National Socialist settlement and population policy. As director of the University of Leipzig "Institute for Race and Ethnology," Reche served on the consulting board of the North und East Ethnic German Research Society.[80] In addition, he was adviser to Günther Pancke, the head of the SS Rasse- und Siedlungshauptamt (Race and Settlement Main Office).[81] Reche believed that a "bastardization of German immigrants" in the course of a new settlement policy in Poland had to be prevented at all costs. Jews and Poles should be deported from areas where Germans would settle. In addition, he proposed that ethnic German settlers who entered the Reich in accordance with the German-Soviet pact should be examined on "racial-hygienic" grounds to determine whether they could be integrated into the Reich's population.[82] Reche had cooperated closely with Eugen Fischer, one of Germany's leading theoreticians of racial hygiene, since the 1920s. Together with Fritz Lenz, who held the first chair for racial hygiene at the University of Berlin, Otto Reche succeeded in pushing through his views against the opposition of a "Breslau school" centered on Egon von Eickstedt. Unlike Eickstedt, Lenz and Reche believed external characteristics, such as blue eyes or blond hair, should not factor too heavily during *Umvolkung*, the process of relocating German people from the East. Instead, *Volksliste* registration should be carried out in accordance with more precise and thorough racial hygienic standards. Lenz and Reche received support from Albert Brackmann.[83]

In contrast to Otto Reche's and Erhard Wetzel's papers, Schieder's memorandum was not intended to be a policy plan.[84] Instead, Schieder wanted to stake a claim for the Berlin *Ostforschung* working group in the field of race and settlement policy at a time when the political responsibilities of researchers had not yet been clearly delineated. Therefore, Schieder sent his memorandum only to the Interior and Foreign Ministries, to the Abwehr (the Wehrmacht's intelligence service), and the German Labor Front (DAF) not, however, to the SD. Nevertheless, the Berlin *Ostforscher* working group's activities occurred in the context of the resettlement and extermination plans developed under the guidance of SD chief Reinhard Heydrich in November 1939.[85]

Ostforschung in the "Battle for Ethnic Heritage" in Poland and the "Final Solution of the Jewish Question"

Resettlement and extermination were two variants of a policy planned and later implemented by various Reich agencies following the occupation of Poland in September 1939. The first plan for the occupied areas' immediate future was developed by Reinhard Heydrich. Heydrich intended to deport the Polish and Jewish populations from the newly annexed territories of the Warthegau into the Generalgouvernement, which the Reich occupied but did not incorporate. These deportations were intended to create space for ethnic Germans resettled from the Baltic states.[86] Heydrich's long-range plan, developed in 1940, foresaw additional deportations from Poland's annexed western areas to make room for ethnic German resettlers from the Soviet Union and South Tyrol. The Landratsämter (district administrative offices) in the newly occupied territories were charged with compiling lists of people to be deported. These offices had to focus on two political objectives. First, those Polish and Jewish groups deemed unfit for integration into the German population were to be deported. These included all Polish citizens not considered to have an important economic function. Second, all members of the Polish intelligentsia, priests, teachers, scientists, and Poles of a national democratic orientation were selected to immediate liquidation. Prior to their deportation, people had to be registered in a census. Those who failed to register would not receive a certificate of registration and faced the possibility of immediate execution.[87] In parallel with the deportation of Poles and Jews, the "cleared" areas were to be settled by ethnic Germans. Only Polish citizens of German nationality and those Germans who had adopted Polish language and culture would be registered for future integration into new German settlements. In order to achieve these two goals, all agencies involved in the various aspects of the project—the central offices in Berlin as well as regional branches operating in the areas projected for settlement—depended on expert research to facilitate the resettlement process. The expertise they needed had long existed within the network of the North East Ethnic German Research Society.

The Publication Office (P-Stelle), which served as the Berlin *Ostforschung* working group's operational branch, had cooperated as early as 1938 with the SD. The P-Stelle maintained the *Volkstumskartei* (ethnic group index), a catalogued all members of "foreign" ethnic groups in the German Reich, who had been required to register with the P-Stelle Berlin-Dahlem following the annexation of Austria and dismemberment of Czechoslovakia in 1938.[88] The P-Stelle also administered the *Deutsche Volksliste* (German National List or DVL). Reich agencies and party Gau administrations used these two lists in the annexed eastern areas to categorize the ethnically "mixed" societies in the occupied areas of Eastern Europe into individual, more easily managed ethnic groups. As early as 7 October 1939, State Secretary Karl Wilhelm Stuckart presented Adolf Hitler with P-Stelle first comprehensive population statistics for categorizing the eastern areas. The data, which reflected conditions in formerly German territories absorbed by Poland in 1919 as well as the "core areas" of the Polish state, showed the latest population and nationalities statistics.[89] These statistics enabled the Publications Office in Berlin-Dahlem to achieve Reich status as a research institute specializing in race and settlement policy. The P-Stelle operational branch processed into quantitative statistics raw data that it received from SS Sondereinsatzkommandos (special task forces) following relocations to the Reich of ethnic Germans from the Baltic states, the Soviet Union, and South Tyrol.[90] In addition, the publications office also conducted qualitative analyses of the ethnic composition of entire regions. The influence of P-Stelle research on party and government settlement and population policy remains to be studied. In any case, the expertise of P-Stelle went far beyond "objective" statistical analysis. P-Stelle papers contained openly evaluative estimations of "foreign nationalities." When Georg Leibbrandt, head of the NSDAP's Foreign Office, received a report on "Population conditions in the Generalgouvernement" in April 1940, he was primarily interested in the "question of the *Lemken* and *Goralen*" in the Carpathian regions. Wolfgang Kohte, the Office's specialist for statistics and nationality questions, evaluated these people negatively, rejecting any notion that they represented a "special" ethnic category.[91] As a result, they were refused integration into new German settlement areas, since only people exhibiting "racially valuable characteristics" could be settled in these "ethnically sensitive" regions.

The *Ostforschers'* quantitative research projects were regionally grounded for good reason. Their close ties to the Gauleiter in Breslau, Oppeln, Königsberg, and Danzig made sense, because the Gauleiter also headed the regional administrative offices. These agencies prepared the deportation lists for Jews and non-Jewish Poles. The Gauleiter even controlled the inclusion of ethnic German Polish citizens on the German *Volksliste*.[92] How deeply intertwined research and policymaking had become on the regional level is evident in the research program of the Landesstelle für Nachkriegsgeschichte (Regional Office for Postwar History) in Königsberg. In March 1940, the director of that office, Theodor Schieder, presented the local Gauleiter Erich Koch with a detailed plan for studying the territories annexed to East Prussia. Koch wanted to know what political, social, and ethnic conditions prevailed in those areas.[93] To that end, Schieder sent two reports to the Gau leadership in March 1940. The first contained a detailed estimate of the numerical strength and influence of Polish national democracy down to the local level.[94] The second reported on the operations of the Prussian settlement commission dating to the late eighteenth century and on residual settlements from that earlier operation.[95] The past project most relevant to the concerns of National Socialist settlement and extermination policy was a population inventory conducted around the turn of the nineteenth century in the East Prussian district of Zichenau and in the county of Suwalki.[96] The data collected in the eighteenth and nineteenth centuries evidently provided a basis for segregating ethnic Germans from their Jewish and "Slavic" spouses within the context of the German *Volksliste* project.[97]

The "General Plan East" and the "Final Solution of the Jewish Question" in the "Struggle for Ethnic Heritage"

After Germany invaded the Soviet Union in June 1941, the work of *Volkstum* researchers entered its final, most radical phase. *Ostforscher* participated in the settlement planning of the "General Plan East" and in the "Final Solution of the Jewish Question."[98] On 17 January 1942, only three days before he attended the Wannsee Conference to coordinate the "Final Solution,"[99] Georg Leibbrandt presented the plans of the Ostministerium (Reich Ministry for the Occupied Eastern Territories or RMO) at the annual Ethnic German Research Societies' board of directors meeting in Berlin. The RMO planned to smash the multiethnic Soviet state into individual ethnic group fragments and to decimate these "foreign populations," so that the German population would never again be threatened by the "steamroller" from the East. *Völkische* historiography would continue its "ethnic revision of history" and remain available for practical assignments."[100] The "*Sammlung Leibbrandt*" (Leibbrandt Collection) represented the locus within *Ostforschung* institutions where National Socialism's two large-scale projects, ethnic "reordering" and the "Final Solution," overlapped. The "Leibbrandt Collection" referred to the P-Stelle Ost, that section of the P-Stelle devoted to the eastern territories, which produced ethnic settlement maps of the region's Jewish, Polish, and German populations for Leibbrandt in preparation for the "Final Solution" and "ethnic reordering."[101]

The "know-how" developed between 1939 and 1941 within the NOFG and in the "regional offices for postwar history" found direct application to political practice in 1942. In that year, VoMi operative Gerhard Wolfrum, Schieder's former assistant in Königsberg who had previously worked under Hermann Aubin in the Silesian "Regional Office for Postwar History,"[102] was responsible for compiling the German *Volksliste* in Ukraine, together with racial policy specialists in the Reichskommissariat Ost (Reich Commissariat East). The experts' guidelines were clear: ethnic Germans who had been active on behalf of the NSDAP and who did not have any "foreign blood," primarily members of rural German communities without Russian or Jewish relations, would be placed in the first and second categories of the *Volksliste* and receive German citizenship. In contrast, "russified urban Germans" were placed in the third category. Those people placed in the fourth category, partners in German-Jewish "mixed marriages," would receive "special treatment" according to guidelines established at the Wannsee Conference.[103] In the euphemistic jargon of the "Final Solution," "special treatment" meant liquidation.[104]

In two respects, the *Ostforscher* participated directly or indirectly in the deportation and genocide of those Jews considered to be not "racially mixed." First, the *Ostforscher* collected statistics on the ethnic segregation of "eastern areas." Second, the evacuation of those areas provided potential new social and cultural research programs. When Theodor Schieder wrote his eighth report in 1942 on ethnic conditions in Bialystok, he remarked favorably, that "the Jews" were encountered only "at a distance" and only in the "ghettoes of the cities." At the same time, he reported on thee "Bolshevist organization of Jewish-Russian functionaries" in Bialystok.[105] Schieder received exact information on the question of whether a region was *judenfrei* (free of Jews) from top secret files of Konrad Meyer's regional Bodenämter (land offices).[106]

Peter Heinz Seraphim was the only *Ostforscher* to speak publicly in support of the "Final Solution of the Jewish Question," in March 1941, together with Walter Groß, head of the NSDAP's "race-political office."[107] Following the invasion of the Soviet Union in June 1941, Seraphim stated that by December of that year, between 150,000 and 200,000 Jews had been executed in that country. Among those murdered were elderly people, women, and children. Seraphim criticized the mass murder as poorly conceived but only because he considered the policy economically counterproductive.[108] Seraphim later became director of the regional office of the NSDAP's "Institute for Research on the Jewish Question" in Lodz, where he worked with the ghetto administration and, from expropriated Jewish goods, prepared materials on "world Jewry" for National Socialist foreign propaganda.[109]

Following the invasion of the Soviet Union, the NOFG *Ostforschers'* political ideas diverged from the models developed by Theodor Oberländer, as Oberländer's sharp criticism of the settlement and extermination policy suggests. During the war, Oberländer distanced himself from Konrad Meyer in several memoranda and privately voiced his negative views, specifically about Seraphim. These criticisms made Oberländer a target for the SS. The SS Reich Security Main Office (RSHA III B, *Volkstum*) explicitly noted that Oberländer was not "in line" on the "Slavic question."[110] As a member of the Abwehr, Oberländer wanted to arm the "foreign peoples" (i.e., non-Russians) in Ukraine and the Caucasus region to build a united front against the Red Army. He did not discuss the "Jewish question."[111] Similar hostile statements from SS quarters or party administration about other *Ostforscher* from the NOFG's inner circle have so far not been found by historians.

A final curious example of *Ostforschers'* visions for repopulating ethnically cleansed territories surfaced in 1943.[112] Werner Essen, responsible for race and settlement policy in the Reichskommissariat Ostland, proposed that the Pripyat Marshes in the Belorussian S.S.R.—already cleared of Jews—be drained by the Dutch. The responsible functionary, Erich Keyser, even wanted to send spies into archives in the Netherlands to uncover new sources that would support the notion of a Dutch eastern colonization.[113] Karin Schönwälder correctly interprets this idea as an absurd attempt to "sell the Dutch the war and settlement in the East as their own tradition-bound concern."[114]

Conclusion

How individual historians, as "chastened democrats," interpreted the "Final Solution of the Jewish Question" after the war can be determined in only a few cases. Walter Bußmann, a Wehrmacht general staff officer in the war administration department in Berlin, had the task of transmitting radio reports not only from the front but also on the Einsatzgruppen (Mobile Killing Units) killings of Jews to the Reich Chancellery and Wehrmacht high command. Bußmann knew about the SS plans to murder Jews, which at the time were not as controversial as the notorious "Commissar Order" (which instructed German soldiers to execute Red Army political commissars on the spot). According to Bußmann, the army leadership was only concerned with the question of "how to avoid a breakdown of the Eastern Front and at the same time end the war without Hitler."[115] The fact that in 1983 Bußmann used his position as a historian to question Helmut Krausnick's study about the killings of Jews, because Krausnick failed to account for a *Befehlsnotstand* (the requirement to carry out orders against one's own moral compunctions) encountered by German officers is not merely an irony of history, but an intentional inversion of the victims' perspective. Bußmann's stance reveals the self-image of a scholarly elite that may not have achieved its wartime objectives but nevertheless maintained a powerful position in German academia from which it could shape the historical evaluation of its own failures. While Bußmann, a prominent critic of critical research into the Jewish genocide, at least had the honesty to admit his exact role and awareness of the genocide during the war, other historians maintained an eloquent silence about their own roles during the National Socialist period. It is one of the most noteworthy problems of postwar German historiography that the same historians who helped plan deportations of Jews and Poles under National Socialism assumed responsibility for researching the deportations of Germans from East-Central Europe after 1945.[116] The result is an apologist historiography that continues to exercise strong influence in German academic and public spheres to this day.

Notes

I thank Kathrina Hering for her stimulating comments, and Christof Morrissey and Sace Elder for correcting my English.

1. See Klaus Zernack, "'Ostkolonisation' in universalgeschichtlicher Perpektive," in *Universalgeschichte und Nationalgeschichten*, ed. Gangolf Hübinger (Freiburg, 1994), 108. Harmut Boockmann, *Ostpreußen und Westpreußen* (Berlin, 1992), 60ff.; Willi Oberkrome, "Historiker im Dritten Reich. Zum Stellenwert volkshistorischer Ansätze zwischen klassischer Politik- und neuerer Sozialgeschichte," in *Geschichtswissenschaft und Unterricht* 50 (1999): 9ff.
2. Christoph Kleßmann, "Osteuropaforschung und Lebensraumpolitik im Dritten Reich," in *Wissenschaft im Dritten Reich*, ed. Peter Lundgreen (Frankfurt am Main, 1985), 356f.
3. Imre Lakatos, "Die Geschichte der Wissenschaft und ihre rationale Konstruktion," in *Kritik und Erkenntnisfortschritt*, ed. Imre Lakatos and Alan Musgrave (Braunschweig, 1974), 282f.
4. See Karl-Heinz Grundmann, *Deutschtumspolitik zur Zeit der Weimarer Republik. Eine Studie am Beispiel der deutsch-baltischen Minderheit in Estland und Lettland* (Ph.D. diss., Berlin, 1975), 269; Norbert Krekeler, *Revisionsanspruch und geheime Ostpolitik der Weimarer Republik. Die Subventionierung der deutschen Minderheiten in Polen* (Stuttgart, 1973), 13ff., 34ff., 149f.
5. See also Michael Fahlbusch, *"Wo der deutsche ... ist, ist Deutschland!" Die Stiftung für deutsche Volks- und Kulturbodenforschung in Leipzig 1920–1933* (Bochum, 1994), 104–165, esp. 71ff.
6. The term literally means "German ethnicity and land cultivation." It refers not only to territories occupied by ethnic Germans in the present but also evokes cultural and territorial claims to all lands in the East where Germans once lived in the past, before they were later expelled or assimilated into non-German populations.
7. See Wilhelm Volz, ed., *Der ostdeutsche Volksboden. Aufsätze zu den Fragen des Ostens* (Breslau, 1926); Karl Haushofer, *Grenzen in ihrer geographischen und politischen Bedeutung* (Berlin, 1927), 36; GStAPK (Geheimes Staatsarchiv/Preußischer Kulturbesitz), Rep. 77, Tit. 856, Nr. 298, Bd. 1, Nr. 62, pp. 148–150; Gustav Aubin, "Agrarverfassung und nationale Frage," in *Protokoll über die Tagung zu Marienburg vom 10.–12. 10. 1925*: 37ff.
8. See Martin Broszat, *Zweihundert Jahre deutsche Polenpolitik* (Frankfurt am Main, 1972), 229.
9. GStAPK, Rep. 77, Tit. 856, Nr. 298, Bd. 1, Nr. 62, pp. 91f.), Max Hildebert Boehm, "Der großdeutsche Gedanke," in *Protokoll der Tagung für Deutschtumspflege der Deutschen Mittelstelle für Volks- und Kulturbodenforschung vom 29. August bis zum 1. September 1925 in Freiberg/Sachsen.*
10. Wilhelm Volz, "Lebensraum und Lebensrecht des deutschen Volkes," in *Deutsche Arbeit* 24 (1925): 169–174, 173.

11. See also Gabriele Camphausen, "Die wissenschaftliche historische Russlandforschung in Deutschland 1892–1933," in *Forschungen zur Osteuropäischen Geschichte* (Wiesbaden, 1989), 47; Klaus Schwabe, *Wissenschaft und Kriegsmoral. Die deutschen Hochschullehrer und die politischen Grundfragen des Ersten Weltkrieges* (Göttingen, Zürich, and Frankfurt, 1969), 90f.; Fritz Fischer, *Griff nach der Weltmacht* (Düsseldorf, 1962), 214ff., and Imanuel Geiss, *Der polnische Grenzstreifen 1914–1918* (Lübeck and Hamburg 1960), 53, 183.
12. GStAPK, Rep. 178, XVI, 3, 3AB4, pp. 349ff., Wilhelm Volz to the Prussian Ministry of Interior from 17. October 1928; GStAPK, Rep. 178, XVI, 3, 3AB4, pp. 347f., Prussian Ministry of Interior to Volz, 9. October 1928.
13. Karl Christian von Loesch, "Der Deutsche Schutzbund. Die Ziele," in *Volk unter Völkern*, ed. Karl Christian von Loesch (Breslau, 1925): 10–15.
14. See Haushofer, *Grenzen*, 124 (note 135, p. 331), 317 (note 242, p. 242) and 323 (note 281, p. 242); Graf von Baudissin, "Innere Kolonisation. Grundsätzliches und Praktisches," in Wilhelm Volz, ed., *Der ostdeutsche Volksboden*, 375–388.
15. See Willi Oberkrome, "Geschichte, Volk und Theorie. Das 'Handwörterbuch des Grenz- und Auslandsdeutschtums,'" in *Geschichtsschreibung als Legitimationswissenschaft 1918–1945*, ed. Peter Schöttler (Frankfurt am Main 1997), 109.
16. Politisches Archiv des Auswärtigen Amtes (PA), R 60351, Walter Goetz to Carl Severing, 12. January 1930.
17. See also Walter Goetz, "Nation und Völkerbund" (Berlin, 1920).
18. Georg G. Iggers, "Geschichtswissenschaft in Deutschland und Frankreich 1830 bis 1918 und die Rolle der Sozialgeschichte. Ein Vergleich zwischen zwei Traditionen bürgerlicher Geschichtsschreibung," in *Bürgertum im Vergleich*, vol. 3, ed. Jürgen Kocka (Munich, 1988), 176.
19. Werner Essen, *Die ländlichen Siedlungen in Litauen mit besonderer Berücksichtigung der Bevölkerungsverhältnisse* (Leipzig, 1930).
20. BArch (Bundesarchiv), Berlin Document Center (BDC), Werner Essen was born 1910, membership in NSDAP 1931. Institut für Zeitgeschichte, MA 259, Bl. 926, see the "Rundschreiben des Reichskommissars für das Ostland" to the "Generalkommissare in Riga, Reval und Minsk," the "Erlaß" and the "Richtlinien für die Behandlung der im Ostland ansässigen Volksdeutschen und Deutschstämmigen," 11 September 1942.
21. Michael Fahlbusch, *Wissenschaft im Dienst der nationalsozialistischen Politik? Die "Volksdeutschen Forschungsgemeinschaften" von 1931–1945* (Baden-Baden, 1999), 134f.
22. Cf. Eric J. Schmaltz and Samuel D. Sinner, "The Nazi Ethnographic Research of Georg Leibbrandt and Karl Stumpp in Ukraine, and its North American Legacy," in this volume.
23. Protokoll der Wannsee-Konferenz, in *Akten zur Deutschen Auswärtigen Politik 1918–45*, Serie E, Bd. I (Göttingen, 1969), 267–275.
24. See also Rüdiger vom Bruch, "Historiker und Nationalökonomen im Wilhelminischen Deutschland," in Klaus Schwabe, ed., *Deutsche Hochschullehrer als Elite 1815–1945* (Boppard, 1983), 121; Fritz K. Ringer, *Die Gelehrten. Der Niedergang der deutschen Mandarine 1890–1933* (Munich, 1987), 130ff.
25. BArch, R 15.06, 249, p. 68, Hans Rothfels to the president from the Historical Commission of the Reich, 2 March 1932.
26. Ibid., 68f.
27. Max Hildebert Boehm, *Das eigenständige Volk. Grundlegung der Elemente einer europäischen Völkersoziologie* (Göttingen, 1932), 9; see also Stefan Kühl, *Die Internationale der Rassisten. Aufstieg und Niedergang der internationalen Bewegung für Eugenik und Rassenhygiene im 20. Jahrhundert* (Frankfurt am Main and New York 1998), 114.
28. See Ingo Haar, "'Revisionistische' Historiker und Jugendbewegung: Das Königsberger Beispiel," in Schöttler, *Geschichtsschreibung als Legitimationswissenschaft*, 65, 78f.
29. See Siegfried Mattl and Karl Stuhlpfarrer, "Angewandte Wissenschaft im Nationalsozialismus. Großraumphantasien, Geopolitik, Wissenschaftspolitik," in *Willfährige Wissenschaft. Die Universität Wien 1938–1945*, ed. Gernot Heiß (Vienna, 1989), 283–299.

30. BArch, NL Rothfels, 12, Hans Rothfels, *Der deutsche Staatsgedanke von Friedrich dem Großen bis zur Gegenwart*, 1933, January, 8f.

31. According to Arthur Moeller van den Bruck´s definition, "[a] German is not only whoever speaks German, has roots in Germany, or even holds German citizenship. Land and language are the natural foundations of a nation but it receives its historic individuality from the manner in which people of its (common) blood prevalue life in spirit. Living in consciousness of one's nation means living in consciousness of its values." (Deutscher ist nicht nur, wer deutsch spricht, wer aus Deutschland stammt oder gar, wer dessen Staatsbürgerschaft besitzt. Land und Sprache sind die natürlichen Grundlagen einer Nation, aber ihre geschichtliche Eigentümlichkeit empfängt sie von der Art, wie ihr das Leben von Menschen ihres Blutes im Geiste vorgewertet wird. Leben im Bewußtsein seiner Nation heißt Leben im Bewußtsein seiner Werte.) See Arthur Moeller van den Bruck, *Das Dritte Reich*, 3rd ed. (Hamburg, Berlin, and Leipzig, 1931), 303.

32. Archiv der deutschen Jugendbewegung, Witzenhausen, 400242/1, Theodor Schieder, "Unsere Stellung zum Nationalsozialismus" (February 1930).

33. GStAPK, Rep 76 Va, Sekt. 11, Tit. IV, Abt. IV, Nr. 21, Bd. XXXIV, Bl. 449, The Reich Ministry of Justice to Rudolf Heß and Hermann Rauschning, 9 August 1934; see also Hans Mommsen, "Hans Rothfels," in *Deutsche Historiker*, vol. 9, ed. Hans-Ulrich Wehler (Göttingen, 1982), 138f.

34. GStAPK, Rep 76 Va, Sekt. 11, Tit. IV, Abt. IV, Nr. 21, Bd. XXXIV, p. 449, National Leadership of NSDAP to Reich Ministry of Science, Education, and Popular Culture, 22 February 1934.

35. See also Georg G. Iggers, "Geschichtswissenschaft in Deutschland und Frankreich 1830 bis 1918 und die Rolle der Sozialgeschichte. Ein Vergleich zwischen zwei Traditionen bürgerlicher Geschichtsschreibung," in Jürgen Kocka, ed., *Bürgertum im Vergleich*, vol. 3 (Munich, 1988): 197.

36. See Haar, "'Revisionistische' Historiker," 70ff.

37. BArch, R 153, 1269, Otto Hoetzsch was a member of the NOFG from 1933 to 1935, and president of the German Society for the Study of Eastern Europe (Deutsche Gesellschaft zum Studium Osteuropas). Heinrich Himmler denounced Hoetzsch as a friend of the Soviet Union. See "Der Reichsführer der SS und Chef des Sicherheitshauptamtes, *Erfassung führender Männer der Systemzeit. Wissenschaftler*" (June 1939), 10. See also Gerd Voigt, *Rußland in der deutschen Geschichtsschreibung 1843–1945* (Berlin, 1994), pp. 246–256.

38. BArch, ZAV 157, p. 1. See Theodor Schieder's personnel file.

39. Albert Brackmann, Curriculum vitae (BArch, R 153, 1039).

40. Archiv der Max-Planck-Gesellschaft, Abt. I., Rep. 1A, 924/4, 78f., Johannes Stark, Über die Notwendigkeit des Aufwandes größerer Mittel zur Förderung der deutschen Forschung (1934).

41. See Fahlbusch, *Wissenschaft*, 188f.

42. See for example Siegfried Schütt, *Theodor Oberländer. Eine dokumentarische Untersuchung* (Munich, 1995), 116f.; Robert Ernst, *Rechenschaftsbericht eines Elsässers* (Berlin, 1955), 199. PA, R 60442, Protokoll der interministeriellen Besprechung zwischen Hans Steinacher und den Referenten für Minderheitenpolitik aus dem Auswärtigen Amt und dem Reichsinnenministerium, 14 December 1933. According to the latter document, all statements on race issues shall therefore be closely coordinated between the VDA/BDO and the ministries, because "various German ethnic groups abroad feared disadvantageous ramifications for their already imperiled life opportunities from the race laws planned in the Reich."

43. BArch, R 153, 1277, Albert Brackmann to Erich Krahmer-Möllenberg, 16 June 1934.

44. Jan Skala, "Assimilation—'Dissimilation'—Renationalisierung. Grundsätzliche Erwägungen zur volkstumspolitischen Terminologie," *Kulturwehr* (1934): 78f., 81ff.

45. Ibid., 85; see Susanne Heim and Ulrike Schaz, *Berechnung und Beschwörung: Überbevölkerung—Kritik einer Debatte* (Berlin, 1996), 40.

46. Jan G. Smit, *Neubildung deutschen Bauerntums. Innere Kolonisation im Dritten Reich. Fallstudien Schleswig-Holstein* (Kassel, 1983), 61–67, 143f.

47. Adolf Diestelkamp, "Das Staatsarchiv Stettin seit dem Weltkriege," *Monatsblätter der Gesellschaft für Pommersche Geschichte und Altertumskunde* 52 (1938): 70ff.

48. See Theodor Schieder, *Deutscher Geist und ständische Freiheit im Weichsellande. Politische Ideen und politisches Schrifttum in Westpreußen von der Lubliner Union bis zu den polnischen Teilungen (1569–1772/93)* (Königsberg, 1940); Karl Kasiske, *Beiträge zur Bevölkerungsgeschichte Pommerellens im Mittelalter* (Königsberg, 1942); Erich Maschke, *Polen und die Berufung des deutschen Ordens nach Preußen* (Danzig, 1934); Maschke, "Zur Kulturgeschichte des mittelalterlichen Deutschtums in Polens," *Deutsche Monatshefte in Polen* 2 (1935): 26–33; Maschke, "Deutschland und Polen im Wandel der Geschichte," *Neue Jahrbücher für Wissenschaft und Jugendbildung* 12 (1936): 219–232, 354–366; Rudolf Craemer, *Deutschtum im Völkerraum—Geistesgeschichte der ostdeutschen Volkstumspolitik*, vol. 1 (Stuttgart, 1938); and Werner Conze, *Hirschenhof. Die Geschichte einer deutschen Sprachinsel in Livland* (Berlin, 1934).

49. BArch, R 153, 1270, Vermerk des Reichsminister des Innern, 3 February 1934, über die Besprechung vom 30 January 1934 betreffend der NOFG.

50. PA, R 60442, E 611284, Sitzungsprotokoll über die Zusammenarbeit der Referenten der Reichs- und Preußischen Ministerien in Volkstums- und Minderheitenfragen, 10 November 1933.

51. BArch, R 153, 879, Reichs Ministry of Science, Education, and Popular Culture (August 1936), decree "Dissertationen über historisch-politische Stoffe, Volkstums-, Grenz- oder auslandsdeutsche Angelegenheiten sowie über Fragen, die das außenpolitische Gebiet überhaupt berühren."

52. Haar, "'Revisionistische' Historiker," 54–73. See also Ulrich Herbert, "'Generation der Sachlichkeit.' Die völkische Studentenbewegung der frühen zwanziger Jahre," in *Arbeit, Volkstum, Weltanschauung. Über Fremde und Deutsche im 20. Jahrhundert*, ed. Ulrich Herbert (Frankfurt am Main, 1985), 31–58.

53. PA, R 60273, E 062017-18, Theodor Oberländer, "Die Grenzkampfaufgaben im deutschen Osten," in *Bericht über das Ostschulungslager des BDO und der deutschen Dozentenschaft in Marienbuchen vom 20. bis zum 28. 3. 1935.*

54. Ibid., also Werner Essen and Peter-Heinz Seraphim.

55. BArch, Dy 6, vol. 1360 und ZA VI, 1354.

56. PA, R 60273, E 062018-E 062019, see Peter-Heinz Seraphim, "Das Judentum im osteuropäischen Raum," in *Einige Hauptprobleme deutscher Ostwissenschaft. Gedankengänge anläßlich des Osttreffens deutscher Dozenten in Jablonken vom 18.–24. 10. 1937*, 52–62; Seraphim, "Das ostjüdische Ghetto," in *Jomsburg* 1 (1937): 439f.

57. See Götz Aly and Susanne Heim, *Auschwitz und die Pläne für eine neue europäische Ordnung* (Frankfurt am Main, 1991), 92ff., 102ff.

58. PA, R 60276, Theodor Schieder, Bericht über die Studienfahrt nach Finnland und Estland vom 1. bis zum 12. 6. 1936.

59. BArch, R 73, 10614, Werner Conze, Plan meiner Arbeit, 3 June 1936.

60. BArch, R 153, 94/BArch, 8043, 1149, pp. 79, 80f., 90f., see Gunther Ipsen's presentation at the "Tagung des Volkswissenschaftlichen Arbeitskreises des VDA," 3–4 January 1937.

61. Hermann Raschhofer was associated with Hermann Kier, a fellow of the Kaiser Wilhelm Institut. See *25 Jahre Kaiser-Wilhelm-Gesellschaft zur Förderung der Wissenschaften*, vol. 1 (Berlin, 1936), 194–195.

62. Hermann Raschhofer, "Nationalität als Rechtsbegriff," in *25 Jahre Kaiser-Wilhelm-Gesellschaft zur Förderung der Wissenschaften*, vol. 3 (Berlin, 1937), 348, 338, 373. See Michael Stolleis, *Geschichte des öffentlichen Rechts in Deutschland. Vol. 3: Staats- und Verwaltungswissenschaft in Republik und Diktatur 1914–1945* (Munich, 1999), 385. For analysis of the terms "Bevölkerungsdruck" und "Volksgruppenrecht," see Franz Neumann, *Behemoth. Struktur und Praxis des Nationalsozialismus 1933–1944* (Frankfurt am Main, 1993), 188ff., 203ff.

63. See Martin Broszat, *Die nationalsozialistische Polenpolitik 1939–1945* (Stuttgart, 1961), 1ff.

64. BArch, R 8043, 1168, pp. 186f., Theodor Oberländer, *Der Kampf um das Vorfeld* (June 1937).

65. Ibid. Oberländer means that the Polish peasants can profit from the German "Reichs-erbhofgesetz" from 29 September 1933. This was a new national-socialist order to distribute the land to a lot of small farms, where the farmer was the owner. The character of this property-law was racistic. The farmer couldn't be Jewish.

66. Götz Aly and Susanne Heim, *Vordenker der Vernichtung*, 111, 118ff.

67. Gunther Ipsen referred primarily to the French *jus solis* citizenship principle. BArch, R 49.01, 2979, p. 121, Gunther Ipsen to Reich Ministry of Science, Education, and Popular Culture, 2 February 1938.

68. BArch, R 49.01, 2979, p. 292, List of presenters and topics at the Sociological Congress.

69. Werner Conze, "Die ländliche Überbevölkerung in Polen," in *Die Arbeiten des XIV. Internationalen Soziologen Kongresses in Bukarest. Mitteilungen der Abteilung B—das Dorf*, vol. 1, ed. Dimitrie Gusti (Bucharest, 1940–1941), 40f.

70. Ibid., 46.

71. Ibid., 48.

72. Bruno Wasser, *Himmlers Raumplanung im Osten. Der Generalplan Ost in Polen 1940–1944* (Basel, Berlin, and Boston, 1993), 19ff.; Rolf Dieter Müller, *Hitlers Ostkrieg und die deutsche Siedlungspolitik* (Frankfurt am Main, 1991), 11ff.

73. BArch, R 153, 291, Theodor Schieder, Report on settlement and *Volkstum* questions in the reclaimed territories, Findings of the Berlin working circle, 29 September–3 October 1939.

74. BArch, R 153, 289, Walter Kuhn, *Deutsche Dörfer in Mittelpolen, unmittelbar und jenseits der alten Reichsgrenze*, 5 September 1939.

75. Ibid., Theodor Schieder, Aufzeichnung über Siedlungs- und Volkstumsfragen in den wiedergewonnenen Gebieten.

76. Broszat, *Die nationalsozialistische Polenpolitik*, 23f.

77. Institut für Zeitgeschichte, MA 125/9, pp. 380572–380597, Erhard Wetzel and G. Hecht, *Die Frage der Behandlung der Bevölkerung der ehemaligen polnischen Gebiete nach rassepolitischen Gesichtspunkten*, 25 November 1939.

78. See Broszat, *Die nationalsozialistische Polenpolitik*, 21.

79. See also Werner Conze, *Polnische Nation und deutsche Politik im Ersten Weltkrieg* (Cologne and Graz, 1958), 339.

80. BArch, R 153, 288, Otto Reche, *Leitsätze zur bevölkerungspolitischen Sicherung des deutschen Ostens*, 24 October 1939.

81. BArch, R 153, 288, Otto Reche to Albert Brackmann, 14 November 1939.

82. See Michael Burleigh, "Die Stunde der Experten," in Mechtild Rössler and Sabine Schleiermacher ed., *Der "Generalplan-Ost." Hauptlinien der nationalsozialistischen Planungs- und Vernichtungspolitik* (Berlin, 1993), 351–355.

83. BArch, R 153, 1356, Otto Reche to Johannes Papritz, 25 November 1941; Wolfgang Kohte to Fritz Lenz, 15 December 1941; Fritz Lenz to Wolfgang Kohte, 19 December 1941, and Fritz Arlt to Fritz Bracht, 29 July 1942.

84. See Götz Aly, *'Endlösung.' Völkerverschiebung und Mord an den europäischen Juden* (Frankfurt am Main, 1995), 17f.

85. See Broszat, *Die nationalsozialistische Polenpolitik*, 38ff. Götz Aly provides details on resettlement of ethnic Germans and extermination of Jews, *"Endlösung,"* 38–44, 69f.

86. Institut für Zeitgeschichte, Eichmann-Prozeß, Beweisdokument 1461, Der Höhere SS-und Polizeiführer beim Reichsstatthalter in Posen als Beauftragter des Reichskommissars für die Festigung deutschen Volkstums. Amt für die Umsiedlung der Polen und Juden, Erfahrungsbericht über die Umsiedlung von Polen und Juden aus dem Reichsgau "Wartheland," 26 January 1940.

87. Institut für Zeitgeschichte, Beweisdokument 1460, Reinhard Heydrich to die Höheren SS- und Polizeiführer in Krakau and Posen, 28 November 1939. Ibidem, Beweisdokument 1459, Geheime Staatspolizei/Staatspolizeistelle Danzig to Höhere SS- und Polizeiführer in Krakau, Breslau, Posen, Danzig and Königsberg, 28 November 1939.

88. Götz Aly and Karl Heinz Roth, *Die restlose Erfassung. Volkszählen, Identifizieren, Aussondern im Nationalsozialismus* (Berlin, 1984), 78ff.; BArch, R 153, 810, P-Stelle Berlin-Dahlem to Werner Essen, 25 June 1941, and "Vermerk für das Reichsministerium des Innern über die Volkstumskartei."

89. Staatsarchiv Marburg, 340, C12d, 77, pp. 4–11, Johannes Papritz, "Gliederung der Ostgebiete nach dem Vortrag beim Führer," 7 October 1939, überreicht von Staatsekretär Karl Wilhelm Stuckart.

90. Staatsarchiv Marburg, NL Johannes Papritz, C12d, 64 a,b,c,d, *Kleiner Umsiedlungsspiegel*, 1942/43, and "Listen der Sondereinsatzkommandos der SS," October 1939–April 1944.

91. BArch, R 153, 286, Wolfgang Kohte to Georg Leibbrandt, 26 March 1940, and report "Die Bevölkerung des Generalgouvernements."

92. See Broszat, *Die nationalsozialistische Polenpolitik*, 49f., 118–137.

93. BArch, R 153, 317, Albert Brackmanns to Ernst Vollert, 8 March 1940, "Bericht über die neuen Arbeiten zur Bevölkerungsgeschichte in den Grenzgebieten," 8 March 1940.

94. BArch, R 153, 1196, Landesstelle Ostpreußen für Nachkriegsgeschichte: *Der Regierungsbezirk Zichenau im Spiegel der früheren polnischen Sejmwahlen* (Königsberg, 1940).

95. BArch, R 153, 317, Landesstelle Ostpreußen für Nachkriegsgeschichte: Die preußische Kolonisation von 1795–1807 im Regierungsbezirk Zichenau, Bericht Nr. 1 (Königsberg, 1940), 1.

96. BArch, R 153, 317, Albert Brackmann to Ernst Vollert, 8 March 1940, and "Bericht über die neueren Arbeiten."

97. Ibid., Landesstelle Ostpreußen für Nachkriegsgeschichte, *Fragebogen für deutsche Siedlungen im Regierungsbezirk Zichenau und Kreis Suwalken*, Anlage zum Bericht Nr. 1 der Landesstelle über die "preußische Kolonisation."

98. See Fahlbusch, *Wissenschaft*, 512–522, 602–614; Karl Heinz Roth, "'Generalplan Ost'— 'Gesamtplan Ost.' Forschungsstand, Quellenprobleme, neue Ergebnisse," in Rössler and Schleiermacher, *Der Generalplan Ost*, 25–45.

99. Minutes of the Wannsee-Konferenz of 20 January 1942, in *Akten zur deutschen auswärtigen Politik 1918–1945*. Serie E: Bd. 1, 12 Dezember 1941–28 February 1942 (Göttingen, 1969), 267–275.

100. BArch, R 57 alt, 1224, pp. 63–66, Georg Leibbrandt, Vortrag für die Leiter der Volksdeutschen Forschungsgemeinschaften, 17–18 January 1942.

101. Staatsarchiv Marburg, NL Papritz, C12d, 6, Emil Meynen, *Die Volksdeutschen Forschungsgemeinschaften. Ein Zehnjahresbericht*, 1 April 1941.

102. Mathias Beer, "Die Landesstelle für Schlesien 1934 bis 1945. Geschichtswissenschaft und Politik im Lichte neuer Aktenfunde," in *Silesiographia. Stand und Perspektiven der historischen Schlesienforschung* (Würzburg, 1998), ed. Matthias Weber, 142. After the war, Gerhard Wolfrum served as Theoder Oberländer's assistant in the federal ministry for expellees.

103. Institut für Zeitgeschichte, MA 259, p. 913, Besprechung über die Ausführungsbestimmungen zum Volkslistenverfahren in der Ukraine, 23 November 1942.

104. Hellmuth Auerbach, "Der Begriff 'Sonderbehandlung' im Sprachgebrauch der SS," in *Gutachten des Instituts für Zeitgeschichte*, vol. 2 (Munich, 1966), 188.

105. GStAPK Berlin-Dahlem, Rep. 178, F, Kasten 9079, Theodor Schieder, "Die völkischen Verhältnisse des Bezirks Bialystok und ihre geschichtliche Entwicklung. Bericht Nr. 8 der Landesstelle Ostpreußen für Nachkriegsgeschichte" (Königsberg, 1942), 3, 19.

106. BArch, R 153, 96, 946, Kreisberichte der Bodenämter aus den eingegliederten polnischen Gebieten in Ostpreußen. Abschnitt "Gebietseinteilung und Bevölkerung."

107. See "Die Judenfrage im Spiegel der Wissenschaft," *Frankfurter Volksblatt*, 28. 3. 1941.

108. Peter-Heinz Seraphim, "Judenfrage," privater Bericht zur persönlichen Unterrichtung des Chefs des Wehrwirtschafts- und Rüstungsamtes im Oberkommando der Wehrmacht, 2 December 1941, in *Der Prozess gegen die Hauptkriegsverbrecher vor dem Internationalen Militärgerichtshof*, vol. XXXII (Munich, 1989), 73.

109. Institut für Zeitgeschichte, MA 251, pp. 460–463, Die Hohe Schule der NSDAP/Institut zur Erforschung der Judenfrage to Reichsschatzmeister der NSDAP, 14 July 1942; agreement between Peter Heinz Seraphim and the Osteuropainstitut in Breslau, 2 July 1942.

110. Philipp Christian Wachs, *Der Fall Oberländer* (Ph.D. diss., Munich, 1999), 196–201.

111. BArch, R 153, 1673. According to Oberländer, the Slavic peoples of the East should be considered racially nordic. See Theodor Oberländer "20 Thesen zur Lage," 5 April 1943.

112. GStAPK, Rep. 178, VII, 3 A 4, Bd. 1, pp. 102–112, Forschungsbericht zur Niederländerforschung und Übersicht über die wichtigsten Arbeiten über die Beziehungen zwischen den Niederlanden und Polen.

113. GStAPK Berlin-Dahlem, Rep. 178, VII, 3 A 4, p. 133, Erich Keyser, presentation on regional and *Volkstum* research in West Prussia, in Protokoll der Besprechung der NOFG in Posen, 25–27 February 1943.

114. Karen Schönwälder, *Historiker und Politik. Geschichtswissenschaft im Nationalsozialismus* (Frankfurt am Main 1992), 203.

115. Walter Bußmann, "Politik und Kriegsführung. Erlebte Geschichte und der Beruf des Historikers," in *Fridericiana. Zeitschrift der Universität Karlsruhe* 32 (1983): 6f., 15.

116. See Mathias Beer, "Das Grossforschungsprojekt 'Dokumentation der Vertreibung der Deutschen aus Ostmitteleuropa,'" *Vierteljahrshefte für Zeitgeschichte* no. 46 (1998): 345–389.

Chapter 2

THE ROLE AND IMPACT OF GERMAN ETHNOPOLITICAL EXPERTS IN THE SS REICH SECURITY MAIN OFFICE

✦ ✦ ✦

Michael Fahlbusch

Preface

The Conference of German Historians (Deutscher Historikertag) at Frankfurt in 1998 was devoted to a controversial topic unparalleled in German historiography. It was a subject that had attracted much public attention even before the conference had started. The question under discussion was whether German historians had not only supported the NS regime ideologically, but also contributed to the Holocaust policy via their scientific research.[1] The papers delivered demonstrated that the major interest of some of the historians had indeed been not the teaching and study of history, but rather the pursuit of so-called *Volksgeschichte* and *Volkstumsforschung* (i.e., ethnopolitical research into the ethnic Germans and their history). This controversial discussion actually culminated in the International Conference on Southeast European Research during the Third Reich in Munich in October 2002 and arose even in the United States among the descendants of German-Russians.[2] These topics had begun to dominate cultural sciences during the 1930s. Michael Burleigh's book on German *Ostforschung* (1988) was the first serious scholarly attempt to focus attention on this topic. Since then, however, it has been ignored by German scholars. Meanwhile, new research results revealed the highly organized network in which *Volkstumsforschung* was realized and the extent to which this network collaborated with the SS. All this has been concealed for more than forty years.

This could be interesting as well in comparison to the Brain Trusts in the United States, which in contrast were examined in unrestricted discussion

Notes for this chapter begin on page 47.

after World War II. In 1948 the sociologist Talcott Parsons reported that World War II and the research for the intelligence services had given rise to several new approaches to sociology in the United States. The professionalization of cultural experts succeeded in producing several think-tanks like the research and analysis branch of the Office of Strategic Services (OSS). Their objective was enemy analysis, as we know so far from studies on the intelligence services.[3] The magnitude of the entanglement of science and politics becomes apparent when we take into account that about forty American historians and several leading geographers worked for the OSS during World War II.[4]

Unlike the discussion in the United States in the late 1940s, the break up of the wall of silence concealing the German scientific secret service seems now in particular a task for the present "young" generation of historians. The objective of this essay is to analyze the network of ethnic experts who were entangled in the *Volksdeutsche Forschungsgemeinschaften* (ethnic German research societies) and the SS Reich Security Main Office (RSHA), in the foreign intelligence branch of the SS.

Introduction

It is well worthwhile to enquire more closely into the NS regime's science policy and the organization of scholarship during the Third Reich. Postwar accounts maintain that the *Landes-* and *Volksforschung* in the Third Reich had been conducted in a serious, scientifically innovative way and had not been subject to National Socialist infiltration. Hence, sophisticated studies showing the extent of the *Volkswissenschaftler*'s involvement with Nazism are few and far between. The question of this science's relative importance within the framework of *Volkstumspolitik* has not been recognized as particularly salient.

Contemporaries' testimonials have suggested that there were no permanent institutions devoted to "special research" in the Third Reich. Even the *Volkstumsforschung* (research on ethnic Germans abroad), founded by geographers in the early 1920s, is said to have been initiated as an interdisciplinary field under the auspices of historians. Emil Meynen, speaking to the British intelligence service in 1947 at Camp Dustbin, stated that "it is not without interest [in] the history of its development that the first attempt [toward] concentration of forces in the beginning of the twenties ensued under a definite geographic leadership; ten years later, historical research takes the lead. And another feature [has become evident]: it is no more an isolated investigation of a single field, but [rather the realization] of regional and historical connections which leads again and again fruitfully to new research. And ... there was never fixed any unification of those regional research groups."[5]

This assessment is only partly true: it had indeed been German geographers who had initiated the research program of *Volkstumsforschung* during the Weimar Republic, but there was close interaction among those regional research groups. Meynen himself serves to illustrate this close interaction. He was no small fry in the nets of the British intelligence service: like the well known American geographer Richard Hartshorne, who chaired the Projects Committee of the OSS Board of Analysts in the U.S.,[6] Meynen had played a crucial part (up to 1945) as director of the Central Business Office of the *Volksdeutsche Forschungsgemeinschaften*, the six ethnic German research societies, as well as of the *Handwörterbuch des Grenz- und Auslanddeutschtums*. In addition, he had held numerous offices: secretary of the German *Geographentag* and of the central commission for scientific *Landeskunde* of Germany, head of the department of *Landeskunde*, head of the Publikationsstelle Ost (Publications Office East), and head of the population-political inventory for the *Generalplan Ost* (a strategic development plan created by the SS for the brutal incorporation into the Reich of a Germanic Eastern Europe). It appears that Meynen, when he was arrested, had already worked out his statement that *Volkstumsforschung* had not been organized as a scientific network structure during the NS regime. In the Allies' internment camps, this view emerged into a legend that has persisted until today. It is highly probable that the British secret service was well aware that Meynen's statements were at best distortions of the truth, because at the same time Wilfried Krallert, the director of the RSHA's department VI G and the branch of the Southeast German Research Society (SOFG) in Vienna, was being interrogated by the British intelligence service while the Brain Trust of the SS was "discovered" in July 1945. In addition, the RSHA VI G (the foreign intelligence branch of the SS) was endowed with the considerable sum of RM 2 million per year to be used solely for *Volkstumsforschung*.[7] Nevertheless, this assumption cannot be held on the strength of the secret service's thin interrogation protocols. It is, however, safe to assume that the Allies were perfectly well acquainted with the German *Volkstumsforschung* at the time they conducted their interrogations, because they dealt with their "scientific" knowledge and experience of Russia.[8]

It is notable that the connection between *Volkstumspolitik* and external cultural policy, as well as the fact that the promotion of *Kulturpropaganda* was a complementary part of ethnic policy, remain yet to be acknowledged by historiography. It has led to fatal historiographical simplifications, as in point of fact the *Deutschtumspolitik* had been the concern of at least two central offices, the Ministry of Interior and the Foreign Ministry, for almost one hundred years. During the Nazi period alongside these two ministries, Alfred Rosenberg's Ministry for the Occupied Eastern Territories was involved as well as the SS.

The Brain Trust

During the era of the NS regime, the *Volksdeutsche Forschungsgemein-schaften* recruited their personnel staff from a network of cultural sciences, founded in 1931, that had been covertly designing a conceptual framework for National Socialist ethnic policy. This network comprised a group of political consultants from the core of the young conservatives' movement who had already exerted their influence on political committees during the Weimar Republic through think-tanks and lobbying.

The claim of the nonexistence of an NS regime science policy must too yield to the facts. Apart from National Socialist staff policy in the universities, the promotion of the sciences in the Third Reich alone testifies to a strengthening of investments in that sector. The Reich Ministry of Science and Research doubled its budget to RM 22 million between 1935 and 1938; by 1942 its expenditures had risen to RM 97 million. The Reich Ministry of Interior (RMI), another important subsidizer, expended roughly RM 43 million on the sciences in 1935; this amount increased to RM 131 million in 1942.[9] The RMI therefore was the chief provider for research activities. Since a working partnership was in operation with the Deutsche Ausland-Institut at Stuttgart, *völkisch* science could control a total budget of at least RM 20 million. This substantial expansion of research activities, which, considering the general scarcity of funds in the state, could have been put into effect only by a coordinated science policy, throws a telling light on the investments in the NS science system.

The analysis presented in this chapter shows that after the Nazis' seizure of power in 1933, many *Volkstumsforscher* continued their careers without interruption. Toward the end of the 1930s, the Ethnic German Research Societies' staff comprised around 1,000 persons, including some of the conservatives mentioned above. Two hundred of them were archivists in the state archives administration, integrated into the Ethnic German Research Societies by their director Albert Brackmann and his successor Ernst Zipfel, who was also deputy chairman of the Westdeutsche Forschungsgemeinschaft (West German Research Society). Another 800 persons who were members of the Ethnic German Research Societies were engaged in work on the *Handwörterbuch des Grenz- und Auslanddeutschtums* (Handwörterbuch). The Ethnic German Research Societies' personnel can be further divided up as follows: 300 of the 800 were attached to the Deutsches Ausland-Institut at Stuttgart, which was in charge of the *Handwörterbuch*'s overseas volume. The remaining 500 persons belonged to the six other research societies. The Nordostdeutsche Forschungsgemeinschaft (North East Ethnic German Research Society, NOFG), with a staff of 150 by far the largest of the research groups, controlled more than four hundred research projects.

A board of eighteen directors operated on the strategic level and determined the scientific and political development of *Volkswissenschaft* in the

Third Reich. Its members were the directors of the six research societies and of their branches as well as the respective officials from the RMI and the Foreign Ministry. They came from the Juniklub and then the Volksdeutscher Klub, a populist circle of right-wing intellectuals that had emerged from the former in 1924/25 to assume cultural leadership during the Weimar Republic and bring about radical revisionism and the antidemocratic alliance between the conservative right and the National Socialists on the occasion of the campaign against the Young Plan. From 1937 on, the SS exerted its influence through the representatives of the Volksdeutsche Mittelstelle (VoMi), and after 1943 directly through the RSHA's branches III B and VI G. The board of directors consisted of twelve historians, three geographers, three archivists, one geologist, and one economist, who were joined by officials of the ministries and a VoMi representative. It is notable that most of this assembly's members had been born before the turn of the century. Albert Brackmann, the oldest of them, had been born in 1871 and was therefore 62 years old when the Nazis came into power. The managers of the branches of the six regional research societies that belonged to the operational level were born after the turn of the century (with the exception of Paul Wentzcke). The youngest executive, only 25 years old in 1937, was a member of the SS. Out of a total of 25 executives, only 6 did not belong to the NSDAP. There was a strong disposition toward joining the SS, especially among the executives born after 1900.

The group of cultural experts and archivists that formed the Ethnic German Research Societies were mostly servile functionaries with deeply rooted instincts of obedience to orders who surrendered themselves unconditionally to the service of politics. This elite of functionaries may be divided into three types of officials:

1. University teachers, born before 1890, who had fought in World War I and who blamed the losses sustained by the German Reich on parliamentarism and democracy. Members of *völkisch*-nationalist factions and partly of the Young Conservatives, they constituted the Ethnic German Research Societies' strategic executive council with contacts with top-level offices in Party and Government. The Ethnic German Research Societies' board of directors was the central strategic leadership body.[10]
2. Scholars born between 1890 and 1905. Only some of them had fought in World War I, but most came from the *völkisch* youth movement and were susceptible to conservative and *völkisch* anti-Semitic doctrines. They integrated themselves into *völkisch* associations and the Young Conservatives and collaborated with them without compunction. At the beginning of the Third Reich most of them held their Ph.D.s or were engaged in their *Habilitation* (the degree needed to obtain a professorship). As the future academic

elite they were the main field of recruitment for the *Volkswissen-schaften*. They constituted the Ethnic German Research Societies' operative management and were in charge of the six regional research societies' branches.

3. Scholars born after 1900 who were beginning their university education or finishing their doctorate at the beginning of the NS regime. They constituted the main potential for the SS and its subdivisions. At the beginning of World War II they were young, highly motivated experts, aged 30 to 35, who were recruited for special missions. They may also be found in the RSHA.

This Brain Trust for *Volkstumspolitik*, the Ethnic German Research Societies, was divided into six regionally and functionally distinct research societies and institutions with branches in all neighboring countries. Because their classified subject matter was restricted to the issues and problems raised by these respective states, this Brain Trust was never recognized for what it was by independent experts or the Allies' intelligence services. Even when Paul Norman Förster, a member of the Künsberg Sonderkommando, a special SS commando unit of cultural scientific experts specializing in the looting of regional statistics and scientific libraries for the occupation authorities, finally managed to be picked up by the Red Army in 1942 in the East European theatre of the Kalmyk Steppe, we can assume that the intelligence service of Russia was not well informed about his activities.[11] The regional division is reflected in the hierarchical and functional structure that regulated this large-scale scientific organization. The Brain Trust supplied relevant information to the Foreign Ministry, the Ministry for the East, the RMI, Himmler's strategic planning bureaucracy, and the leadership of so-called *Volksdeutsche* organizations, including the Volksbund für das Deutschtum im Ausland (VDA) and the League of the German East (Bund Deutscher Osten, BDO). Research was conducted in the shape of an interdisciplinary and project-focused cooperation between geographers, historians, archivists, *Volkskundler* (folklorists), sociologists, *Rassenkundler* (racial experts), and art historians.

For their designs of the future German *Lebensraum* the SS was able to draw various types of information from the memoranda composed by these experts. The material supplied included publications, translations, maps, art collections, the German National List (*Deutsche Volksliste* or DVL), and the German *Volkstumskartei*, as well as registers of persons and institutions that were also passed on to the Gestapo. Political advice was offered concerning the course of frontiers (such as in the preparation of the 1938 Munich Treaty or the division of Poland in 1939 and Yugoslavia in 1941), the handling of minorities and other populations (such as in the 1938 and 1940 Vienna agreements), and resettlement projects and looting of cultural goods in the occupied countries.

This chapter will elaborate on three distinct spheres of influence that illustrate the societies' complicity in ethnic cleansing: The Ethnic German Research Societies exerted their influence over the German leadership of *Volksgruppen* and more than thirty separatist factions and *Volksgruppen* organizations in the occupied states. They managed the minorities within the Reich and ascertained their relation to Germandom. Moreover, the Ethnic German Research Societies supported the establishment and scientific legitimization of the Reich's *Volksgruppenpolitik*. As experts on the courses of frontiers, they contributed to the ethnic segregation of Europe into culturally homogenous districts (*Kulturräume*). They participated in ethnic cleansing and provided the Holocaust with scientific endorsement. In 1947, geographer Emil Meynen euphemistically termed his search for objective criteria of a scientifically endorsed racism the "registration of remnants of German settlements according to population-hygienic viewpoints."[12] By way of the *Deutschtumsforschung* (studies on German regions and people in Europe), the Ethnic German Research Societies supported the NS regime's racial and ethnic policy as well as their geopolitical aims. These may be called the complementary sides of the same coin of Germany's policy of furthering a cultural hegemony of Germany, which was conceived as a society of fate, thought and culture.

Four concepts borrowed from cultural science were instrumental in the promotion of this goal of politics. In order to preserve the unity of Germandom, the Polish minorities were defined as Germans under the heading of *Kulturgemeinschaft*, the Alsatians were subsumed under the German *Sprachgemeinschaft* (linguistically related), the *Schlonsaken* (in Poland) were qualified as Germans as members of the same *Denkgemeinschaft*, and, finally, the *Windischen* (in Caryntnia) were made Germans by the concept of *Blutgemeinschaft* (virtual descent by Aryan blood). Whenever a people had no ethnological features in common with the Germans, the concept of *Denkgemeinschaft* was reverted to. This artificially constructed concept of ethnicity served as a safeguard for a national "German" identity, based on the exclusion of Jews and Slavs in cases where a common language was no longer traceable. Apart from that, the *Volkstumswissenschaftler* granted small linguistic societies such as the Rätoromanen (in the Swiss Grisons and in South Tyrol) their cultural independence, provided they could be shielded from the influence of Italian cultural imperialism.

The aim of the German ethnopolitical strategy, as determined by Albert Brackmann, leader of the NOFG, was to be population transfer (*Umvolkung*).[13] *Umvolkung* meant the germanization of German-friendly peoples in the conquered territories and the allocation of particular peoples to areas of settlement appropriate for them. It was the Ethnic German Research Societies' political privilege to select the minorities to be officially defined as such. For the purpose of shifting these minorities according to "German blood" the Dahlem branch of the NOFG kept a copy of the German National List.

Centralization of the Ethnic German Research Societies by the SS and the German Intelligence Service in 1943

Even before the Ethnic German Research Societies were subordinated to the SS in the autumn of 1943, *Volksforschung* underwent a process of radicalization: while at the beginning of the war the Ethnic German Research Societies' members participated in the settling of border questions and conferences on the partition of conquered territories, after 1941 they also took part in looting cultural goods with the Künsberg Sonderkommando and Reichsleiter Rosenberg's *Einsatzstab* (special unit Rosenberg's in looting cultural goods). Already in the spring of 1941, before the attack on Yugoslavia, the historian and director of the Southeast German Research Society in Vienna, Otto Brunner presented the Balkan germanization policy exactly as it was implemented in practice a short time afterward. In the autumn of the same year a first review of the Balkan *Volksgruppen* policy was drawn up by the Foreign Ministry in the presence of the Ethnic German Research Societies' directors. In the fall of 1941, a meeting of the political department of the Ministry for the Occupied Eastern Territories was attended by the board of directors. A couple of days before the Wannsee Conference, which Georg Leibbrandt attended, he intimated his plans for a future ethnic policy during a meeting with the board of directors. They were therefore well aware of the overall goals of the disintegration of the East European peoples by ethnic research.[14]

The progress of the war and the expansion of the SS's power at last entailed a considerable shifting of competencies within the mechanisms of political power. The political leadership was supported in its "wisdom" by the *Volksforscher*. After the fall of Under State Secretary Martin Luther in the Foreign Ministry, the department "Germany" was dissolved and reorganized into divisions Inland I and Inland II by the spring of 1943. The *Volkstum* organizations and research facilities were placed under the authority of Inland II, the division that was also responsible for keeping in touch with the SS (see figure 2.1).[15]

The RMI was Himmler's next objective. In a close discussion with the state secretary of RMI, Wilhelm Stuckart, and in a proposal addressed to Himmler via the Chef der Sicherheitspolizei und des SD Ernst Kaltenbrunner on 28 May 1943, Wilfried Krallert managed to concentrate all relevant research institutes in his new office of RSHA VI G.[16] In the course of the reallocation of statistical authority over research fields and regional studies services (*landeskundliche Information*) the charges of the RMI's division VI were transferred to the RSHA's branch VI G in the autumn of 1943. Prior to that, the Waffen-SS had tried several times to take control over the research facilities. Likewise, the Künsberg Sonderkommando's future was in jeopardy: it was eventually dissolved, and part of the staff was transferred to RSHA VI G.[17] To judge by Jens Banach's study, the RSHA is conspicuous for the top-level young technocrats that figured on

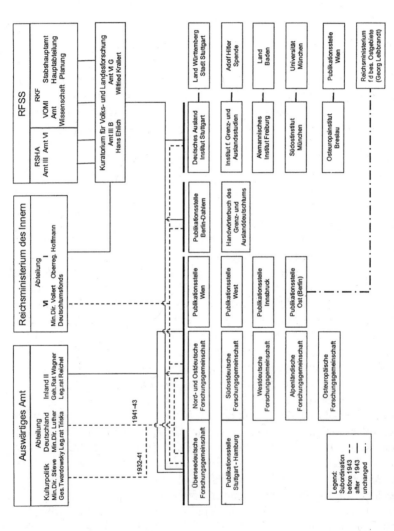

FIGURE 2.1: The Subordination of Institutes and Associations of the Kuratorium für Volkstums- und Landesforschung before and after 1943. *Source:* PRO WO 208/5228, Personal File Wilfried Krallert, First Interrogation Report.

its payroll. This applies to Werner Best, the SS's administration expert, Reinhard Heydrich himself, and the heads of the two intelligence services.[18] Even the division leaders of RSHA III B and VI G, physician Hans Ehlich and geographer and historian Wilfried Krallert, represented a new type of morally uninhibited administration specialists whose confidence in handling a weapon equaled their skills with pen and ink.

All of the facilities conducting *Volkstumsforschung, Landes-* and *Volksforschung*, formerly controlled by the RMI, were newly placed under the authority of Amtschef RSHA VI (*SD-Ausland*) SS-Oberführer Walter Schellenberg, in cooperation with RSHA III (*SD-Inland*) under the direction of Otto Ohlendorf, while the Foreign Ministry continued to fulfill its superintending function. Within the RSHA the responsibility for foreign intelligence lay with Group G, the "scientific-methodical research-service." It was directed by Wilfried Krallert in cooperation with his assistant, the specialist on the Baltic states Jürgen Hehn of the NOFG, while the historian Hans Joachim Beyer was in charge of the Reinhard Heydrich Foundation in Prague. Through the office of RSHA III B (*Volkstum*), founded in 1939, renamed in 1940 and headed by SS-Standartenführer Hans Ehlich, the SS intelligence service commanded the major institutions of regional studies. The *Amtsgruppe* RSHA III B alone numbered around 300 *Volkstum* specialists who had been working well behind the military lines for resettlement and genocide since 1937/38.

Schellenberg was in command of at least ten divisions including research and analysis branches, which were in turn headed by group VI experts such as SS-Sturmbannführer Martin Sandberger, SS-Standartenführer Eugen Steimle, or SS-Obersturmbannführer Otto Skorzeny. Many of Schellenberg's employees in department VI had been leaders of Special Units of the SS (*SS-Einsatzgruppen*) in the East. The continuous growth of its power led to a concurrence of two functions in the SD, described by Heinz Höhne: "Espionage in foreign countries and serving as a rallying point for all those who were to lead task forces and Special Units in World War II, carrying political terror and racial slaughtering into Hitler's Europe."[19] Other members of RSHA VI were the linguist Manfred Pechau, himself a task-force leader, and Giselher Wirsing, the future chief editor of the conservative newspaper *Christ und Welt.*[20]

The RSHA VI G's map department and the surveying and processing office for looted libraries were accommodated in the Vienna evacuated branch office of the Southeast German Research Society at the Abbey of St. Lambrecht in Steiermark, Austria. This former abbey also housed an outstation of the Mauthausen and Ravensbrück concentration camps comprising around 120 prisoners, of whom at least four were dispatched for work in the branch at the demand of the RSHA VI G. The SS, who confiscated St. Lambrecht in 1938 and parceled out its estates into *Reichserbhöfe*, used the abbey as a storage place for over 200,000 volumes of Russica.[21] Since some stocks had been damaged by Allied bombing raids, a centralization at St.

Lambrecht of all branches' stocks was under consideration. Belorussian library stocks from Minsk and Baranowitsch were to be transferred there as well.[22] The British 8th Army discovered this branch by chance when they interrogated SS member Heinz Pedyna on 29 July 1945. Until then the British intelligence service had been aware only that the German intelligence service had scientific branches of the Regional Research Society related to the Foreign Ministry and the RMI.[23]

In February 1944, 16 SS members belonged to the intelligence branch VI G; by until July 1944 membership had increased to 80 persons. The continuous extension of the RSHA VI G's responsibilities during the year led to the engagement of 10 more staff members as well as, finally, 20 members of the Wannsee Institute.[24] By January 1944, scientific institutions with a total of 300 employees were subordinated to the Dienststelle Dr. Wilfried Krallert (an alias for RSHA VI G) along with the Ethnic German Research Societies and their branches. Krallert's office used aliases to cloak its activities: "Central Office for Regional and Ethnic Research of the RMI" and, as of the summer of 1944, officially Der Reichsführer SS-Kuratorium für Volkstums- und Länderkunde. What is particularly interesting about this *Kuratorium* is that it brought together representatives of the RMI, the VoMi and the RKF (Reichs commissioner for the strengthening of Germandom). The RSHA was officially in charge; the Foreign Ministry was only consulted informally.[25]

The Reinhard Heydrich Foundation was founded in 1942 at the Deutsche Karls-Universität in Prague. This third Reichsuniversität next to Posen and Strasbourg was an SS stronghold. The Reinhard Heydrich Foundation was supervised by Hans Joachim Beyer (born in 1908). Since his beginnings as a *völkisch* journalist in the fringe of the journal *Tat*, he had developed into an ethnopolitical expert for the RSHA III. There is evidence that he was responsible for drawing up the list of Polish university teachers singled out for execution in Lvov in July 1941. In Prague, where important members of the Southeast German Research Society taught ethno- and population-political disciplines, Beyer was commissioned as director of a newly founded department for *Volkslehre* and *Nationalitätenkunde*. He also took over what had originally been called the Reichsstiftung für deutsch-slawische Forschung. After Heydrich's death it was renamed the Reinhard Heydrich Foundation. Formally, it was headed by the rector of the University of Prague. Karl Hermann Frank was appointed its curator; law historian Wilhelm Weizsäcker officiated as head of the administration. It was structured into four departments: law and economy, directed by Weizsäcker; philology and history, under Heinz Zatschek; *Volkswissenschaft,* under Hans Joachim Beyer; and natural science, under geologist Arthur Winkler-Hermaden. Its financial future was secured by RM 1.5 million drawn from the confiscated Masaryk Foundation and the Lausitz Wenden-Stiftung, which had been impounded by the RSHA. The new foundation's aim and task was to promote the assimilation of the Czechs, i.e., to overcome the "peculiarity of the Czech individual" and to determine the "significance of Judaism for German-Czech relations."[26] In practice, this meant the establishment of eight departments of cultural science with a total of over 90 employees, headed by the Austrian members of the Southeast German Research Society mentioned above.[27] Their library stocks of about 70,000 volumes were assembled over the course of several large-scale plundering flings in various libraries.

Intelligence Service Duties

The most significant feature of this new Reichsstiftung für Länderkunde (Regional Research Society) of the RSHA was that it coordinated all of the regional research groups, including the Wannsee Institute, in its role as "substantial auxiliary organization for the foreign intelligence service."[28] However, the true significance of this unification can be appreciated only when the projected unification of the two foreign intelligence services, the military's and the Security Service's (SD), is taken into account. The decree on the unification of the foreign intelligence services that was issued by the chief of the Sipo and the SD (Security Police and Security Service) on 3 May 1944 following Hitler's orders thus also impinged on the Ethnic German Research Societies branches' activities. "The Group VI G will take over the management and working direction of these units.... Thereby, all major areas [*Grossräume*] will have been brought into this research net.... A basic condition for these institutes is [that] as scientific establishments of different types ... the connection with the SD must not be discernible from the outside, and known only within the narrowest circle of collaborators."[29] Krallert's office, RSHA VI G, was now responsible for the standardization of the press bulletins, which, however, still had to be modified to fit regional circumstances. Simultaneously, the production of maps was reorganized by the RSHA VI G in agreement with the Oberkommando des Heeres's (Headquarter of the German Army) war maps department.[30]

In the final stages of the war, in the summer of 1944, the head of the RSHA III B, Hans Ehlich, explained to the Ethnic German Research Societies' board of directors the significance of the measures that were being taken by the SS. He emphasized that the new regulation placing the Ethnic German Research Societies under the RSHA's authority was not meant to tie scientific work to the political leadership's apron strings. However, the shift of the charges to the Reichsführer SS would entail "that we should like to give you political directions and indicate to you the overall political goal to guide your scientific work by." This was presented as part of the rationalization of work due to the critical "Nachwuchsproblem" (shortage of junior experts): "We can say that the younger generation is practically nonexistent." He therefore suggested to the *Volkstumsforscher* that Heinrich Himmler should exempt talented specialists from Wehrmacht duties via

General Keitel. He elaborated on the future value of the research already carried out by the *Volkstumsforscher*: "We do not yet agree about the significance of our work in relation to the end of this war. We cannot yet form a clear conception of how the problems will be solved in the future; however, there can be no doubt that the work carried out by you is of the utmost significance for future development and planning." He then named the four most important tasks—not all of them really new—that the *Volkstumsforschers* should devote themselves to in the future:

1. He designated *Erhaltung und Stärkung des Deutschtums* (preservation and strengthening of Germandom) as of the first priority. The Freiburg Alemannische Institut regional and ethnic projects were presented as models for this kind of work.
2. "Winning back buried *Deutschtum*" was necessary where *Deutschtum* who had been *umgevolkt* (absorbed) centuries ago lay concealed among foreign peoples. He emphasized that a *Volk* was not only a "racially connected Society of the blood," but also a "community of fate." He was not concerned with solving incidental problems of *Umvolkung* in the sense of germanization, but with sifting the neighboring peoples for German blood and "trying to win it [the blood] back to the German *Volk* by a process of education." This was, indeed, necessitated by the Germans' "biological condition" alone.
3. He stressed the "raising of the overall Germanic consciousness" in National Socialist propaganda, in order to intensify cultural-political work among other European peoples of "Germanic" extraction by pointing out features held in common with the Germans.
4. The "analysis and discussion of foreign *Volkstümer* within our *Raum* as well as outside our frontiers" was to be promoted as a *volkspolitische* duty.[31]

These precepts, presented to the Ethnic German Research Societies' board of directors so plainly upon the reorganization of *Volkstumsarbeit* in the summer of 1944, are reflected almost completely in the Ethnic German Research Societies leaders' reports. The only novelty was a certain disillusionment at the prospect of the prolonged crisis-handling that the future seemed to hold in store for them. But this does not alter the fact that they served as accessories to a regime of terror and that some of them boasted of having had a hand in things, even after the war.

A Normal Nazi Shooting Star: Wilfried Krallert's Biography

Krallert, alias Fritz Bergmann, was born on 23 January 1912 in Vienna, the son of a senior official of the Ministry of Transport. At only sixteen he began his political career when he formed a local branch of the Deutsche Mittelschülerbund, an extremist right-wing association of secondary schoolboys under the auspices of the SA. From 1930 to 1932 he was a member of the Deutsche Wehr, a right-wing paramilitary organization, and of Ludendorf's Tannenbergbund. During this time he was appointed *Landesleiter Vienna* of the Deutsche Mittelschülerbund. In April 1933 he joined the National Socialist Party in Austria with Party No. 1,529,315; he became a *Blockwart* in June of the same year. Three months later he joined the newly formed Mittelstandarte Vienna, which was converted into SS-Standarte 89 in April 1934. According to the Nazi plot of the same year he was to participate in the assassination of Austrian Chancellor Dollfuss as the official NSDAP historian, but owing to a last-minute confusion with his brother Reinhold, who finally attended to this assassination, and was therefore refused admission to the University of Vienna, Wilfried did not do so. After the failure of the plot he was promoted to SS-Hauptscharführer and employed as a staff member of *SS-Standarte 89*. He joined the intelligence section of the Standarte in autumn and organized a secret mail service with the Nazi inmates of the detention camp Wöllersdorf, where, for example, the geographer Friedrich Metz—later head of the West German Research Society—was detained. In the same year he joined the SD as a detached member of the staff of the SD-Hauptamt. From 1934 to 1941 he made a number of journeys in the Balkans, under cover of research work, on behalf of that office and later of department VI of the RSHA.

He studied history and geography at the University of Vienna under Hans Hirsch and Hugo Hassinger, both heads of the Southeast German Research Society. On the completion of his studies with a Ph.D. in 1935, he was appointed secretary to this society in Vienna and became later, after the Anschluss, director of the branch office of this society as well as a member of the Blockstelle Vienna, the predecessor of RSHA VI/E of the RSHA. From this time onward he traveled for business under the alias Bergmann. In July 1938 he was promoted to SS-Untersturmführer, and in spring 1939 he was officially attached to Amt VI of the RSHA; he was promoted to SS-Obersturmführer that July. In April 1941 he was named *Sonderführer "Z,"* and he took part in the Yugoslav campaign with the Künsberg Sonderkommando of the Foreign Ministry. In this document section he collected population statistics and maps from the unpublished Yugoslavian census data of 1931. These documents were data-processed, and maps were immediately distributed to the special units of the SS in Yugoslavia and the Wehrmacht. During this time, he was involved in the Vienna Treaty between Hungary and Romania in August 1940 where he met, for example, the population expert of the Romanian government, Sabin Manuilă, who provided Krallert with territorial population data. Immediately after the clash against Belgrade, Krallert attended the Vienna peace conference of Italy and Germany on the April 1941 partition of Yugoslavia, during which he supported State Secretary of the RMI Wilhelm Stuckart and his know-how. In the summer of 1941 he accompanied the Künsberg Son-derkommando to Russia, where early in 1942 it was converted to the Waffen-SS. Krallert was promoted to SS-Hauptsturmführer in June 1942. In the course of his document collections he established a distribution center by the branch office in Vienna. The cooperation of the Publications Office Vienna with the Special Units of the SS reached its tragic climax between July 1941 and 1944. In this context, a division of work developed between Reichsleiter Rosenberg's *Einsatzstab*, the Special Units of the SS, and the Publications Office Vienna. Their work concentrated above all on the collection and processing of information for the political and military leadership. In March 1943 Krallert was recalled by the RSHA, and in October 1943 of that year he was appointed as acting Gruppenleiter of the newly created RSHA VI G for the duration of the war and director of the Kuratorium für Volkstums- und Landesforschung des Reichsführers SS. After receiving his appointments, Krallert spent a third of his time in Berlin and the rest with the Publications Office Vienna. During this time he visited Paris for the purpose of obtaining maps and documents. According to translated documents, in autumn 1944 he was apparently promoted to SS-Sturmbannführer.[32]

In his capacity as a geographer and historian, Krallert was invited to participate in the planned Nazi assassination of Austrian Chancellor Dollfuss, but through a slip-up, he missed out on the event. A cartographer and ethnographic expert on Southeastern Europe, he worked for the foreign intelligence branch (department VI) of the RSHA and headed the Austrian Wannsee Institute. As Amt VI G Gruppenleiter, he also served as secretary of the so-called Kuratorium (III/VI), which coordinated domestic and foreign intelligence research. At the end of the war he was arrested and interned by the British, who interrogated him and eventually released him in 1948. There were reports that French intelligence used him thereafter, and the Gehlen organization picked him up in 1952. Then he may have been associated with the Federal Office for the Protection of the Constitution (Bundesnachrichtendienst), the West German equivalent of the FBI. Documents from 1963 and 1964 indicate some CIA concern about Krallert's wartime activities (and presumably his susceptibility to Soviet pressure), but the file ends on an inconclusive note.[33] He died in the 1960s.

In the spring of 1944, Wilfried and his brother Reinhold supported Adolf Eichmann and Wilhelm Höttl in the Hungarian campaign. An action, in which the scholars of the Publications Office Vienna participated in 1944, was to be directed toward the confiscation of the stocks of Jewish and antiquarian bookshops in Budapest containing literature of interest to the SS research institutes. The owners were to be apprehended for possessing anti-German propaganda materials and handed over to the Gestapo. The planning of this action lay completely and entirely in the hands of Wilfried Krallert, and therefore of the Southeast German Research Society. For the advance clarification of this task with the Hungarian state police, he led discussions in Budapest with State Secretary of Interior László Baky and with Government Councilor Peter Hain. On 5 May 1944, a "spontaneous action" was executed against approximately 150 Jewish bookshops and antiquarian bookshops. The searching of the bookshops lasted only a weekend. The possession of antistate materials served as a pretext. The action was carefully prepared, "since in view of the planned total solution of the Jewish question in Hungary, first of all the Jewish businesses in Budapest themselves may not yet be encroached upon and the final closure of the bookshops carried out beforehand could trigger deep unrest as well as interventions from the Minister of Interior and from Horthy." This fear of Krallert was, in view of the scale of the SS actions in Budapest, unfounded. For the three-and-a-half-day action, 30 to 50 businesses most important to the RSHA VI G were chosen. "The entire action means for [the RSHA] VI G the unique opportunity, in a country known for its extraordinarily highly developed bookshop and antiquarian bookshop system, to investigate this material and for the institutes to receive them."[34] For this action came six commandos, each under the leadership of a member of the RSHA VI G who led the persons knowledgeable in the region and the subject at hand. These were recruited from the Publications Office Vienna. In addition to SS-Hauptsturmführer Wilfried Krallert, the following participated in the action: his wife, Gertrud Krallert (SOFG), and his brother, SS-Untersturmführer Reinhold Krallert; also SS-Sturmbannführer Fesel, SS-Obersturmführer Alfred Karasek (SOFG), SS-Obersturmführer Leo, and SS-Obersturmführer Hachmeister, as well as Katharina Klaftenegger and Irma Steinsch, both of the Publications Office Vienna. The Foreign Ministry in Berlin was represented by the former leader of the *Volkstums* department (*Volkstumsreferat*) Helmut Triska, who at the time was active as a cultural attache in Budapest. The Carlton and Gellert hotels provided accommodation to the special units. The *Volksgruppenführung* in Hungary, which along with the SS profited from the aryanization of Jewish property, was informed and had from SOFG assistant Irma Steinsch probably three further assistants to place. The intended destruction of the cultural heritage was not only a violation of national rights, but an integral element of the "Final Solution."

What was the use of this action? According to Wilfried Krallert's representation, the main thing was to sort out, on the basis of prepared lists, Jewish authors such as Heinrich Heine or fairy tale books edited by Jewish publishers. Extensive amounts of scientific literature, such as Krallert had originally assumed, were evidently not to be found here. Under Reinhold Krallert's supervision, a few days later the sorted books were loaded onto three freight carriers and transported into a depot in Sonnberg (Naphegy). After World War II, a part of the stolen books was returned to Budapest from Prague.[35]

Thanks to Reinhold Krallert's "prudent manner of work" in the *Einsatzkommando*, the RSHA VI G carried away "extensive material finds in the Badoglio-Italian and Polish offices of Budapest." With "great success" he further led the "lucrative action against the Jewish bookshops in Buda-pest."[36] Without a doubt the SD's force directed itself also against the Ital-ian embassy of the Badoglio government. Over and above this, Reinhold Krallert found a diary with over twenty addresses of Polish exile organi-zations in Great Britain whose pamphlets were immediately translated by the Publications Office Dahlem and analyzed by the SD.[37]

The example of the scrupulous planning by the Publications Office Vienna leader and the execution of this action demonstrates the scope of action in which the *Volkstumsforscher* operated. The Hungarian govern-ment's first measures against the Jewish bookshops were already unleashed on 30 April with the promulgation of a decree concerning "The Protection of Hungarian Intellectual Life from the Literary Works of Jewish Authors," which led to the banning of Jewish authors. All such books were confis-cated. Excepted at first were libraries and bookshops with scientific works by Jews. László Baky was regarded as a "notorious anti-Semite." Both of Wilfried Krallert's contacts were servile functionaries of the SS. Beginning on 3 May all Jewish houses in Budapest were marked with the yellow star of David.[38] In a subsequent move, as documented by Randolph Braham, the closing of all bookshops in Jewish possession was officially demanded from the Hungarian side. The climax was the book-burning action on 16 June 1944 in Budapest when nearly 450,000 books fell victim to the flames. The coordinated action against the Jewish businesses in Budapest—of 30,000 businesses, 18,000 were closed, leading to deep disruptions of the Budapest economy—ended with the liquidation of the business owners. The Aryanization of the Jewish businesses had certainly already begun in March 1944 under the personal leadership of the RSHA head, Ernst Kalten-brunner.[39] The evacuation of the first zones with Jewish populations oc-curred, at the time of the book action. The deportees were murdered in Auschwitz. This example unambiguously proves that under Wilfried Krallert's overall leadership, RSHA VI G indirectly participated in the extermination of Jews, and that the action was coordinated meticulously with Hungarian and Austrian collaborators. In contrast with the actions carried out by Reichsleiter Rosenberg's *Einsatzstab* in other European countries, where as a general rule stores of booty were hoarded into tem-porary storerooms, the possibility presented itself to the RSHA VI G of its research institutes being able without delay to collect specialized South-east European literature.

Here we must ask whether the SS foreign intelligence service during the Third Reich had indeed never held "a really influential position, not even as an advisory authority."[40] This cynical assessment by Wilhelm Höttl lowers indeed the importance of the German intelligence service. It has, however, been proved false by new findings. He had himself enjoyed the fruits of the German intelligence service's activities during his posting in Hungary. The records of the British intelligence service indicate that the SS exerted its influence very directly. Höttl of course was involved with the Jung Affair, i.e., the "flourishing traffic in gold and other valuables" to Austria and eventually Switzerland.[41]

In the British documents, Wilfried Krallert stood in the rank of SS-Sturmbannführer. Given his age—only 33—this would meant that his career as a Nazi scientist was outstanding, but this is a title that never was verified during my research. In the last days of the war, Krallert evacuated the Publications Office Vienna to St. Lambrecht Abbey and in addition traveled to Graz until his arrest on 30 May 1945 in order to assist in the evacuation of the Wannsee Institute to St. Lambrecht. He was interned at 373 PW Camp by the British army. Over the years, British and American intelligence services were in close contact concerning Krallert.

In fact, the assessment of the British intelligence service seems to be reliable; Krallert

> spent large sums of money on his journeys, and wild parties at Melle eventually caused the dismissal to the British staff. The general opinion on Krallert, gathered from our desk officers who knew him or of him during and after the war, may be summed up as follows: A man of intelligence and great ambition. Conceited, ruthless, boasting and (despite his ambition) lazy. An Austrian of the worst type (from another Austrian!) a Nazi of the worst type. He appears also to have possessed the 'finest' collection of pornographic literature in Germany: a hobby for which he used his official appointments. While exercising his control over the Wannsee Institute, he secured the dismissal of Achmeteli—then Director—and the appointment of his old tutor Prof. Hans Koch, with whom he still has close contact. Koch is now head of the Ost-Europa-Institute of University of Munich and must be expected strongly to support Krallert. Information on Krallert's position around the time of the capitulation could probably be obtained from Dr. Harald Speer, who was with the Wannsee Institute in Graz, and is now with the Landesamt für Verfassungsschutz, Stuttgart. There is evidence on the files that Krallert, while employed by DRS, was actually selling his information elsewhere. He was dismissed on this suspicion and for his general incompetence around February 1951, when he returned to Austria. Since his dismissal he appears to have acted as collector of material for various institutes and organizations, particularly for Prof. Valjavec in Munich (Süd-Ost-Europa-Institute), for Prof. Koch and for the Gehlen organization. There are rumours that his patrons have found him expensive. A summing up might read: An intriguer who uses his position to introduce his friends, and his friends to increase his position. An expensive and unproductive luxury for any organization.[42]

But not for the Cold War-experienced German Federal Office for the Protection of the Constitution (*Bundesnachrichtendienst*).

Conclusion

In spite of the numerous studies on the fate of ethnic Germans in Eastern Europe, the *Volkstumsforschung* has attracted only modest attention; this neglect is unjustifiable, since *Volkstumsforschung* played a strategic role within National Socialist *Volkstumspolitik*. *Volkstumspolitik* was, on the one hand, a revisionist policy that emerged from the Treaty of Versailles and is in evidence along the whole of the German frontiers, especially in the new states in East-Central Europe. On the other hand, it continued the German Empire's Pan-German expansionist tradition with its ideal of a germanized Eastern Europe. But the overall goal of the NS regime's clandestine foreign policy had always been the establishment of an Irredenta, not only in the territories of the German Empire, i.e., the Baltic, East-Central European and Southeast European states, but also in the neutral states, especially after 1939. According to National Socialist *völkisch* Empire ideology, these countries had always been under German influence, an assertion that until today has not been properly acknowledged by current historiography and, in some cases, has even been denied. *Volkstumspolitik* was an important feature of German foreign policy (concerning itself with German minorities or minorities with so-called ethno-German roots) and population politics. Its goal was to divide the population of the occupied states into groups according to ethnic, political, and socioeconomic criteria.[43]

The intention after 1939 was to segregate from the occupied territories those ethnic minorities that had already been sequestered by the Nuremberg Laws of 1935 or could not be germanized by National Socialist *Volksgruppenrecht* for strategic reasons. Simultaneously, *Volkstumspolitik* concentrated on investigating the *Volksdeutschen* and determining their cultural classification. Integration into the *deutscher Lebensraum* was a matter of great concern to the so-called *Zwischenvölker* (a derogatory term for Slavic minorities), i.e., the *Wenden* (Sorbs) in the Lausitz, the *Schlonsaks*, the *Masurians*, the *Windischen* in Carynthia, and the so-called *Wasserpolen* (bilingual Poles) in Upper Silesia.

In order to succeed in segregating the ethnic groups in the occupied states, *Volkstumspolitik* sought scientific advice from numerous research societies and highly specialized scientific institutions. The activities of these institutions focused on two objectives: the social and cultural experts supplied basic geographical and historical data used for verification or falsification of territorial claims, which in turn were instrumental in segregating ethnic groups in the occupied territories; and they served as consultants for the intelligence services of the SS (RSHA), the Wehrmacht (Ic), and other institutions of cultural policy belonging to German military or civil authorities in the occupied territories.

The presence within the Ethnic German Research Societies of representatives of Otto Ohlendorf's and Walter Schellenberg's offices, as well as Interior and foreign intelligence branches (i.e., RSHA III B and VI G), indicates that the Ethnic German Research Societies served as a typical accessory to the fact, either supplying and processing relevant intelligence materials or solving ethnic questions of practical concern. The fact that members of the Research Societies had been working for the SS even before it was incorporated into the Kuratorium für Volks- und Länderkunde (one of RSHA VI G's aliases) and had served as consultants on questions of *Volkstumspolitik* for the task forces substantiates this further. It was not sufficient just to accumulate an abundance of "scientific" data from foreign countries (i.e., the occupied territories). Only by processing this multitude of population-political, regional, and statistical materials could the logical unity of the SS's information and terror apparatus be warranted. The "mental warfare in science, mass communications and art" expresses this to a point.[44] A new objective of the SS's work that had emerged with the beginning of the war, i.e., involving foreign peoples more strongly in the *volksdeutsche Arbeit*, was the real background of such a consciousness.

Regardless of their crimes against humanity, these German *völkisch* experts of the RSHA were involved in the postwar period too. This was the case for the German espionage service, as the example of Wilfried Krallert shows: as a member of the SS RSHA specialists, he was interrogated by the British intelligence service when he was a prisoner of war in Austria. But surprisingly he was one of the few who where not accused in the Nuremberg tribunal against war crimes. Even though the documents from his Vienna office, including his diaries, are known as not available up to now despite the fact that they were seized and transferred to Great Britain in 1946. However, in the Public Record Office in London several files of the Control Commission for Germany and Austrian intelligence bureau give an intimate insight into his collaboration with the Allied intelligence service until 1955.[45]

Notes

This essay is dedicated to Horst Kissmehl, who motivated me to further studies on this subject and who died in 1995, and to Meir Buchsweiler, Kibbuz Beeri, Israel. The author thanks also Antonia Bertschinger in Basel, Switzerland, for the translation. I am indebted to James H. Freis Jr. in Basel, Richard Benert in Belgrade, Montana, and Eric J. Schmaltz and Samuel D. Sinner in Lincoln, Nebraska, for their corrections and additional information and helpful remarks.

1. See Winfried Schulze and Otto Gerhard Oexle, eds., *Deutsche Historiker im Nationalsozialismus* (Frankfurt am Main, 1999). This essay is an extended version of lectures delivered at the Leipzig Conference on "Institutionalization of Historical Research and Teaching" (23–25 September 1999), at the Conference on "Intelligentsia and/or Intellectuals: The Forthcoming Reality of the 21st Century" at Moscow Lomonossov State University (5–6 October 1999), and at the 24th Annual Conference of the German Studies Association in Houston (5–8 October 2000).

2. Tagungsbericht: Südostforschung im Schatten des Dritten Reiches (1920–1960). Institutionen, Inhalte, Personen, Südostdeutsche Historische Kommission, Tübingen, 24.–26. 10. 2002, Munich in http://hsozkult.geschichte.hu-berlin.de/index.asp?id=148&pn =tagungsberichte; Mathias Beer and Gerhard Seewann, eds., *Südostforschung im Schatten des Dritten Reiches (1920–1960). Institutionen-Inhalte-Personen* (Munich, 2004).

3. Talcott Parsons and Bernard Barber, "Sociology 1941–46," *The American Journal of Sociology* 53 (January 1948): 245–257; Michael Burleigh, *Germany Turns Eastwards: A Study of Ostforschung During the Third Reich* (Cambridge, 1988); Barry M. Katz, *Foreign Intelligence: Research and Analysis in the Office of Strategic Services 1942–1945* (Cambridge, 1989); Christopher Simpson, *Science of Coercion: Communication Research and Psychological Warfare 1945–1960* (New York and Oxford, 1994); Alphons Söllner, ed., *Zur Archäologie der Demokratie in Deutschland. Analysen politischer Emigranten im amerikanischen Geheimdienst, vol. 1, 1943–1945* (Frankfurt am Main, 1982).

The think-tanks included: (1) The Research Branch of the Information and Education Division of the War Department, directed by S.A. Stouffer; (2) the Foreign Morale Analysis Division of the Office of War Information, directed by Alexander Leighton and Elmer Davis; (3) the Research and Analysis Branch of the Office of Strategic Services, directed by the historian W. L. Langer; (4) Psychological Warfare Division of the U.S. Army, directed by Robert McClure; (5) the Division of Program Surveys at the Department of Agriculture; and (6) the War Communication Division at the Library of Congress, directed by Harold Lasswell.

4. Burleigh, *Germany Turns Eastwards*; Katz, *Foreign Intelligence*, xii. For a brief introduction, see also Eric J. Schmaltz and Samuel D. Sinner, "The Nazi Ethnographic Research of Georg Leibbrandt and Karl Stumpp in the Ukraine, and Its North American Legacy," *Holocaust and Genocide Studies* 14, no. 1 (2000): 28–64; Ingo Haar, "Deutsche 'Ostforschung' und Antisemitismus," *Zeitschrift für Geschichtswissenschaft* 48, no. 6 (2000): 485–508; Gideon Botsch, "Geheime Ostforschung im SD. Zur Entstehungsgeschichte und Tätigkeit des Wannsee-Instituts 1935–1945," *Zeitschrift für Geschichtswissenschaft* 48, no. 6 (2000): 509–524.

5. Public Record Office London (PRO) Foreign Office 1031/140, Bericht E. Meynen et al., *Der Drang nach dem Osten, Camp Dustbin 1947*, 82.

6. Katz, *Foreign Intelligence*, 15.

7. Bundesarchiv (BArch) R58/101, Note 18 January 1944, 18f.

8. PRO WO 208/5228, Secret Memorandum of James E. Vine, 9 June 1955.

9. Kurt Zierold, *Forschungsförderung in drei Epochen. Deutsche Forschungsgemeinschaft. Geschichte—Arbeitsweise—Kommentar* (Wiesbaden, 1968); Notker Hammerstein, *Die Deutsche Forschungsgemeinschaft in der Weimarer Republik und im Dritten Reich* (Munich, 1999). Frank R. Pfetsch, *Datenhandbuch zur Wissenschaftsentwicklung, Die staatliche Finanzierung der Wissenschaft in Deutschland 1850–1975*, 2nd ed. (Cologne, 1985), 352.

10. Hessiches Staatsarchiv Marburg 340 NL Papritz, C 12d6 E. Meynen, Die VFG. Ein Zehnjahresbericht, 1 April 1941, 27.

11. Anja Heuss, *Kunst- und Kulturgutraub. Eine vergleichende Studie zur Besatzungspolitik der Nationalsozialisten in Frankreich und der Sowjetunion* (Heidelberg, 1999); Michael Fahlbusch, *Wissenschaft im Dienst der nationalsozialistischen Politik? Die "Volksdeutschen Forschungsgemeinschaften" von 1931–1945* (Baden-Baden, 1999), 492.

12. PRO FO 1031/140, Bericht E. Meynen et al., *Der Drang*, 108.

13. In a paper for the board of the NOFG, Albert Brackmann pointed out his urgent "population hygienic programme," which had to be finished by autumn 1943. See Politisches Archiv des Auswärtigen Amts (PA) Inl. II C 33/1 NOFG Bd. 10, Brackmann Rundschreiben an die Beiräte der NOFG No. 20, 6 August 1943, No. D630914.

14. Fahlbusch, *Wissenschaft im Dienst*, 538ff., 603ff.; Peter Longerich, *Politik der Vernichtung* (Munich and Zürich, 1998), 466ff.

15. Hans-Jürgen Döscher, *SS und Auswärtiges Amt im Dritten Reich: Diplomatie im Schatten der "Endlösung"* (Frankfurt am Main, 1991); Peter Longerich, *Propagandisten im Krieg. Die Presseabteilung des Auswärtigen Amtes unter Ribbentrop* (Munich, 1987).

16. PRO WO 252/1184, Supplement to Special Document Report No. 1, September 1945, pp. 9ff.

17. BArch R58/101, Notice of Krallert about Unternehmen Lieben 17 May 1944, No. 68f. See Heuss, *Kunst- und Kulturgutraub*. The contemporary assessment of the British intelligence

service that the Künsberg Sonderkommando was the "German equivalent of our Document Sections" neglected the fact that members of the Kommando were involved in killing actions in South Russia. PRO WO 252/1184 Special Document Report No. 1, The Benedictine Abbey St. Lambrecht, 13 July 1945, p. 2. Also see Andrej Angrick, *Die Einsatzgruppe D. Struktur und Tätigkeiten einer mobilen Einheit der Sicherheitspolizei und des SD in der deutsch besetzten Sowjetunion* (Hamburg, 2003).

18. Jens Banach, *Heydrichs Elite. Das Führerkorps der Sicherheitspolizei und des SD 1936–1945* (Paderborn et al., 1996).

19. Heinz Höhne, *Der Orden unter dem Totenkopf. Die Geschichte der SS* (Gütersloh, 1967), 238.

20. See Walter Schellenberg, *Memoiren*, ed. Gita Petersen (Cologne, 1959), and PRO FO 1031, ibid.

21. BArch Film Nr. 2694, Notice of W. Krallert about R. Krallert regarding the granting of the *Kriegsverdienstkreuz II. Klasse mit Schwertern* (undated). See also BArch Film No. 2694, No. 2973524, Letter of RSHA VI G concerning KZ-prisoners 22 March 1944; Dietmar Seiler, *Die SS im Benediktinerstift. Aspekte der KZ-Außenlager St. Lambrecht und Schloß Lind* (Graz et al., 1994).

22. BArch R58/101, Notice Krallert from 18 December 1943, No. 8.

23. Details on the St. Lambrecht Abbey in PRO WO 252/1184 Special Document Report No. 1, The Benedictine Abbey St. Lambrecht, 13 July 1945. All personal records and files of Wilfried Krallert were registered and sent to Great Britain via the Document Section in Klagenfurt.

24. Groupleader SS-Hauptsturmführer Wilfried Krallert, Ernst Hachmeister, Viktor Paulsen, Jürgen Hehn, Jörn Leo, Alfred Max, Viktor Dieser, Heinz Pedyna, Willy Händler, Hermann Schleifer, Walter Schmidt, Christian Schramm, Erich Thomas, Alfred Ulner, and a secretary. BArch Film No. 2694, Verzeichnis der Gruppe VI G 14 February 1944, BArch, ibid., No. 2973953-958; ibid., Film Nr. 2693, Correspondence of Wannsee-Institute 1944. See also Gerd Voigt, *Rußland in der deutschen Geschichtsschreibung 1843 bis 1945* (Berlin, 1994), 258f.

25. In Ehlich's opinion they were the best "*Gefolgschaftsmitglieder.*" BArch Film No. 2694, Ehlich/Chef der Präsidialkanzlei Lammers 18 January 1944.

26. The biography of H. J. Beyer and the role of the Reinhard Heydrich Foundation in Czechoslovakia is described by Karl Heinz Roth, "Heydrich's Professor. Historiographie des 'Volkstums' und Massenvernichtungen: Der Fall Hans-Joachim Beyer," in *Geschichtswissenschaft als Legitimationswissenschaft 1918–1945*, ed. Peter Schöttler (Frankfurt am Main, 1997), 262–342.

27. Members of the Southeast German Research Society branch in Vienna were medievalist Franz J. Beranek, economic historian Anton Ernstberger, slavists Gerhard Gesemann and Eugen Rippl, folklorists Josef Hanika and Edmund Schneeweiss, ecclesiastical historian Eduard Winter, Heinz Zatschek, and economist Ferdinand Ulmer. See also Roth, *Heydrich's Professor*, 301–308.

28. BArch R58/101, Notice of Krallert about a meeting with Wilhelm Stuckart and a negotiation with Heinrich Himmler 3 May 1944, Bl. 53, ibid., R58/101, Brandt/Kaltenbrunner 15 September 1944, 152.

29. PRO WO 208/5228 Dr. Wilfried Krallert, vol 1, 1945–55, Political Intelligence Department of the Foreign Office, Ref. No. 158, 21 December 1945 (translation of Document No. 1, W. Krallert to W. Schellenberg, Vortragsnotiz für RFSS über die Errichtung und Aufgaben der Gruppe VI G, 20 October 1943).

30. BArch R58/125, Krallert/Branch Innsbruck 19 September 1944, 256f.

31. Politisches Archiv des Auswärtigen Amtes (PA) Inl. II C 38/3 VFG vol. 14, Vermerk über die Arbeitstagung in Prag v. 9/10 March 1944, no. D 653382-384.

32. Summarized and cited without quotations from PRO WO 208/5228 Dr. Wilfried Krallert, vol. 1, 1945–55, First Detailed Interrogation Report on SS-Sturmbannführer Wilfried Krallert (September 1945) Copy No. 32, 1ff. Ibid. Appendix "G" Translation of an Introductory Summary to a Memorandum Concerning the Ideal Coordination of all German

Intelligence Agencies, compiled by Lt-Col. von Dewitz and SS-StubaF Krallert in December 1944, from 18 December 1944. Cf. detailed research in M. Fahlbusch, *Wissenschaft im Dienst*, 257f.

33. See declassified CIA files: National Archives, Name Files RG 263.
34. BArch, Film Nr. 2431, Notes W. Krallert v. 22 und 23 April 1944, Aufn.Nr. 971616-620, as well as ibid., Film Nr. 2704, W. Krallert/Schellenberg v. 15 March 1945, Aufn.Nr. 2990368f. See as well ibid., Film Nr. 2694, Paulsen/Krallert v. 27 April 1944, Aufn.Nr. 2974238f. The center of the Special Units of the SS was in Astori Hotel; see Randolph Braham, *The Politics of Genocide: The Holocaust in Hungary*, 2 vols. (New York, 1993), 516. On the role of the leadership of the German Volksgruppe in Hungary, see Lorant Tilkovszky, *Ungarn und die deutsche "Volksgruppenpolitik" 1938–1945* (Budapest, 1981), 302, 322.
35. Letter of R. Krallert dated 6 April 1997 to the author; see notice of archivist Szabolcs Szitas in Budapest 27 February 1997.
36. BArch, Film Nr. 2693, file entry of W. Krallert on R. Krallert regarding the granting of a *Kriegsverdienstkreuzes II. Klasse mit Schwertern* (undated). The arrest of the Badoglio government representative is documented in Braham, *The Politics of Genocide*, 511.
37. See BArch, Film Nr. 2431, file entry of Krallert v. 26 April and 1 June 1944, Aufn.Nr. 971623-628; see also Voigt, *Rußland in der deutschen Geschichtsschreibung*, 278; Burleigh, *Germany Turns Eastwards*, 245f.
38. Baky, who refounded the Nazi Party in Hungary, is regarded as one of those responsible for the Jewish tragedy in Hungary. On Hain and Baky, see Braham, *The Politics of Genocide*, 424f.; and also the chapter there on the Budapest Jews, ibid., 850–860.
39. The most thorough treatment of the topic is Braham, *The Politics of Genocide*, 528–542. See further Martin Broszat, "Das deutsch-ungarische Machtverhältnis nach dem 19. 3. 1944 und die antijüdischen Maßnahmen in Ungarn," in *Gutachten des Instituts für Zeitgeschichte* (Stuttgart, 1958), 214–221.
40. Walter Hagen (alias of Wilhelm Höttl), *Die geheime Front. Organisation, Personen und Aktionen des deutschen Geheimdienstes* (Linz and Vienna, 1950), 478. Cf. Braham, *The Politics of Genocide*.
41. PRO WO 208/5228 Dr. Wilfried Krallert, vol. 1, 1945–55, First Detailed Interrogation Report on SS-Sturmbannführer Wilfried Krallert (September 1945) Copy No. 32, 15f.
42. PRO WO 208/5228 Dr. Wilfried Krallert, vol 1, 1945–55, Secret Memorandum of James E. Vine, 9 June 1955.
43. Rudolph Michaelsen, *Der europäische Nationalitätenkongreß 1925–1928* (Bern et al., 1984). For a brief introduction to German ethnopolitics, see Burleigh, *Germany Turns Eastwards*; Guntram H. Herb, *Under the Map of Germany: Nationalism and Propaganda 1918–1945* (London and New York, 1997); Anthony Komjathy and Rebecca Stockwell, *German Minorities and the Third Reich: Ethnic Germans of East Central Europe between the Wars* (New York, 1980).
44. PA Inl. II C 33/4 NOFG vol. 13, Koßmann/AA 30 May 1944, No. D631257.
45. PRO WO 208/5228 Dr. Wilfried Krallert, vol. 1, 1945–55; ibid., 252/1184 Special Document Report No. 1 (and supplement): The Benedictine Abbey, St. Lambrecht.

Chapter 3

THE NAZI ETHNOGRAPHIC RESEARCH OF GEORG LEIBBRANDT AND KARL STUMPP IN UKRAINE, AND ITS NORTH AMERICAN LEGACY

✦ ✦ ✦

Eric J. Schmaltz and Samuel D. Sinner

Introduction: Nazi Scholarship, Genocide, and Postwar Genealogy

In recent years a new generation of scholars has increasingly turned its attention to the problem of academicians, "technocrats," and middle managers who put their knowledge and skills at the disposal of the Nazi regime. Certainly not members of any "lunatic fringe," this educated elite collaborated with the Nazis voluntarily and enthusiastically. In the field of *Ostforschung* (research on Eastern Europe) a number of scholars helped advance grandiose policies of racial imperialism in the occupied territories. This sophisticated segment of German society served the Nazi machinery of death, then went on to pursue successful post–World War II professional careers.

Tapping into the darker side of intellectual endeavors, the Nazi regime in the course of the late 1930s and early 1940s politicized and utilized Germany's scholarly disciplines for its own designs and purposes. In his 1988 study of the *Ostforscher*, Michael Burleigh underscored the reasons the Nazi state required the contributions of modern experts to realize its imperialist aims:

> As scholarly experts on the East, the *Ostforscher* had a distinctive contribution to make to the accurate "data base"—the statistical and cartographical location of persons—upon which *all* aspects of Nazi policy in the East, as elsewhere, ultimately rested. Deportations, resettlements, repatriations, and mass murder were not sudden visitations from on high, requiring the adoption of some

Notes for this chapter begin on page 78.

commensurate inscrutable, quasi-religious, meta-language, but the result of the exact, modern, "scientific" encompassing of persons with card indexes, card-sorting machines, charts, graphs, maps and diagrams. All that an individual was, or was going to be allowed to be, could be precisely expressed through cards and index tabs. The existing methods and preoccupations of German *Ostforschung* dovetailed usefully with Nazi policy. That was why the subject received generous funding.[1]

Enlisted into the service of the Nazi state, such experts now found the opportunity to turn ideas into realities. As the Reich projected its prestige and influence in order to attract ethnic German minorities abroad into the greater German *Volk*, many émigré scholars living in Germany proved well-suited to act as Nazi contacts, propagandists, informants, and goodwill ambassadors among their former compatriots.

For more than five decades beginning in the 1920s, Georg Leibbrandt (1899–1982) and Karl Stumpp (1896–1982) contributed to the academic and popular literature on Eastern Europe's German ethnic minorities, particularly those in the Soviet Union.[2] The National Socialists' ideology of *Blut und Boden* (blood and soil) coincided with Stumpp's and Leibbrandt's own personal and professional aspirations, for the party's leadership envisioned a "re-establishment of Germandom" in the East. With the expansion of the "race" forming the ideological core of Nazism, the young Hitlerite regime sought professionals who could devise concrete developmental plans. The intelligentsia's collaboration with the regime, of course, augured ill for the *Untermenschen*, the East's soon-to-be subjugated populations. For Stumpp and Leibbrandt, both émigrés from Soviet Ukraine, the Nazi state's *Drang nach Osten* offered "salvation" to their persecuted co-ethnics, soon to rejoin the *Herrenvolk* (ruling race).

Their intimate contact with the ethnic German minorities permitted Stumpp and Leibbrandt to perform various administrative roles in the Nazi machinery of racial imperialism and mass murder. For most of World War II, Leibbrandt functioned as a high official in the political department of Alfred Rosenberg's Ministry for the Occupied Eastern Territories (RMO). By late 1941, Leibbrandt was making top-level policy decisions concerning the liquidation of East European Jews. He attended the 20 January 1942 Wannsee Conference, which officially planned the implementation of the "Final Solution." He served as Stumpp's immediate superior between late 1941 and early 1943, when the latter headed an eighty-member special-action unit (*Sonderkommando*) in western Ukraine. Leibbrandt's decision-making role demonstrates his more direct involvement in the Nazis' extermination policies. As one of countless mid-level "ethno-specialists" in the occupation's administrative apparatus, Stumpp was more of an indirect participant in the Holocaust, although circumstantial evidence has pointed to his unit's direct involvement in isolated killing actions. Leibbrandt's office assigned Kommando Dr. Stumpp, as the special unit was later called, to carry out behind the front lines a comprehensive demographic, cultural, and racial survey of ethnic Germans in Nazi-occupied Ukraine.

Practicing the Nazis' rigorous card indexing of individuals and groups, this unit identified at least three hundred German villages and settlements, extensively documenting the systematic annihilation and "resettlement" of tens of thousands of Jews, "mixed race" individuals, Romany (Gypsies), and even ethnic Germans. More than eighty of their comprehensive village reports (*Dorfberichte*) now reside in the German War Records, most concerned with the history, cultural life, education, health, and economic status of the region's ethnic German villages.[3]

Undoubtedly devoted to the *Volksdeutsche*, Stumpp and Leibbrandt also shared deep concerns about the degree to which the Nazi regime recognized their ethnic compatriots as "racially pure." Inspired by Nazi ideology and by anti-Bolshevism, and most eager to reverse the Ukrainian Germans' Soviet-influenced cultural "deficiencies," Stumpp and his agents stressed their biological "resilience," even going so far as to mask thousands of ethnic German deaths suffered under Lenin and Stalin. Their concerns stemmed in part from the intense political rivalry and jurisdictional disputes between the Rosenberg ministry and the SS over the occupied regions. In the *Herrenvolk-Untermenschen* paradigm, successful efforts to "rehabilitate" the Ukrainian Germans supposedly would have increased the Rosenberg ministry's prestige in Berlin at the SS's expense, brightening Stumpp's and Leibbrandt's professional prospects. Falling under Leibbrandt's direct supervision, Stumpp fully understood the wider political, ideological, and racial context in which he carried out his duties as a Nazi Sonderkommando.

The overall irony of Stumpp's and Leibbrandt's professional services to the Nazi state is that much of their Nazi-era research and findings later appeared in apolitical postwar academic publications.[4] In many respects their evolution is a journey from genealogy to genocide, then back to genealogy. Their postwar "rehabilitation" exemplifies the banality of the Nazi organization of terror, the blurring of the roles of perpetrators and bystanders, the rapid erosion of historical truth and memory, and the traditional respect enjoyed by German academicians. Perhaps most importantly, the Cold War altered political perceptions of committed anti-Communists such as Stumpp and Leibbrandt. One significant result of their Nazi activities and their "return to normalcy" was the North American Russian-German ethnic community's growing fascination with family and village history research—research based in part on 1930s and 1940s Nazi racial fact-finding and record-keeping.

This study seeks to shed light on the relative obscurity surrounding the careers of Stumpp and Leibbrandt, who remained lifelong associates. Both men enjoyed distinguished reputations and popularity in the field of ethnic German scholarship. After 1950 both participated extensively in some of West Germany's ethnic German cultural organizations (*Landsmannschaften*).

In the 1960s and 1970s, Stumpp's efforts proved pivotal in establishing two ethnic German heritage societies in North America.[5] On both sides of the Atlantic, the German community remembers them mostly for their post–World War II academic, organizational, and cultural contributions. Both were so successful in their many endeavors that Leibbrandt's complicity in the "Final Solution" and Stumpp's special action unit were soon forgotten. The majority of short biographies testify to their accomplishments and dedication to the ethnic group, making little or no mention of their Nazi past. Many researchers, including contemporary scholars in North America, remain ignorant of the nature and extent of Leibbrandt's and Stumpp's Nazi complicity. Thus, nearly a generation after both men passed away in 1982, this essay represents the first critical investigation of their lengthy careers and roles in the Nazi machinery of death.[6]

Background to Mid 1941

Leibbrandt's and Stumpp's academic careers in the study of ethnic Germans began in the early 1920s, after they fled the newly established Soviet state. After 1933 the Nazis supported them and other émigrés working to alleviate the plight of their "brethren in need" (*Brüder in Not*) in their former homelands.[7]

Born in 1896, Karl Stumpp came from German Lutheran stock that had helped establish the village of Alexanderhilf near Odessa, Ukraine, in the early nineteenth century.[8] A promising student, he received his primary education in neighboring Grossliebental and his higher education in Dorpat and Odessa. In 1918, at the end of World War I, he left with the departing German occupation troops to undertake graduate studies in Germany. Attending the University of Tübingen, he earned a doctorate in geography and natural science. Although he evaded the Russian Civil War's turmoil, he never forgot the peasant world he had left behind, as is suggested by his 1922 doctoral dissertation, a study titled *Die deutschen Kolonien im Schwarzmeergebiet, dem früheren Neu- (Süd-) Rußland, ein Siedlungs- und Wirtschaftsgeographischer Versuch* (The German Colonies in the Black Sea Region, in the Former New- [South-] Russia: A Demographic, Economic and Geographical Experiment). Between 1922 and 1933 Stumpp taught at a German girls' school in Tarutino, Bessarabia—a region Romania had recently annexed from the former Russian Empire. Tarutino was close to his beloved Ukrainian homeland, then experiencing increasingly oppressive Communist misrule. Besides teaching, he engaged in various cultural activities in Tarutino and neighboring communities, establishing a youth organization, training choirs, conducting genealogical research, and lecturing on the history of Russia's Germans.[9]

Georg Leibbrandt's early years were quite similar to Stumpp's. Born in 1899 in the German Lutheran village of Hoffnungsfeld near Odessa, Ukraine,

Leibbrandt attended his church's primary school and then the high school in the nearby mother colony of Hoffnungstal. By 1919 he had successfully completed his secondary education in Dorpat and Odessa. In 1920, while the Russian Civil War still raged, he journeyed to Weimar Germany to pursue his graduate studies in theology, philosophy, history, and economics at the universities of Tübingen and Leipzig. After earning his doctorate in 1927 he studied international law and international relations at the French Sorbonne and the London School of Economics. The University of Leipzig subsequently appointed Leibbrandt Assistant at the Institute of Culture and World History.

Leibbrandt's professional prospects further brightened when the Association of German Science commissioned the young scholar to conduct research on the Soviet Union's ethnic Germans. Utilizing Soviet archival materials, Leibbrandt published reports about his 1926–1927 travels through the USSR, including a short book on emigration. Following his brief employment at the Reichsarchiv (1929–1931), a Rockefeller Scholarship from 1931 to 1933 allowed Leibbrandt to resume his studies in France, Switzerland, the United States, and Canada. During this time he established numerous contacts among the ethnic Germans living abroad. In Germany, he had already joined the SA (Brownshirts). Between 1933 and 1940, he was commissioned by the German Foreign Office to complete a study on the peoples of Eastern Europe while he taught at the University of Berlin's foreign studies department.

As early as 1933 Alfred Rosenberg had requested Leibbrandt's services as Director of the Eastern Division of the NSDAP's Foreign Policy Office. When the Reich Ministry for the Occupied Eastern Territories was established under Rosenberg in 1941, Leibbrandt became its Director of Political Development. In this capacity he worked as a liaison official for the various ethnic German émigrés until forced out of his various posts by the rival SS in mid 1943.[10]

Stumpp returned to Germany after the Nazis' conquest of power. By 1933 the Romanian government was requesting that he become a Romanian citizen, but Stumpp decided that it was in a revitalized Fatherland that his services could make the most impact. Yet the Nazi leadership, contrary to his and other expatriates' high expectations, initially showed little interest in the Soviet Union's ethnic Germans. Aside from the fact that the issue yielded pride of place to German foreign policy considerations, Hitler and his associates had assumed that these Germans had been either killed off or "Bolshevized." In fact, the common perception, going back all the way to Bismarck, was that the ethnic Germans were already "Russianized."[11] As a result, émigrés felt obliged to convince the Nazi authorities that the USSR's ethnic Germans were not a lost cause.

The expatriates made their case by seeking out three political avenues during the last half of the 1930s.[12] A first political ally to which the ethnic German supporters turned was the Anticomintern, an organization established to engage in ideological struggle against Soviet Communism. This political body fell under Joseph Goebbels's Reich Ministry for Propaganda. The expatriates' second, and perhaps most obvious, choice was the network of semi-academic and quasi-scientific institutions. A third political route was the NSDAP's Foreign Policy Office under Alfred Rosenberg, a Nazi ideologue of Baltic German descent.[13] By this time Leibbrandt was already Rosenberg's political adviser.[14]

Upon arriving in Stuttgart in 1933, Stumpp took the position of business manager of the Verein für das Deutschtum im Ausland or VDA (Association of Germans Abroad). During the five years he spent in this capacity, he gave hundreds of lectures on the history of Russia's ethnic Germans. Further professional opportunities awaited. He soon became involved with the Stuttgart-based Deutsches Ausland-Institut or DAI (German Foreign Institute), established in 1917 to collect information on German culture abroad. In this role, Stumpp was able to establish contacts with Germans in North and South America, especially those interested in family genealogies.[15] In the late 1930s his DAI responsibilities included the compilation of a central archival index of Germans living abroad. Besides the DAI, a second agency called the Verband der Deutschen aus Rußland or VDR (Association of Germans from Russia) also played a role in relations between the Russian-German émigrés and the NSDAP. In mid 1938 the DAI and VDR established the Forschungsstelle des Rußland-deutschtums im Deutschen Ausland-Institut or FstR (Research Office of the Russian Germans in the German Foreign Institute), with Stumpp serving as the director. The new organization's main goal was "to do family-oriented and racial-biological research on all Russian Germans across the world."[16] It especially sought to collect information about ethnic Germans under Soviet rule.[17] For two years, Stumpp's FstR remained in Berlin, but in mid 1940 (despite some VDR protests), the VDR's archive was transported from Berlin to Stuttgart.

The DAI-VDR merger was supposed to foster administrative efficiency under the NSDAP. By 1938, *Gleichschaltung* (the NSDAP's "coordination," or, more accurately, *subordination* of civic institutions) had essentially reduced the DAI to an information-gathering agency. The Nazi leadership was taking an increasingly practical interest in the Soviet Union's ethnic Germans and other *Volksdeutsche* for its own expansionist and racial aims. In 1941 Stumpp's various DAI activities fell to Rosenberg's Reich Ministry for the Occupied Eastern Territories (RMO), under the direct authority of Leibbrandt, the director and émigré liaison official of the ministry's political department. Since it was already merged with the DAI, the VDR also logically fell under the Rosenberg ministry's direction. Overseeing both the VDR and DAI, then, Leibbrandt ultimately turned Stumpp's FstR into a special action unit (*Sonderkommando*) stationed in Ukraine. Thus did these Russian-German émigrés tie their ambitions to the Nazi establishment during the course of the late 1930s and early 1940s. Their fateful decision ultimately held grave consequences for the ethnic populations in the East, especially as the SS assumed more administrative control over ethnic German affairs. By 1939, when World War II broke out, most other agencies handling ethnic German affairs, especially those of Russian-German émigrés, were either abolished or left with little jurisdiction.[18]

Early in World War II, Stumpp received new orders that put him into ever closer contact with the ethnic German settlements. In the summer of 1940, the Soviet Union forced Romania to surrender its claim to Bessarabia. The Soviets also signed an agreement with Nazi Germany for the transfer of the Bessarabian Germans to Germany. Because of his familiarity with the region and its people, Stumpp was one of several officials assigned to Bessarabia that fall. The first special mission was to supervise the relocation of 90,000 ethnic Germans to the Greater German Reich (*Aktion Heim ins Reich*).[19]

Early on, the SS's racial aims were obvious to officials working in other governmental and military departments, including the DAI and Rosenberg's ministry. Among the various DAI officials sent to Bessarabia in 1940 was Dr. Hermann Maurer.[20] After the Nazi invasion of the USSR, Maurer was stationed in a German army unit in western Ukraine. In an August 1941 intelligence report sent to the DAI president in Stuttgart, he provided details about the population's health, "character," and attitudes toward work. This report notes the preparation of documents certifying German ethnicity in the Kuchurgan enclave (a cluster of ethnic German villages near Odessa), indicating the SS's predominance in the region and the DAI's supporting role. On the arrival of the Kommando of Einsatzgruppe D, Maurer writes:

> An SS-Special Command, first stationed in Tiraspol and then transferred to Kandel, has taken over police protection of the German population and has contributed much to pacification. This service issues personal certificates for those clearly proved to be of German blood. In this way the foundation is being laid for a census survey of people of German stock.... The SS-Special Command is presently making investigations which will lead to the arrest and, if necessary, the liquidation of persons who gave harsh treatment to their ethnic compatriots bodily or through seizure of property during the Bolshevik era.[21]

Maurer implies that the Bolsheviks and their supporters would get what they "deserved." And indeed, in August 1941 the "pacification" and "liquidation" of "politically tainted elements" were just beginning. Making these observations exactly when the SS killing units were arriving, he indicated that the executions would include particular ethnic Germans, notably directors of collectives and Communists.

Richard H. Walth's village research in the region seems to confirm Maurer. Walth, who traced his ancestry to the ethnic German village of Neu-Glückstal in Ukraine, compiled a list of the approximately 800 persons who lived there before the Nazis' 1944 mass evacuation to the West.

Brief remarks shed light on the fates of those missing, including those whom the Soviets had "banned" prior to the Nazi invasion, males who died while serving in the German armed forces, and a limited number whom the SS shot during the last half of 1941. These latter reflect the ideology behind Alfred Rosenberg's calculation that ten to fifteen percent of the Soviet Union's ethnic German population consisted of "human scrap."[22]

SS policies afforded ethnic German occupation officials returning to their old homelands the opportunity to exact revenge for earlier Soviet mistreatment. In late July 1941, Stumpp was one such ethnic German making his way toward the Eastern Front, preparing for his new appointment as leader of a *Sonderkommando*. Anticipating the liberation of his *Volksdeutsche*, Stumpp still claimed family in the region, including individuals who had experienced the 1930s Soviet terror.[23]

Heading the DAI Research Office, Stumpp was well informed of the SS activities. Like Maurer, he arrived in the region in July 1941, when many of the SS's early "special actions" were taking place. Behind Operation Barbarossa's advancing front lines, *Einsatzgruppe* C was to carry out its exterminations in northern and central Ukraine, *Einsatzgruppe* D in Bessarabia, southern Ukraine, the Crimea, and the Caucasus.[24] Ingeborg Fleischhauer has disassociated Stumpp from the SS's special actions, maintaining that his special unit investigated only villages the SS had earlier "cleansed."[25] Yet in 1983, one year after Stumpp's death, Fleischhauer also stated that Stumpp's *Dorfberichte* were not simple or innocent genealogical and ethnographic studies, but "racial-biological" research "which arose from a historicizing and statistical over-zealousness [and] may ... have in many cases served as a guide for the *SS-Kommandos*, who were 'cleansing' the German regions."[26] Even if Stumpp were never personally involved in the executions, some of his intelligence work may have contributed to their efficiency.

Michael Fahlbusch's extensive 1999 study on the connection between German scholarship and National Socialist policies supports the contention that Stumpp's registration of the ethnic German population was part of "racial-hygienic" policy, and notes that since 1939 Stumpp had been occupied with "racial-biological" *Mischlinge*, persons born to mixed marriages. Fahlbusch concludes that the Nazi ethnographers compiling village reports were "directly" informed about the extermination of Jews. They had to maintain at least some contact with the SS and SD over matters of policy and information-gathering.

When they arrived at the villages, the ethnographers usually had to collect data on persons who had already been liquidated; their reports could not be completed without the SS and SD information about Jewish and other victims. For Fahlbusch, Stumpp's village reports constituted the Nazi authorities' "final check" on the region's "population transfer" (*Umvolkung*)—that is, official confirmation of "human extermination." He also contends that Ukraine's ethnic German population—those not personally assisting in the "ethnic cleansing"—were well informed about the extermination of their Jewish neighbors.[27]

Concurring with Meir Buchsweiler, Fahlbusch stresses Stumpp's "indirect role in the extermination process,"[28] also acknowledging (like Fleischhauer) that the ethnographer's fact-finding may have been occasionally necessary for carrying out additional "mopping-up" operations. He emphasizes broader political dimensions of Nazi ethnographic research, designating the village compilers as "ethno-political advisers," "ethno-specialists," and "ethno-politicians" (*volkstumspolitische Berater, Volkstums-spezialisten*, and *Ethnopolitiker*). Serving as advisers to the occupation authorities, these roaming field researchers sometimes provided demographic information to the SS *Einsatzgruppen* that worked in the area's ethnic German villages. Fahlbusch cites the example of Hans Joachim Beyer, whom he identifies as an "ethno-political adviser" to *Sonderkommando* 4a of SS *Einsatzgruppe* C stationed in Galacia and northern Ukraine. In November 1941, Beyer compiled for the Nazi Munitions Inspector of Ukraine a comprehensive report including findings on the "ruthless mass shootings." Fahlbusch states that we can conclude with certainty that Stumpp should be counted among those "'ethno-political advisers,' who ascertained this genocide's 'resulting quota.'"[29] Indeed, Fahlbusch notes that as late as August 1942 the region's SS special units carried out executions of people from these villages, individuals who fell under the "Racial Category IV" of the German National List (*Deutsche Volksliste* or DVL), including ethnic German villagers and others whom the Nazis deemed to be at the lowest level of "racial purity" or ideological conformity. Stumpp's special unit began its official duties in November 1941 and operated until March 1943, a period covering most of the killing actions. Though the literature mentions SS opposition to Kommando Dr. Stumpp, ironically Stumpp himself was a member of the SS. Most of the *Dorfberichte* (village reports) were compiled in the course of mid to late 1942, with some appearing as late as early 1943. When Nazi ethnographers like Beyer, Karl Götz of *Sonderkommando* R, and Stumpp determined to which "ethnicity" (or to what degree of "ethnicity") a villager belonged, their assignment could mean life or death.[30] Fahlbusch quotes Nazi geographer Emil Meynen's words that Stumpp compiled the *Dorfberichte* "according to population-hygenic [sic] viewpoints."[31]

After compilation, Stumpp's *Dorfberichte* were sent back to Berlin. There they were further processed in various administrative offices grouped under the heading Osteuropäische Forschungsgemeinschaft (The East European Research Society or OEFG), sometimes known as the Leibbrandt Collection (Sammlung Georg Leibbrandt) or the Publications Office East (P-Stelle Ost), a vast central information-gathering agency that was operating by 1942. This agency was concerned with all aspects of Eastern European affairs—above all, with occupation and settlement policies and the promotion of National Socialism among the Russian Germans.

Much like Kommando Dr. Stumpp, this agency had close ties with Leibbrandt's ministerial posts, having grown out of a special collection on Russian-German materials Leibbrandt had started in the 1920s. By the fall of 1943 the SS completely took over Leibbrandt's duties and formally turned Sammlung Leibbrandt into P-Stelle Ost,[32] in the words of Fahlbusch the "'scientific' element of the Nazis' human extermination program."[33]

In early August 1941, Kommando Dr. Stumpp went into action. For much of 1942, Stumpp's field staff filed numerous reports and statistical tables on the "racial" composition of villages in western Ukraine. The DVL data collected were, therefore, by their very nature, political, ideological, and racial.[34] The special unit not only functioned as one part of the Nazi machinery of death, but also painstakingly documented the mass killings in Ukrainian villages at the height of the Nazi racial war.[35]

The Mundane and the Murderous: Kommando Dr. Stumpp and the Documentation of Destruction

Among the United States National Archives' Captured German Records are materials concerned with the Soviet Union's ethnic Germans.[36] Specifically, Stumpp's unit prepared more than eighty reports for Ukrainian-German villages, all except six on settlements west of the Dnieper River, most in a small area of central Ukraine between the Dnieper and Ingulets. Stumpp's special action unit enjoyed a privileged semimilitary status from November 1941 onward, establishing its headquarters in Dnepropetrovsk early the next year.[37] When the Nazis carried out their cataclysmic withdrawal from the Soviet Union in 1943 and 1944, much of the material collected by Stumpp was lost, at least temporarily. After the war, however, many DAI records eventually turned up among the Captured German Documents.[38] In addition to the dozens of *Dorfberichte*, at least twelve confidential reports (diaries or *Tagebuchfrontberichte*) written by Stumpp between August 1941 and May 1942 to the Reich Ministry for the Occupied Eastern Territories (RMO) survived.[39]

The village reports varied in quality and thoroughness, even though their compilation constituted the special command unit's primary task. They consisted of a cover sheet; the narrative itself; the listing of families in the village; the listing of the inhabitants (including age groupings); questionnaire forms for ethnic German genealogical information; extra lists for victims of Soviet repression and economic policy, as well as those ethnic Germans serving in the Red Army; geographical sketches and maps; biographical sketches; and "control sheets" for additional information.[40] Despite the mountains of sometimes mundane details, the reports served to inform the Nazi authorities, including the SS, about the demographic and racial character of the ethnic Germans and their neighbors.

Stumpp enlisted the services of about eighty men from Germany to help his unit conduct surveys, including a number of ethnic German expatriates from Russia, some of whom after the war became prominent in the Landsmannschaft der Deutschen aus Rußland (the émigré National Association of Germans from Russia). Interestingly, several Protestant pastors and community leaders, including Mennonites, worked as staff assistants. Besides their official duties, they were particularly interested in reintroducing religious practices to the occupied region. One was the Mennonite Gerhard Fast, who prepared the reports for the Mennonite village of Chortitza and others. Protestant pastor Friedrich Rink headed the organization in the province of Volynia. The Lutheran pastor Heinrich Roemmich, a dedicated organizer of the Landsmannschaft in the 1950s and 1960s, served on the staff.[41] Stumpp's diaries and various reports indicate his strong sense of purpose as a Nazi liberator of his *Volk*. Collecting information on the Russian Germans and assisting them in cultural and economic matters, he also reveals his anti-Jewish and anti-Bolshevik views. Recent interpretations of his motives and activities vary.

In 1984, just two years after Stumpp's death, Canadian Adam Giesinger, considered one of the deans of North America's Russian-German historiography, explained Stumpp's anti-Jewish statements in the confidential reports as a temporary aberration. A postwar colleague of the late Stumpp, he lets his readers decide for themselves the significance of this chapter in Stumpp's life. Yet this publisher of edited translations of the twelve diary reports also stands as one of North America's few Russian-German scholars who have recognized Stumpp's complex motivations. Giesinger states in his introduction to Stumpp's confidential reports that "in reading these reports, we must remember when they were written. Hitler was then at the height of his power. His success in the war up to that point had created great enthusiasm for him throughout Germany."[42] Giesinger, however, does not mention (or does not know) that, long before the euphoria of military victory, Stumpp's DAI was already publishing much racially motivated "scholarship."[43] Giesinger was only partly correct in the following interpretation:

Dr. Stumpp was caught up in this enthusiasm. With many other German expatriates from Russia then living in Germany, he saw in Hitler the savior of his beloved people in Russia, their liberator from Communist tyranny. He saw the war against the Soviet Union as a holy crusade against the evils of a regime that was threatening all mankind. The Nazi theory that there was a Bolshevik-Jewish conspiracy to enslave all nations looked rational to him. His unkind remarks about Jews, which appear here and there in these reports and which will surprise some of our readers, must be judged in this light.[44]

This view is valid in the sense that Stumpp felt part of a national crusade against Bolshevism. Yet, at the time, Stumpp's special military mission was not a temporary aberration or professional side-note. Ingeborg Fleischhauer qualifies Stumpp's enthusiasm, when she argues that after the late 1930s he exhibited a degree of superficiality in his conformity to Nazism. She does point out, though, that he maintained "certain anti-Semitic tendencies."[45] Although initially Stumpp had been more of an anti-Bolshevik than an anti-Semite, it is clear that following Hitler's seizure of power he embraced Nazi racial theories, thereafter writing as if all Jews were Communists.

A number of unkind remarks about the Jews appear in Stumpp's private reports to the Reichsminister. It is best to let Stumpp speak for himself here, since he makes matters quite clear. In Report No. 1 of 6 August 1941, Stumpp notes that, while driving by car to Lvov, "we see the first columns of Jews with their white armbands going out to work.... Here and there a grave comes into view, with a steel helmet on the cross; many a brave soldier had to give his life for the liberation of Germany and Europe from the Bolshevik-Jewish plague." And yet in the same report the author contradicts the identification of Bolshevism with Judaism: "All without exception, I believe even the majority of the Jews are glad to be liberated from Bolshevik rule." Suggesting his familiarity with the "lazy" capitalist or *sovkhoz*-director stereotype of Jews,[46] he elsewhere repeats the common perception that to see Jews engaged in physical labor had been rare under the Soviets. And yet Stumpp also observed, "Every morning [Jews] appear in our service building [in Lvov] to clean the rooms or to load automobiles. They can finally tackle a job—and how they tackle it! There's a particular Jew who appears at my office door every morning, makes a deep bow and cleans up my room. When he is finished, he bows very low again and disappears out of the door backwards. Outside women wash the floors and men clean the windows."[47]

Stumpp seems to have been most willing to talk to representatives of other nationality groups, including Russians and Ukrainians. This attitude may have reflected the Rosenberg ministry's racial policies toward non-Jews, policies that were relatively "less rigid" than those of the SS. A practical consideration was Rosenberg's desire to turn the East European peoples against the Soviets and Jews; certainly, the RMO could glean useful information from the indigenous nationalities as well as enlist their support for the Nazi crusade against communism. Discussing Jews, Stumpp describes a conversation he had with a young Russian prisoner of war in Lemberg (Lvov):

> I could see how this young man, who had no notion of the old Russia nor of foreign countries, struggled with himself, how the light dawned on him about things that he did not want to believe but yet had to admit were true. You are right, he said again and again; it has struck me that there are no Jews among our [Soviet] flyers, for that takes courage. He had no notion that [former People's Commissar of Foreign Affairs] Litvinov was a Jew (he had never heard the name Finkelstein); he did not know that [current Commissar of Foreign Affairs] Molotov's wife was a Jewess. He was speechless and one could read from his face: now everything was becoming clear to me. When such a lieutenant is

unaware of such matters, what can one expect from the broad masses of the people. If only such persons could now speak to their people.[48]

Stumpp and his associates encouraged the various POWs to make protests against the Soviet regime. Returning as a liberator to his persecuted homeland, Stumpp in fact was performing "politico-educational" duties in addition to his scholarly ones. He continues,

> Yesterday we attempted to accomplish this. Five [Soviet] prisoners were placed before microphones. They were young fellows, three of them sons of kulaks, who had been forced into the army, and two poor farmers' sons. They agreed voluntarily to speak. Two of them even mentioned their names and their army units, although we had to warn them against the dangers of that. I can testify that no pressure of any kind was exerted on them. On the contrary, we constantly had to put on the brakes, because they didn't want to stop talking. One of them even wrote a letter to the *Führer*; I have the letter. They declared unanimously that conditions in Russia were terrible.[49]

Stumpp's unit provided information to the various Nazi occupation authorities and knew of SS activities in the Odessa region;[50] as the unit commander, Stumpp knew the fate of Jews and other "undesirables" in the region through the compilation of the village reports. In Report No. 4, 27 August to 9 September 1941, he addresses the question of mixed marriages and "foreigners" living in the villages. Local ethnic Germans acted as Stumpp's informants, but Stumpp's keen eye is also evident. In one of many references in Report No. 4 to ethnically mixed villages, he observes: "Especially valuable were reports from boys from Kandel, Elsass, Baden and Strassburg. These four Catholic villages have remained completely German. There is not a single Russian family living there. In Elsass there are three Jewish and one Gypsy family. The one Jew is chairman of the collective, the second a bookkeeper and third is in the cooperative store. In Baden there are two Jewish families and in Strassburg there are said to be none."[51]

As Richard H. Walth's extensive research in the *Bundesarchiv* illustrates, the staffers underlined the names of villagers of "foreign" origin in blue, while children of mixed marriages were marked in red.[52] Documentation of mass murder is excluded, however. Meir Buchsweiler correctly notes that the blank columns for 1942 in the village reports tacitly indicate that the villages had been cleansed of their Jewish populations; the columns for 1941 list the number of who had been present at the time of the Germans' arrival.[53] All written references to "resettlement" must be understood in terms of euphemism and innuendo. To substantiate this crucial charge, Buchsweiler cites the case of the village of Kalinindorf, where it was known that on 16 September 1941 a mass execution of Jews took place. Kalinindorf's population had been nearly 79 percent Jewish. Out of the 1,670 Jews living there before June 1941, Stumpp's village report of Kalinindorf listed *no* Jews in the 1942 tally—the column is left blank. The

Nazis murdered an additional 205 Soviet citizens in the village on that day, for a total of 1,875. A memorial for the Kalinindorf victims, built by the Soviets and inscribed in Russian and Yiddish, still stands at the massacre site.[54]

In this manner, then, Kommando Dr. Stumpp tabulated extermination actions. In this examination of the DAI archival records, at least 259 villages have statistics, which the special unit broke down into at least ten regional charts. By no means the definitive list of DAI records, these charts with the 259 villages include the following: (1) the districts of Zhitomir and Lutzk (Volynia); (2) the regions of Zhitomir and Chudnov (Volynia); (3) the district of Emilchino; (4) the regions of Radomyshl, Korostyshev, Olevsk, and Ovruch; (5) the region of Zviahel; (6) the general district of Dnepropetrovsk; (7) the region of Krivoy Rog; (8) the region of Chortitza; (9) the region of Kronau; and 10) the region of Korosten.[55]

In 1941, the summary listed 41,642 Jews living in seventy-eight of the villages or settlements covered. In 1942, the ten regional charts made it appear that 41,592 Jews could not be accounted for. The "blank columns" for 1942, listing both families and individuals, stand in stark contrast to the previous year's statistics-laden columns. Occasionally, individual Jewish survivors are tabulated, suggesting the meticulous care that Stumpp's unit took in preparing the lists. Thus, by mid 1942, only fifty Jews were still resident in the seventy-eight communities. The few surviving Jews were probably providing skilled labor or other services to the occupation authorities, but the reasons for their being spared remain unknown. The death rate was therefore about 99.9 percent, or, in other words, only about 0.12 percent survived the 1941 and 1942 death squads. These statistics, it should be noted, do not even include the dead or missing Ukrainians, Russians, offspring of mixed marriages, and even ethnic Germans. Hence, the actual death total easily runs into several tens of thousands.

Careful analysis of these records reveals features besides the population "shifts." No "zeros" are ever used in the tabulation of "missing" Jews or other victim groups.[56] Giesinger stated in 1977 that the consistently empty columns may sometimes reflect the unavailability of data on Jews and other peoples; yet elsewhere he recognized the heart of the matter:

> There is another Nazi policy of which the Reports of 1942 remind us. This was the liquidation of the Jews in the occupied territories. A few German villages had substantial numbers of Jews when war broke out in June 1941.... By May 1942, when the reports for these villages were prepared, there were no Jews left.... The population statistics for both June 1941 and May 1942 are given in the reports but nothing is said about the fate of the vanished Jews. Presumably the writer [of the reports] did not know, or dared not say.[57]

This assessment is correct as far as it goes, but Giesinger does not point out that Stumpp's unit regularly left "blanks" in chart tabulations for targeted groups, and that "zeros" never appear in these columns. Since Jews experienced the brunt of the "special actions," the incriminating evidence must be read between the lines; down to the single person, all survivors were tabulated.

Indeed, many of Stumpp's records detail the drastic population decrease in the number of Jews living in the mixed communities, as the euphemistic term "resettled" (*ausgesiedelt*) was understood to mean something else (*erschossen* or *hingerichtet*—shot or executed). As Buchsweiler notes, some of the *Dorfberichte* even plainly state that various persons were shot on the spot (*erschossen*).[58] The *Dorfbericht* for Friesendorf indicates the following:

> The village, founded in 1924 as a Jewish settlement and given the name Tshe-merinsk, was renamed Stalindorf in 1928, and the county administration was moved here at the same time. When the German Wehrmacht entered in 1941, the village was renamed "Friesendorf." In 1942 the Jews were resettled and replaced with ethnic German settlers from neighboring villages.... At the outbreak of the war, many Ukrainians were mobilized, and the Jews were pressed into acting as guards of the village. They moved their families ... to safety, drove off their live-stock, and after that the rest of the Jews fled as well.... Immediately after the arrival of German troops, calm was [restored], everyone breathed a sigh of relief, and even the Ukrainian population was happy to have been delivered from the Jewish yoke.[59]

Viewed as a whole, the work of the Sonderkommando Dr. Stumpp reflects not only Nazi-oriented research on German descendants, but also shows support of the SS-Raumplanung with all its lethal effects for the Jews of Ukraine. In 1942–1943, Himmler launched a settlement experi-ment in the Zhitomir district in Ukraine. Instead of creating a German ter-ritory in the Zhitomir district, he planned new "showcase settlements" modeled after the already existing SS and police support bases (SS- und Polizeistützpunkte) in western Ukraine. Under war conditions, settlement experts of the RKF concentrated over 30,000 ethnic Germans from German villages across Ukraine into three settlement areas close to Zhitomir, Hegewald, and Försterstadt. Of course, the forced expulsion (deportation) of about 15,000 Ukrainians from these areas to the Dnepropetrovsk district constituted the first step in that process. The annihilation of the Jews in the Dnepropetrovsk district represented the second step taken before the Ger-man resettlement began in November 1942.[60]

Einsatzgruppen C and D performed most of the area's mass killings be-tween mid 1941 and mid 1942; Stumpp's unit began most of the tabula-tions between mid and late 1942, completing them by early 1943. In the DAI records, several statistical compilations document the mass extermi-nation. In 1941, for example, the small city of Summe (Sumy) claimed 4,818 Jews, about 5 percent of the population. The 1942 report listed only 5 remaining.[61] Other cases include Gorodnitsa (3,784 Jews "missing," 11 remaining), Radomyshl (5,840 Jews "missing," "0" remaining), Slovechno (5,591 Jews "missing," 9 remaining), and Malin (8,745 Jews "missing," "0" remaining), and so forth.[62] In short, Stumpp possessed clear evidence about what was going on, and relayed this information back to Rosenberg and Leibbrandt in Berlin. Although deeply concerned about the pressing needs of the *Volksdeutsche*, Stumpp's unit nevertheless took time to document the killings, almost to the point of making them appear banal.[63]

Near Odessa beginning in July 1941 the villages of Selz, Kandel, Bischofsfeld (Jeremovka), Hoffnungsfeld, Mannheim, Sebastiansfeld, Lichtenfeld, Worms, Landau, Rosenfeld, and Rastatt witnessed the executions of not only children of mixed marriages, but their German fathers or mothers, too. The principal victims were Jews who had fled from the region of the Beresan villages. According to the eyewitness Katharina Tröster of Rastatt, no one was ignorant of these atrocities; even children could observe the burning pits nearby.[64] As Fahlbusch notes, in many cases the Nazi authorities themselves informed local populations about executions in various regions unrelated to Tröster's testimony.[65] Fleischhauer speculates that SS units may even have used some of Stumpp's village information for planning isolated cases of ancillary killing actions.[66] Although Sonderkommando Stumpp was involved in the Zhitomir region concurrently with the SS Einsatzgruppen C and D, the general view is that the majority of scholars like Stumpp were only indirectly involved in the mass murders, indeed, that the SS executions were finished before Stumpp's arrival. One source alleges Stumpp's personal involvement in some shootings, but no supporting evidence has been presented.[67]

Leibbrandt and the "Final Solution," April 1941 to Late 1942

As early as 29 April 1941, prior to Operation Barbarossa, Alfred Rosenberg's Ministry for the Occupied Eastern Territories (RMO) was organizing to handle "problems" in the occupied East. Directing the ministry's political department, Dr. Georg Leibbrandt and his assistant, Otto Bräutigam, were to formulate "political goals" for the East, including nationalities policy. The political department had to determine a "temporary solution" regarding the Jews, whether forced labor or the creation of ghettos.[68]

The evidence clearly points to Leibbrandt's direct administrative involvement in the "Final Solution." Reacting to the August 1941 Soviet deportation of the Volga and other ethnic Germans to Siberia and other remote regions, Leibbrandt issued guidelines for Nazi radio broadcasts to make it "absolutely clear that, in the case of the plan ... to banish the Volga Germans, Jewry in the areas located in the German field of power ... will be repaid manyfold for the crime."[69] However, as Fleischhauer notes, these directives came "at a time when already great parts of Central European Jewry were concentrated in the extermination locations ... and when hundreds of thousands of East European Jews had [already] fallen to

Heydrich's Einsatzkommandos." Planning for the Wannsee Conference was already well under way, and, "as a competent man in these questions," Leibbrandt would be invited. Fleischhauer concludes that, "seen in this light, the guidelines of the *Ostministerium* could be assessed only as a propaganda instrument for the covering up of the true facts."[70] In other words, Leibbrandt justified the Holocaust in the occupied USSR as a punishment for an act that had not as yet taken place.

On other occasions, Leibbrandt demonstrated initiative with regard to the "Final Solution." At one point in late 1941 the Reichskommisariat Ostland was considering the transport of 25,000 Jews to a new labor camp being constructed near Riga and the remaining 25,000 to the ghetto in Minsk. In context, this relocation would have constituted a prelude to the Jews' ultimate liquidation. But in the Reich Commissioner Hinrich Lohse's absence, his political adviser Trampedach decided to stop the shipments, perhaps motivated by the need to protect a supply of skilled labor. Since the RMO oversaw Ostland, Trampedach approached Leibbrandt for his approval. Leibbrandt, however, replied that there was no need to be so concerned about the Jews, since in any case they would soon be transported "farther east," i.e., killed, as Raul Hilberg correctly interprets it.[71]

On 31 October, Leibbrandt sent what was phrased as an inquiry, but was actually an instruction, to the Reichskommissar Ostland: "[T]he Reich Security Main Office [i.e., SS] has complained that the Reich Commissioner for the East has forbidden executions of Jews in Liepaja [Libau]. I request a report in regard to this matter."[72] On 15 November 1941, Trampedach (then in Riga) responded to his superior, Leibbrandt, in Berlin with both an explanation and a contritely phrased query: "I forbade the wild [i.e., indiscriminate] executions of Jews in Liepaja [Libau] because they were not justifiable in the manner in which they were carried out. I should like to be informed whether your inquiry of 31 October is to be regarded as a directive to liquidate all Jews in the East? Shall this take place without regard to age and sex and economic interests (of the Wehrmacht, for instance in specialists in the armaments industry)?"[73] Evidently, Trampedach interpreted Leibbrandt's 31 October inquiry as a directive calling for the extermination of the Jews without consideration of economic necessity; he apparently sensed that Leibbrandt, taking his cue perhaps from the SS's complaints to Berlin, was bothered by the decision to forestall the liquidations. And indeed, Leibbrandt's communication was just this: the RMO's head of the political division wanted to know why the executions had not yet occurred.

On 1 December 1941 Leibbrandt replied tentatively to Trampedach, apparently in his own hand (it is signed only "L.")[74] and on the original 15 November document he had received from Riga: "Of course, the cleansing of the East of Jews is a necessary task; its solution, however, must be harmonized with the necessities of war production. So far I have not been able to find such a directive either in the regulations regarding the Jewish question in the 'Brown Portfolio' [*Braune Mappe*] or in other decrees."[75]

After several days' study on the matter, Leibbrandt's Berlin office reached a final position, excluding in this case the policy of balancing "the cleansing of the Jews" with the "necessities of war production" in favor of a more ideologically inspired politics. Henceforth economic considerations were *not* to be taken into account when affairs concerned the liquidation of the Jews. Therefore, on 18 December 1941—one month before the Wannsee Conference convened—Leibbrandt's deputy, Otto Bräutigam, signed the following declaration concerning the matter addressed in the recent correspondence: "Clarification of the Jewish question has most likely been achieved by now through verbal discussions. Economic considerations should fundamentally remain unconsidered in the settlement of the problem. Moreover, it is requested that questions arising be settled directly with the Senior SS and Police Leaders."[76]And so, despite their political rivalry, the SS and Leibbrandt now supported the same policy: the indiscriminate execution of Libau's Jews.

In 1981, Gerald Reitlinger documented that around this time Leibbrandt even forwarded to Reich Commissioner Lohse the first proposal for a permanent gas chamber near Riga.[77] Another political question was the possible execution of 68,000 to 75,000 Jews still remaining in the ghettos of the Reichskommisariat Ostland as of fall 1942. Leibbrandt sent a 23 October letter to Generalkommisar Wilhelm Kube in Ostland. Kube had temporarily postponed the killing of skilled laborers, but an impatient Leibbrandt wrote to request "a report about the Jewish situation in the Generalbezirk Belo Russia, especially about the extent to which Jews are still employed by German offices, whether as interpreters, mechanics, etc. I ask for a prompt reply because I intend to bring about a solution of the Jewish question as soon as possible."[78] After a long delay, Kube replied that, with the Security Police's cooperation, he was translating Leibbrandt's initiative into action.

Thus, long before the Wannsee Conference, Leibbrandt held an important position in the Nazi machinery of death. Even as he directed the executions of tens of thousands, he supervised the duties carried out by Kommando Dr. Stumpp. Leibbrandt's two jurisdictions revealed the Nazis' *Herrenvolk-Untermenschen* dichotomy. In other words, he helped oversee the subjugation and extermination of "subhumans" while simultaneously seeing to the welfare of the "ruling race." Without a more complete understanding of Leibbrandt's responsibilities, the full impact of Stumpp's activities in Nazi-occupied Ukraine remains obscure.

Cultural "Deficiency" and Racial "Resilience"

In his various reports, Stumpp implies the ethnic Germans' Nationalist Socialist outlook and racial "superiority," but there appears to be some question about how honestly he represented even basic facts. Soviet archival evidence refutes Stumpp's claims of German fecundity and biological "resilience" in the face of Bolshevik repression and famine. Moreover, Stumpp was at pains to demonstrate the ethnic Germans' political and ideological loyalty to Hitler and Nazism.

Although many ethnic Germans welcomed liberation from communism, some of the Nazi occupation authorities questioned their ideological fervor and racial purity. According to Buchsweiler, other authorities' observations occasionally contradicted Stumpp's more positive reports.[79] For instance, upon his arrival in Transnistria in the summer of 1941, the "ethno-specialist" Karl Götz of *Sonderkommando* R (SS VoMi) observed that many of the German soldiers were startled and disappointed when they first entered the ethnic German villages. In August 1941, Dr. Hermann Maurer of the DAI expressed a similar opinion. He writes about the time when his army unit marched three days in the Kuchurgan village enclave near Odessa: "The impression ... that the Germans in Russia have suffered very badly under the twenty years of Bolshevist repression and are worn down, broken, starved, intimidated, and hardly capable of independent work and decision-making anymore has completely confirmed itself."[80] In contrast with Stumpp's claim that the ethnic Germans in Ukraine had read Hitler's *Mein Kampf*, Maurer reported that they had not yet even seen the Führer's photograph.[81]

The more critical Nazi observers pointed out the populace's lack of initiative, a sure sign of "Bolshevization" and racial "deterioration." Maurer observed the ethnic Germans' prevalent "laziness." The SS did not fail to take note. *Einsatzgruppen* C and D accordingly initiated the elimination of those ethnic Germans identified as communists, Soviet officials, and the racially "suspect." At a 1942 Nazi meeting in Rovno (Reichskommissar for Ukraine Erich Koch was there), one observer wrote that "owing to the deportation of the best [German] elements, [the German villages] are not in the condition to economize independently."[82]

To a certain extent, then, Stumpp's view of the *Volksdeutsche* differed from that of fellow Nazis, especially the SS. Stumpp's motivations were complex. Although quick to point out his people's pressing need, he often took the opportunity to emphasize their "resilience" and their unwavering devotion to the Fatherland. His notion of the *Herrenvolk-Untermenschen* dichotomy suggested that the people he studied would either thrive or die under the New Order.[83]

It is important to bear in mind that Stumpp worked under the Rosenberg ministry, at that time a bitter rival of the SS for control over the occupied East. Therefore, success in Stumpp's efforts to "rehabilitate" the ethnic Germans would have pleased his Berlin superiors. In Report No. 8, his diary for 13–25 January 1942, Stumpp mentions an encounter he had with a "Ukrainian" family (presumably German) as he traveled east. Finding them warmly receptive, he spoke to them about the glory of Hitler and the German cause:

In W. there was no night accommodation. I talked to a Ukrainian boy that I saw standing at the farmyard gate. He invited us with sincere hospitality and we came to a house in which there were 8 children but where room was found for us nevertheless. In the evening the teachers assembled and asked me to talk to them.... They are concerned [because] there is no enlightenment from the German side and no counter-propaganda. Deeply touched, those present gulp down every word that I told them about Germany and its *Führer*. "Please send us more men who can speak our language and enlighten our people"—that was the unanimous entreaty of these people.[84]

Stumpp's reports (along with other documentary evidence) suggest that the *Volksdeutsche* embraced the Nazi invaders almost immediately as liberators. It was a general reaction to the effects of twenty years of Soviet terror. Stumpp states in Report No. 11 of April–May 1942 that

> education meetings for ethnic German teachers took place in the German settlements of Chortitza and Kronau. There's little doubt that the German pedagogues from the *Reich* had never had a more grateful audience than these teachers, who swallowed with great hunger everything that was offered to them on pedagogical and political questions. For me also it was a profoundly moving experience to speak at these gatherings about research on emigration, on genealogy and on family history.[85]

Although ideological pacifists, some Mennonites (20 percent of the area's remaining German population) expressed ardent support for the occupiers. Buchsweiler correctly observes that in times of anti-German sentiment in the old Russian Empire, the Mennonites often had referred to themselves as "Dutch," and not as "Germans." Under the Nazis, however, they again called themselves "Germans."[86] Report No. 10, 12 February to 10 March 1942, speaks of Stumpp's successful "politico-educational" efforts in the Mennonite village of Chortitza and in the city of Zaporozh'e: "It has never happened to me before that farm women want to rise to applaud in the midst of my presentation; they controlled themselves with difficulty on this occasion. A teacher told me: after all that we heard up to this time, we respectfully esteemed the *Führer*, but now we love him." Non-Mennonite ethnic Germans also welcomed Stumpp with open arms. In the same report, Stumpp notes another productive "political-educational" visit, with the mayor of the city of Zaporozh'e:

> The German mayor was sitting in dignity on his official leather chair; above him hung a huge portrait of the *Führer*. This intelligent official of the old type readily gave me information about everything. His assistant ... was busy over a large volume in which he was inscribing the genealogical information for the whole community. I told him that I was not in a position to present him with an Iron Cross, first class, but could give him a copy of *Mein Kampf*. A [pleased] smile passed over his face.[87]

The ethnic Germans supposedly recognized the Führer's role in the crusade to reclaim the *Volksdeutsche*, thanks partly to Stumpp's own efforts. In Report No. 4, covering the period 27 August to 9 September 1941, he recalls another special moment:

> In Pulin-Huta we stopped to talk to 80-year-old Ferdinand Holz.... Old man Holz listened devotedly to my descriptions of Germany and particularly to information about the *Führer*. Tears ran down his cheeks. When I told him about the attempt on the *Führer*'s life in Munich [this reference may pertain to the 1939 Georg Elser bomb assassination attempt in Munich], he grasped my hand and said: "Sir, we heard about that. My neighbors came to me and we fell on our knees in gratitude that the *Führer* has been preserved." You have to realize that these people were completely cut off from Germany, were not allowed to read papers and were strictly forbidden to listen to foreign news broadcasts.[88]

More importantly, Stumpp tried to make a statistical case for the racial "superiority" of the *Volksdeutsche*.[89] Consequently, Kommando Dr. Stumpp tended to obscure the Soviet terror's disastrous demographic impact. The eighty-plus village reports that Stumpp assembled in Nazi-occupied Ukraine constitute an important source of village statistics on famine losses.[90] Stumpp's statistics must not be uncritically accepted, however, for other contemporary evidence suggests that they contain incomplete mortality figures.[91] In one 1941 entry Stumpp claims that the "German population in the individual villages, as well as altogether, has increased in comparison with 1914." But this observation contradicts accompanying reports that during the Russian Civil War under the Ukrainian anarchist Makhno "almost every village" lost twenty to fifty inhabitants to murder.[92] Elsewhere Stumpp promotes the myth of German "resilience," writing, for example, that "in most German settlements, in spite of famine years and deportations, the German population has not declined in comparison with 1914, but even increased."[93] In another report he tells his readers that "only one German died of hunger [in the village of Fassova Rutni], while in the neighboring Russian village 240 died. This phenomenon is general."[94] Soviet archival data clearly contradict Stumpp's presentation. Although statistics are complicated by ethnic "ambiguity" and shifting group and individual identities, official Soviet documents still indicate a significant population decline among Russian Germans. Even the 1939 Soviet census, deliberately inflated to hide the extent of the famine losses following collectivization, shows a rise in the Ukrainian-German population between 1926 and 1930 from approximately 394,000 to 450,000, followed by a decrease to 392,000. In 1930 the ethnic Germans' population in the USSR probably stood at around 1,380,000 or 1,400,000. The more accurate 1937 Soviet census, kept secret until the early 1990s, shows only about 1,152,000 remaining. Based on their previous growth rate, in 1939 this should have been about 1,700,000, but even the falsified 1939 Soviet census shows only 1,423,545.[95]

Stumpp was attempting to lead his readers to believe that, despite two world wars, revolution and civil war, two devastating famines, massacres, the Stalinist purges, and extensive deportations, the Ukrainian Germans did not decrease in number, but rather increased. This claim would contradict the experience of every other ethnic group in Ukraine during the same period.

For some time, Stumpp's Nazi superiors had voiced concerns over the "unsuitability" of "Bolshevized" ethnic Germans. With Leibbrandt's apparent support and understanding, Stumpp apparently tried to influence them by demonstrating that his Ukrainian *Volksdeutsche* were indeed biologically and racially "fit," so that they would not abandon them. Stumpp recorded the words of Alfred Rosenberg during his brief visit to Ukraine in June 1942: "In Chortitza, the Minister spoke to several thousand *Volksdeutsche* [and said,] 'I will report to the *Führer* that here I have found a piece of Germany.'"[96] No small accomplishment for Stumpp, considering Rosenberg's claim that "ethnic scrap" constituted ten to fifteen percent of the Soviet Union's ethnic German communities.[97]

Did Stumpp's ideology hamper the accuracy of his statistical data?[98] Perhaps his sympathy for his people (at the expense of others) compelled him to mask their shortcomings, so that the Nazi regime would spare more of them from the fate awaiting the *Untermenschen*. Not least of all, Stumpp, a Rosenberg ministry official, could claim a special role in "reclaiming" the *Volksdeutsche*. Did political considerations prevent him from being more critical of his sources or from checking whether data were complete and accurate? Did he seek to determine if a given village's population in 1941 was the same that had lived there during World War I or collectivization? These and other questions deserve more careful attention in the light of recently opened Soviet archives.

The argument has been advanced that possibly the 1933 famine did not affect the Ukrainian Germans as severely as the Volga Germans. Supposedly the Ukrainian Germans could have lived off wild vegetation and fish from local bodies of water. The argument, however, ignores the fact that even Stumpp's reports reveal that the non-German villages in the same areas experienced high mortality rates. For instance, although the German village of Münsterberg was supposedly hardly touched at all by the famine, the neighboring Russian village of Shesternaya lost half its population in 1933. Stumpp claimed that only one German died of starvation in Fassova Rutni. Though Stumpp generalized such cases to the entire Ukraine, available evidence strongly suggests that the mortality level in the villages was higher than the *Dorfberichte* claim.[99]

How is one to account for the profound differences between the Russian and ethnic German mortality rates found in Stumpp's *Dorfberichte*? Despite the fact that other hypotheses could be advanced, the possibility that Stumpp was consciously or subconsciously distorting his data in order to manipulate his superiors should not be completely dismissed: much of the evidence presented above favors this interpretation. That

Stumpp's reports portray the socioeconomic and educational "backwardness" of his ethnic compatriots does not contradict his belief in their racial "superiority." He blamed the Ukrainian Germans' cultural and economic inferiority on years of Bolshevik oppression in order to create sympathy for them. In the 1930s and the early 1940s, Stumpp's and others' arguments for the biological "superiority" of the Russian Germans appeared in the Berlin-based *Deutsche Post aus dem Osten* and similar Nazi publications. In the village reports, too, Stumpp argued that the Ukrainian Germans were no lost cause.[100]

Conclusions: From Genocide to Genealogy

Despite almost two years of intensive activity, Stumpp's command unit ran out of time. Even before the Soviets pushed the Nazis out of Ukraine, the old political rivalry between the Rosenberg and Himmler fiefdoms finally culminated in the SS's dissolution of Kommando Dr. Stumpp. Although receiving a temporary extension from Leibbrandt to complete some tasks in Ukraine, the special unit was disbanded officially on 31 March 1943. In the preceding weeks and months, Stumpp had already had to pack up his central office and archive, soon to be transported to Leibbrandt.[101] Unfortunately, during the process of relocation a good portion of the material was lost. Under the U.S. military government in Germany, however, some of it was later retrieved with Stumpp's apparent assistance.[102]

After his command, Stumpp spent the next few months working as a Rosenberg ministry staffer. In this capacity he helped organize the materials he had collected in Ukraine.[103] By the fall of 1943, however, his patron Leibbrandt himself had been forced to step down. After years of intergovernmental jurisdictional struggles, the powerful SS had finally forced Leibbrandt's resignation, and SS-Obergruppenführer Gottlob Berger replaced him.[104] Leibbrandt spent the remainder of the war in the German navy, after which time he served a brief prison sentence under the Allies (1945–1949).[105]

In the fall of 1943, Stumpp, now without Leibbrandt's patronage, was assigned to help coordinate the ethnic Germans' relocation from the Soviet Union. Growing depressed, disillusioned, and isolated as the war turned against Germany, he increasingly viewed the *Volksdeutsche* as the pawns of the National Socialist administrative apparatus.[106] By the spring of 1945 Stumpp found himself in Allied-occupied western Germany, although his family was still in Berlin. Fearing capture by the Soviets, he went under an assumed name and survived as a farm hand in Württemberg. Ultimately, his wife and children joined him in Tübingen, where he found employment as a teacher in the *Uhlandgymnasium*.

In 1950, with the establishment of the émigré organization Landsmannschaft der Deutschen aus Rußland in Stuttgart, Stumpp found a new lease on life as a Russian-German administrator, researcher, lecturer, author, and editor for another three decades.[107] He also provided valuable assistance to Chancellor Konrad Adenauer in late 1955, when the West German government entered into negotiations with Moscow over the release of German POWs and amnesty for the USSR's ethnic Germans. In 1966, the Federal Republic of Germany awarded Stumpp the Distinguished Cross of Merit, First Class, in "recognition of services performed on behalf of the state and the people."[108] Generating little controversy and receiving much international acclaim, Stumpp continued working tirelessly until his 1982 death in Stuttgart. In the late 1960s and early 1970s, he supported the establishment of various Russian-German organizations abroad. He even served as an honorary president of such heritage associations.[109]

With his late 1940s "denazification"—one of thousands of middle-tier Nazi officials—Stumpp publicly disassociated himself from his Nazi past by claiming that he had followed the Nazis only for what he understood to be the good of his *Volk*. But Stumpp's wartime duties in Ukraine still cast a dark shadow over his subsequent work. According to a highly reliable source from North America's Russian-German ethnic community and formerly of U.S. Military Intelligence, Stumpp plea-bargained with Allied occupation officials by helping retrieve missing Nazi documents, some now housed at the U.S. National Archives in Washington, D.C. Another corroborating source says that on one occasion he personally read a U.S. Military Intelligence file on Stumpp, which had many sections blacked out for security reasons. Sources also speak of having seen an old World War II photograph of Dr. Stumpp seated in an armored vehicle and wearing a dark military uniform. During one trip to Stuttgart, a source learned that Stumpp's personal files at the Landsmannschaft remain under lock and key, probably to protect the Stumpp family's privacy rights.[110] A former SS member reports that "it is beyond doubt" that Stumpp personally shot innocent Jews in Ukraine. But as long as all these sources insist on remaining anonymous, their claims can only constitute hearsay evidence at best.

The great irony is that so much of Stumpp's postwar research came out of the period in question, making questions about his past motivations difficult to avoid. As recently as the mid 1990s, for instance, a public outcry erupted when the German Interior Ministry funded the publication of a Landsmannschaft booklet titled *Volk auf dem Weg—Deutsche in Rußland und in der GUS, 1763–1993*, based partly on the late Stumpp's revised manuscripts. Some public figures criticized its apparently "positive" portrayal of the Nazi "liberation" of Russian Germans. In a press statement at the time, German parliamentary delegate Annelie Buntenbach of Bündnis 90/Die Grünen called the ministry's financial backing of this brochure "an unbelievable scandal."[111]

Leibbrandt's demonstrative postwar "silence" was rather public, but it is now mostly forgotten. In 1947 (while himself serving in prison), Leibbrandt was a key witness in the case against the Nazi Foreign Ministry. Robert M. W. Kempner, the lawyer who cross-examined Leibbrandt at Nuremberg, provides revealing information about Leibbrandt's complicity at Wannsee. In 1961 Kempner reflected that Leibbrandt "showed little inclination to ... admit to his participation at the Heydrich-Eichmann conference [Wannsee]."[112] During his testimony, Leibbrandt did, however, refer to the "Final Solution" as *Wahnsinnpolitik* (a policy of insanity). He even claimed that after the conference he had protested to Rosenberg, insisting that he would not participate in such policies. But although it is true that Leibbrandt opposed some of the SS's policies toward the Slavic peoples—whom he deemed potential allies against the Soviets—the Nuremberg documents show that he was directly and actively involved in ordering the mass executions of Jews.[113] In the course of cross-examining Leibbrandt, Kempner posed a rhetorical question: "You are a sensible man. Think about the meeting and the murder plan once more, with whom you spoke and so forth. Not one of you stood up and said, 'here I stand and cannot do otherwise.' Is that correct?" Leibbrandt remained silent.[114]

Leibbrandt's denial of complicity in the "Final Solution" already had been refuted by his immediate superior, Alfred Rosenberg. On 17 April 1946 during the Nuremberg trials, Rosenberg admitted to Allied prosecutors that his assistants—including Erich Koch, Hinrich Lohse, Wilhelm Kube, Otto Bräutigam, and Georg Leibbrandt—were fully informed of the program to eliminate the Jews. The court's president asked him, "Do you agree that these five people were engaged in exterminating Jews?" Rosenberg replied, "Yes. They knew about a certain number of liquidations of Jews. That I admit, and they have told me so, or if they did not, I have heard it from other sources."[115]

Some members of the ethnic German community have subsequently picked up on Leibbrandt's excuses. Many never knew the whole truth. People close to activists like Leibbrandt and Stumpp naturally find this issue difficult to confront. Only a generation after their deaths and those of their closest associates can we begin putting the issue into better perspective. In 1975 one short biography claimed that Leibbrandt worked in vain to prevent Nazi foreign policy excesses, and that, in his official capacities, he protested the "Final Solution"; it implied that Leibbrandt voluntarily resigned from his post in 1943. Nor was there any mention of Wannsee.[116] As to the other biographical sketches, articles, and obituaries on Leibbrandt, the Wannsee Conference and Allied war crimes trials receive little or no mention at all. Especially as events recede further in time, the sheer ignorance concerning them increases. Today this historical "amnesia" does not necessarily stem from any ulterior motives, but the fact remains that the events are unknown to most Russian Germans—indeed, to most scholars.

Though the Allied prosecution had made a clear case against Leibbrandt and his deputy Bräutigam, they were never prosecuted, and by 1950 all charges had been dropped against them. This decision, made as the Cold War intensified, reflected the notion that only the highest-ranking Nazis should bear the responsibility. But, was not serving as a ministerial representative at the Wannsee Conference "high-ranking"? Merciless men like Leibbrandt and Bräutigam once again became "respectable" citizens. After the trial Leibbrandt served as an economic adviser in Bonn and resumed his studies on the Russian Germans. For thirty years, he contributed to and participated in the Landsmannschaft. At these organizational gatherings, one could often find Stumpp and Leibbrandt, sometimes sitting near each other. Leibbrandt's most recent publication appeared in 1980, two years before his death. A career diplomat, Bräutigam worked for many years in the West German Foreign Office, and his name was actually considered for the list of experts who were to accompany Chancellor Konrad Adenauer on his September 1955 summit meeting in Moscow.[117]

In North America, the Russian-German ethnic community founded two heritage societies—the American Historical Society of Germans from Russia (AHSGR), and the Germans from Russia Heritage Society (GRHS). Members of both societies have generally viewed Stumpp's and Leibbrandt's work (some of the village reports aside) as genealogical gems having no connections to a historical context. At least since the 1930s, Stumpp had encouraged genealogical research among the world's ethnic Germans. To point to its political uses does not gainsay the meticulousness and factual value of the "dean's" work on the conditions of village life, history, culture, language, and demographics; yet it must be borne in mind that only after the war was it depoliticized and made to look "matter-of-fact." Though knowing far more about Stumpp's activities than do many of his associates, Canadian Adam Giesinger viewed Stumpp's wartime service as chiefly academic and non-ideological. Not making fully clear that his colleague's wartime service was more complex and conflicting than generally assumed,[118] he declared in 1977:

> Without minimizing the [academic] value of the [Village] Reports of 1942, which are my subject here today, I think it can be said that this unofficial work of Kommando Dr. Stumpp [in uncovering the Dnepropetrovsk Archives' genealogical records] is of far greater importance than the preparation of the reports, which was the official purpose of its mission. Dr. Stumpp, a tireless worker, whose accomplishments in a few short months are almost unbelievable, did not neglect the task for which he had been sent to Russia.[119]

In the city of Dnepropetrovsk, Stumpp found the Russian government archive with census records on the early nineteenth-century German settlers. For Giesinger,

> the choice of this city as headquarters site was a great good fortune for American descendants of Black Sea Germans, particularly those interested in genealogy.... [Stumpp] put a number of people to work transcribing these census lists, brought the transcriptions to Germany, and eventually, with financial support

from AHSGR, published them [thirty years later] in his monumental … *The Emigration from Germany to Russia in the Years 1763 to 1862.*[120]

Thus, at least in North America, the Stumpp-Leibbrandt legacy is primarily appreciated for its contributions to scholarship and genealogical and village research. Yet this approach leaves much out of the picture. Those interested today in Russian-German family history are the indirect beneficiaries of Stumpp's Nazi commitment and his wartime activities in Ukraine. With Stumpp having played the longtime role of catalyst and organizer, the intense fascination of some Russian Germans in Canada and the United States with genealogy continues to grow in the wake of post–Cold War Russia's decision to open up its archives. To be fair, the compilation of family histories has increasingly become an American and Canadian pastime, a natural reflection of the human longing for rootedness, self- and group-affirmation, and continuity in an ever-changing mass society. After the 1960s Stumpp's promotion of family and village history research thus coincided well with popular interest in both immigrant societies.

For obvious reasons, the fascination with ancestry in post-Nazi Germany is subdued. North America's genealogical trend has mostly run counter to the greater emphasis of the Russian-German Landsmannschaft placed upon politics of émigré integration and cultural activities. The latter grew partly from the Nazis' connection of ancestry to a supposedly inherent biological hierarchy of races. At one time the compilation of detailed pedigree charts had been primarily a practice of the European aristocracies; the Nazis adapted it to an "aristocratic" racial notion useable on a mass scale for the "Aryans." In contrast, for many Germans in North America the compilation of family history has taken on a *personal* urgency. Like the Mormons, the Russian-German ethnic community here ranks as one of the most devoted to the writing of family histories, thanks partly to the efforts Stumpp resumed in the 1960s. As a result of several decades of assimilation, one of the few common links that the remnant of North America's Russian Germans still holds is their ancestral heritage and the Old World's traditional village. Perhaps Stumpp, himself a product of profound turn-of-the-century socioeconomic modernization, pursued such postwar research activities in order to preserve what little remained of the group. But in North America today, with the growing loss of the various German-language dialects, ethnocultural practices, and even traditional religious beliefs, the remaining Russian Germans can no longer claim those old ethnic ties that once expressed a deeper and more urgently felt meaning in everyday life.

Considering that a significant number of members of both Russian-German heritage societies in the United States and Canada fought against the Nazis during World War II, the erosion of historical memory regarding Stumpp assumes an ironic character. One of the prominent founders of

AHSGR, a Russian-German native of Colorado (now deceased), served in 1948 and 1949 on General Lucius Clay's legal staff in Berlin, with the Office of Military Government, and with the Intelligence Division in Nuremberg and Bad Nauheim.[121] Another founding member participated in the American liberation of Dachau. This study raises questions about a convoluted history. Stumpp's special unit dutifully helped document both the ethnic composition of western Ukraine and SS genocide. Leibbrandt made certain that both missions were enacted. Though previously enthralled by a totalitarian regime, they and their academic associates, like so many others, returned to "normal" lives after the war, almost as if nothing had happened. With wartime memories fast fading, the information they collected became ethnographic, apolitical, and academic to North American heritage societies unaware of the Nazi origins of much of Stumpp's and Leibbrandt's data.

Notes

The authors thank Oxford University Press for permission to republish parts of this essay. The article originally appeared in Eric J. Schmaltz and Samuel D. Sinner, "The Nazi Ethnographic Research of Georg Leibbrandt and Karl Stumpp in Ukraine, and Its North American Legacy," *Holocaust and Genocide Studies* 14, no. 1 (2000): 28–64.

1. Michael Burleigh, *Germany Turns Eastwards: A Study of Ostforschung in the Third Reich* (Cambridge, 1988), 10. For more information, see also Götz Aly, "The Planning Intelligentsia and the 'Final Solution,'" in *Confronting the Nazi Past: New Debates on Modern German History*, ed. Michael Burleigh (New York, 1996), 140–153; and Michael Fahlbusch, *Wissenschaft im Dienst der nationalsozialistischen Politik? Die "Volksdeutschen Forschungsgemeinschaften" von 1931–1945* (Baden-Baden, 1999).
2. See "Abschied von Dr. Leibbrandt 5.9.1899 bis 19.6.1982," *Volk auf dem Weg* (Stuttgart) 8–9 (August–September 1982): 9; "Dr. Karl Stumpp," *Volk auf dem Weg* 2 (February 1982): 3; "Dr. Karl Stumpp 12.5.1896–20.1.1982," *Volk auf dem Weg* 5 (May 1996): 5; "Dr. Karl Stumpp gestorben," copy of the 1982 newspaper clipping of Stumpp's obituary in the *Kanada Kurier*, which is in the file "Karl Stumpp Chronicles" located at the American Historical Society of Germans from Russia Headquarters, Lincoln, Nebraska; Arthur E. Flegel, "Memories of Dr. Karl Stumpp," *Journal of the American Historical Society of Germans from Russia* 5, no. 1 (1982): 5; Adam Giesinger, "Dr. Karl Stumpp (1896–1982): A Life of Service to His People," *Journal of the American Historical Society of Germans from Russia* 5, no. 1 (1982): 1; Emma S. Haynes, "Dr. Karl Stumpp—In Memoriam," *Journal of the Historical Society of Germans from Russia* 5, no. 1 (1982): 3; Joseph S. Height, "Dr. Georg Leibbrandt: Scholar, Author, Publisher" and "Dr. Karl Stumpp: Scholar, Author, Lecturer," in *Homesteaders on the Steppe: Cultural History of the Evangelical Lutheran Colonies in the Region of Odessa, 1804–1945* (Bismarck, N.D.: North Dakota Historical Society of Germans from Russia [Germans from Russia Heritage Society], 1975), 395–396, 399–400; Sidney Heitman, "Introduction (Germans)," *Guide to the Study of the Soviet Nationalities: Non-Russian Peoples of the USSR* (Littleton, Colo., 1982), 232; Fred C. Koch, "A Bibliographic Survey," *The Volga Germans in Russia and the Americas, From 1763 to the Present* (University Park and London, 1977), 326; James W. Long, *From*

Privileged to Dispossessed: The Volga Germans, 1860–1917 (Lincoln, Nebr., and London, 1988), 256; Franz Usselmann, "Karl Stumpp," *Volk auf dem Weg* 2 (February 1982): 3.

3. The mountains of evidence scattered in the German War Records can be intimidating. Hundreds of Ukrainian villages are listed in various charts, but a smaller number of villages (between eighty-one and ninety-nine) relate to the so-called *Dorfberichte*. According to Adam Giesinger, eighty-one village reports were completed on Ukraine's German villages. Yet Richard H. Walth argues that up to ninety-nine villages were documented. Stumpp's twelve diary reports (*Tagebuchfrontberichte*) are also found among these. Giesinger, "Captured German Documents," *American Historical Society of Germans from Russia Work Paper No. 13* (December 1973): 12; Giesinger, "Reports of 1942–43 from German Villages in the Ukraine," *American Historical Society of Germans from Russia Work Paper No. 24* (1977): 19–23; Richard H. Walth, *Flotsam of World History: The Germans from Russia between Stalin and Hitler*, 2nd rev. ed. (Essen, 1996), 328–336, 338–372. See also *Guides to German Records Microfilmed at Alexandria, VA: No. 21: Records of the Deutsches Ausland-Institut Stuttgart: Part II: The General Records* (Washington, D.C., 1961).

4. Some of their postwar works were self-published. Ethnic German organizations and publishing houses in Germany and North America later republished some.

5. The two North American Russian-German historical societies include the American Historical Society of Germans from Russia, or AHSGR (Lincoln, Nebr.), established in 1968; and the Germans from Russia Heritage Society, or GRHS (Bismarck, N.D.), created in 1971. At various times, Dr. Stumpp held the office of honorary president of both. One must note that most members of these organizations, who number in the thousands, know little or nothing about the details of Stumpp's and Leibbrandt's careers. The "controversy" is confined to a small number of academically trained members. On Stumpp's visits to heritage society conferences in North America, see Michael M. Miller, ed., *Researching the Germans from Russia: Annotated Bibliography of the Germans from Russia Heritage Collection* (Fargo, N.D., 1987), 174–175.

6. Only a few contemporary scholars have discussed this, mostly in the 1970s and the 1980s. Though typically only a few pages treated Stumpp and Leibbrandt, this essay is indebted to them, especially the Israeli historian Meir Buchsweiler, (West) German Jewish historian Ingeborg Fleischhauer, German émigré scholar Richard H. Walth, and Canadian scholar Adam Giesinger.

7. Ingeborg Fleischhauer and Benjamin Pinkus, *The Soviet Germans: Past and Present*, ed. Edith Rogovin Frankel (New York, 1986), 94–95.

8. Meir Buchsweiler, *Volksdeutsche in der Ukraine am Vorabend und Beginn des Zweiten Weltkriegs—ein Fall doppelter Loyalität?* (Gerlingen, 1984), 21; Ingeborg Fleischhauer, *Das Dritte Reich und die Deutschen in der Sowjetunion* (Stuttgart, 1983), 33; Fleischhauer and Pinkus, *Die Deutschen in der Sowjetunion: Geschichte einer nationalen Minderheit im 20. Jahrhundert* (Baden-Baden, 1987), 18, 220–226; Giesinger, "Dr. Karl Stumpp," 1.

9. Buchsweiler, *Volksdeutsche in der Ukraine*, 21; Fleischhauer, *Das Dritte Reich*, 33; Fleischhauer and Pinkus, *Die Deutschen in der Sowjetunion*, 220–221; Giesinger, "Dr. Karl Stumpp," 1; Height, "Dr. Georg Leibbrandt: Scholar, Author, Publisher," 395. See also Dr. Karl Stumpp's DAI personnel file in the microfilmed German Records T-81, Roll 349, Frame 5078430 (e.g., GR T-81, R 349, F 5078430). See also Stumpp's own account of the early days in "Ein Leben für mein Volkstum," in *Heimat-Kalender der Bessarabiendeutschen 1978* (Hanover, 1978), 94–106.

10. Buchsweiler, *Volksdeutsche in der Ukraine*, 21; Height, "Dr. Georg Leibbrandt: Scholar, Author, Publisher," 399–400; Walth, *Flotsam of World History*, 45–46, 49.

11. Long, *From Privileged to Dispossessed*, 60–61.

12. Fleischhauer and Pinkus, *The Soviet Germans*, 94–95; Fleischhauer and Pinkus, *Die Deutschen in der Sowjetunion*, 210–211.

13. Fleischhauer and Pinkus, *The Soviet Germans*, 94–95.

14. Buchsweiler, *Volksdeutsche in der Ukraine*, 21; Fahlbusch, *Wissenschaft im Dienst*, 591; Walth, *Flotsam of World History*, 45–46, 49. Note that in addition to the *Ostabteilung*,

Leibbrandt directed with Rosenberg the *Abteilung zur Bekämpfung des Bolschewismus im Außenpolitischen Schulungsamt der NSDAP.*

15. For example, see an excerpt from the 17 August 1939 letter by Jacob Volz (York, Nebraska) to Dr. Stumpp, in GR T-81, R 606, F 5396424. Genealogy is discussed.

16. Buchsweiler, *Volksdeutsche in der Ukraine*, 83. Cf. Stumpp, "Zur Volksbiologie des Rußlanddeutschtums," GR T-81, R 608, F 5399053-56 (1940); "Gesundheitsübersicht vom Gebiet Emiltschino," GR T-81, R 606, F 5396990.

17. Buchsweiler, *Volksdeutsche in der Ukraine*, 21, 46–52, 64–85; Fleischhauer, *Das Dritte Reich*, 33; Fleischhauer and Pinkus, *Die Deutschen in der Sowjetunion*, 220–221; Giesinger, "Dr. Karl Stumpp," 1; Stumpp, "Ein Leben für mein Volkstum," 100–106; Walth, *Flotsam of World History*, 69.

18. Buchsweiler, *Volksdeutsche in der Ukraine*, 21; Fleischhauer, *Das Dritte Reich*, 33; Fleischhauer and Pinkus, *Die Deutschen in der Sowjetunion*, 215–221; Giesinger, "Dr. Karl Stumpp," 1.

19. Giesinger, "Dr. Karl Stumpp," 1–2. Cf. Stumpp, *Von der Urheimat und Auswanderung der Deutschen in Bessarabien* (Stuttgart, 1938).

20. Cf. Buchsweiler, *Volksdeutsche in der Ukraine*, 270 (fn. 472).

21. Hermann Maurer (trans. Adam Giesinger), "A Report Sent Home to Germany by a Sergeant in a German Army Unit Stationed in the Kutschurgan Villages 13–28 August 1941," *Journal of the American Historical Society of Germans from Russia* 7, no. 1 (1984): 1–3, 5–6. Cf. GR T-454, R 20.

22. "Einwohnerverzeichnis (mit Ergänzungsliste) des Ortes Neu-Glückstal (1944 Neu-Glückstal Family Register with Supplementary List and Notes), comp. in Walth, *Auf der Suche nach Heimat: Die Rußlanddeutschen—In Search of a Home: The Germans from Russia* (Dülmen, 1990), 195–238. Cf. Fleischhauer and Pinkus, *The Soviet Germans*, 98.

23. In Diary Report No. 5, 13–23 September 1941, Stumpp refers to his family's village of Alexanderhilf: "In Kirovograd there live many Germans, above all from the Odessa region. Here I met the first ethnic German woman from my own home village; she had been with my sister in banishment." In Stumpp (trans. Giesinger), "In the Wake of the German Army on the Eastern Front, August 1941 to May 1942," *Journal of the American Historical Society of Germans from Russia* 7, no. 3 (1984): 33.

24. Fleischhauer, *Das Dritte Reich*, 97–98; Walth, *Flotsam of World History*, 327. Cf. J. Noakes and G. Pridham, *Nazism, 1919–1945: Vol. 3: Foreign Policy, War and Racial Extermination: A Documentary Reader* (Exeter, 1988), 1086ff.

25. Fleischhauer, *Das Dritte Reich*, 97.

26. Ibid., 98.

27. Fahlbusch, *Wissenschaft im Dienst*, 607–609, 613.

28. Ibid., 607. Cf. Buchsweiler, *Volksdeutsche in der Ukraine*, 364–383.

29. Fahlbusch, *Wissenschaft im Dienst*, 613. Cf. Buchsweiler, *Volksdeutsche in der Ukraine*, 315–324, 364–383; Fleischhauer, *Das Dritte Reich*, 101–116.

30. Fahlbusch, *Wissenschaft im Dienst*, 607–609, 613.

31. Nazi geographer Emil Meynen (in English) cited in Fahlbusch, ibid., 609.

32. Fahlbusch, *Wissenschaft im Dienst*, 102, 590–609, 613. Cf. Stumpp, *Bericht über das Gebiet Chortitza im Generalbezirk Dnjepropetrowsk* (Berlin, 1943), 10; Stumpp, *Bericht über das Gebiet Kronau-Orloff (Orloff jetzt Marienburg)* (Berlin, 1943), 7.

33. Fahlbusch, *Wissenschaft im Dienst*, 609. Along with Stumpp, Emil Meynen, Friedrich Metz, and Hugo Hassinger are still regarded by many as the "academic fathers" of Germany's geography discipline. Receiving little public notice is the fact that they were all associated with the various "coordinated" Reich ministries and the SS, perfecting their craft during the Nazi era. Like his colleague Stumpp, geographer Emil Meynen worked under Leibbrandt for the RMO's Publikationsstelle Ost (Publications Office East). For more critical discussion of the geography profession's role under National Socialism, see also Fahlbusch, "Die verlorene Ehre der deutschen Geographie. Bis heute wird die

Mittäterschaft der akademischen Väter am Völkermord der Nationalsozialisten verdrängt," http://www.fs-geographie.de/vergangenheit.html.

34. The DVL expressed the SS's purpose of placing all ethnic Germans into a hierarchy of four racial categories: Group 1, "racially pure" Germans with German or National Socialist "consciousness"; Group 2, "racially pure" Germans without German "consciousness," but capable of becoming true National Socialists; Group 3, people with predominantly "German blood," deemed capable of being "regermanized"; and Group 4, persons who possessed only some "German blood" or those who were assimilated into other nations, refused to become German citizens, or were deemed unable to be "regermanized." See Fleischhauer, *Das Dritte Reich*, 68; Fleischhauer and Pinkus, *The Soviet Germans*, 96–97.

35. See examples of *Dorfberichte* in Buchsweiler, *Volksdeutsche in der Ukraine*, 252–253, 370; Fahlbusch, *Wissenschaft im Dienst*, 612; and Walth, *Flotsam of World History*, 301ff.

36. Giesinger, "Reports of 1942–43 from German Villages in the Ukraine," 20.

37. Ibid.

38. Giesinger, "Dr. Karl Stumpp," 2.

39. Giesinger, "Captured German Documents," 12; Stumpp (trans. Giesinger), "In the Wake of the German Army on the Eastern Front, August 1941 to May 1942," *Journal of the American Historical Society of Germans from Russia* 7, no. 4 (1984): 17.

40. Walth, *Flotsam of World History*, 76–79. Walth also points out that each village report contained the following categories: (1) village name; (2) number of inhabitants, according to nationality; (3) number of mixed marriages; (4) breakdown of German residents in terms of men, women, and children; (5) origin of the colony's residents; (6) information about education; (7) information about cultural affairs; (8) information about health and welfare; (9) records on church registration; (10) economic data, primarily about the farmers and the village's infrastructure; and (11) economic and political concerns under Bolshevik rule.

41. Giesinger, "Reports of 1942–43 from German Villages in the Ukraine," 20.

42. Stumpp, "In the Wake of the German Army on the Eastern Front, August 1941 to May 1942," *Journal of the American Historical Society of Germans from Russia* 7, no. 1 (1984): 10. Cf. German Records T-175, Roll 580.

43. See also Stumpp, "Zur Volksbiologie des Rußlanddeutschtums," GR T-81, R 608, F 5399053-56 (1940).

44. Stumpp, "In the Wake of the German Army," 7, no. 1 (1984): 10.

45. Fleischhauer, *Das Dritte Reich*, 33 (fn. 69).

46. Stumpp writes in one report: "(The Germans) were taken by the work-shy Jews and exploited as slave labor ([Die Deutschen] wurden von den arbeitsscheuen Juden gerne aufgenommen und als Arbeitssklaven ausgenützt)." Cited in Buchsweiler, *Volksdeutsche in der Ukraine*, 380.

47. Stumpp, "In the Wake of the German Army," 7, no. 1 (1984): 10–11. This particular report continued with the author's—perhaps unwitting—observation of the desperate plight of Lvov's Jews: "In many business places, coffee houses, hair-dressers, there are notices: 'Jews not desired' or even 'Jews are forbidden to enter.' One day the streets were blocked so that one could hardly get through. Jews were standing there in large numbers offering all sorts of household objects for sale: gold jewelry, silver cutlery, watches, fountain pens.... An imposed sum of twenty million rubles has to be raised in a few days. Surprising only is the fact that the buyers are mostly German soldiers. For the first time in the history of this city, its beautifully planted parks will be free of Jews on Sundays."

48. Ibid., 11.

49. Ibid.

50. Maurer, "A Report Sent Home to Germany," 1–3, 5–6.

51. Stumpp, "In the Wake of the German Army on the Eastern Front, August 1941 to May 1942," *Journal of the American Historical Society of Germans from Russia* 7, no. 2 (1984): 24.

52. Walth, *Flotsam of World History*, 78.

53. Buchsweiler, *Volksdeutsche in der Ukraine*, 368–369. See also fn. 298 (p. 368) concerning Giesinger's possible misinterpretation of *ausgesiedelt*.

54. See published copy of the Kalinindorf report and photograph of the memorial in Buchsweiler, *Volksdeutsche in der Ukraine*, 369–371. Cf. Fahlbusch, *Wissenschaft im Dienst*, 608.

55. It remains uncertain how many more villages Stumpp's special unit recorded. GR T-81, R 606–607. Cf. Walth, *Flotsam of World History*, 330–331.

56. GR T-81, R 606–607. Cf. Walth, *Flotsam of World History*, 338ff.

57. Giesinger, "Reports of 1942–43 from German Villages in the Ukraine," 22.

58. Buchsweiler, *Volksdeutsche in der Ukraine*, 368–369.

59. Quoted in Walth, *Flotsam of World History*, 93.

60. See the report of RKF-official in Hegewald, SS-Standartenführer Theodor Henschel to Heinrich Himmler, 25 November 1942, in BArch, R49/2427. Cf. Isabel Heinemann, "Towards an 'Ethnic Reconstruction' of Occupied Europe: SS Plans and Racial Policies," in *Annali dell'Istituto storico italo-germanico in Trento*, vol. 27 (2001), 512f.

61. Walth, *Flotsam of World History*, 360.

62. GR T-81, R 607, F 5397081, 5397088.

63. GR T-81, R 606–607.

64. Fleischhauer, *Das Dritte Reich*, 131ff., 141.

65. Fahlbusch, *Wissenschaft im Dienst*, 609.

66. Fleischhauer, *Das Dritte Reich*, 98; Fahlbusch, *Wissenschaft im Dienst*, 608–609.

67. Wishing to remain anonymous, a source formerly active in U.S. military intelligence and possessing sensitive information has told the authors that Stumpp was involved in SS killing actions against Ukrainian Jews during the time the *Dorfberichte* were being compiled. The informant did not imply that Stumpp participated in an SS Einsatzgruppe's actions, but that Stumpp, who himself belonged to the SS, committed isolated and apparently self-initiated executions as the leader of his special Sonderkommando unit. According to this highly reliable source, some members of the émigré community and Stuttgart Landsmannschaft have also expressed their private concerns over various allegations concerning Stumpp's activities in Ukraine. For documentation of Stumpp's SS membership and rank, see GR T-81 R 374 = DAI Film (58), "Potsdam, Rundbrief Nr 23 Stuttgart. 23 September 1942. Haus des Deutschtums. An die Kameraden bei der Wehrmacht." Michael Fahlbusch supplied this reference. The authors were themselves surprised to hear the claim that Stumpp personally shot Jews. While recognizing that the claim is questionable, they nevertheless felt that if they were not to publish the claim, they would have made themselves vulnerable to the charge of suppressing evidence, even if of a problematic nature. Especially after receiving independent testimony to the same effect, the authors felt obliged to publish the claim.

68. See Document 1024-PS in vol. 26, 560ff. of the International Military Tribunal, *Trial of the Major War Criminals*, Nuremberg, 1947–1949 (in German). Cf. Document 1024-PS, 685ff. in vol. 3 of the Office of United States Counsel for Prosecution of Axis Criminality, *Nazi Conspiracy and Aggression*, Washington, D.C., 1946–1948 (in translation). See also Otto Bräutigam's autobiography concerning the SS-RMO rivalry and his boss, Georg Leibbrandt: *So hat es sich zugetragen: Ein Leben als Soldat und Diplomat* (Würzburg, 1968), 380–388, 622–625, 627ff.

69. Leibbrandt, "Abschrift. Fernspruch aus Berlin vom 13. September 1941. Reichsminister Ost, gez. Leibbrandt," GR T-454, R 20, F 374. Cf. Fleischhauer, *Das Dritte Reich*, 157.

70. Fleischhauer, *Das Dritte Reich*, 158.

71. Document 1024-PS in vol. 26, 560ff. and Document 3663-PS in vol. 32, 435–436 of *Trial of the Major War Criminals*. Cf. Document 1024-PS, 685ff. in vol. 3 and Document 3663-PS, 401–402 in vol. 6 of *Nazi Conspiracy and Aggression*. See also Raul Hilberg, ed., *The Destruction of the European Jews*, rev. ed., vol. 1 (New York and London, 1985), 352. Cf. "Leibbrandt to Reichskommisar Ostland," 13 November 1941, Occ E 3-32.

72. Document 3663-PS, vol. 6, in *Nazi Conspiracy and Aggression*, 401. Cf. Document 3663-PS, vol. 32, in *Trial of the Major War Criminals*, 435–436.

73. Document 3663-PS, vol. 6, in *Nazi Conspiracy and Aggression*, 401–402. Cf. Document 3663-PS, vol. 32, in *Trial of the Major War Criminals*, 436.
74. Over the years, scholars have differed over whether the "L." signed on the 15 November 1941 document stood for Georg Leibbrandt or Hinrich Lohse. It is known that Trampedach, Lohse's deputy in Riga, was sending this correspondence to Berlin, and that Leibbrandt's Berlin office was replying to these inquiries. Possibly Lohse was in Berlin at this time, and even had an opportunity to review the correspondence. However, the initial response to Riga's inquiry came from Leibbrandt himself. In any case, it remains clear that Leibbrandt's department authorized these killing actions. On 17 April 1946 during the Nuremberg trials, Alfred Rosenberg testified on this matter that it "could hardly be Lohse. I do not know Lohse's initial. I do not know.... It could also be Leibbrandt; I do not know." In the end, Rosenberg was not willing to say that the handwritten part of the 15 November letter was from Lohse. Consult vol. 11, *Trial of the Major War Criminals*, 555–556.
75. Document 3663-PS, vol. 6, in *Nazi Conspiracy and Aggression*, 401–402. Cf. Document 3663-PS, vol. 32, in *Trial of the Major War Criminals*, 435–436. The "Brown Portfolio" consisted of directives on the Four-Year Plan for the Nazis' economic exploitation of the East.
76. Document 3666-PS, vol. 6, in *Nazi Conspiracy and Aggression*, 402–403. Cf. Hilberg, *The Destruction of the European Jews*, vol. 1, 376–377.
77. Gerald Reitlinger, *The SS: Alibi of a Nation, 1922–1945* (Englewood Cliffs, 1981), 186.
78. Hilberg, *The Destruction of the European Jews*, vol. 1, 384. Cf. "Leibbrandt via Lohse to Kube," 23 October 1942, Occ E 3-45.
79. Buchsweiler, *Volksdeutsche in der Ukraine*, 314–316.
80. Our translation. Buchsweiler, ibid., 315.
81. Ibid., 272–273, 314–315.
82. Our translation. Buchsweiler, ibid., 315.
83. Stumpp relates what he considers to be his people's desperate circumstances. In Report No. 3, August 1941, Stumpp writes: "In Berdichev I was able to find 21 German families and three German girls married to Poles.... The children know scarcely any German, for they learn only Ukrainian in school. It was forbidden to speak German at home and so the parents had to speak Ukrainian to their children.... They must definitely be removed from here into a German environment or they will be lost as Germans." In Report No. 7, November–December 1941, he writes: "Fate brought me to Berdichev on this day and I was invited to an ethnic German Christmas celebration. I found it very depressing. The children stood in a circle and sang Ukrainian songs.... These children had never experienced a German Christmas celebration. Only after an address by me did a festive mood ensue.... It is urgently necessary that these Germans, who migrated to the cities to escape from forced labor, be resettled in their villages as soon as conditions permit. There has been much Russification in the language spoken in the home, and the number of mixed marriages is considerable." See Stumpp, "In the Wake of the German Army," 7, no. 1 (1984): 15; Stumpp, "In the Wake of the German Army," 7, no. 4 (1984): 18.
84. Stumpp, "In the Wake of the German Army," 7, no. 4 (1984): 18.
85. Ibid., 21.
86. Buchsweiler, *Volksdeutsche in der Ukraine*, 111–113.
87. Stumpp, "In the Wake of the German Army," 7, no. 4 (1984): 20.
88. Stumpp (trans. Giesinger), "In the Wake of the German Army," 7, no. 2 (1984): 20.
89. Stumpp, "Zur Volksbiologie"; "Gesundheitsübersicht vom Gebiet Emiltschino."
90. The statistical data in these reports were extracted and published in Walth, *Flotsam of World History*, 361–364.
91. Consult Samuel D. Sinner, *The Open Wound: The Genocide of German Ethnic Minorities in Russia and the Soviet Union, 1915–1949 and Beyond/Der Genozid an Rußlanddeutschen 1915–1949*, prefaces by Eric J. Schmaltz and Gerd Stricker (Fargo, N.D., 2000).
92. Stumpp, "In the Wake of the German Army," 7, no. 3 (1984): 34.

93. Ibid., 36.
94. Stumpp, "In the Wake of the German Army," 7, no. 2 (1984): 18.
95. The statistics are documented in Sinner, *The Open Wound*, 59–62; *Der Genozid*, 69–70, 76–79.
96. Stumpp, "Bericht über den Besuch des Reichsministers Rosenberg, die Schulfeier in Chortitza und die Lage der Volksdeutschen auf der Halbinsel Krim und östlich von Dnjepropetrowsk," GR T-81, R 606, F 5396710, 2.
97. Fleischhauer and Pinkus, *The Soviet Germans*, 98.
98. In this context, consult Stumpp's propaganda piece, "Zur Volksbiologie." Stumpp pays particular attention to ethnic German fertility and birthrates. Cf. "Gesundheitsübersicht vom Gebiet Emiltschino."
99. Some villages no doubt experienced lower mortality levels in the 1930s than others. But exceptions should not be generalized. Some contemporary historians have also misinterpreted exceptional cases.
100. In the 1930s, not only Karl Stumpp and Georg Leibbrandt, but the latter's brother Gottlieb, were frequent contributors to *Deutsche Post aus dem Osten* (*DPO*). Gottlieb's articles consisted mostly of anti-Semitic and anti-Bolshevik slogans and propaganda. After the war, Gottlieb emigrated to Canada. Cf. Adolf Eichler, "Die völkische Widerstandskraft der Rußlanddeutschtum" in *DPO*, no. 3 (1938): 2–5/no. 4 (1938): 9–12; Joseph Geiger, "Die rassische Beschaffenheit der rußlanddeutschen Kolonisten" in *DPO*, no. 2 (1936): 23–25; and Stumpp, "Zur Volksbiologie des Rußlanddeutschtums" in *Volk und Reich*, vol. 16 (1940): 124–127.
101. Walth, *Flotsam of World History*, 68–70, 73–75, 326.
102. According to one highly reliable source formerly of the U.S. military intelligence community (who wishes to remain anonymous), part of Stumpp's "rehabilitation" under the Allied occupation authorities in Germany stemmed from his help in relocating some of the missing German War Records in question.
103. GR T-81, R 606, F 5396899.
104. Bräutigam, *So hat es sich zugetragen*, 627ff.; Fahlbusch, *Wissenschaft im Dienst*, 591; Fleischhauer, *Das Dritte Reich*, 100–101; Walth, *Flotsam of World History*, 68–70, 73–75. Fahlbusch cites as the reason for Leibbrandt's forced resignation his engagement with the Mennonites, whose pacifism made the SS suspicious. In fact, when in the United States in the early 1930s, Leibbrandt had begun studying this group, publishing some of his findings in the *Mennonite Quarterly Review* in Goshen, Indiana.
105. Height, "Dr. Georg Leibbrandt: Scholar, Author, Publisher," 400; Walth, *Flotsam of World History*, 46.
106. Fleischhauer, *Das Dritte Reich*, 100–101.
107. Giesinger, "Dr. Karl Stumpp," 2; Walth, *Flotsam of World History*, 46, 49. Resulting from his archival collections, three of Stumpp's best known postwar works include: *The German-Russians: Two Centuries of Pioneering* (Bonn, Brussels, New York, 1967 [1964]); *Das Schrifttum über das Deutschtum in Rußland* (Tübingen, 1980 [1958]); and *Die Auswanderung aus Deutschland nach Rußland in den Jahren 1763–1862* (*The Emigration from Germany to Russia in the Years 1763–1862*), rev. ed. (Lincoln, Nebr., 1978 [1973]). This thousand-page tome is the product of forty years of genealogical research. Besides the Landsmannschaft der Deutschen aus Rußland, Stumpp was also an active member in the Landsmannschaft der Bessarabiendeutschen (Stuttgart).
108. Height, "Dr. Georg Leibbrandt: Scholar, Author, Publisher," 396.
109. See also Giesinger, "Germans from Russia in Germany in the 1950s: The Early Years of the Landsmannschaft," *Journal of the American Historical Society of Germans from Russia* 4, no. 1 (1981): 26–33; Giesinger, "The History of the AHSGR: The Important Role of Dr. Stumpp in the Early Years: Based on the Documents in the Society Files," *Journal of the American Historical Society of Germans from Russia* 5, no. 2 (1982): ii-3.
110. The authors are still in the process of locating a copy of Stumpp's "denazification" file in Washington, D.C.

111. Concerning the brochure publication controversy, refer to the Internet article "Rasse-biologie vom BMI" in *Forum Wissenschaft 1/96*, http://www2.hrz.tu-darmstadt.de/fsmathe/BdWeb/Forum/96-1/nari.html.

112. Robert M. W. Kempner, *Eichmann und Komplizen* (Zürich, Stuttgart, Vienna, 1961), 155.

113. Again, consult Document 1024-PS in vol. 26, 560ff. and Document 3663-PS in vol. 32, 435–436 of the International Military Tribunal, *Trial of the Major War Criminals*, Nuremberg, 1947–1949 (in German). Cf. Document 1024-PS, 685ff. in vol. 3 and Document 3663-PS, 401–402 in vol. 6 of the Office of United States Counsel for Prosecution of Axis Criminality, *Nazi Conspiracy and Aggression*, Washington, D.C., 1946–1948 (in translation); Leni Yahil, *The Holocaust: The Fate of European Jewry* (New York and Oxford, 1990), 315, 701.

114. Kempner, *Eichmann und Komplizen*, 155–157. Compare the published English translation of this cross-examination in Gitta Sereny, *Albert Speer: His Battle with Truth* (London and Basingstoke, 1995), 349–350. Leibbrandt's reaction to the cross-examination should be compared with other Wannsee witnesses at Nuremberg. Cf. Kempner, *Das Dritte Reich im Kreuzverhör* (Munich and Esslingen, 1969), 188–193; and Kempner, *SS im Kreuzverhör* (Munich, 1964), 208–222, 291–293.

115. For Rosenberg's admission of Leibbrandt's knowledge of the liquidation of Jews in Ukraine, see Rosenberg's testimony of 17 April 1946 recorded in vol. 11 of *Trial of the Major War Criminals*, 560–561. For related incriminating evidence against Leibbrandt in Rosenberg's testimony, see ibid., 540, 544–546, 554–556.

116. See Height, "Dr. Georg Leibbrandt: Scholar, Author, Publisher," 399–400.

117. Reitlinger, *The SS: Alibi of a Nation, 1922–1945*, 186. Concerning Jewish Americans' outrage over Leibbrandt's post-trial release from prison, please see the newspaper article "Judenmörder laufen frei herum," *Aufbau* (New York) 8 December 1950, 3.

118. Cf. Giesinger, *The Way It Was: A Family History and Autobiography* (Winnipeg: Hignell, 1993 [Adam Giesinger, 1992]). This book is located at the AHSGR archives in Lincoln, Nebraska.

119. Giesinger, "Reports of 1942–43 from German Villages in the Ukraine," 20.

120. Ibid.

121. "David J. Miller, Esq. 1906–1993: Founder and First President," *Journal of the American Historical Society of Germans from Russia* 16, no. 2 (1993): 53. Cf. Giesinger, *The Way It Was*.

Chapter 4

VOLK, BEVÖLKERUNG, RASSE, AND RAUM
Erich Keyser's Ambiguous Concept of a German History of Population, ca. 1918–1955

◆ ◆ ◆

Alexander Pinwinkler

Introduction: The Current State of Research

Recent debates on the role of German historians and of German historiography in the period encompassing the Weimar Republic, the Third Reich, and the early Federal Republic assign a relatively minor function to the person and work of Erich Keyser (1893–1968). Hermann Aubin, Werner Conze, and Theodor Schieder are much more conspicuous topics of current discussion than is the historian Keyser, a member of the faculty at Danzig, then at Marburg after 1945. Much greater influence on the development of postwar German historiography is attributed to these other historians than to Keyser. In overviews of the history of the discipline, Keyser is usually portrayed as a representative of ethnically oriented (*völkisch*) groups during the Weimar Republic who later openly supported the Nazis during the Third Reich.[1] Nevertheless, his professional career after 1945 has remained virtually unnoticed in the literature. Keyser's publications and his ethically questionable activities aimed at the "scientific" legitimation and the technocratic realization of Nazi racial and genocidal policies have also only rarely been a matter for detailed study.[2]

The purpose of this essay is to outline the image of a *völkisch* historian[3] who as early as the 1920s considered history of population (*Bevölkerungsgeschichte*) to be an appropriate instrument for restoring Germany's lost position as a superpower. Keyser, who had been socialized within the conservative cultural and educated elite of Danzig, was unreservedly committed by 1933 at the latest to a National Socialist transformation of Europe. Under these political conditions, his concept of history of population[4] or, more precisely, of a population history of Germany, had much greater chances than during the Weimar Republic of exerting widespread influence among historians and folklorists (*Volksforschern*) and of influencing state population policy.

Biographical Elements: Erich Keyser's Career and Professional Influence within the Context of Nazi Population Policy in Occupied Poland

Born in Danzig on 12 October 1893, Keyser studied history in Freiburg, Halle, and Berlin. His doctoral thesis, published in 1918, dealt with issues related to the earliest settlement and economic history of his home town. In 1920, he took on a position at the State Archives in Danzig.[5]

The publications of this Danzig historian can be correctly assessed only in the light of his specific political mentality. Keyser's political views were formed after World War I, when he experienced the loss of Germany's claim to hegemony over parts of Poland. In the Free City of Danzig, the existence of which was allegedly threatened by its Polish neighbors, ethnically oriented (*völkisch*) historiography supposedly attained an immediate political significance. One of the roots of the political radicalization of the German discipline of history was the social milieu of municipal and regional history in West and East Prussia, the milieu that fostered Keyser's rise as a historian of more than regional renown.[6]

Appointed an extraordinary professor at Danzig Technical College in 1931, Keyser transformed his studies on history of population into what was virtually his own branch of the academic discipline of history. In 1938, these efforts led to the publication of *Bevölkerungsgeschichte Deutschlands* (Population History of Germany). His programmatic essay on this topic was published as a pamphlet under the title *Die Geschichtswissenschaft—Aufbau und Aufgaben* (History: The Discipline's Structure and Concerns) in 1931. Also during the 1930s, Keyser began work on a multi-volume project of German municipal history, an attempt to broaden the scope of his earlier research on the history of Danzig in the direction of a comparative perspective.[7]

Keyser was not only an archivist and a university lecturer, but also a museum director and an effective organizer of academic activities. In addition to his professional work, he actively propagated nationalist ideas within the public sphere;[8] he became a member of the National Socialist German Workers' Party (NSDAP) on 1 May 1933.[9]

In various journals of regional history and geography, Keyser published essays on the municipal history of Danzig and on the regional history of West and East Prussia. In 1926, he created the State Regional Museum of Danzig History in Danzig-Oliva; he remained its director until 1945. The establishment of a committee of historians concerned with regional research on East and West Prussia in Königsberg in 1923 occurred in response to a suggestion made by Keyser. He became president of the West

Prussian Historical Society in 1938. And from 1941 on, he was director of the research unit dealing with West Prussian regional history within the regional studies research department of the *Reichsgau* Danzig-West Prussia. In addition, Keyser worked at the Danzig Ostland Institute founded in 1927, then a branch of the Leipzig Stiftung für Volks- und Kulturbodenforschung (Foundation for Research on German Ethnicity and Land Cultivation), and at a later date of the North East Ethnic German Research Society (NOFG). This institute was entrusted with "controlling Polish academic studies."[10] During World War II, Keyser also directed a research unit for regional and ethnic studies that was instituted in the course of a meeting of the Königsberg Main Council (*Oberpräsidium*) in 1939. Organizationally, this research unit was linked to the NOFG and furthered the cause of an ethnic reallocation of land in the eastern regions of the Reich. To this end, the department planned demographic studies of the population in those areas.[11]

During the autumn of 1940, Keyser attended the Conference on History of Population in Berlin as a representative of the Office of Regional Studies in Danzig. Among the other scholars attending the conference were Hermann Aubin and Theodor Schieder. Some of the historians there involved directed regional studies research units located along the Polish borders that were under the supervision of the respective district administrations (*Gauleitungen*) and that were designed to form the nucleus of a future Reich Office of Regional Studies. At the conference, Aubin and Walter Kuhn, a settlement historian and ethnic researcher on linguistic "islands" (*Sprachinseln*), spoke on issues concerning "national policy problems involved in representing population developments."[12] Keyser reported on the plans of his West Prussian regional history research unit, which was expected to complete the following four projects: (1) compilation of expert reports on regional history for the district offices, (2) collaboration on germanizing the names of localities in the newly formed *Reichsgau*, (3) research on the history of the province, and (4) a history of the population in the area along the Vistula River in order to provide materials for future population policy measures.[13]

Within the scope of the so-called Germanization of the Danzig-West Prussia region, Keyser participated in the compilation of the German National List (*Deutsche Volksliste*, DVL). Using data from the German census of 1939, Wilhelm Löbsack, the district office director and general adviser on issues concerning ethnic German traditions (*Volkstumsfragen*), calculated along with Keyser and his assistant Krannhals, "who selected the groups to be assessed, that approximately 30,000 families should be considered for Germanization."[14] The self-administrative district agencies played a significant role in the realization of Nazi population policy. At the regional level, the collaboration between academic disciplines, administration, and politics seemed to function quite smoothly.[15]

After the collapse of the Third Reich, Keyser was active in (re-)establishing the network of *völkisch* researchers. At the University of Hamburg, he helped to establish Hans Harmsen's German Academy of Population Studies,[16] and he was one of the leading members of the Ranke Society, which supported a revision of German history along national-conservative and ethnocentric lines.[17] Furthermore, Keyser was one of the founders of the Herder Research Council in Marburg/Lahn in 1950. Until 1959, he was the director of the J. G. Herder Institute; he remained co-editor of the institute's journal, the *Zeitschrift für Ostforschung*, up to the time of his death on 21 February 1968.[18]

Volk and *Bevölkerung* in Erich Keyser's Œuvre: Topics Relevant to a History of Population (*Bevölkerungsgeschichte*)

Keyser's history of population was intended to study "a group of people who inhabited the same region."[19] For Keyser, the term *Bevölkerung* (population) refers to those ethnically and racially classified segments of the population who lived on "land cultivated by the Germans"; thus, *Bevölkerungsgeschichte* included not only German, but also non-German groups—but only insofar as these had come into contact with Germans in the past. Accordingly, the region of the population, i.e., "the area occupied as a coherent settlement by the German people at the time of its greatest expansion"[20] could include several nations and races. In much the same way as, for instance, Hans Joachim Beyer or Werner Conze, Keyser was opposed to "individualistic" definitions of *Bevölkerung*. In his view, one such definition was the "statistical" concept of population, which did not go beyond a statistical survey of a number of individuals.[21]

Keyser was largely dependent on the historian and folklorist Adolf Helbok for his definition of *Volk* as "a historically developed communal life of persons who, due to their family descent, form a blood community and a functional community and, in this way, set themselves apart from other peoples."[22]

In Keyser's view, history of population should encompass the following four thematic areas:

- the region inhabited by the population (*Bevölkerungsraum*) as the "living space" of certain "human communities." This "space" can also be occupied by several "nations" or "races";[23]
- the quantity of the population (*Bevölkerungszahl*). The work of the economists and statisticians Karl Bücher and (Karl) Julius Beloch, which Keyser valued quite highly,[24] provided the methodological model for this particular sphere of history of population (the study of the current state of the population and of migration);
- the groups constituting the population as "natural units of the population" (persons, families, estates, tribes, peoples). According to Keyser,

"social history" is one component of population history, for both disciplines are concerned with the "stratification" of the population. In this view, a history of familial lineage is also to be undertaken within the framework of a more general history of population—this subdiscipline should provide insight into the "birth rates and ethnic make up of the population." In addition, Keyser refers to a specific "personal history" concerned with the individual, also a discipline closely connected to the history of population. Within this concept, the "history of tribes and nations" refers to individual ethnic groups and "peoples." Keyser expected the history of population to provide a "historical counterpart"[25] to Wilhelm Winkler's book, *Statistisches Handbuch des gesamten Deutschtums* (1927).[26]

- the nature of the population "according to physiological and psychological characteristics or to the racial make up of the population and its groups."[27] Ancillary disciplines to be included in such studies were anthropology and the psychological study of national character traits (*Völkerpsychologie*). As Keyser explicated in ever more detail during the following years, he found close cooperation between *Bevölkerungsgeschichte* and *Rassenforschung* to be essential, for "racial history" could "not be understood without knowledge of the history of population." The historian himself was especially interested in the "racial categorization of the *current* population of Germany and in the racial classification of physiological remains from the centuries of the past" (emphasis added).[28]

Keyser was convinced that a complete reconstruction of German ethnic history (*Volksgeschichte*) from the beginnings up to the present could enjoy some prospect of success only if, in close cooperation with archaeology, a systematical study of the findings from all eras of (pre-)history were undertaken. Fundamental to Keyser's concept is his focus on the immediate present. In order to make an assessment of the "essence" and "value" of contemporary "Germandom," it is of fundamental significance for Keyser to inquire into its racial-biological "core" and, in this context, to determine the point in time at which "foreign" elements entered the "body of the German people" (*Volkskörper*).

Between Regional History and History of the People (*Volksgeschichte*): Keyser's Research on the Population and the Radicalization of *völkisch* Historical Thought in the Nazi Era

Keyser aimed at a breakthrough for history of population both at the regional level and at the more general level of a history of the German people. In what follows I will discuss two studies by Keyser that can be assigned to these spheres. The first is entitled *Die Geschichte des deutschen Weichsellandes* (1939), the second is Keyser's *Bevölkerungsgeschichte Deutschlands* (1938–1943).

In 1938, Keyser openly placed the regional history of the area along the Vistula River at the service of political interests. His primary concern was with the history of the region during the High Middle Ages, for which he wished "to determine the boundary between the Baltic Pruzz in the East and the Slavic Pomoranes in the West."[29] The arguments of the relevant studies were based primarily on an analysis of names designating towns and rural areas; the studies were "carried out by the State Regional Museum of Danzig History in Danzig-Oliva on the orders of Reichsführer-SS Himmler."[30] With his conception of *"Weichselland,"* Keyser created the myth of a historical region that in fact had never really existed as such, for the area along the Vistula had never been a unified territory along the lines of a politically and legally integrated (early) modern state. Keyser's efforts to retrospectively fabricate such a unity of "space" and "land" were all the more distinct and emphatic. For Keyser, "space" was something more or less naturally determined; the spatial hub of the Vistula region was formed by the lower reaches of the most important river, i.e., of the Vistula itself. Keyser delved far back into geological history to find historical support for his argument.[31] In his view, the sociopolitical conflicts within the region were also predetermined by the natural characteristics of this "space": "This struggle [i.e., between the peoples of the region] is a law of space. Such oppositional nature [i.e., between plain and plateau, between the Vistula and its tributaries] is not characteristic of all geographical regions." In addition to timeless spatial unity, Keyser also attempted to offer proof of a continuous Teutonic-German settlement of the Vistula region. He contended that the Germanic "Norsemen" (i.e., Normans, Vikings), whom he also called "men of the Nordic race," were the first to infuse the region with "a unified characteristic" by means of their settlements and cultivation practices. Thus, from the beginning, or at least from the beginning of a "history" reconstructible from written records, "people" and "space" were irrevocably connected to one another.[32]

All of those earlier studies that Keyser had undertaken since the late 1920s informed his *Bevölkerungsgeschichte Deutschlands*. It was his explicit intention not simply to describe the influx of settlers into so-called German cultivated land, but to depict the "origin and development of the German people."[33] One of the basic principles of this work is the construction of a social and "racial" opposition between "Germans" and "Jews" since the Middle Ages. In this view, the majority of "Germans" were hostile toward the "Jews" to such an extent that, before Jewish assimilation in the nineteenth century, there had only rarely been family or other ties between the two groups.[34] Keyser apprehends the history of the German population by means of the specific combined effects over time of the following three structures: the "quantity of the population," the "nature of the population," and the "region of the population." In a review of the first edition of the book, Helmut Haufe, an assistant lecturer to Gunther Ipsen, saw this as an attempt to proceed "from previously conventional issues of the economic and social sciences to a theoretical foundation of '*Volk*.'"[35]

Haufe's remarks on the book's content structure are not at all incorrect in their contention that the presentation extends over an extremely wide range of historical data and thus restricts itself "to the great lines of history."[36] The demographer Roderich v. Ungern-Sternberg also found fault with such disparities of the presentation in his critique of the third edition of Keyser's *Bevölkerungsgeschichte*. "Hardly a third of the book" dealt with the nineteenth and twentieth centuries, although there were fairly substantial statistical sources available for precisely this time period.[37]

A more pressing question than whether Keyser was able to master the abundant content of his study, or whether his work was in accord with contemporary demographic research, seems to be whether and to what extent the three editions differ in content and whether they somehow reflect the experience of the intensification of the German War of Annihilation in the East. In any case, Keyser did expand his study by one hundred pages from the first to the second edition and by approximately 130 pages from the second to the third edition. Corresponding to this expansion of the book are certain content-related alterations, of which I would like to emphasize the following: For the second edition in 1941, Keyser replaced the original general "introduction" with a separate introductory chapter entitled "The People and Academic Research" (*Volk und Forschung*) and bearing section headings such as "What is the Nature of the German People?" and "People and Population."[38] Keyser added another section entitled "People and Race" to the introduction for the third edition of 1943. Furthermore, in another new subchapter of the book entitled "Aliens in Germany," he also discussed "the first appearance of the Jews," "National Socialist population policy," and "the immortality of the German people."[39]

Such additions reflected the rapidly unfolding debate within the demographic sciences on the presumed interconnections among concepts of *Volk*, *Rasse*, *Raum*, and *Bevölkerung*—interconnections that, for their own part, were primarily stimulated by the direct or indirect, prospectively legitimizing participation of academic scholars in Nazi population policy. In 1943, the year of the escalation and the turning point in the War of Annihilation in the East, Keyser maintained that "the will of the German people to cleanse itself of undesirable racial components"[40] was the driving force behind the study of such connections. *Volk* was now no longer, as it had been five years previously, determined by the dualism of "blood community and functional community." Instead, it was semantically restricted to a "blood community" in the sense of an "hereditary and ... reproductive community."[41]

Back to the Roots of *völkisch* Historical Discourse? Erich Keyser's Essay "Die Erforschung der Bevölkerungsgeschichte" (1956)

In the essay "Die Erforschung der Bevölkerungsgeschichte" (Researching Population History), Keyser makes emphatically affirmative use of *völkisch* concepts and terminology. He perceives demographic developments since 1945 as an expression of a far-reaching crisis of the German people. The terminology employed by a contemporary demography of Western provenience is of no significance here. On the evidence of this essay, it is not difficult to demonstrate the continuity of *völkisch* thought in Keyser. In 1956, it is not the concept of population, but, once again, that of *Volk* that is the major factor in the conceptual horizon of this author. *Volk* now appears as the "community of fate," the community of those persons uprooted and expelled after 1945. Yet it is no longer constituted by a presumed organic interrelationship of *Blut*, *Boden*, and *Raum*. On the contrary, "sociological" terms of so-called communities of origin, such as "family," "clan," "tribe," and "people" are superimposed on the genetic-racist vocabulary—terms that themselves are difficult to separate from their biologically deterministic implications. "Man," who forms such "communities" (more or less the keyword of this short text, appearing in it a total of thirteen times), also brings about (not further specified) changes in them. The history of population arises from the interaction between "man" and "community," thus, between "man" and "*Volk*." In addition to the "communities," a further concern of Keyser's history of population is the role of the individual, of the personality[42]—no longer in the heroic, combative sense that had been noticeable in Keyser's apologetics and active appropriation of the Führer principle in 1935,[43] nor in a sense more appropriate to an individualistic, liberal, more modern conception of society. Here "man" is not primarily perceived as an autonomous agent, but much more as an entity bound to community, in natural and inevitable dependence on the "community."[44]

According to this view, even social change is not to be understood as a sequence of temporal events or as secular conflicts among social classes or strata, but instead as a biological process of "maturation" and "decline." This specific view of social change also corresponds to Keyser's definition of the research program for demography, stated as follows: "Demography is concerned with existence and non-existence, with the development and decline of humans within those groups and formations that have evolved in the course of history." Thus, human "communities" have a specific life span that depends primarily on the "reproductive capacities" of the peoples.[45]

Keyser, who here also emphasizes the specific "peculiarities of East German man" and in this way reproduces the myth of a regeneration of German "tribes," sees the loss of the eastern territories (*Ostraum*) as a genuine and fundamental catastrophe.[46] Henceforth—after the demise of the

German settlement of eastern and southeastern Europe—history of population must come to terms with the task of imparting the historical significance of the East to the German people once again.[47] In doing so, Keyser maintains, other peoples are also to be taken into account; yet in contrast to his earlier work, Keyser now wishes to refrain from making judgements on these other peoples.

Summary

Conceptually, Erich Keyser drew a strict distinction between the territorially confined population (*Bevölkerung*) and the *Volk*, which consisted of certain ethnically or racially determined segments of the population. As a primary historical discipline related to spatial conditions, history of population (*Bevölkerungsgeschichte*), together with demographic surveys and demographic theory (*Bevölkerungskunde* and *Bevölkerungslehre*), should, in Keyser's view, become one of the three subdisciplines of "population studies." For Keyser, this overarching discipline was synonymous with "research on the body of the people" (*Volkskörperforschung*), "studies of national tradition" (*Volkstumskunde*) or "folklore" (*Volkskunde*).[48] Within this conception, "population studies" was to provide methodological clarification for related disciplines (such as anthropology, statistics, race theory) and to provide politics with expert opinions directly pertinent to a course of action. Based on long-lasting traditions of *völkisch* research, the central inquiry into the "essence" of the German people, then, was directly geared to the terminological grasp of racially undesirable elements that had over time through immigration and marital ties found their way into the German population, to the separation of such "elements" from the "body of the German people," and thus to the definition of a specific racial-biological core of the German *Volk* that seemed to be identical to the Nazi myth of Nordic man. In this way, Keyser designed an anachronistic image of *the* German, whose physical (racial-biological) and psychological characteristics had allegedly never changed since the early Indo-Germanic era.[49]

Keyser's attempt to discursively generate an alleged new domain and to assign it a special disciplinary status within a more comprehensive "population studies" or *Volkswissenschaft* was also a manifestation of the unavoidable ambivalence of such inexplicable categories as *Volk*, *Bevölkerung*, *Rasse*, and *Raum*. The terms of reference between the individual categories were never clarified and remained notoriously controversial among the individual *Volksforscher*. The research planned and conducted by the historian from Danzig tended to blend history of population with an obscure "racial science" that was largely dependent on the corresponding teachings of the social anthropologist and race researcher H. F. K. Günther. With this research program, which more or less dissolved at its edges and became increasingly blurred, Keyser was not far removed from schemes that preached a vague *völkisch* universalism and, for their part, took recourse to ideas of the self-proclaimed conservative revolutionaries Max Hildebert Böhm and Arthur Moeller van den Bruck. But with his research strategy, Keyser may have tended to exceed the human resources and institutional capacities of his discipline. This might help to explain—in addition to certain rivalries among the *Volksforscher* still requiring more detailed analysis—why Keyser's work did not attain the recognition among his colleagues that he had probably hoped for. Notwithstanding the diversified responses of the critics, the three editions of Keyser's book *Bevölkerungsgeschichte Deutschlands* reflected the cumulative radicalization of the mutual relations between the spheres of history of population and "race theory."

On the subject of whether Keyser's studies were in any way innovative, one can contend that the use of simple statistical scales and ratios and the application of basic demographic methods does not in itself comprise any sort of "innovation."[50] However, we can certainly maintain that the scientific schemes of identification and segregation of individual segments of the population, as such schemes were developed by Keyser, were readily adaptable to realization in the form of the inhumane practice of racist social engineering.

After 1945, the specific ambivalence of Keyser's view of history resulted from the fact that it contained traces of widely varied *völkisch* discourse and patterns of thought that were interwoven into a peculiar amalgam. Keyser hardly took notice of genuine methodological developments or of certain liberal traditions in the domain of demography—demonstrated, for instance, by the work of Karl Theodor v. Inama-Sternegg or Paul Mombert.[51] In this way, Keyser's work indirectly indicated that by the 1950s at the latest German population studies had become methodologically and conceptually ossified. To be sure, he did remove Nazism's specific emphasis from *völkisch* terminology (there is, e.g., no longer a conceptual link between *Blut* and *Blutströmen*). As the 1956 essay cited above readily demonstrates, Keyser's political stance was influenced by West German discourse on Europe in the midst of the Cold War. Yet the *völkisch* frame of mind managed sustain itself practically undiminished in Keyser's work.[52] The way he engaged in research on the history of population was a compelling manifestation of a "new" conservatism during the 1950s. At that time, in reaction to the (shared) experience of impotence at the "loss of community," a conservative way of thinking opposed certain forms of an Americanized consumer society that had a substantial influence on the *Zeitgeist* and lifestyle of the postwar period. After many of the former *Volksforscher* had experienced insecurity about their very material existence during the first postwar years, there was a return to specific "time-honored values." For many of the nationalistically inclined academics under *völkisch* influences, this ideologically motivated, backwards-looking projection went along with regaining secure career positions. This was also the case for Erich Keyser, who was the director of the J. G. Herder Institute during the 1950s. Only after Keyser's death did the Marburg-based institute begin to gradually become receptive to a form of historical research on Eastern Europe that was not ethnocentrically oriented, but was interested in studying all of the ethnic groups inhabiting the region on an equal basis.[53]

— *Translated by Thomas La Presti*

Notes

1. With reference to Keyser's essay "Die völkische Geschichtsauffassung," Winfried Schulze remarks that in 1933 Keyser provided a nearly "official" definition of an ethnocentric conception of history. Schulze, *Deutsche Geschichtswissenschaft nach 1945* (Munich, 1993), 291. Cf. E. Keyser, "Die völkische Geschichtsauffassung," *Preußische Jahrbücher* 234 (1933): 1–20; Bernhard vom Brocke, *Bevölkerungswissenschaft Quo vadis? Möglichkeiten und Probleme einer Geschichte der Bevölkerungswissenschaft in Deutschland* (Opladen, 1998), 82–83, 106, 110.
2. Still, cf. the recurrent mention of Keyser in Michael Fahlbusch, *Wissenschaft im Dienste der nationalsozialistischen Politik? Die "Volksdeutschen Forschungsgemeinschaften" von 1931–1945* (Baden-Baden, 1999), 189, 535, 560, 577–578, 581, 585.
3. Cf. Wolfgang Weber, "Völkische Tendenzen in der Geschichtswissenschaft," in *Handbuch zur "Völkischen Bewegung" 1871–1918*, ed. Uwe Puschner, Walter Schmitz, and Justus H. Ulbricht (Munich, 1996), 834–858; here especially a definition of "völkischer Historie" (835–836).
4. According to Keyser, it was in 1934 that the journal *Jahresberichte für deutsche Geschichte* began to include a subsection *Bevölkerungsgeschichte* in its section VII (genealogy). Cf. Keyser, "Neue Forschungen über die Bevölkerungsgeschichte Deutschlands," *Vierteljahrschrift für Sozial- und Wirtschaftsgeschichte* 29 (1936): 46.
5. There is still no book-length biography of Keyser. Cf. the positive evaluations by Hermann Aubin "Zu den Schriften Erich Keysers," in *Studien zur Geschichte des Preußenlandes. Festschrift für Erich Keyser zu seinem 70. Geburtstag*, ed. Ernst Bahr (Marburg, 1963), 1–11, and Bahr's obituary, "Nachruf auf Erich Keyser," *Zeitschrift für Ostforschung* 17 (1968): 288–291.
6. Cf. Keyser, "Die Entwicklung der landesgeschichtlichen Forschung in Ost- und Westpreußen," *Mitteilungen des Grenzmarkdienstes Posen-Westpreußen*, 14. April 1929; Keyser, "Die Historische Kommission für ost- und westpreußische Landesforschung," *Zeitschrift für Ostforschung* 1 (1952): 525–529.
7. Keyser, *Die Geschichtswissenschaft, Aufbau und Aufgaben* (Munich, 1931); Keyser, *Bevölkerungsgeschichte Deutschlands* (Leipzig, 1938; 2nd ed. 1941; 3rd ed. 1943; Keyser ed., *Deutsches Städtebuch. Handbuch städtischer Geschichte. I. Nordostdeutschland* (Berlin, 1939); II. *Mitteldeutschland* (Stuttgart and Berlin, 1941); III. *Niedersächsisches Städtebuch* (Stuttgart, 1952), *Westfälisches Städtebuch* (Stuttgart, 1954), *Rheinisches Städtebuch* (Stuttgart, 1956), IV. *Hessisches Städtebuch* (Stuttgart, 1957), *Badisches Städtebuch* (Stuttgart, 1959), *Württembergisches Städtebuch* (Stuttgart, 1962); V. *Bayerisches Städtebuch* (Stuttgart, 1971/1974).
8. With reference to these efforts on the part of Keyser, Hermann Aubin esteemed him as an "educator of the people" (*Volksbildner*). Hermann Aubin, "Zu den Schriften Erich Keysers," 2.

9. Bundesarchiv Berlin (formerly BDC), NSDAP-Gaukartei, Prof. Dr. E. Keyser. Within the same year, Keyser also became a member of the NSLB (on 1 October 1933) (Bundes-archiv, formerly BDC).

10. Fahlbusch, *Wissenschaft*, 189.

11. Ibid., 535, 577. Fahlbusch does not mention whether the "research department" speci-fied actually carried out the planned demographic studies. On the biographical details listed above, cf. Bahr, "Nachruf," 288–291.

12. Michael G. Esch, *"Gesunde Verhältnisse." Deutsche und polnische Bevölkerungspolitik in Ostmitteleuropa 1939–1950* (Marburg, 1998), 578.

13. Ibid., 581–582. Keyser's staff, especially Dr. Max Aschkewitz, completed numerous unpublished studies of the history of the settlement and population of the region. Cf. Herder-Institut Marburg, Dokumentensammlung, Materialien Forschungsstelle für westpreußische Landesgeschichte Danzig-Oliva, "Hand- und maschinschriftliche Auf-zeichnungen." (See also note 18 below.) Even during the late 1960s, Aschkewitz published a study, "The Jews in West Prussia," that developed from his activities during the war: Max Aschkewitz, *Zur Geschichte der Juden in Westpreußen* (Marburg, 1967).

14. Cited in Esch, *"Gesunde Verhältnisse,"* 237.

15. Cf. Ingo Haar, "'Ostforschung' und 'Lebensraum'-Politik im Nationalsozialismus," in *Geschichte der Kaiser-Wilhelm-Gesellschaft,* ed. Reinhard Rürup and Wolfgang Schieder vols. 1–2, 2: *Bestandsaufnahme und Perspektiven der Forschung,* ed. Doris Kaufmann (Göt-tingen, 2000), 461.

16. Apart from the organization's president Harmsen, the officials of the academy included the following demographers and sociologists: H. Muckermann, K. Horstmann, K. V. Müller, and H. Schelsky, some of whom had compromised themselves through their involvement in Nazi population policy. Burgdörfer became an honorable member of the society in 1956. Among the more prominent of the academy's twenty-four founding members were the following: F. Burgdörfer, H. Harmsen, G. Ipsen, E. Keyser, S. Koller, G. Mackenroth, H. Schubnell, and O. Frhr. v. Verschuer (Statistisches Bundesamt, Archiv Wiesbaden) (StBA, Archiv), Deutsche Akademie für Bevölkerungswissenschaft, Protokoll der Gründungssitzung der Akademie v. 23. February 1953).

17. Other leading members of this society included Karl Alexander v. Müller, Heinrich v. Srbik, Harold Steinacker, and Otto Brunner, who had all identified themselves more or less closely with National Socialism during the Third Reich. The founder of the Ranke Society, the well-known anti-Semite Gustav Adolf Rein, had become a member of the NSDAP in 1933. Schulze, *Geschichtswissenschaft*, 204–205.

18. Cf. Bahr, "Nachruf," 289–290. Keyser's personal effects are divided between the Herder Institute in Marburg and the Institute for Comparative Municipal History in Münster (Westphalia). According to information provided by Dr. Peter Wörster, to whom I am most grateful for his assistance, the portion located at the Herder Institute includes 210 archival units and requires 3.5 m of shelving space. The index to *Bevölkerungsgeschichte* in Keyser's personal effects, referring only to items from the time after 1945, includes references to Keyser's correspondence with persons and institutions concerning issues of population studies.

19. Keyser, *Bevölkerungsgeschichte Deutschlands* (Leipzig, 3rd ed. 1943), 13.

20. Keyser, "Die Zeitalter der Bevölkerungsgeschichte Deutschlands," *Archiv für Bevölke-rungswissenschaft und Bevölkerungspolitik* 4 (1934): 134, 148.

21. Cf. Keyser, "Bevölkerungswissenschaft und Geschichtsforschung," *Archiv für Bevölke-rungswissenschaft und Bevölkerungspolitik* 5 (1935): 155–156.

22. Keyser, "Rassenforschung und Geschichtsforschung," *Archiv für Bevölkerungswissen-schaft und Bevölkerungspolitik* 5 (1935): 3.

23. Keyser, *Geschichtswissenschaft*, 132. Here, Keyser is explicitly opposed to the concept of *Volks- und Kulturboden* (133), since he felt that this concept, which could be traced back to the geographer Albrecht Penck, was nationally restricted. Cf. Michael Fahlbusch,

*"Wo der deutsche ... ist, ist Deutschland!" Die Stiftung für deutsche Volks- und Kulturboden-
forschung in Leipzig 1920–1933* (Bochum, 1994).

24. Keyser, *Geschichtswissenschaft*, 131.
25. Keyser, *Geschichtswissenschaft*, 128–129, 131.
26. Wilhelm Winkler ed., *Statistisches Handbuch des gesamten Deutschtums*, im Auftrag der
    Stiftung für deutsche Volks- und Kulturbodenforschung in Leipzig, in Verbindung mit
    der Deutschen Statistischen Gesellschaft (Berlin, 1927).
27. Keyser, "Bevölkerungswissenschaft," 148.
28. Keyser, "Neue Forschungen," 47.
29. Keyser, *Die Geschichte des deutschen Weichsellandes* (Leipzig, 1939), 48.
30. Keyser, "Bevölkerungsgeschichtliche Forschungen im Staatlichen Landesmuseum für
    Danziger Geschichte," *Archiv für Bevölkerungswissenschaft und Bevölkerungspolitik* 8
    (1938): 48–49.
31. Keyser, *Geschichte*, 7ff.
32. Ibid., 12, 15, 14.
33. Cited in Helmut Haufe, "Zur bevölkerungsgeschichtlichen Forschung," *Archiv für
    Bevölkerungswissenschaft und Bevölkerungspolitik* 8 (1938): 277.
34. Consistent with this line of thought, Keyser viewed Nazi policy as a—positively con-
    noted—revival of cultural practices that had already been a substantial part of the cus-
    toms of the German people during medieval times. Cf. Keyser, *Bevölkerungsgeschichte*
    (2nd ed., 1941), 295, 452ff.
35. Haufe, "Forschung," 277. Haufe criticizes Keyser for not having taken recourse to Gun-
    ther Ipsen's essay in *Handwörterbuch des Grenz- und Auslandsdeutschtums* in connection
    with the discussion of the essential characteristics (*Wesen*) of the German people. For
    Haufe, Keyser's negligence in clarifying the concept of *"Volk"* was a substantial meth-
    odological deficit of the book.
36. Ibid., 279.
37. Cf. Roderich v. Ungern-Sternberg, "Erich Keyser, Bevölkerungsgeschichte Deutsch-
    lands, 3rd ed., Leipzig 1943," *Allgemeines Statistisches Archiv* 32 (1943/44): 172–173.
38. Cf. Keyser, *Bevölkerungsgeschichte* (2nd ed., 1941), 1–23.
39. Keyser, *Bevölkerungsgeschichte* (3rd ed., 1943), 3ff. ("Volk und Rasse"), 128ff. ("Volks-
    fremde in Deutschland"), 572ff. ("Die nationalsozialistische Bevölkerungspolitik"),
    585ff. ("Die Unsterblichkeit des deutschen Volkes").
40. Ibid., 2.
41. Ibid., 5.
42. E. Keyser, "Die Erforschung der Bevölkerungsgeschichte," *Studium Generale* 9 (1956): 496.
43. Keyser, "Rassenforschung," 1.
44. Keyser, "Erforschung," 497.
45. Ibid., 496–499.
46. Nowhere in this essay does Keyser make direct or indirect mention of the Holocaust.
47. Keyser, "Erforschung," 498.
48. Cf. Keyser, *Bevölkerungsgeschichte* (3rd ed., 1943), 16–17.
49. At the same time, Keyser now no longer ignored the fact that mutual assimilation and
    acculturation had also influenced so-called German territory.
50. Originally, the theme of innovation was brought up as a possibility by Christoph Kleß-
    mann, "Osteuropaforschung und Lebensraumpolitik im Dritten Reich," in *Wissenschaft
    im Dritten Reich*, ed. Peter Lundgreen (Frankfurt am Main, 1985), 350–383, esp. 353; for a
    critical view, see Peter Schöttler, "Einleitende Bemerkungen," in *Geschichtsschreibung als
    Legitimationswissenschaft 1918–1945*, ed. Peter Schöttler (Frankfurt am Main, 1997), 18;
    Axel Flügel, "Ambivalente Innovation. Anmerkungen zur Volksgeschichte," *Geschichte
    und Gesellschaft* 26 (2000): 653–671.
51. On Inama-Sternegg, see Valerie Müller, *Karl Theodor v. Inama-Sternegg. Ein Leben für
    Staat und Wissenschaft* (Innsbruck, 1976). A study that more pointedly emphasizes
    Inama-Sternegg's role in the development of historical statistics is still to appear. No

work has yet been published on Paul Mombert; hence, this remains a desideratum of historical research.

52. Even in the 1970s and 1980s, Wolfgang Köllmann's specific way of thinking in terms of collective groups was still quite remarkable. In Köllman's view, *Bevölkerungsgeschichte* should concern itself with "demographic structures and the processes of structural change in territorially defined social collectives." Köllmann, "Bevölkerungsgeschichte," in *Sozialgeschichte in Deutschland*, Bd. 2, ed. Wolfgang Schieder and Volker Sellin (Göttingen, 1986), 18.

53. To mention only one example: the title of the journal Zeitschrift für Ostforschung was not changed to Ostmitteleuropa-Forschung until 1995. Renaming the journal had been a matter of discussion among the editors since 1969. See Manfred Kittel, "Preußens Osten in der Zeitgeschichte. Mehr als nur eine landeshistorische Forschungslücke," *Vierteljahrshefte für Zeitgeschichte* 50 (2002): 457.

Chapter 5

ETHNIC POLITICS AND SCHOLARLY LEGITIMATION

The German Institut für Heimatforschung
in Slovakia, 1941–1944

✦ ✦ ✦

Christof Morrissey

In the independent state of Slovakia (1939–1945), the National Socialist-oriented German Party (Deutsche Partei, hereafter DP) exercised political leadership over the country's small but influential ethnic German minority.[1] The DP's primary goals included strengthening the Germans' special position, both in relation to the country's other ethnic groups and within the structure of the Slovakian state. Out of the various German-speaking settlements within the territory of Slovakia, the DP strove to forge a culturally homogenized "Carpathian German" ethnic group (*Volksgruppe*), politically unified along National Socialist guidelines and subordinated to the Reich's foreign policy.[2] Cultural politics, including scholarship, played a central role in the realization of these goals.

The DP and its overlords in the Reich consciously instrumentalized scholarship to legitimize their political aims. Reich German scholars—historians, ethnographers, anthropologists, linguists, art historians, even musicologists—eagerly responded to their call. Their scholarship of legitimation aimed not only to boost German claims of having brought civilization to Slovakia in medieval times and consequently deserving special rights in the country, particularly in the stewardship of land and cultural "leadership."[3] It also supported the National Socialist leadership of the DP in its program of forging a homogenous *Volksgruppe* out of distinctly diverse, particularist German-speaking settlements in Slovakia.[4] Ultimately, this sort of scholarship would have laid the intellectual groundwork for an eventual absorption of the Slovak lands and people into Greater Germany.

Notes for this chapter begin on page 107.

The Institut für Heimatforschung (Institute for Local Historical Studies; hereafter IHF) in Käsmark (Slovak: Kežmarok), a town in northeastern Slovakia, played a key role in facilitating a National Socialist "scholarship of legitimation" and culturally aligning the German minority in Slovakia. Initially conceived by local patriots seeking mainly to memorialize German achievements in the historic Zips region, this seemingly modest institute was integrated into a vast network of research institutions that laid the intellectual groundwork for National Socialist expansionism and ethnic cleansing.[5] Not only does the IHF present an intriguing case study of the relationship between regional scholarship and ethnic politics in the German diaspora; its story also helps illuminate how the National Socialist apparatus of scholarly legitimation incorporated regional research into its program of ethnically reordering Central and Eastern Europe.

The Institut für Heimatforschung was established on 9 January 1941 in Käsmark, a small, historically German town in the Upper Zips (Slovak: Horný Spiš) region of northeastern Slovakia. At the time of its establishment, the DP's Main Cultural Office (Hauptkulturamt) and the German Institute for the Abroad (Deutsches Ausland-Institut or DAI) in Stuttgart acted as its main sponsors. The project's main visionary, however, was Johann Liptak, a native Zipser and teacher at the German Lutheran *Lyzeum* (academic high school) in Käsmark. Liptak served as the IHF's official director throughout its existence and had excellent credentials for the job. He was a member of the Working Community for Zipser Local Research, which disbanded in 1939, and was widely considered the region's leading local historian thanks to a number of publications in the 1930s.[6]

The idea for an institute that would promote the local history of the Zips and "Carpathian" Germans of Slovakia appears to have originated with Liptak. But the realization of Liptak's vision required the political and financial backing of the DP, as well as the main Reich agencies involved in "Germandom" politics. The IHF came into being only through the involvement of Third Reich ethnic functionaries and the leadership of the DP, based in Bratislava (German: Preßburg). These groups vigorously opposed what they considered the reigning particularism of the Zipser Germans. From the moment of its birth, the IHF served a decidedly political mission that outweighed any scholarly accomplishments. Nonetheless, local staff members who had absorbed the pro-Hungarian particularist outlook characteristic of the region's intelligentsia influenced the institute's everyday functions to a considerable extent. As a result, the IHF did not always uphold the antiparticularist, anti-Magyar orientation to Berlin and Preßburg's satisfaction.

At a scholarly level, the IHF was charged with "organizing all colleagues in the field of Carpathian German local research [*Heimatkunde*], nominating a research council, and assuming responsibility for promoting a new scholarly generation. For this purpose, the institute should expand its library, establish a photo collection and archive, support publications in the field of local research [*heimatkundliche Schriften*] and establish ties to other similar institutions." These responsibilities were outlined in a DAI memorandum to Reichsführer-SS and top "Germandom" functionary Heinrich Himmler in February 1941.[7] During its three and one-half years of existence, the IHF largely succeeded in achieving these goals.

At its inception, the IHF included a division dedicated to ethnic characteristics (*Volkstum*) and traditions, a folk song and folk music archive, and a section for genealogical and family research (*Sippenkunde*). Responsibility for the latter area initially belonged to Margarete Urban, a native Zipser whom the DAI in Stuttgart made available to the institute in Käsmark. The Lutheran *Lyzeum* allowed the IHF to move into its old schoolhouse and made available the school library of approximately 30,000 volumes.[8] Liptak hoped eventually to move into an "aryanized Jewish house" that the German Lutheran church was to purchase and make available to the institute. This plan remained unfulfilled, however.[9] A supervisory research council (*Forschungsrat*) that eventually included seventeen members was founded, something addressed in greater detail below.

Neither the DAI nor the academics on the supervisory council, however, proved to be the main pillars of the IHF. Instead, the cultural department of the Berlin-based SS organization Ethnic German Liaison Agency (Volksdeutsche Mittelstelle or VoMi), under the direction of Wilhelm Luig, and the DP's Hauptkulturamt, headed by the Sudeten German engineer Hans Friedl, increasingly defined the institute's agenda. These groups openly sought to instrumentalize the IHF for promoting National Socialist Germandom policies, for example, through close cooperation with German schoolteachers in Slovakia, who were organized in the DP's Carpathian German Teachers Corps (Karpatendeutsche Erzieherschaft or KE), as well as with other party organizations.[10] By publishing regular press reports and articles on Zipser German or Carpathian subjects, a tradition established by the defunct Zipser Working Community, the IHF directly and indirectly helped spread the DP's political message.

At the official IHF opening ceremony in March 1942, the presence of Hanns Ludin, German minister in Bratislava, Embassy Counsel Hans Gmelin, Ethnic Group Leader (*Volksgruppenführer*) and DP chief Franz Karmasin, and other leading party functionaries underscored the fledgling institute's political importance. In his remarks, Karmasin defined the IHF's threefold political mission as strengthening Germandom in Slovakia, binding the country's ethnic Germans to the Reich, and exploring "new forms of relations between various ethnic groups" in Slovakia. Karmasin referred primarily to relations between Germans and Slovaks. Other ethnic groups in the region, such as the Hungarians, played only a subordinate role in the institute's planning, the Jews and Romany, almost none at all. Another speaker, cultural office chief Friedl, announced that the IHF would "combat any and all local particularism." Minister Ludin described the IHF as a "spiritual bracket for all Germans in Slovakia," where there should be no "Deutsch-Probener, no Zipser or Preßburger Germans, but only Germans."[11]

In fact, VoMi and Foreign Ministry functionaries viewed the IHF as a key instrument for their wide-ranging efforts to weld often disparate, localist German diaspora settlements into a unified "Southeast European Germandom." Once unified and aligned along National Socialist lines, these ethnocrats anticipated, the Germans of Southeastern Europe could be easily harnessed for the Reich's war effort and "ethnic reordering" schemes.[12] The establishment of the IHF should be considered in the context of these efforts to bind the German diaspora communities more closely to one another as well as to the Reich. Events such as the "cultural week" held in Käsmark in July 1943, which representatives of almost all German *Volksgruppen* attended, underscored the importance of regional research institutions such as the IHF to the process of creating a "Southeastern Germandom."[13]

Furthermore, the DP leadership in Bratislava attempted to use the IHF as a weapon in its own struggle against the regional particularism of the Zipser Germans. In that region, the intelligentsia and upper middle classes had typically cultivated a pro-Hungarian world-view (Magyarophilia) since the last decades of the nineteenth century. Many Zipser patriots rejected the DP's "non-native" cadre of leaders, most of them transplanted Sudeten Germans. The DP's rivalry with the Zipsers' own regional political party in the Czechoslovak republic before 1938 and its campaign against the local Zipser press only aggravated these resentments. Although Reich Germandom agencies frequently criticized Karmasin's cronyism, his indecisiveness, and his often confrontational tactics toward the regions, they naturally backed the DP's efforts at centralization as a necessary precondition for their own aims of a unified, politically aligned "Southeastern Germandom."

Despite (or perhaps because of) their suspicions of the Zipser Germans, both the DP leadership and Reich agencies considered it politically indispensable to maintain the IHF in Käsmark, in order fully to integrate the Zips into the National Socialist "cultural effort." Despite interagency rivalries, the Reich authorities concerned with the cultural and political affairs of Slovakia's Germans—the SS agencies VoMi, SD, and Waffen-SS replacement office, as well as the Foreign Office and Bratislava embassy—pursued largely the same all-German goals. These goals, and the antiparticularist stance of the DP's leadership, could coexist with the "Magyarone" orientation and "separatism" of the Zipser notables only with great difficulty. It should be pointed out that the SD (*Sicherheitsdienst*) and DP intelligence sections charged with sounding out internal attitudes often tended to overestimate dissent in the ethnic German population. Even seemingly insignificant occurrences, such as the publication of a field guide to Zipser flora (*Volkspflanzen*), aroused the security services' hostility. In their view, the nature guide came from a "Magyarone" author and possessed no "ethnic political value."[14]

In order to counter any manifestations of Zipser "separatism" in the IHF, VoMi and the DP orchestrated the assignment of a Sudeten German husband-wife team, Franz Josef Beranek and Hertha Wolff-Beranek, to the institute. Franz Beranek, who researched settlement history, transferred to Käsmark in May 1942 from the technical college in Tetschen (Czech: Děčín), Bohemia. His wife, a folklorist, joined him in July 1942. In contrast to the director Liptak, the Beraneks represented "modern" academic research in the Third Reich and boasted good ties to leading networks of *völkisch* scholars. The SD and VoMi considered them more "politically reliable" than Liptak. In his younger years, the director had belonged to a Masonic lodge, as well as the particularist Zipser German Party. He was also married to a "Hungarian" woman. Nevertheless, the SD did register Liptak's newly discovered *völkisch*-German orientation after 1938.[15]

During their twenty months in Käsmark, the Beraneks took over most of the IHF's research tasks.[16] Franz Beranek worked with ethnic German teachers and for their journal, the *Karpatendeutscher Erzieher* (Carpathian German Educator), collected material on the history of German settlements (with reportedly skimpy results),[17] and wrote a folklore column for the the the weekly DP organ *Deutsche Stimmen* (German Voices). Hertha Wolff-Beranek built up a voluminous folklore collection. Johann Liptak, the institute's actual director, worked only in a voluntary capacity, suffered from poor health, and remained generally passive. Apparently, he felt a scholarly inferiority to the Beraneks and may have worried about his social status in the close-knit community.[18] Franz Beranek himself summarized the "true purpose" of his assignment to the IHF: "Compensating his [Liptak's] shortcomings and [acting] as a counterweight to his regional orientation." Beranek also claimed that, prior to assuming his office in Käsmark, he had been given the following friendly insight: "In Preßburg, they [the DP leadership] need a dummy who will wrestle around with Liptak."[19]

Despite its political and personnel peculiarities, the IHF enjoyed a reputation as an academically interesting institution in the relevant scholarly circles. In addition to Ludin and Gmelin from the German embassy in Bratislava, DP leaders Karmasin, Friedl, and propaganda chief Karl Hauskrecht, as well as the Bratislava university lecturer Aurel Emeritzy, the supervisory research council boasted some of the Reich's leading scholars of ethnic Germandom. Alongside the Beraneks, these included: Josef Hanika, a Prague-based folklorist and expert on the Carpathian Germans; Bruno Schier of Leipzig, a visiting professor in Bratislava; Hans-Joachim Beyer and Wilhelm Weizsäcker of the Reinhard-Heydrich-Stiftung in Prague; art historian Erich Gierach and geographer Hugo Grothe of Munich; Hugo Hassinger and Kurt Willvonseder of Vienna; and the Eisenstadt archivist Heinrich Kunnert.[20] The fact that several council members, such as Beyer and Kunnert, were career or part-time SD officials reveals the Reich Security Main Office's (Reichssicherheitshauptamt or RSHA) considerable interest in the Käsmark institute.[21]

During the first IHF "working meeting" in February 1943, which VoMi representatives, the DP political leadership, and several members of the research supervisory council attended, Franz Beranek itemized the institute's accomplishments to date. These included establishing a folklore archive, registering "field names" (*Flurnamen*) as evidence of historical German settlement, analyzing German place names in Slovakia, and cataloguing German settlements in the country. Beranek announced plans to reorganize the institute into the following functional categories: history, folklore, linguistic research, art history, economics, sociology, racial science, the "Jewish Question," statistics, migration studies, Slovak and Magyar studies. Projects for the coming year included the study of borrowed German words in the Slovak language, compiling a bibliography of Slovakia's Germandom, and beginning work on a dictionary of German dialects in Slovakia.[22] These tasks, however, largely stalled in the planning stage.[23] Even Beranek's pet project, reorganizing the institute, was only partially implemented.

The Beraneks, whom observers considered "personally eccentric people," ran afoul of some leading Zipser citizens. Beranek himself blamed a unified "front of the Upper Zipser" for the couple's social isolation.[24] Both Beraneks proved incapable of working constructively with Liptak and Urban.[25] Furthermore, Franz Beranek had to contend with accusations that he accomplished little for the institute while exploiting his position there to collect material for his own research projects. In fact, Beranek's reluctance to return borrowed institute materials after his withdrawal from Käsmark provoked threats of legal action on the part of VoMi cultural chief Wilhelm Luig. This incident resulted in a permanent split between VoMi and the DP on the one hand and the Beraneks on the other.[26] In December 1943, the Beraneks were transferred from Käsmark to Prague. Following their departure, a number of employees, mainly teachers from the Käsmark *Lyzeum*, attempted to continue their work on a part-time or temporary basis.[27] Between February and November 1944, only the young VoMi folklorist and ethnologist Ingeborg Kellermann, who became one of the leading ethnologists in the postwar Federal Republic, worked full-time at the institute. The rapidly changing staff and evolving war situation appear to have rendered further systematic, goal-oriented work at the IHF impossible.[28]

The IHF attempted to win additional renown by releasing a small series of publications and organizing academic conferences. The conferences were co-organized and funded by the DP's cultural office, since the IHF lacked even the personnel resources, to say nothing of financial ones, to organize such events on its own.[29] In September 1942 and September 1943, the IHF hosted a "German Higher Education Week" (*Deutsche Hochschulwoche*), essentially academic conferences dealing with Germandom in Slovakia. The first of these conferences was dedicated to "historical and higher education" themes (especially to the origins of the German presence in Slovakia),[30] while the second (and final) meeting addressed issues of "economics, property rights, and sociology." A third *Hochschulwoche* examining "educational questions" and "cultural autonomy" was planned for early fall 1944 but never materialized on account of the war situation. Leading scholars, especially from Prague and from Austria, participated in both *Hochschulwochen*. They included Josef Hanika, Egon Lendl, Bruno Schier, Hugo Grothe, and Karl Christian von Loesch. The presence of top DP functionaries and, at the 1943 meeting, VoMi chief Werner Lorenz, attested to the institute's political importance.[31]

The IHF also served as a weapon in the DP's "ethnic struggle" (*Volkstumskampf*) against the Slovaks. Possibly provoked by the politicized scholarship of the IHF, Slovak politicians, cultural functionaries, and academics took up their own *Heimatforschung* with new energy. DP culture chief Friedl reported to VoMi in February 1943 that Slovak authors were increasingly producing works that challenged the findings of German scholars.[32] Archeological digs, such as the "ring walls" at Svety Jur (German: St. Georgen) in the Morava Valley, became subjects of ethnic-nationalist controversy.[33] According to Friedl, the Slovak interior ministry secretly decreed that all historically important towns, especially those with a sizeable German-speaking population or a German history, should form *Heimatforschung* associations. These associations were to emphasize the Slovak contribution to local history, even "invent" one if necessary. Such reactions to German researchers' scholarship of legitimation also reflected the Slovaks' growing desire to distance themselves from the Germans after the tide of war turned against the Reich.

The increasing threat to the Germans of eastern Slovakia, brought on by the Slovak "National Uprising" in late summer 1944 as well as the advancing Eastern Front, abruptly terminated the existence of the IHF. Most of the institute's materials were evacuated to Kunnersdorf (Czech: Kunratice) in Bohemia. Johann Liptak fled first to Austria, later to Bavaria.[34] Although Carpathian German expellee organizations (*Landsmannschaften*) soon emerged in both the Federal Republic and Austria, the IHF was not reestablished. Until his death in 1958, Liptak was active in the West German Carpathian *Landsmannschaft*, publishing the organization's annual yearbook (*Karpatenjahrbuch*).[35] Most academic members of the supervisory council continued their careers in West Germany or Austria more or less without interruption.

In what directions the IHF in Käsmark would have evolved had the war turned out differently remains pure speculation. Given examples from other regions, however, a probable scenario emerges. If the moment had ever come for "germanizing" the Western Carpathian region, including Slovakia, something several DP functionaries and SS officers speculated about,[36] the IHF in Käsmark would have been perfectly situated to endow such dubious plans with a pseudo-scholarly cachet.

Notes

1. Population estimates for the German minority in Slovakia (which before the era of National Socialism still included sizeable numbers of Jews) are necessarily inexact. They can vary significantly according to source and date. For most of independent Slovakia's history, the German minority appears to have numbered approximately 150,000, or no more than 5 percent of the country's population. For general historical accounts of the German minority in Slovakia, including the process by which the DP gained its dominant position within the minority, see Lubomir Lipták, "The Role of the German Minority in Slovakia in the Years of the Second World War," *Studia Historica Slovaca* 1 (1963): 150–178; Valdis Lumans, "The Ethnic German Minority of Slovakia and the Third Reich, 1938–1945," *Central European History* 15, no. 3 (1982): 266–297; Rudolf Melzer, *Erlebte Geschichte: Rückschau auf ein Menschenalter Karpatendeutschtum, Teil 2. Von 1939 bis 1945 und wie es weiterging* (Stuttgart, 1998).
2. See Dušan Kováč, "Das nationale Selbstverständnis der deutschen Minderheit in der Slowakei," *Österreichische Osthefte* 33, no. 2 (1991): 77–92; and Jörg Hoensch, "Die Entwicklung eines Geimeinschafts- und Volkstumsbewußtseins unter den Karpatendeutschen in der Zwischenkriegszeit," *Südostdeutsches Archiv* 30–31 (1987–1988): 112–128.
3. A typical example of the spirit in which German scholars of the period approached German-Slovak cultural relations is the following excerpt by Bruno Schier: "Of all influences from neighboring peoples that Slovakdom experienced in the course of its thousand-year history at the foot of the Carpathians, the German cultural influence stands dominantly in the foreground." Schier, "Aufbau der slowakischen Volkskultur," in *Deutschtumsfragen im Nordkarpatenraum* (Käsmark, 1943), 166.
4. These included three major settlement regions, known as "linguistic islands" (*Sprachinseln*) in the ethnological jargon of the day: Preßburg (Slovak: Bratislava) and its environs in the southeast, the central region around Deutsch-Proben (today Nitrianske Pravno, before 1945 Nemecké Pravno) and Kremnitz (Kremnica), which became known as the "Hauerland"; and the Zips (Spiš) in the northeast. Furthermore, separate German communities existed in rural areas throughout the country and in most larger cities, such as Tyrnau (Trnava), Kaschau (Košice), and Sillein (Žilina). From the DP's racialist point of view, people of German descent who had culturally assimilated to their Slovak or Magyar-speaking surroundings should be "reclaimed" as Germans. These included the "Habaner" in western Slovakia, a group apparently descended from sixteenth-century Anabaptist emigrants and a favorite subject of DP functionaries and Reich-based academics alike.
5. See Michael Fahlbusch, *Wissenschaft im Dienst des Nationalsozialismus? Die "Volksdeutschen Forschungsgemeinschaften von 1931–1945"* (Baden-Baden, 1999); and Peter Schoettler, ed., *Geschichtsschreibung als Legitimationswissenschaft, 1918–1945* (Frankfurt am Main, 1997).
6. For Liptak's career, see P. Rainer Rudolf and Eduard Ulreich, *Karpatendeutsches Biographisches Lexikon* (Stuttgart, 1988), 195; Melzer, *Erlebte Geschichte*, 409–410; *Grenzbote*, 24 September 1943.
7. Deutsches Ausland-Institut to Reichsführer-SS, 5 February 1941, BArch, former Berlin Document Center files, Franz Josef Beranek.
8. RSHA III B 14 (Böhrsch) to "Sonderbeauftragten des RFSS" (special representative of the RFSS), Preßburg, 6 March 1941, BArch, R70 Slowakei 47/110/6 and "Bericht einer Vertrauensperson" (Report of a reliable agent), 20 October 1942, BArch, R70 Slowakei 47/110/33.
9. "Bericht über die Arbeitsbesprechung des Instituts für Heimatforschung in Käsmark" (Report of the IHF working meeting), 19 February 1943, BArch, R70 Slowakei 47/110/38 and "Bericht über die Tätigkeit des Instituts für Heimatforschung" (Report on the IHF's activities), 6 March 1944, BArch R70 Slowakei 47/110/229-230.
10. Melzer, *Erlebte Geschichte*, 234.

11. BArch, R70 Slowakei 47/110/10. See also *Grenzbote*, 24 March 1942.
12. As early as 1937, Karmasin, then still right-hand man for the Slovak lands to Sudeten German Party chief Konrad Henlein, wrote that the Germans of Slovakia needed to unify their separate linguistic enclaves and link their political fate to that of Germandom as a whole, while also stressing their common links to other Southeast European German minorities. It is probable that such thinking helped convince VoMi that Karmasin was the right man to "lead" the German *Volksgruppe* in Slovakia. See Karmasin, "Die Aufgaben des Karpatendeutschtums," in *Das Karpatendeutschtum im Jahre 1937* (special insert to the *Sudetendeutsches Jahrbuch* 1938): 1–4.
13. Politisches Archiv des Auswärtigen Amtes (PA), Abteilung Inland IIc., R10038, Bd. 9, 1941–1943.
14. Kunnert to SD Zlin, 13 April 1944, BArch, R70 Slowakei 47/110/212-215.
15. SD Prague to RSHA III B (Hummitzsch), 19 February 1942, BArch, R70 Slowakei 47/110/20.
16. Melzer, *Erlebte Geschichte*, 395.
17. Kurt Hofer (head of the DP's internal intelligence service) to SD Preßburg, 13 November 1943, BArch, R70 Slowakei, 47/110/56-57.
18. Friedl to Gmelin, 1 April 1943, BArch, R70 Slowakei 47/110/58-63; RSHA III B 1 (Böhrsch/Busija) to RSHA III B (Ehlich), March 1943, BArch, R70 Slowakei 47/110/201.
19. Franz Beranek to Friedl, 23 February 1944, BArch R70 Slowakei 47/110/207.
20. "Bericht über die Tätigkeit des Instituts für Heimatforschung" (Report on the IHF's activities), 22 September 1943, BArch R70 Slowakei 47/110/147-158).
21. On the dominant role of the SS and especially the RSHA in *Volkstum*-oriented research, see Fahlbusch, *Wissenschaft im Dienst des Nationalsozialismus?* 86–89.
22. "Bericht über die Arbeitsbesprechung des Instituts für Heimatforschung in Käsmark" (Report of the IHF working meeting), 19 February 1943, BArch, R70 Slowakei 47/110/38-44.
23. "Bericht über die Tätigkeit des Instituts für Heimatforschung" (Report on the IHF's activities), 6 March 1944, BArch R70 Slowakei 47/110/227.
24. Franz Beranek to Friedl, 18 February 1944 and Franz Beranek to Luig, 23 February 1944, BArch R70 Slowakei 47/110/206-207.
25. The mutual antipathy culminated in a "slapping incident" (*Ohrfeigenszene*) between Hertha Wolff-Beranek and Margarete Urban on 10 December 1943. After Liptak complained to the DP cultural office, the Beraneks were immediately transferred from Käsmark. See BArch R70 Slowakei 47/110/187-195.
26. Kunnert to SD, Prague, 23 February 1944, BArch, R70 Slowakei 47/110/200.
27. Liptak to Kunnert, 3 February 1944, BArch, R70 Slowakei/70.
28. Melzer, *Erlebte Geschichte*, 396.
29. The cultural office's funding mechanisms did not always function smoothly. In December 1942, the DP had yet to reimburse Franz Beranek Ks 40,000 that he had spent from his own budget on the *Hochschulwoche* in September of that year. See BArch, R70 Slowakei 47/110/37.
30. See the published collection of papers from this conference, *Deutschtumsfragen im Karpatenraum* (Käsmark, 1943).
31. BArch, R70 Slowakei 47/110/97.
32. Friedl to Gmelin, 1 April 1943, BArch, R70 Slowakei 47/110/58-63.
33. BArch, R70 Slowakei 47/110/244-262.
34. "Vermerk" (file note), 16 November 1944, BArch, R70 Slowakei 47/110/90. By this time, Ingeborg Kellermann was already active organizing care for refugees for the Volksbund für das Deutschtum im Ausland (League for Germans Abroad or VDA) in Vienna.
35. "In Memoriam Dr. Johann Liptak, 1958–1968," *Karpatenjahrbuch* (1969): 32–34.
36. According to DP functionary Ruprecht Steinacker, "We have the advantage that, owing to the betrayal of the Southeastern peoples, consideration for them will no longer be

necessary when the ethnic group is rebuilt after the war," 6 March 1945, BArch, R70 Slowakei 4/41-5. The SS-Hauptamt representative in Slovakia, Obersturmbannführer Viktor Nageler, claimed in his "political situation report for Slovakia": "The racial substance of the Slovak people is the largely the same as that of the Germans … [in that respect] all preconditions for an assimilation are given." SS-Hauptamt-Chief Gottlob Berger to Heinrich Himmler, 19 February 1943, BArch, NS19/2042/8-9. In his study of the relationship between "race" and "folk culture," Bruno Schier remarked on "the high percentage of the fair races in the composition of the Slovak people" without explicitly anticipating the Slovaks' assimilation. See Schier, "Aufbau der slowakischen Volkskultur," 140–150.

Chapter 6

THE SWORD OF SCIENCE
German Scholars and National Socialist
Annexation Policy in Slovenia
and Northern Italy

✦ ✦ ✦

Michael Wedekind

In the backwash of the Balkan war of April 1941 and, subsequently, after the German occupation of Italy, in September 1943, the Third Reich realized a lesser known expansionist strategy that focused on the annexation of provinces south of its 1938 (former Austrian) border. In both cases, the underlying political design had been launched and successfully advocated by leading circles of Austrian National Socialists. Even though no definite conceptions of the future status of the occupied territories had previously been worked out, the expansionist model was integrated into the general dispositions concerning German domination of Yugoslavia and, two years later, of Italy. Herewith a political strategy was realized that can be regarded as a pointed imperialist derivation from expansive pre-1918 Austrian borderland designs and later revisionist aspirations—a strategy that, as far as Italy was concerned, had been inhibited, until 1943, by the National Socialist leadership and its political and military alliance with Fascist Italy. The following concise analysis concentrates on the hitherto little-studied function "cognitive pools" of scholarly elites had in planning and legitimizing aggressive conceptions of National Socialist territorial reorganization in the alpine and upper Adriatic area, in delineating essential elements of German nationality policy and radical social "rebuilding" in the annexed territories as well as in academic knowledge transfer to the administrative bureaucracy of the Third Reich, and on their direct involvement in execution procedures.

In the course of the territorial dismantling of Yugoslavia by the Axis powers and their allies in 1941, Germany had reclaimed the northern area

Notes for this chapter begin on page 133.

of Slovenia, leaving its southern part (Lower Carniola, German: Unter-krain) to Italy and conceding to Hungary a small district on the left bank of the Mura River.[1] The German occupation zone was divided into two administrative units, the "Lower Styria" (German: Untersteiermark) region and the "occupied territories of Carinthia and Carniola" (Upper Carniola, German: Oberkrain).[2] This cordon of semi-annexed provinces was accomplished in 1943, when Italy, after the armistice with the Western Allies, was widely occupied by German troops. Whereas most of the country was placed under military administration, German civil administration was introduced into the so-called Operational Zones of the Prealps[3] and of the Adriatic Littoral,[4] situated in the area between Lake Garda and the city of Fiume (Croatian: Rijeka).[5]

The National Socialist occupation regimes installed in the bordering provinces of Yugoslavia and Italy showed great similarities. Although not formally annexed, the occupied territories were subordinated to the sovereignty of the Reich, albeit to very different extents. The administration was headed by the highest-ranking party exponents of the neighboring German regions, namely by the respective party leaders and regional Representatives of the Reich (Gauleiter and Reichsstatthalter). Similar regimes had previously been installed in those occupied territories that were destined to be annexed by the end of war.

On 14 April 1941, Hitler nominated the chiefs of civil administration in occupied Slovenia: Siegfried Uiberreither (1908–1984?), Gauleiter and Reichsstatthalter of Styria, took over the area of Lower Styria, whereas Franz Kutschera (1904–1944), vice Gauleiter and Reichsstatthalter of Carinthia, was assigned to Upper Carniola. On 18 November 1941, he was succeeded by Friedrich Alois Rainer (1903–1947), who in September 1943 was able to significantly enlarge his sphere of influence when appointed *Oberster Kommissar* (Supreme Commissioner) in the Operational Zone of the Adriatic Littoral. At the same time Franz Hofer (1902–1975), Gauleiter and Reichsstatthalter of Tyrol, was given charge of the Operational Zone of the Prealps.

The ethnic structure of these regions was rather heterogeneous. Lower Styria (6,800 km²; 523,000 inhabitants) and Upper Carniola (3,200 km²; 180,000 inhabitants) were predominantly Slovenian, whereas the German-speaking minority had decreased notably since 1918, numbering 32,000 to 35,000 persons in Lower Styria[6] and roughly 1,500 in Upper Carniola by the 1930s. In the Adriatic Littoral (21,820 km²; 2,092,000 inhabitants) the Italians, with a population of 680,000, were the largest ethnic group, spread all over the region, except in the province of Ljubljana. They were followed by about 650,000 Slovenians living mainly in the eastern provinces, roughly 500,000 Friulians in the province of Udine and neighboring zones, and some 230,000 Croatians in the south and east of the Istrian Peninsula. German minorities, while sparsely scattered over the rest of Lower Carniola (there were around 2,600 in 1941, mainly in the city of

Ljubljana), had settled densely in the region of Kočevje (German: Gott-schee) (about 12,500 in 1941). In the Kanal Valley (German: Kanaltal, Slovenian: Kanalska dolina) (with approximately 6,600 Germans in 1939) they mixed with Slovenians and Italians. Even in the zone of the Prealps (17,270 km²; 903,000 inhabitants) the Italians were the dominant ethnic group, numbering about 716,000 people. However, whereas the popula-tion of the provinces of Trento and Belluno was prevalently Italian,[7] in 1943, 176,000 Germans still lived alongside 105,000 Italians and 11,000 Ladinians in South Tyrol. Some 11,800 other Ladinians settled in the neighboring Dolomite valleys of the provinces of Trento and Belluno.

With the more or less overt annexation of these territories, the Third Reich expanded into an area that had mostly been a centuries-long Habs-burg dominion. In the last decades of Austrian rule, it was the seat of heavy ethnic conflicts over socioeconomic potentials, national emancipa-tion, and regional autonomies—conflicts in which the Germans, as the most influential nationality of the monarchy, attempted to safeguard acquired privileges by means of ever more offensive and aggressive strat-egies, often mitigated or stopped, however, by the Austrian authorities. Characterized by profound political mobilization and nationalization, these ethnic clashes, in which traditional forms of supranational identifi-cation, solidarity, and discipline were increasingly replaced by ethnocen-tric patterns of group identity and loyalty, had a decisive influence on the growth of national intolerance in the region. The conflict was aggravated even more by the collective experiences of World War I, which since 1915 had had its theatre on the Tyrolean Dolomites, in the Carnian and Julian Alps, and especially along the Isonzo River. The aftermath of the war—the dissolution of the Habsburg Empire, heavy territorial losses, the inclusion of some 380,000 borderland Germans into Italy and Yugoslavia, the mili-tary and propagandistic struggle for Southern Carinthia from December 1918 to October 1920—as well as the oppression of German minorities by Yugoslavia and the Fascist regime in Italy, not only produced deep disap-pointment and damaged the German sentiment of national superiority, but also widely resulted in a radicalization of political thought, reinforced xenophobia, and incited revenge.[8]

Beyond revisionist claims and internal resettlement programs in ethni-cally mixed or non German areas of Carinthia, Styria, and the Burgenland,[9] genuine Austrian imperialist concepts regarding the alpine and Adriatic area had emerged since the mid 1920s. Shortly after the 1938 Anschluss (union) of Austria with Germany, Hugo Hassinger (1877–1952), a promi-nent scholar of historical, political, and anthropological geography, stated that "here in the *Ostmark*, due to its geographical position, to its nature and history, pursuing matters of spatial reorganization necessarily implies going beyond the German national space and considering greater Central-European areas."[10] Actually, the claim to the southeastern alpine foreland, to access to the Adriatic Sea, to establishing German hegemony in Central

Europe in order to expand to East-Central and Southeast Europe was a remake of traditional, pre-1918 models. During the interwar period they were propagated by geographers such as Karl Haushofer (1869–1946), Hugo Hassinger, Johann Sölch (1883–1951), Friedrich Metz (1890–1969), and Hans Bobek (1903–1990), as well as by publicists or nationalistic activists such as Friedrich Lange, Felix Kraus (1887–1950), Friedrich Wallisch (1890–1969), Karl Springenschmid (1897–1981), and Kurt Trampler. Following the "German national and cultural soil" thesis in order to trace future German borders—a theory that in prewar Germany had already been opposed to an etatistic conception of the nation—Kurt Trampler, then assistant of the Südost-Institut (Southeast Institute) in Munich, stated in 1934 that "in the South, the border of [German] culture stretches significantly beyond the ethnic border: incontestably it includes the Romansh and Ladinian regions as well as the Slavic foreland of Carinthia and Styria."[11]

In this matter, as early as 1931, Otto Maull (1887–1957), professor of geography at the University of Graz, one of the leading experts of ethnocentric geopolitics, and author of a standard work on political geography (1925) had, together with Helmut Carstanjen (1905–1991), demanded "a more thorough scientific knowledge" of the (German) borderland questions and a "more precise specification of [territorial] claims," particularly by cartographic methods.[12] In 1932, with respect to Lower Styria and Carinthia, Carstanjen additionally requested a concerted study of the southern settlement and nationality frontiers, thus "passing from the former position of defense … to a position of offense" by "most decisively opposing the German idea of 'unredeemed Lower Styria' to the Slovenian nationalistic idea of 'unredeemed Southern Carinthia'."[13]

In the years to come, the Südostdeutsche Forschungsgemeinschaft (Southeast German Research Community) and the Alpenländische Forschungsgemeinschaft (Alpine Research Community), as well as the Südostdeutsche Institut (Southeast German Institute) in Graz (in particular since 1938), took on a decisive role in this research. They focused on preliminary studies for ethnic cleansing in Carinthia and territorial revision in northern Yugoslavia.[14] The cognitive interests, themes, and methods of the scholars involved—whether orientated toward *Volkswissenschaften* or multidisciplinary spatial planning and "sociotechnical" population research—relate to the Third Reich's designs for a radical transformation of the social structures in (occupied) Europe. In fact, statistical, sociodemographic, sociogeographic, and cartographic techniques characterize the studies on Lower Styria by Helmut Carstanjen (1933, 1935), Hans Pirchegger (1936), Schmidt and Neumann (1937), Walter Neunteufl (1939, 1943), Wilhelm Sattler (1942, 1943), and Manfred Straka[15] (1938, Straka and Neunteufl 1941).

When, in the summer of 1940, German expansionist and annexationist designs regarding Yugoslavia started taking shape, the institutions mentioned above assumed consultative functions in the process of political decision-making. Alongside peripheral party offices in Styria and Carinthia,[16] they produced several minutes, memoranda, and other documents that, submitted to leading representatives of the regime, laid claim to Slovenia by emphasizing linguistic, historical, cultural, and economic aspects. Particularly the Südostdeutsche Institut was engaged in expansionist planning concerning Lower Styria. In 1940, on behalf of the institute, the social and demographic historian Manfred Straka (1911–1990) produced two ethnic maps of Yugoslavia, which were attached to the *Militärgeographische Beschreibung von Jugoslawien* published by the German Army General Staff in June 1940. Later on, together with Wilhelm Sattler, he elaborated a repertory of place names to be used in the future annexation of the territories of Lower Styria, Mežiška Valley (German: Mießtal), and the Prekmurje region. In June 1940, again on behalf of the Südostdeutsche Institut, Hermann Ibler, lecturer at the University of Graz, prepared a study on the question of the southern borders of Styria that was presented to Hitler and Foreign Minister Joachim von Ribbentrop by Gauleiter Uiberreither. Concerning the future organization of Yugoslavia, the Foreign Minister, applying in July on his own behalf to the Reichsstelle für Raumordnung (Reich Office of Spatial Planning), requested data concerning the linguistic and economic situation.

Helmut Carstanjen, a fellow member of the NSDAP, was appointed Director of the Südostdeutsche Institut. He embodies to a striking degree the mental and cognitive vicinity of these scholarly circles to bureaucratic registration techniques, as well as their will to influence politics or even to intervene immediately in the administrative sphere. Carstanjen had been a collaborator with the Volksbund für das Deutschtum im Ausland (League for Germans Abroad or VDA), as well as with the Alpenländische Forschungsgemeinschaft, and, before 1941, an informant of the Reichssicherheitshauptamt (Reich Security Main Office or RSHA) on Slovenian issues. As of 1941, he was directly engaged in the Third Reich's efforts to racially restructure Slovenia. As head of the Styrian main office of the Volksdeutsche Mittelstelle (Ethnic German Liaison Office or VoMi), a principal instrument of the German population policy, and in his additional functions as "National-Political Consultant" not only to the chief of civil administration in Lower Styria but also to the leadership of the Steirischer Heimatbund (Styrian Popular League) and, temporarily, to the Maribor office of the Reichskommissar für die Festigung deutschen Volkstums (Reich Commissioner for Strengthening Germandom or RKF), Carstanjen was directly involved in the deportation of Slovenians and in germanizing Lower Styria—although in the autumn of 1941, after a conflict on competences between the power center of the SS and the RKF on the one hand and the regional power pole of the Gauleiter on the other, Carstanjen, as the deputy of the latter, lost his influence over the RKF office in Maribor. He had, however, partial authority on the commissions established in order to examine, from a racial as well as from a political point of view, all those Slovenians and Germans who, mainly induced by intimidations, appealed for membership in the Steirischer Heimatbund,[17] the preliminary

National Socialist Party organization and key instrument for germanizing the annexed territory. Based on previously accumulated sociodemographic and statistical knowledge, in 1943 Carstanjen elaborated a precise settlement strategy for the extension of the German linguistic frontiers in Lower Styria.[18] Following the model of the nationalistic association Südmark, which in 1906 had started a German settlement program around Šentilj (German: Sankt Egydi) in the Hills of Slovenske Gorice (German: Windische Büheln), Carstanjen proposed the strengthening of a German linguistic "bridgehead" in that very area, in order to gradually establish a German-speaking strip between Styria and the city of Maribor. Other "bridge-heads" were supposed to be built up along the axis Eibiswald in Styria—Radlje (German: Mahrenberg)—Muta (German: Hohenmauthen) in the upper Drava Valley, and between the biggest cities, thus weakening the existing linguistic frontiers. Carstanjen's plan symptomatically marks the point of juncture between rational scholarly research and its perversion and exploitation for expansionist spatial planning, denationalization, mass deportation, and resettlement.

Actually, determined by an aggressive expansionism and anti-Slavism, based on bureaucratically designed scenarios of population transfers as well as on spatial planning, a vast project of ethnic cleansing and resettlement aiming at the complete alteration of the regional population structures according to political and "racial" criteria was started in Lower Styria and Upper Carniola almost immediately after the German occupation. The deportation of the Slovenians had already been decided on 8 and 9 April 1941 during a conference in Graz, at which the secretary of state in the Ministry of Interior, Wilhelm Stuckart (1902–1953), an "ambitious SS officer with a strong geopolitical bent and keen interest in Großraumverwaltung,"[19] had convoked the future chiefs of the civil administration, Siegfried Uiberreither and Franz Kutschera.

In two phases (7 June to 5 July and 11 July to 27 September 1941), 14,634 Slovenians and Serbs from Lower Styria were deported to Serbia and Croatia, whereas simultaneously (6 to 10 July) 2,337 Slovenians were expelled from Upper Carniola and transported predominantly to Serbia. Additionally, as already established in May 1941, 107 people from the former Carinthian Mežiška Valley were destined to be transferred to Germany and another 2,631 were to be "evacuated." The largest deportation project, expelling some 36,000 Slovenians from the area along the rivers of Sava and Sotla in Lower Styria and transferring them to several camps of the VoMi in Germany, where they were employed in forced labor, was realized between 23 October 1941 and 30 July 1942.[20] Although by that time the deportations in the rest of Slovenia had already nearly been stopped due to the intervention of Heinrich Himmler, the Sava-Sotla plan was carried out all the same in order to facilitate the resettlement of Germans from the Kočevje region. According to Himmler's intentions this area was to become "the most Germanized … of all Styria."[21]

The deportations were preceded by the work of racial examination teams that inspected and classified the population, assigning each person to one of four scaled categories that had been established on the basis of presumed racial criteria and judgement of individual political attitudes. These racial examination teams, which between 23 April and 15 September 1941 classified 433,934 people in Lower Styria as well as 63,334 people in Upper Carniola, decided the destiny of hundreds of thousands of Slovenians.

Head of the examination commission in both territories was SS-Obersturmbannführer Bruno Kurt Schultz (1901–1997),[22] a physical anthropologist who in the late 1930s, on behalf of the Rasse- und Siedlungshauptamt (Race and Settlement Main Office), had composed a set of racial criteria for SS candidates in order to form a racial elite. In his capacity as head of the Arbeitskreis "Die bäuerliche Lebensgemeinschaft" (Study Group "The Rural Community"), part of the Forschungsdienst of the Reichsarbeitsgemeinschaft der Landbauwissenschaften (Research Service of the Reich Study Group for Agricultural Sciences), he was involved in research on the genetic and sociological conditions of rural populations with the intention of gaining a general idea of their hereditary factors.[23] In April 1941, in Upper Carniola and Lower Styria, Schultz took over Division II (Racial Examination) of the "Resettlement Staff" of the Kommandeur der Sicherheitspolizei und des Sicherheitsdienstes (Commander of the Security Police and Security Service) in Bled (German: Veldes).

While the deportation of Slovenians was still under way, the first German settlers arrived in Lower Styria, and by the end of October 1943 10,666 people from the Kočevje region, 156 South Tyroleans, 297 Germans from Bessarabia, and 247 from Dobrogea (Romania, Black Sea Littoral) had been transferred.[24] Only 1,200 Germans, originating from Ljubljana, Kočevje, the Kanal Valley, and South Tyrol, had been moved to Upper Carniola by the middle of May 1943, however.[25]

Yet the first activities by partisan groups in the summer of 1941 showed that German deportations were provoking an increasing potential for resistance. The subsequent reorientation in German occupation policy in Slovenia was considered at the latest from the moment when Himmler in August 1941 ordered the suspension of the deportations until the end of the war. In fact, escalating German violence and repression had been criticized by the Ministry of Interior and by the chief of the Main Staff Office of the RKF, Ulrich Greifelt (1896–1949), as well as by different Carinthian party officials. As early as May 1941, at a moment when the Styrian Gauleiter Uiberreither was still making complaints about the "incomprehensible German restraints" in deportation affairs,[26] the historian Karl Starzacher (1913–1945), chief of staff of the RKF office in Upper Carniola, criticized the current germanization program in a memorandum. Starzacher, who in Carinthia had an important role not only in National Socialist "population management"[27] but also in the regional scientific community, had graduated from the University of Vienna in 1935 and become director of the Klagenfurt record office in 1939. His reserve concerning German deportations originated from mere efficiency aspects—he thought a mass expulsion of the Slovenians technically impossible. While not renouncing the deportation of intellectuals and the physical liquidation of "racially inferior people," SS-Obersturmführer Starzacher pleaded for germanization by means of German acculturation and school teaching:

> The first goal is the formation of a middle class which considers itself part of the Reich and of Carinthia, as the smaller regional entity.... Basically, it has to be carried out the same systematical denationalization process that in former Carinthia made it possible that [in 1918/19] the Windisch population, in a communion of destiny, fought the defensive battle [against Yugoslavia] alongside the Germans.... Additionally, more than any other, this apparently moderate, but in fact much more clear-sighted method is the most likely to guarantee successful germanization; furthermore, [avoiding] producing a persisting atmosphere of conflict, the Reich could prevent spoiling all sorts of its projects in neighboring South-East [Europe].[28]

The foundation of the Institut für Kärntner Landesforschung (Institute for Carinthian Regional and Cultural Studies) in October 1942 was at least partially a result of giving up systematic mass deportations in favor of denationalization measures. As Ferenc points out, in Lower Styria the German occupation regime was much more efficient in realizing its germanizing goals than in Upper Carniola.[29] Besides the fact that, having based itself on the German-speaking minority of the province, the regime in Lower Styria managed to gather a larger basis of public consensus, a decisive factor is to be found in more systematic and far-reaching preliminary studies that consented to operate according to a more complete and uniform design. In fact, the central figure of National Socialist denationalization and deportation of Slovenians in Carinthia, SS-Obersturmbannführer Alois Maier-Kaibitsch (1891–1953), who in Upper Carniola had been chief of the RKF office in Bled and "National-political consultant" to the chief of the civil administration since October 1941, complained about a "total deficiency of German scientific studies"[30] on the recently occupied region. Actually, Styria had these institutions of intellectual guidance in German expansion, Carinthia not. Additionally, Carinthian borderland scholars had been predominantly engaged in what could be called "internal colonization" until the end of the 1930s. Their studies, highlighting cultural, linguistic, geographical, economic, and, increasingly, racial aspects,[31] were inspired by the leitmotiv of German cultural superiority and focused mainly on the linguistically mixed and Slovenian-speaking areas of Lower Carinthia. They were targeted toward "defending" the supposed geographic and cultural "unity of the province" and toward constructing a "Carinthian national" identity—a concept intended to subject the local Slovenian minority to German socioeconomical as well as political guidance and supremacy, and, finally, to denationalization. In this process of

German assimilation the invention of a linguistically and ethnically distinct, so-called *Windisch* identity, artificially separating the Slovenians of Carinthia from those south of the Karawanken Mountains, was a decisive instrument, developed mainly by the Carinthian historian Martin Wutte (1876–1948).[32] Since 1941, this strategy was basically supposed to also be applied to the process of germanizing occupied Upper Carniola.

The task of the Institut für Kärntner Landesforschung, whose foundation had been ventilated since mid 1941, was to guide and support National Socialist germanization policy and to ensure the "mental conquest" of Upper Carniola. In June 1941, in requesting that "now as ever, science ought to stand by the side of the sword," Franz Kutschera, a hard-liner in German oppression policy in Slovenia, had already defined a catalogue of essential research topics, such as archeological and historical studies on the migration of the peoples, Lombard and German settlements, racial composition of the population, "German achievements and creations in all sectors of public and cultural life,"[33] and German linguistic influences on Slovenian dialects. Maier-Kaibitsch, however, called for more "practical" support for the German goal of the "creation and awakening of a specific Upper Carnolian identity": "Any scientific evidence is still lacking, up to now, for such a national-political orientation of the Slovenians in Upper Carniola.... For that purpose the employment of an entire team of scholars is needed."[34]

Due to internal conflicts among different groups of Carinthian National Socialist officials over German policy in Slovenia and the related question of the nomination of a new Gauleiter, the establishment of the Institut für Kärntner Landesforschung was delayed until autumn 1942. Although annexed to the University of Graz, it depended mostly on the directions of the Carinthian Gauleiter. This, together with the collaboration with the SS-Ahnenerbe, introduced a strong political influence to all the "scientific" activities of the institute, which thus became an instrument of the political leadership.[35] As was officially pointed out in September 1942, the task of the institute was "to develop in an irrefutable manner the ideology of the German claim to Upper Carniola as a land of ancient Germanic settlement."[36]

Eberhard Kranzmayer (1897–1975), who, after having been a lecturer at the University of Munich, had held the professorial chair for "Dialectology and Borderland Studies" at the University of Graz since 1 October 1942, was appointed director of the institute. Kranzmayer was an expert in German linguistic history (especially in Bavarian dialectology), in geolinguistics, minority languages, and dialects (with special regard to German, Bavarian dialects in Northern Italy, Slovenian, and Ladinian), as well as in settlement history in the Eastern Alps and in folklore, "borderland" and place name studies. Wounded in World War I, he had participated in the borderland struggles in Carinthia in 1919 and Upper Silesia in 1921. Inspired "from the bottom of his heart by a profound love of the German people and their earth, which they gained thanks to hard pioneer and colonization work and which they are tenaciously determined to defend, despite all unjustified claims,"[37] Kranzmayer considered his scholarly studies a continuation of these ethnic conflicts by other means. His mostly philological contributions on the southern German-speaking borderlands,[38] and especially his works on cultural and linguistic influences on the Slovenians, made him believe in "an enormous cultural superiority of the German nation compared to the whole East."[39] With "unreachable clarity," Kranzmayer could finally present "the long-established Slovenians as an adaptive component of the German cultural community."[40] Pervaded by a concept of German cultural expansionism, the other Carniola-related contributions of the institute mostly treated historical aspects of settlement geography and regional civilization characteristics (*Siedlungs- und Kulturlandschaftsgeographie*): Karl Dinklage (1907–1987) from the University of Graz, head of the pre- and early history section of the institute, contributed studies on early medieval settlements in Carinthia, Lower Styria, and Upper Carniola;[41] the geographer Günter Glauert (1905–1982) continued to publish on the historic settlement geography of Upper Carniola.[42] On the other hand, Georg Graber (1882–1957)[43] treated racial and folkloristic questions, whereas Viktor Paschinger (1882–1963)[44] studied geographical aspects of the annexed territory. The general tenor of all these studies was to demonstrate "that Upper Carniola is a province of ancient German civilization in the fullest sense of the word and had mainly been a German settlement territory, although due to slovenization all German bonds have deliberately been cut off or even turned inside out."[45]

Though the deportations mentioned above had been stopped in 1941, National Socialist rule in Upper Carniola was nonetheless characterized more than ever by a climate of brutal repression.[46] The struggle against the partisan movement, which had soon been perverted to an arbitrary terrorization of the civil population, was increasingly meant to continue the German settlement policy by deporting insurgents and their relatives, by shooting hostages, and by the devastation of entire villages. Deportations and germanizing measures went on notwithstanding internal criticism, even after Franz Kutschera was replaced by Friedrich Rainer on 18 November 1941.

Yet only some days after the nomination of Friedrich Rainer to Supreme Commissioner in the Adriatic Littoral in September 1943, Martin Wutte, the doyen of Carinthian historiography and "inventor" of the *Windischen* theory who had flanked the anti-Slovenian denationalization policy of the regime in Carinthia as well as in Upper Carniola, directed a written appeal to Rainer recommending a more moderate nationality policy in his sphere of responsibility, especially in the province of Ljubljana. Wutte, although pervaded as much as ever by a strong feeling of German cultural superiority, asked after the excesses of 1941 and 1942 that Slovenians be conceded autonomy in the cultural and, to some extent, the administrative sector in order to demonstrate that "henceforth Slovenian nationality will be recognized and that security will be given to support and preserve it within the German Empire."[47] Like the political leadership, Wutte intended, after the German occupation of Italy, to reunite the territories of former Carniola as a German protectorate. Although doubtlessly a courageous act, his intervention was primarily meant to assure the realization of National Socialist spatial planning and to make German occupation policy more dynamic and effective.

In the autumn of 1944, even the chief of the Main Staff Office of the RKF, Ulrich Greifelt, influenced by the Reich's general military situation and by the increasing power of the resistance movement, and doubting the success of German denationalization policy "in such an [ethnically] compact settlement area as the Slovenian," recommended a complete stop to deportations and proposed autonomy for Upper Carniola and the province of Ljubljana, as well as to the foundation of an independent Slovenia under German control. For Greifelt, abandoning the *Windischen* theory or other pseudo-scientific constructs on German acculturation of the Slovenians, the collaboration aspect prevailed over germanizing the region, "as the preponderance of German resettlement will not be in the South, but in the East."[48]

Rainer, however, showed no inclination to alter his political line in Upper Carniola, although some insignificant concessions of autonomy had been made to the Slovenians on the cultural and administrative field. Driven by a marked spirit of ethnic intolerance, Rainer considered the deportations to be "the last possibility to lay our hands on Slovenian soil"[49] in order to guarantee the settlement of Germans from the Reich. In the semi-annexed provinces of the Adriatic Littoral, however, National Socialist nationality policy toward the Slovenians differed from that in Upper Carniola. Even before receiving Wutte's aforesaid memorandum, Rainer had favored a more moderate political line that, by conceding a certain cultural and administrative autonomy to the Slovenians, should distinguish in a positive way the German from the odious former Italian policy, thus guaranteeing the collaboration of the population. In agreement with Hitler and Himmler, this strategy, dictated by the increasingly shattered German position of power, removed the restrictions on Slovenian cultural life and language usage, that had been introduced in Friuli-Venezia Giulia by the Fascist regime.[50] Actually, however, these measures had hardly any influence on the real circumstances of daily life in the Adriatic Littoral, which was dominated by the German repression of the partisan movement, by deportations, by the extermination and spoliation of the Jewish population, and by a series of extremely brutal reprisals, as well as by compulsory conscriptions for military or labor service.

The expansion to Trieste and the Adriatic Sea, which was begun by the institution of a National Socialist civil administration in the Adriatic Littoral in 1943, was part of a greater design of German political and economic imperialism in Southeast Europe and of strengthening German hegemony on the continent. Within this concept, Carinthia seemed to be guaranteed a long-desired decisive role.[51] Martin Wutte rejoiced: "today even the small Yugoslav barrier between the Karawanken Mountains and the Adriatic Sea has been destroyed. The window facing South is open: Carinthia looks towards new great duties."[52] Thus, in 1943 even the activity field of the Institut für Kärntner Landesforschung was enlarged. There is evidence that the institute, in close touch with the political leadership, was concerned with delineating the general setup of the German occupation system in the Adriatic Littoral and had especially been working on issues of spatial planning.

Although postponed until the end of the war, a new ethnic and political configuration of the territory had already been contemplated in this preparatory phase. In a telegram to Foreign Minister von Ribbentrop, dated 9 September 1943, Gauleiter Rainer considered the future institution of Reich protectorates in Gorizia County, Istria, and Carniola.[53] Shortly afterwards, an analogous system was even considered for Friuli. Yet during a preliminary phase, the German occupation regime, renouncing plans to modify the existing borders, aspired to

> a gradual separation of this territory from the Italian administrative corpus and to its assimilation into the institutions of the Reich.... Considering its nationality aspects, the problem of Europe's huge and only Germanic-Romanic-Slavic transit area is a problem of German leadership which can definitely be resolved if its historic and regional conditions are taken into consideration. Backed by the power of the whole Reich, it will be the duty of the Reichsgau of Carinthia to give this foreland area not only order but also the consciousness of its position in a rearranged Europe and to orient it to the natural center of gravity in the middle of the continent.[54]

German rule in the Adriatic Littoral was to be legitimized by a conglomerate of geopolitical and economic, historic, ethnic, and political reasons, while for the different regions and nationality groups new specific identities were to be designed. Apparently, the Institut für Kärntner Landesforschung was engaged in this task right from the outset, thus sustaining National Socialist policy in the Adriatic Littoral as it already had in Carinthia and Upper Carniola. Its publications, as well as the German mass media propaganda that instigated and supported centrifugal aspirations in the region, followed a strategy of "ethnic segmentation," but also of ethnic antagonism. The ethnic complexity of the region was to minimize the legitimacy of Italian supremacy, additionally called into question by affirming the complete failure of Fascist minority policy. As the *Deutsche Adria-Zeitung* pointed out, Germany was destined to succeed as a stabilizing power and called upon to establish a new, "natural" spatial order. Trying to flank this thesis, Günter Glauert,[55] in a booklet on Istria published by the institute in 1943, offered a historical fundament that excelled in eclecticism:

In this borderland of races and peoples, of languages and cultures, it is extremely difficult to trace a frontier line which is fair in terms of nationality and in the meantime satisfactory from a military as well as political and economic point of view. Therefore, it was good fortune that, for nearly a millennium, German state systems assumed the function of a stabilizing power and that German lords and nobles encouraged the economic and administrative development of the country.

Alluding to the medieval German Empire and the Habsburg monarchy, Glauert, as well as Martin Wutte and the SS-guided German propaganda paid special attention to the historic development of Trieste. Wutte pointed out that "Trieste owes its rise exclusively to the union with Austria. If it had remained under Venetian rule, it would have continued to be a small city as the Istrian towns did.... Venice had no interest in the rise of Trieste."[56] On this issue the Carinthian historians constructed a continuity of economic antagonism that had divided Italy and Trieste up to the present, opposing it to the advantages of National Socialist *Großraumwirtschaft* and of the "New European Order" which would restore access to the traditional hinterland of Trieste lost in 1918 and again bring the city new economic prosperity.

Little is still known about the German concept for nationality policy in Friuli (province of Udine), the western part of the Adriatic Littoral. It is evident, however, that it was based on the idea of denationalization and that Carinthian scholars had decisive influence. In the above-mentioned telegram to Foreign Minister von Ribbentrop, Gauleiter Rainer had already emphasized that "ethnically even Friuli is not Italian soil." The individuality of the Friulian language and its vicinity to the Ladinian and Romansh idioms rather than to Italian were two factors vindicating the segregation and future separation of the region from Italian national territory. Hence, it was not to be wondered at that, of all the colleagues of the Institut für Kärntner Landesforschung, it was Kranzmayer, a specialist in minority languages, whom the political leadership of Carinthia entrusted with composing a booklet on Friuli. Besides stressing the particularities of the Friulian language and thus confuting the contrarious position of Italian linguists, Kranzmayer highlighted "the profound German influence on the life of the Friulians"[57] by citing not only a series of German loan words and medieval place names, but also by referring to the "march" function of Friuli in the Carolingian and in the early German Empire, as well as to German feudal lords in the region and to its temporary annexation to the Duchy of Carinthia since the late tenth century. Enriched by the thesis of German acculturation, an even more pregnant conclusion was drawn from similar eclectic considerations in an internal paper: "the Friulians ... belong to the German cultural field, as their land has been an ancient land of the German Empire and ever since part of the German vital space."[58] The authorship of this document may possibly be ascribed to Karl Starzacher, who by that time was regional chief of the National Socialist civil administration in Udine and had strong influence on German propaganda. In 1939, the Italian linguist Carlo Battisti (1882–1977) had already realized the impact of such a politico-cultural stratagem, which could be employed by Germany to "declare the Eastern Alps to be part of its vital space in order to push forward to the Adriatic Sea."[59] German newspapers portrayed Friuli as a region of centuries-old Germanic and German settlement, underlining German influence on Friulian customs and popular culture. The National Socialist propaganda written in the Italian language, however, which treated Friulian folklore in various articles and tried to revivify it, designed and presented a concept of a new national identity based on ethnic distinction and particularism as well as on regional autonomy, by recalling the 350 years of national unity and self-rule under the medieval Patriarchate of Aquileia. Besides the offices of the German civil administration, nationality and racial policy related tasks in Friuli were conferred to the Race and Settlement department of the Höherer SS- und Polizeiführer (Higher SS and Police Leader) in the Adriatic Littoral as well as to other offices of the SS, which in April 1944 started a census on the Friulian-speaking population. However, the intense Friulian resistance movement, which in the summer of 1944 managed to liberate large parts of the province from National Socialist occupation, made obsolete all German concepts of nationality policy.

In Austria, the Italian annexation of South Tyrol in 1918 was felt to be the most vital territorial loss of all. In the decades to follow, vast parts of the Tyrolean scientific elite focused their interests and efforts on evidencing the historical unity of the German-speaking Tyrolean regions north and south of the Brenner (Italian: Brennero) Pass. Continuity with the prewar era, in terms of political thought and cognitive interests, was what predominantly characterized the studies contributed by Tyrolean historians. An anti-Italian attitude and a "Pan-German interpretation" of regional history can be regarded as recurrent *topoi* of Tyrolean historiography since the last decades before 1914. Since World War I the highest endeavor had been "contesting the Italian annexation of German South Tyrol with the weapons of science," as was stated by the then assistant professor for Austrian and economic history of the University of Innsbruck, Hermann Wopfner (1876–1963).[60] It was generally taken for granted, however, that the basis of any territorial revision must be the union of Austria with Germany, which was looked upon by nationalist and *völkisch* historiographers as not just an inevitable political and economic need, but the consequential outcome of history and, more and more, a racial necessity. Tyrol's past was thus recomposed from a prevalent "Pan-German" viewpoint—a process that found expression in the region's postwar self-conception, which was mainly determined by Innsbruck historians. The country now passed as Germany's "south-march," as "a German stronghold" whose people were considered a "part of the very same huge [German] ethnic and national community" and whose historical function was presumed to be its "centuries-long borderland task"[61] of defending the "German mother-country." The demonstration of the "German character" of South Tyrol and of its ethnical, historical, cultural, and geographical unity with North Tyrol—an aspect that gained increasing importance as the Fascist regime forced the italianization of the province—was a scientific design that not only originated from a mere revisionist point of view, but was meant to show that Sub-Brenner German Tyrol had to be considered an integral component of the "German and Germanic cultural and living space" in general.

Although this "intellectual defensive battle" witnessed the participation of several disciplines, the Innsbruck historians Hermann Wopfner and Otto Stolz (1881–1957) can be considered its most prominent protagonists. Referring to medieval Bavarian colonization and settlement in South Tyrol, and stressing the ostensible superior moral concept of "German peasant labor" as a distinctive national character, Wopfner claimed a "German right to South Tyrol owed to German labor"[62]—a guidance thesis of Tyrolean historiography in the interwar period. Wopfner thus studied the settlement and economic history, and the toponymical and folkloristic aspects, of Sub-Brenner Tyrol. The foundation, in 1924, of the Institut für geschichtliche Siedlungs- und Heimatkunde der Alpenländer (Institute of Historical Settlement and Regional Studies on the Alpine Countries) reflected Wopfner's concerns.

Even to Otto Stolz[63] the "question of the historical age of German settlements in South Tyrol" was of decisive importance. Ascribed to this range of ideas is, for example, his ponderous four-volume study, *Ausbreitung des Deutschtums in Südtirol im Lichte der Urkunden* (Extension of Germandom in South Tyrol in the Light of Records), which he considered an "arsenal for the historiographic defense of South Tyrolean Germandom."[64] However, Stolz also focused on other topics, such as the historical unity of the country and its self-conception, on its national consciousness during the course of history, and on the right to national self-determination and its incompatibility with the Italian annexation of 1918.

In the years to come, an all but secondary influence on the Tyrolean scientific activities was exercised by the network that the University of Innsbruck had established in the 1920s with nationally determined learned circles in Germany, thus trying to prepare the "intellectual Anschluss" of the country. What mainly materialized were financial grants by German institutions (especially for publications concerning South Tyrol), the appointment of German scholars to Innsbruck professorial chairs, and the institutionalizing and linking of revisionist-oriented research. Particularly important in this context were the appointments of the sociologist Adolf Günther (1881–1958) and the geographer Friedrich Metz, the former a representative of social spatial research and the latter of geography and history combining historic-genetic research (*historisch-genetische Kulturlandschaftsforschung*).

Mostly due to Metz's initiative,[65] the Arbeitsgemeinschaft für alpendeutsche Forschungen (Working Group for Research on the German Alps) was established in Innsbruck in April 1931; some years later this became the Alpenländische Forschungsgemeinschaft (AFG).[66] It was part of a chain of six similar, concealed and informal institutions in Germany and Austria, the so-called *Volksdeutsche Forschungsgemeinschaften* (ethnic German research societies or VFG).[67] Whereas the German Ministry of Interior was responsible for the political alignment, the funding was left to the Foreign Ministry. The AFG activities were targeted toward the "collecting and sighting of all scientific data on the Germans in the Alps"[68] from Styria to Switzerland, the coordination and financing of studies on the borderland areas, the gathering of information on the scientific research and political intentions of neighboring countries, the preparation of the border revision and the "scientific basis for the Reich's policy towards [German] ethnic minorities abroad."[69] Thanks to its founding members, the AFG succeeded in establishing a large network of connections with learned institutions and nationalist agitation societies alike. Despite its changing staff of collaborators and its altering organizational subordination, and regardless of its periodical marginalization imposed by the authorities of the Third Reich in respect of the official German-Italian alliance,[70] the AFG became, and remained until 1945, an important institution and brain trust with leading competence especially in South Tyrolian affairs and with notable influence on opinion-forming among the political decision makers.

While National Socialist Party influence on the VFGs had generally grown since about 1936, the AFG and its supporting ministries had witnessed increasing interference by the Tyrolean party leadership since 1940. Through the Dienststelle für Grenzland- und Volkstumspflege (Office for Borderland and Nationality Affairs), which later on became the Institut für Landes- und Volksforschung (Institute for Regional and Ethnic Studies) of the *Reichsgau* of Tyrol-Vorarlberg, headed by Wolfgang Steinacker (1906–1996), Gauleiter Hofer tried to occupy AFG domains, at least as far as Tyrol, South Tyrol, and Switzerland were concerned. In 1941 the AFG finally had to renounce these issues, henceforth directed by the Dienststelle für Grenzland- und Volkstumspflege, which in an act of partial usurpation was integrated into the structure of the AFG. This change in personnel was finally sealed by installing Steinacker as managing director and by appointing the University of Innsbruck professor of history Franz Huter (1899–1997) chairman of the AFG in 1942. Steinacker in particular, a "borderland activist" and originally a lawyer at the Innsbruck tribunal in charge of persecuting opponents of the regime, introduced a markedly aggressive anti-Italian note with strong connotations of racial ideology. In 1940, considering also the informal Italian claims to southern Switzerland, he demanded "much more thorough German studies on alpine area questions, looking strictly, however, after the interests of German vital space."[71] In Innsbruck, Steinacker was soon considered "indispensable and irreplaceable," and even the Berlin ministries regarded his reports on neighboring

border areas as "indispensable information material ... on nationality policy issues in the alpine regions."[72] In 1943, when they finally took over
central functions in cultural affairs in the Operational Zone of the Prealps,
a primary task for Huter and Steinacker became personal revenge against
the protagonists of Italian nationalist borderland studies and especially
against Ettore Tolomei (1865–1952), the promoter and *maître à penser* of the
italianization of South Tyrol.

Fascist denationalization policy in the Italian-annexed province had
notably increased the percentage of Italians, which in 1939 reached 24.7
percent (1910: 3.0 percent). The German- and Ladinian-speaking populations, in the meantime, had been exposed to harsh measures of cultural
inhibition and socioeconomic marginalization. After the Anschluss of
Austria in March 1938, Hitler had solemnly disclaimed Sub-Brenner Tyrol
on 7 May 1939, two weeks before signing the German-Italian "Steel Pact."
Bilateral negotiations were immediately begun on the future destiny of
the German South Tyroleans and were concluded on 21 October 1939. The
"repatriation" of Germans from South Tyrol and the Kanal Valley (province of Udine) was agreed on. Even the Ladinians from South Tyrol and
the province of Belluno were included in the "repatriation" program,
which was finally extended to the German linguistic exclaves in the province of Trento (the Fersina Valley and Luserna). The idea of "repatriating"
the German population from Italy had first been ventilated by Hermann
Göring in January 1937; it only took shape, however, in a memorandum
composed by Foreign Office official Max Lorenz in March 1938. According
to the German-Italian agreement, the above-mentioned group of people
was required to decide individually, within a few weeks (between the end
of October and 31 December 1939) whether to emigrate to Germany or
keep Italian citizenship by consigning special ballot-papers to the authorities. Massive propaganda exerted by both regimes, however, impeded any
independent, personal decision. In South Tyrol approximately 84 percent,
in the Kanal Valley around 86 percent, among the Ladinians roughly 40
percent of those entitled to vote decided in favor of assuming German citizenship, hence opting for their "repatriation" to Germany. Detailed studies
were conducted on the social structure of the emigrants, and in the months
to follow, nearly 73,000 Germans from South Tyrol (i.e., 31 percent of the
German ethnic group) were transferred to the Reich, alongside about 4,500
Germans (and Slovenians) from the Kanal Valley, around 2,500 Ladinians,
and the majority of the roughly 1,000 Germans who, in the linguistic exclaves of the Fersina Valley and Luserna, had opted for "repatriation."

From the National Socialist viewpoint, giving up "German national soil"
was acceptable only if territory could be regained elsewhere; the "repatriating" groups from northern Italy were thus to be settled in German-occupied
territories, "preferably in an area of a completely different race"[73] from which
the former population had to be removed entirely. Projects concerning resettlement and germanizing measures in northern Moravia, the *Warthegau*

(Poland), Alsace, and Lorraine were rapidly dropped without becoming concrete. A feasibility study, however, was made for settling the South Tyroleans in the Beskid Mountains and in their northern foreland down to the Vistula River in Poland. This settlement geography study was mainly elaborated by Hugo Hassinger, head of the SOFG and director of the "Study community on spatial planning" as well as a professor at the University of Vienna. As stressed in his paper, only the entire transfer of the "repatriating" population would guarantee the preservation of their previous social and economic structure and drive out the Polish inhabitants. Regarding the first aspect, however, decisive differences between agricultural conditions in South Tyrol and the Beskid area materialized, so that the project had already been abandoned by the end of 1939. Subsequently, alternative resettlement and germanizing projects focused on Burgundy (France), Slovenia (Upper Carniola and Lower Styria), and the Crimea, whereas for the Ladinians from the Gardena Valley (German: Grödnertal) resettlement in East Tyrol and, later, in Northern Styria (the Hochschwab Mountains) was considered.[74] Owing to a variety of different motives and difficulties, none of these plans was realized, although some South Tyroleans were established in Slovenia.[75]

Thus, instead of being entirely transferred to a closed settlement area, as had initially been assured, "repatriating" Germans and Ladinians were actually assigned to different regions of the Reich, mostly to northern Tyrol and Vorarlberg, to the remaining areas of the *Ostmark*, and to a lesser degree, to Germany. Following specific germanizing projects, mostly proposed by the staffs of different Austrian Gauleiters, other groups were transferred to southern Carinthia, Upper Carniola, Lower Styria, to the Basin of České Budějovice (German: Budweis) in the Protectorate of Bohemia and Moravia, and to Luxemburg.

When the "repatriation" of the German-speaking population of South Tyrol and the Kanal Valley started, Himmler ordered the constitution of a special scientific working group in order to analyze all testimonies of "German" culture in the two regions. The so-called Kulturkommission, set up on 15 January 1940, was headed by SS-Obersturmbannführer Wolfram Sievers (1905–1948), general director of the Ahnenerbe of the SS.[76] The "commission" was composed of fifteen repeatedly altered teams,[77] comprising, in 1941, 30 German and 26 South Tyrolean full-time collaborators. Their task was to register and analyze the entire stock of local "German" material and spiritual culture and to secure and convey to the Reich all moveable non-public cultural assets of the "repatriating" Germans. Whereas the latter activities of the "commission," sometimes hardly distinguishable from simple theft of cultural possessions, were soon largely paralyzed by Italian-German disputes on the "national" belonging of the objects, the other teams were engaged in extensive folkloristic field research and in the copying of records and parish books, mainly for future racial studies. After the war in Yugoslavia and the agreement on "repatriating" the Germans even from Italian-annexed Lower Carniola, a second Kulturkommission, headed by the geographer and SS-Hauptsturmführer Hans Schwalm (1900–1992), was assembled in order to operate in the Kočevje region.

The widespread activities of the South Tyrolean "commission" were often far removed from real scientific research. This was not only due to the ideological premises of the SS and of the collaborating scholars themselves, but also to the real intentions of the Ahnenerbe, which expected its South Tyrolean registration works to expand to a central and long-term function in National Socialist settlement planning in Eastern Europe and in the reeducation of the new settlers. The Ahnenerbe was thus primarily interested in the practical application and political-ideological exploitation of the folkloristic materials collected, rather than in future scientific publications.

Alongside the ideologically calculated issues of the Kulturkommission there was, however, among most of the collaborating scholars, a lurking incongruity with the official South Tyrol policy of the regime, considered to be in contrast to the ethnocentric theory of German national and cultural space.[78] Disparities had emerged among the "national elites" of Tyrol and even among Tyrolean National Socialist Party members ever since the regime had renounced its claim on Sub-Brenner Tyrol in favor of an alliance with Italy—a renouncement that had been only temporarily tolerated thanks to the Anschluss of Austria in 1938 and the hereby notably augmented prestige of Hitler, as well as to the admiration of German military successes. Obedience and sacrificial devotion to the glorified Führer finally encouraged bowing to the "unbelievable" resettlement of the German-speaking population, despite the enormous delusion and indignation it produced. Even the Tyrolean Gauleiter Hofer, in April 1939, had incredulously addressed himself to Himmler stressing that "once again the question should be put to the Führer whether he is really determined to decree for ever and ever the giving up of the doubtlessly centuries-old German space in South Tyrol."[79] In the end, temporary consolation was found in the vision of a "unique opportunity to furnish North Tyrol with an additional blood stream of 2,750 racially singled out, good South Tyrolean families," thus "safeguarding the frontier-wall in North Tyrol with the best German blood."[80] But as the "resettlement" operation gradually came to a halt, and as the first reverses in Axis warfare were revealed and the prestige of the Fascist regime in Italy faded out, even the consensus with the official party line in the "South Tyrol question" vanished in leading Tyrolean circles—an attitude, however, that did not imply any oppositional stance toward the Führer or National Socialist ideology. The scholars of the Kulturkommission, grotesquely engaged in the "cultural clearance" of a region that for years they had reclaimed for German "living space," increasingly contested the Italian thesis of the Romance character of South Tyrol and became preoccupied with settling the score with their direct Italian opponents. Only two days after the overthrow of Mussolini, on 27 July 1943, Sievers referred to the RSHA in Berlin reporting that in the past the Kulturkommission had

> of course observed all those Italian efforts meant to prove that South Tyrol had ever since been an Italian region and that therefore its cession [in 1919] was based on legal principles. Unbiased and objective research on all cultural fields, however, had alone been sufficient to produce data able to confute these Italian claims, even though this had not originally been our task. … It will be … the task of this study group to gain additional scientific materials as a basis [to invalidate] all probable future Italian claims, which go even in part beyond the Brenner border-line.[81]

Sievers thus emphasized the Ahnenerbe's general and continuing competence in South Tyrolean affairs and delineated its future role, since its former task, after the downfall of Fascism, had actually become obsolete. After talks with Hofer and Himmler, Sievers finally managed to maintain a small special Ahnenerbe branch in Siusi (German: Seis am Schlern) in South Tyrol (Dienststelle Seis des Amtes Ahnenerbe), preserving for his organization an important political-cultural and scientific function in what became the Operational Zone of the Prealps.[82]

Yet, as of September 1943, the Ahnenerbe had to face the rivalry of other power circles within the Third Reich. Reclaiming direct influence on cultural affairs in the occupied territories, Gauleiter Hofer, in his capacity as Supreme Commissioner of the Prealps instituted a particular subdivision within his head office in Bolzano (German: Bozen), into which, in the course of 1944, he also managed to incorporate the Arbeitsgemeinschaft für Landes- und Volksforschung Südtirol (Working Group for South Tyrolean Regional and Ethnic Studies), founded on 28 April 1944 to support and assure the "mental seizure" of South Tyrol. Its objectives had been defined during several meetings between Hofer and Sievers, in which German civil administration and Ahnenerbe officials as well as the highest SS and SD representatives in the Prealps had also participated. In fact, by appointing two collaborators of Hofer's Bolzano subdivision for cultural and educational affairs, Franz Huter and Wolfgang Steinacker, head and deputy head, respectively, of the Working group, a personal union had been attained right from the start with the German civil administration office as well as with the RSHA-guided Alpenländische Forschungsgemeinschaft in Innsbruck, although the Working group was mainly funded by the Ahnenerbe. Since summer 1944, Sievers's organization had lost even more of its earlier influence in South Tyrol, mainly because of competition from the ambitious RSHA, which since the takeover and internal reorganization of the Ministry of Interior by Reichsführer-SS Himmler on 25 August 1943 had gained primacy over the *Volksdeutsche Forschungsgemeinschaften*. Via these research societies, which according to SS-Standartenführer Hans Ehlich, head of RSHA department III B (Nationality), "on the sector of scientific research ought to be more and more enabled to prepare—so to speak—the building blocks of a future European Reich,"[83] the RSHA tried to invade the scientific domain of the Ahnenerbe. Not only did Hofer manage to turn the SS internal contention to his own benefit, gaining a complete hold on the Arbeitsgemeinschaft für Landes- und Volksforschung Südtirol; since March 1944 he had gained ever-increasing influence on Sievers's Ahnenerbe office in Siusi, which as such was de facto closed in the autumn of 1944, whereas from then on the works of the SS scholars mainly depended on the Gauleiter's directives.

Goals and strategies of National Socialist cultural policy and scientific activity in the Prealps had already been delineated in the weeks prior to the German occupation of Italy. Three central aspects emerged: Firstly, the scientific validation of German claims for the "Nordic-Germanic national soil" of Sub-Brenner Tyrol, and the concomitant rejection of the legitimacy of Italian rule. Secondly, the "regermanizing" of South Tyrol and the "strengthening" of its German nationality. Thirdly, the flanking of National Socialist denationalization policy in the Trentino district and towards the Ladinians, whose "affiliation … to the German cultural community"[84] had already been highlighted by the Kulturkommission, but also, for example, by Eberhard Kranzmayer (1937), Friedrich Metz,[85] and, from a racial viewpoint, especially by the social medicine and social hygiene expert Ignaz Kaup (1870–1944).[86]

In the autumn of 1943, the Ahnenerbe was certainly well placed, under these auspices, to dispose of the vast amount of South Tyrolean field research data that had been collected in previous years. The interpretative direction of these data, in the opinion of the Kulturkommission, had simply to be inverted: these materials, "more than any other, allow us to prove unequivocally the German character of this region and its being part of the Nordic-Germanic cultural community for 4,000 years, so that German claims for this disputed borderland can be provided with a definitively assured basis."[87]

In fact, a main issue of the Ahnenerbe in occupied South Tyrol was related to the fieldwork on settlement history and ancient rural architecture initiated in 1940 under the guidance of SS-Obersturmführer Martin Rudolph (1908–1992), lecturer at the Technical University of Brunswick and director of the Ahnenerbe Research Station for Germanic Architecture. The study of traditional farmsteads, of their origins and earliest forms, held a special interest for research on settlement history as well as for investigating the origins of the Germans in Sub-Brenner Tyrol. Actually, the asserted identification of Neolithic, "Nordic-Germanic," and even Lombard architectural style elements, supposed to show particular affinity to primordial Scandinavian forms, was adduced in proof of "Nordic acquisition of the country 4,000 years ago," of "cultural efforts of immigrated Nordic people,"[88] and of their influence on northern Italy. But what is more, these "findings," fitting perfectly to the "Germanomania" and the expectations of the SS, proved to have a practical dimension in National

Socialist settlement policy by "elaborating house-types which can be utilized for the resettlement"[89] of South Tyroleans. Since autumn 1942 the SS
subdivisions in charge of German resettlement in Eastern Europe had also
manifested great interest. On behalf of the SS-Economics Administration
Main Office, Rudolph had been engaged, since the summer of 1944, in
planning issues that, initially concerning Lower Styrian resettlement areas,
were to be extended to the Protectorate of Bohemia and Moravia. As for
South Tyrol, Sievers had already proposed an ambitious project to Hofer
on 7 October 1943 that, directed by the Ahnenerbe, should "re-establish in
its entirety the [region's] former unity between culture and landscape and
simultaneously restore the vigor of the settlement work through powerful
manifestations of revived rural customs." By "forming a complete 'cultural landscape' … we could create something very unique in the Reich, we
could preserve and further a germ cell of genuine popular culture, from
which again and again new genuine German life will originate."[90] In fact,
Rudolph's "Settlement and architecture" sub-division of the Ahnenerbe
office in Siusi was intended to guide "a cultural work aimed at definitively
regaining the Southern alpine region" and at "the future shaping of the
South March."[91] These activities, which for the time being appear to have
been limited to the planning of new settlement areas in South Tyrol and to
the development of new types of farmsteads, were part of a strategy of
massive ideological penetration into the traditional, clerically determined
sphere of alpine peasants as well as diffusion of a National Socialist surro-
gate religion. This project, which had already been initiated in northern
Tyrol, was essentially based on reinterpretation and exploitation of folklore
elements, on designing new or reconstructing existing rural settlement
complexes with annexed special buildings for pseudo-religious National
Socialist festivities (according to the "Neo-Germanic" National Socialist
settlement style developed for Eastern Europe), and on social and economic assistance to the "racially and morally precious"[92] alpine peasants.
These were to be turned into "warrior-peasants," considered to be the
"most secure wall against the invasion of foreign races."[93] Although the circumstances of war prevented this concept from going beyond the initial
planning stage, the Kulturkommission had, however, already used folkloric elements for propaganda purposes in Sub-Brenner Tyrol—elements
that, since 1943, had become part of the occupation regime's strategy for
"regermanizing" South Tyrol.

Already prior to September 1943, the Ahnenerbe had devoted special
attention to the partially extinct German linguistic exclaves in the provinces
of Trento (the Fersina Valley, Luserna, and the Folgaria plateau), Verona
(Giazza, German: Ljetzan, the so-called Thirteen Communities, German:
Dreizehn Gemeinden, Italian: Tredici Comuni), and Vicenza (Seven Communities, German: Sieben Gemeinden, Italian: Sette Comuni). Ahnenerbe
scholars such as Richard Wolfram (1901–1995), Martin Rudolph, Alfred
Quellmalz (1899–1979), and Bruno Schweizer (1897–1958), as well as

Wolfgang Steinacker and the landscape architect and Reich Advocate for the Landscape Alwin Seifert (1890–1972), in investigating the origins of these linguistic islands, defended an ideologically bound ethnogenesis theory asserting Lombard or Cimbrian origins rather than later immigration from southern Germany between the High Middle Ages and the sixteenth century, as evidenced by linguistic aspects. Since scholars such as University of Vienna professor Richard Wolfram, one of the leading figures of "germanocentric" SS folklore studies, considered Germanic "continuity as permanence of 'national substance,'"[94] the asserted Lombard origins of the linguistic exclaves in northern Italy, in the ultimate analysis, were to prove ancient and primogenitary entitlements for German dominion in this area. The Trentino was thus looked upon as an italianized part of the "German cultural and living sphere."[95] It is noteworthy that the Ahnenerbe as well as the "Prehistory" branch of the "Rosenberg Office" made additional efforts to extend Lombard studies—especially the archeological ones—to all of northern Italy. While these projects were greatly hindered by the circumstances of war, the work of confiscation and removal of cultural possessions from Trentino museums and archives, including Lombard and Rhaetian objects as well as documents and testimonies relating to the Italian national movement of the nineteenth and twentieth centuries, was prosecuted until the very last weeks before German surrender. Along with some South Tyrolean scholars, these activities, part of the National Socialist denationalization strategy in the Trentino, saw the involvement of Wolfgang Steinacker, Franz Huter and the Ahnenerbe collaborator and professor of prehistory at the University of Vienna Kurt Willvonseder (1903–1968).

In 1946, when the Italian-Austrian border on the Brenner Pass was once again internationally approved after the war, Franz Huter felt legitimated to voice a general exculpation of Tyrolean historiography and its contribution to flanking German revisionist policy: "This time hardly any guilt can be charged to the living generation of Tyrolean historians"[96] if South Tyrol will once more remain under Italian dominion. Repeating the well-known revisionist claims of *völkisch* Tyrolean scholars, Huter, like many of his colleagues still guided by an attitude of German cultural superiority, showed no inclination either to define a new, mediatorial function for South Tyrol in its position between the German- and Italian-speaking cultural areas or to recognize any responsibility of German scholars for the part they played in National Socialist occupation policy.

Notes

1. Prekmurje region (Hungarian: Muravidék, German: Übermurgebiet), i.e., the district of Murska Sobota (Hungarian: Muraszombat, German: Olsnitz).
2. On German occupation in Slovenia, see Tone Ferenc, "Le système d'occupation des Nazis en Slovénie," in *Les systèmes d'occupation en Yougoslavie 1941–1945. Rapports au 3ᵉ Congrès international sur l'histoire de la Résistance européenne à Karlovy Vary, les 2–4 septembre 1963* (Belgrade, 1963), 47–133; Ferenc, *Nacistična raznarodovalna politika v Sloveniji v letih 1941–1945* (Maribor, 1968); Ferenc, *Quellen zur nationalsozialistischen Entnationalisierungspolitik in Slowenien 1941–1945/Viri o nacistični raznarodovalni politiki v Sloveniji 1941–1945* (Maribor, 1980); Helga H. Harriman, *Slovenia under Nazi occupation, 1941–1945* (New York, 1977); Stefan Karner, ed., *Die Stabsbesprechungen der NS-Zivilverwaltung in der Untersteiermark 1941–1944* (Graz, 1996).
3. Constituted by the Italian provinces of Bolzano (German: Bozen) (i.e., South Tyrol), Trento, and Belluno.
4. Comprising the Italian provinces of Udine, Gorizia, Lubiana (Slovenian: Ljubljana, German: Laibach), Trieste, Pola, Fiume, and the former Italian Civil Intendancy for the Annexed Territories of the Fiumano and the Cupa region.
5. On German military occupation in Italy, see Lutz Klinkhammer, *Zwischen Bündnis und Besatzung. Das nationalsozialistische Deutschland und die Republik von Salò 1943–1945* (Tübingen, 1993); on German civil administration in Northern Italy, see Karl Stuhlpfarrer, *Die Operationszonen 'Alpenvorland' und 'Adriatisches Küstenland' 1943–1945* (Vienna, 1969); Michael Wedekind, "Tra integrazione e disgregazione: l'occupazione tedesca nelle 'zone d'operazione' delle Prealpi e del Litorale Adriatico 1943–1945," *Annali dell'Istituto storico italo-germanico in Trento* 25 (1999): 239–272; Wedekind, *Nationalsozialistische Besatzungs- und Annexionspolitik in Norditalien 1943 bis 1945: Die Operationszonen 'Alpenvorland' und 'Adriatisches Küstenland'* (Munich, 2003).
6. According to contemporary German estimations; see Gerhard Werner, *Sprache und Volkstum in der Untersteiermark* (Stuttgart, 1935), 146; Anton Scherer, "Die Deutschen in der Untersteiermark, in Ober-Krain und in der Gottschee," in *Die Deutschen zwischen Karpaten und Krain*, ed. Ernst Hochberger, Anton Scherer, and Friedrich Spiegel-Schmidt (Munich, 1994), 131. The German minority settled mainly in the city of Maribor (German: Marburg an der Drau) and its surroundings as well as on the Apaško polje (German: Abstaller Feld).
7. German linguistic enclaves are to be found in the upper Fersina Valley (German: Fersental) (1,200 persons), in the village of Luserna (German: Lusern) (760 persons) in the province of Trento, and in Sappada (German: Bladen) (1,500 persons) in the province of Belluno.
8. Prior to the war, aggressive settlement strategies had already played a certain role among German nationalistic associations in Austria, which started colonizing German settlers, e.g., in Lower Styria, and contemplating further such activities in Carniola and in the Littoral in order to establish a German corridor to the Adriatic Sea. In Tyrol, leaders of the Tiroler Volksbund (Tyrolean Popular League), such as Edgar Meyer (1853–1925) and the historian Michael Mayr (1864–1922), fighting Italian irredentism, since 1915 proposed German resettlement of the Trentino. Edgar Meyer in 1916/17 founded the Ausschuss für völkische Belange und deutsche Besiedlung Südtirols (Committee for National Affairs and German Colonization of the Trentino).
9. Alois Maier-Kaibitsch, "Reichsdeutsche Siedler in Kärnten," *Die Welt. Zeitschrift für das Deutschtum im Ausland* 10 (1933): 690–692; Karl Stuhlpfarrer and Leopold Steurer, "Die Ossa in Österreich," in *Vom Justizpalast zum Heldenplatz. Studien und Dokumentationen 1927 bis 1938*, ed. Ludwig Jedlicka and Rudolf Neck (Vienna, 1975), 35–64.
10. Hugo Hassinger, "Die Ostmark," *Raumforschung und Raumordnung* 2 (1938): 396f.
11. Kurt Trampler, "Deutsche Grenzen," *Zeitschrift für Geopolitik* 11 (1934): 25.
12. Otto Maull and Helmut Carstanjen, "Die verstümmelten Grenzen," *Zeitschrift für Geopolitik* 8 (1931): 62.

13. BArch, R 153/1703, *Arbeitsgemeinschaft für alpendeutsche Forschungen*: Report on a conference held in St. Paul i(m) L(avanttal), on 26 and 27 May 1932. Annex: (H. Carstanjen:) Account on the present situation, on scientific problems and studies concerning Germandom in Lower Styria and Carniola.
14. The Alpenländische Forschungsgemeinschaft, for example, supported the Styria-related studies of Helmut Carstanjen, Viktor von Geramb, Otto Reicher, Randolf Rungaldier, Walter Schinner, and Manfred Straka.
15. Straka, for example, had been concerned, since the mid 1930s, with verifying numbers and property of the German population in Lower Styria and with analyzing the land register for the city of Maribor; BArch, R 153/1508 (Raimund von Klebelsberg:) AFG—Report 1935/36 (Innsbruck), undated (1936?).
16. In Carinthia, in this affair, a prominent role was played by SS-Standartenführer Alois Maier-Kaibitsch. Since 1938 he had managed to take over central state and party positions concerned with the local Slovenian minority. Apparently influenced by the then Gauleiter of Salzburg Friedrich Rainer, Maier-Kaibitsch, in his function as chief of the Gaugrenzlandamt (Provincial Borderland Office) in Klagenfurt composed several memoranda, in July and August 1940, claiming to annex border regions of Carniola. In July 1940, Maier-Kaibitsch asked for the annexation of the Mežiška Valley and the district of Jesenice (German: Aßling); on 21 August 1940, for that of the districts of Radovljica (German: Radmannsdorf), Kranj (German: Krainburg), and Kamnik (German: Stein). Finally, in an undated memorandum by Gauleiter Kutschera, presumably composed by the same Maier-Kaibitsch, the annexation of all Carniola and of the regions round Slovenj Gradec (German: Windischgraz), Radlje (German: Mahrenberg), and Gornji Grad (German: Oberburg) was proposed; see Ferenc, *Quellen*, 14ff., 22ff., 30f. Maier-Kaibitsch was also responsible for the "repatriation" of the Germans from the Kanal Valley.
17. It is noteworthy that the Südostdeutsche Institut got an intense hold on the Steirischer Heimatbund (see Ferenc, *Les systèmes d'occupation*, 67f.), as in the past it had already exercised growing ideological, and in particular political-cultural power over the Lower Styrian sections of the Schwäbisch-Deutscher Kulturbund, the central association of all German-speaking people in Yugoslavia.
18. Ferenc, *Les systèmes d'occupation*, 95.
19. Arnold Joseph Toynbee and Veronica Marjorie Toynbee, *Hitler's Europe* (London, New York, and Toronto, 1954), 108.
20. France Škerl, "Nacistične deportacije Slovencev v letu 1941," *Zgodovinski časopis* 6–7 (1952–1953): 768–797.
21. Special order of Heinrich Himmler, 18 April 1941, quoted from Ferenc, *Les systèmes d'occupation*, 61f.
22. On the central importance of Schultz for National Socialist racial science, see Benoît Massin, "Anthropologie und Humangenetik im Nationalsozialismus, oder: Wie schreiben deutsche Wissenschaftler ihre eigene Wissenschaftsgeschichte?" in *Wissenschaftlicher Rassismus: Analysen einer Kontinuität in den Human- und Naturwissenschaften*, ed. Heidrun Kaupen-Haas and Christian Saller (Frankfurt am Main, 1999), 12–64.
23. Volkmar Weiß and Katja Münchow, *Ortsfamilienbücher mit Standort Leipzig in Deutscher Bücherei und Deutscher Zentralstelle für Genealogie*, 2nd ed. (Neustadt an der Aisch, 1998), 97–104.
24. Arnold Suppan, ed., *Deutsche Geschichte im Osten Europas: Zwischen Adria und Karawanken* (Berlin, 1998), 409.
25. RKF ([Günther Stier?]): Note concerning resettlement in Upper Carniola, Berlin, 10 May 1943, quoted in Ferenc, *Quellen*, 609.
26. BArch, R 43 II/1503, Uiberreither to the Ministry of Interior, Maribor, 12 May 1941.
27. Between December 1939 and February 1943, Starzacher was in charge of the SS-dependent German expatriation office (Amtliche Deutsche Ein- und Rückwandererstelle) in Tarvisio (German: Tarvis, Slovenian: Trbiž) in the Kanal Valley and thus responsible for "technical and bureaucratic" aspects of the resettlement. In Upper Carniola he advanced

to chief of staff of the RKF office in Bled. In the Adriatic Littoral, Starzacher later on became "German Adviser" in the province of Udine. On 27 April 1945 he was shot by Italian partisans in Pordenone.

28. Memorandum by Dr. Karl Starzacher, 22 May 1941, quoted in Ferenc, *Quellen*, 115–119.
29. Ferenc, *Les systèmes d'occupation*, 76f.
30. Notice by the Ahnenerbe (Hans Schwalm) on a conference held in Bled on 6 October 1941, Bled, 8 October 1941, in Ferenc, *Quellen*, 295–300.
31. See, for example, Robert Routil, *Völker und Rassen auf dem Boden Kärntens* (Klagenfurt, 1937).
32. In 1932 Wutte stated: "For all German borderland provinces, one of the most important problems is the relationship between language and nationality. It is more and more generally acknowledged that linguistic group-membership has not to be congruent with national group-membership…. Not only the language, but even other forms of identity are important, such as the native region, culture, and economy, commonly experienced destinies, kinship, and sentimental notions…. This is also true for the Slovenian-speaking population of Carinthia. In its linguistically mixed area there are thousands who, besides German, also speak Windisch, although they strongly oppose the Slovenians and demonstrate by their attitude that they do not want to be Slovenians." BArch, R 153/1703, Arbeitsgemeinschaft für alpendeutsche Forschungen: Report on a conference held in St. Paul i(m) L(avanttal), on 26 and 27 May 1932. Annex: Martin Wutte: Account of the state of scientific studies on the Carinthian question.
33. Franz Kutschera to Minister Bernhard Rust, Klagenfurt, 17 June 1941, in Ferenc, *Quellen*, 181–183.
34. Same as note 30.
35. Martin Fritzl, '… für Volk und Reich und deutsche Kultur'. Die 'Kärntner Wissenschaft' im Dienste des Nationalismus (Klagenfurt, 1992), 130. On the Ahnenerbe: Gisela Lixfeld, "Das 'Ahnenerbe' Heinrich Himmlers und die ideologisch-politische Funktion seiner Volkskunde," in *Völkische Wissenschaft: Gestalten und Tendenzen der deutschen und österreichischen Volkskunde in der ersten Hälfte des 20. Jahrhunderts*, ed. Wolfgang Jacobeit, Hannjost Lixfeld, and Olaf Bockhorn (Vienna, 1994), 217–255; Michael H. Kater, *Das 'Ahnenerbe' der SS 1935–1945. Ein Beitrag zur Kulturpolitik des Dritten Reiches* (Munich, 2001).
36. *Kärntner Zeitung*, 30 September 1942, quoted in Fritzl, '… für Volk und Reich,' 134.
37. Prof. Robert Spindler (University of Munich) to the Dean, Prof. Walther Wüst, about Eberhard Kranzmayer, Munich, 30 January 1937 (Bayerisches Hauptstaatsarchiv, Munich, Personal file/Personalakt MK 43.907 "Prof. Dr. Eberhard Kranzmayer").
38. Eberhard Kranzmayer, "Deutsches Sprachgut jenseits der Sprachgrenze in den Alpen, mit besonderer Rücksicht auf das Rätoromanische des Grödnertales," *Deutsches Archiv für Landes- und Volksforschung* 1 (1937): 273–286; Kranzmayer, "Der bairische Sprachraum," *Jahrbuch der deutschen Sprache* 2 (1944): 169–180; Kranzmayer, *Die deutschen Lehnwörter in der slowenischen Volkssprache* (Ljubljana, 1944); and, in general, Herwig Hornung, ed., *Verzeichnis der Schriften von Eberhard Kranzmayer, als Festgabe zu seinem sechzigsten Geburtstag dargebracht von seinen Wiener Freunden und Mitarbeitern* (Vienna, 1957).
39. Kranzmayer, "Sprachraum," 179.
40. Kranzmayer, *Lehnwörter*, 38.
41. Karl Dinklage, "Frühdeutsche Volkskulturen im Spiegel der Bodenfunde von Untersteiermark und Krain," *Mitteilungen der anthropologischen Gesellschaft Wien* 71 (1941): 235–259; Dinklage, "Oberkrains Deutschtum im Spiegel der karolingischen Bodenfunde," *Carinthia I* 131 (1941): 360–391; Dinklage, *Frühdeutsche Volkskultur in Kärnten und seinen Marken* (Ljubljana, 1943).
42. Günter Glauert, *Die Entwicklung der Kulturlandschaft in den Steiner Alpen und Ostkarawanken* (Ph.D. diss., University of Graz, 1936); Glauert, "Zur Besiedlung der Steiner Alpen und Ostkarawanken (das Gebiet Freibach, Kanker, Sann und Mieß)," *Deutsches Archiv für Landes- und Volksforschung* 1 (1937): 457–486; Glauert, "Landschaftsbild und Siedlungsgang in einem Abschnitt der südöstlichen Kalkalpen (Ostkarawanken und Steiner Alpen) und seinen Randgebieten," *Südost-Forschungen* 3 (1938): 457–524; Glauert,

"Ein Kärntner Grenzmarkt in den Karawanken im 17. und 18. Jahrhundert," *Südost-Forschungen* 4 (1939): 643–683; Glauert, "Grundherrschaftsbesitz und Rodung im karantanisch-altkrainischen Grenzgebiet," *Südost-Forschungen* 5 (1940): 864–943; Glauert, "Kulturlandschaftliche Veränderungen im Gebirgslande zwischen Drau und Sawe bis zum Beginn der deutschen Südostsiedlung," *Südost-Forschungen* 7 (1942): 9–52; Glauert, *Siedlungsgeographie von Oberkrain* (Habilitation, University of Munich, 1943).

43. Georg Graber, "Volkskundliches," in *Oberkrain*, ed. Viktor Paschinger, Martin Wutte, and Georg Graber (Kranj, 1942), 67–95.

44. Viktor Paschinger, "Land und Wirtschaft," in *Oberkrain*, 7–35.

45. Karl Starzacher, "Oberkrain—deutscher Kulturboden," *Deutsche Volkskunde. Vierteljahresschrift der Arbeitsgemeinschaft für deutsche Volkskunde* 5 (1943): 69.

46. BArch, NS 19/320, "Guidelines for the execution of actions against partisans and other bandits in Upper Carniola and Lower Styria," 25 June 1941.

47. Wilhelm Neumann, "Martin Wutte und sein Urteil über die nationalsozialistische Slowenenpolitik in Kärnten und Krain aufgrund seiner Denkschrift vom 19. September 1943," *Carinthia I* 176 (1986): 14.

48. BArch, NS 19/2661, Greifelt to Himmler, Enclosure I: "Nationality policy towards the Slovenians," Schweiklberg, 20 October 1944.

49. Ibid.

50. Wedekind, *Nationalsozialistische Besatzungs- und Annexionspolitik*, 397ff.

51. Ibid., 59f. and 383ff.

52. Martin Wutte, *Kärnten—1200 Jahre Grenzland des Reiches* (Carinthia—1,200 years borderland of the Reich) (1945), unpublished manuscript quoted in Fritzl, '... für Volk und Reich,' 216.

53. Telegram Rainer to Ribbentrop, Klagenfurt, 9 September 1943, in *Akten zur deutschen auswärtigen Politik 1918–1945. Aus dem Archiv des Auswärtigen Amtes* (Göttingen, 1979). Series E (December 1941–1945), vol. VI (1 May to 30 September 1943), 520–523.

54. BArch, R 63/252, Felix Kraus to the Südosteuropa Gesellschaft (Southeast Europe Association): Report on a journey to the Adriatic Littoral, Vienna, December 1943. Kraus, an old hand at Austrian nationality and borderland conflicts, was a party official of the Gauleitung of Carinthia, a leading member of the Südosteuropa Gesellschaft in Vienna, and adviser on minority questions for the Supreme Commissioner in the Adriatic Littoral.

55. Günter Glauert, *Istrien: Raum, Geschichte, Bevölkerungsaufbau* (Kranj, 1943), 18.

56. BArch, R 173/131, Martin Wutte: Remarks on the article "Trieste, Istria, Fiume" for the Handwörterbuch des Grenz- und Auslanddeutschtums, Klagenfurt (28 September 1944).

57. Eberhard Kranzmayer, *Das Volk der Friauler* (Klagenfurt, 1943), 3.

58. Typewritten manuscript *Kulturelle und geschichtliche Zugehörigkeit Friauls zum Deutschen Reich* (Friuli—culturally and historically a part of the German Empire) (Library of the Archiepiscopal Seminary of Udine/'Osoppo' Archive of the Resistance movement in Friuli, file B1, folder 14).

59. Carlo Battisti to Ettore Tolomei, 29 December 1939, quoted in Josef Fontana, ed., *Südtirol und der italienische Nationalismus. Entstehung und Entwicklung einer europäischen Minderheitenfrage, quellenmäßig dargestellt von Walter Freiberg*. Part 1: *Darstellung* (Innsbruck, 1989), 190.

60. (Hermann Wopfner), "Die Einheit Deutschtirols," *Denkschrift des akademischen Senats der Universität Innsbruck* (Innsbruck, 1918), 4.

61. Otto Stolz, "Tirol als deutsche Südmark," *Mitteilungen des Deutschen und Österreichischen Alpenvereins* 51 (1925): 208f. For a more detailed analysis of Tyrolean historiography during the interwar period, see Herbert Dachs, *Österreichische Geschichtswissenschaft und Anschluss* (Vienna and Salzburg, 1974); and Laurence Cole, "Fern von Europa? Zu den Eigentümlichkeiten Tiroler Geschichtsschreibung," *Geschichte und Region/Storia e regione* 5 (1996): 194–205.

62. Hermann Wopfner, "Tirols Eroberung durch deutsche Arbeit," *Tiroler Heimat* 1 (1921): 5–38; Wopfner, *Deutsche Siedlungsarbeit in Südtirol* (Innsbruck, 1926); for a critical study, see Reinhard Johler, "Il concetto scientifico di 'deutsche Arbeit' e l'ergologia nell'area alpina," *Annali di San Michele. Rivista annuale del Museo degli Usi e Costumi della Gente Trentina di San Michele all'Adige* 8 (1995): 276–280.

63. Otto Stolz, "Geschichtliche Folgerungen aus Orts-, insbesondere Hofnamen im Bereiche Tirols," *Zeitschrift für Ortsnamenforschung* 7 (1931): 56.

64. Otto Stolz, *Die Ausbreitung des Deutschtums in Südtirol im Lichte der Urkunden* (Munich and Berlin, 1934), 4:v.

65. Metz had previously been secretary of the Stiftung für deutsche Volks- und Kulturboden-forschung, which was founded in Leipzig in 1922 with the aim of secretly and synergetically coordinating, on a common "national basis," all scientific studies on Germandom abroad and in the borderland areas in order to "provide German [revisionist] policy with weapons," BArch, R 57/586, Report on the meeting with Privy Councilor Prof. Dr. [Wilhelm] Volz, Leipzig, 9 January 1927.

66. Michael Wedekind, "'Völkische Grenzlandwissenschaft' in Tirol (1918–1945). Vom wissenschaftlichen 'Abwehrkampf' zur Flankierung der NS-Expansionspolitik," *Geschichte und Region/Storia e regione* 5 (1996): 227–265; and Michael Fahlbusch, "Die Alpenländische Forschungsgemeinschaft—eine Brückenbauerin des großdeutschen Gedankens?" in *Grenzraum Alpenrhein: Brücken und Barrieren 1914 bis 1938*, ed. Robert Allgäuer (Zurich, 1999), 137–233.

67. See Michael Fahlbusch, *Wissenschaft im Dienst der nationalsozialistischen Politik? Die "Volksdeutschen Forschungsgemeinschaften" von 1931–1945* (Baden-Baden, 1999).

68. Raimund von Klebelsberg, *Innsbrucker Erinnerungen 1902–1952* (Innsbruck, 1953), 336.

69. Paper by Dr. (Emil) Meynen, chief of the head office of the *Volksdeutsche Forschungsgemeinschaften*, attached to the Foreign Office note, Berlin, 31 December 1941 (Auswärtiges Amt/Politisches Archiv, Bonn [AA/PA], Inland II g 216).

70. The Foreign Ministry, on 14 May 1938, prohibited any future discussion or publication on South Tyrol: "For us the 'South Tyrol Question' no longer exists." Ribbentrop circular (AA/PA, Pol. Abt. IV, Italien 24, Bd. 1, Bl. D 665.928-D 665.930). Similar instructions were given by Himmler and Heß.

71. Grenz- und Volkstumsinstitut der Gauselbstverwaltung Tirol-Vorarlberg (Wolfgang Steinacker): Third report on borderland politics, Innsbruck, 21 August 1940 (Archiv des Amts der Tiroler Landesregierung/Sachgebiet Südtirol—Europaregion Tirol, 5/II 6.c 19).

72. Letter of the Reich Ministry of Interior/Department VI: Promotion of Steinacker to superior privy councilor, Berlin, 22 April 1943 (BArch/Außenstelle Dahlwitz-Hoppegarten, Reichsministerium des Innern—File "Steinacker, Wolfgang").

73. BArch, NS 19/2070, Himmler: Notice "concerning the South Tyrol Question," Berlin, 30 May 1939.

74. Stefan Karner, "Der Plan einer geschlossenen Umsiedlung der Grödner in die Steiermark 1941," *Zeitschrift des Historischen Vereins für die Steiermark* 69 (1978): 113–123.

75. On the different resettlement projects, see BArch, R 49/2156, R 49/2158, R 57 neu/28 as well as BArch, NS 2/60, NS 19/2070, and NS 19/3457.

76. On the activities of the Kulturkommission in the years 1940–1943, see: Olaf Bockhorn, "Volkskundliche Filme des 'SS-Ahnenerbes' in Südtirol," in *Südtirol im Auge des Ethnographen*, ed. Reinhard Johler, Ludwig Paulmichl, and Barbara Plankensteiner (Vienna and Lana, 1991), 105–135; Anka Oesterle, "Die volkskundlichen Forschungen des 'SS-Ahnenerbes' mit Berücksichtigung der 'Kulturkommission Südtirol,'" in *Südtirol im Auge des Ethnographen*, 76–89; Peter Schwinn, "'SS-Ahnenerbe' und 'Volkstumsarbeit' in Südtirol 1940–1943," in *Südtirol im Auge des Ethnographen*, 91–104; Ludwig Walther Regele, "'Eindeutig rein deutsch?' Die Kommission zur Erfassung der Kulturgüter," in *Die Option. Südtirol zwischen Faschismus und Nationalsozialismus*, ed. Klaus Eisterer and Rolf Steininger (Innsbruck, 1989), 265–274; and Peter Assion and Peter Schwinn, "Migration, Politik und Volkskunde 1940/43. Zur Tätigkeit des SS-Ahnenerbes in Südtirol,"

Kulturkontakt/Kulturkonflikt 1 (1988): 221–226; comprehensively on its activities in the years 1943–1945 and, in general, on scientific studies and cultural politics in the Operational Zone of the Prealps, see Wedekind, "'Völkische Grenzlandwissenschaft.'"

77. In early 1940, the teams of the Kulturkommission were headed by Richard Wolfram (folklore and research on German nationality), Ernst-Otto Thiele (tools and utensils), Gertrud Pesendorfer (national costumes), Friedrich Wilhelm Mai (popular tales and folk poems), Karl Theodor Hoeniger (symbols and heraldic research), Martin Rudolph (research on traditional houses and architecture), Bruno Schweizer (dialect and onomastic research), Franz Huter (archives), Prof. Treber (parish registers), Georg Innerebner (history and geography), Alfred Quellmalz (folk music), Josef Ringler (art, museums, folk art), Erika Hanfstaengl (historical and art monuments), Karl Felix Wolff (ethnohistory [*Volksgeschichte*] and racial origins), and Helmut Bousset (photography and film).

78. Hans Bobek, "Um die deutsche Volksgrenze in den Alpen," *Deutsches Archiv für Landes- und Volksforschung* 1 (1937): 737, 747.

79. BArch, NS 19/2070, Gauleiter Hofer to Himmler, Innsbruck, 14 April 1939.

80. BArch, NS 2/164, SS-Oberführer Curt von Gottberg, supervisory board chairman of the Deutsche Ansiedlungsgesellschaft (German Settlement Company), to Himmler, Prague, 12.7.1939.

81. BArch, NS 19/189, Sievers to von Ramin (RSHA), Berlin, 27 July 1943.

82. The office, led by the South Tyrolean expert in early settlement history Georg Innerebner (1893–1974), was articulated in the divisions "Settlement and Architecture," headed by Martin Rudolph, and "Prehistory," headed by Innerebner.

83. BArch, Ahnenerbe, file Schwalm, Hans–1, Schwalm to Sievers, concerning a conference with SS-Standartenführer Ehlich, Rosenau Castle (Lower Austria), 4 July 1944.

84. *Alto Adige. Eine offiziöse italienische Tendenzschrift über Südtirol. Kritische Anmerkungen zum italienischen Faksimilewerk 'Alto Adige. Alcuni documenti del passato, 3 Bände, Bergamo 1942,'* by Franz Huter, Karl M. Mayr, Alfred Quellmalz, Josef Ringler, Walter Senn, and Otto Stolz, n.p., n.d. (Innsbruck, 1943), 25.

85. Friedrich Metz, "Von den Lebensgrundlagen deutschen Volkstums in Südtirol," *Zeitwende* 8 (1932): 218.

86. Ignaz Kaup, "Die Alpenbewohner im Wandel der Rassensystematik," *Zeitschrift des Deutschen Alpenvereins* 73 (1942): 43.

87. BArch, Ahnenerbe, file Rudolph, Martin—Einsatz in Nord- und Südtirol, Gottschee, Martin Rudolph: Report on the registration of rural settlements and architecture in South Tyrol, undated (summer 1944).

88. Martin Viktor Rudolph, *Die nordisch-germanischen Volkskräfte im südlichen Alpenraum. Ihre Entstehung und ihre Kulturzeugen in Landschaft und Siedlung* (n.p., n.d. [1944]), 23 and 30.

89. BArch, Ahnenerbe, file Rudolph, Martin—Einsatz in Nord- und Südtirol, Gottschee, Sievers to the vice-chancellor of the Technical University of Brunswick (Prof. Herzig), 14 December 1940.

90. Same as note 81.

91. BArch, Ahnenerbe, file Rudolph, Martin—Ahnenerbe-Einsatz, Rudolph to Sievers, Siusi, 28 January 1944.

92. BArch, NS 19/1747, Note from SS-Gruppenführer Ulrich Greifelt for Himmler, 1 September 1942.

93. Sepp Hainzl, "Südmärkischer Bauernwall vom Großglockner bis zur Pußta," *Odal* 8 (1939): 173.

94. Olaf Bockhorn, "Wiener Volkskunde," in *Volkskunde im Nationalsozialismus*, ed. Helge Gerndt (Munich, 1987), 230.

95. M(arius) W. Ravanelli, "Die Herzogswahl im Fleimstal," *Alpenheimat. Familienkalender für Stadt und Land* (1945): 63–65.

96. Franz Huter, "Geburtstagsansprache gehalten am 22. Mai 1946 bei der Feier der Schüler (Hermann Wopfners) im Rahmen der Universität," in *Beiträge zur Geschichte und Heimatkunde Tirols. Festschrift zu Ehren Hermann Wopfners* 1 (Innsbruck, 1947), 11.

Chapter 7

ROMANIAN-GERMAN COLLABORATION IN ETHNOPOLITICS
The Case of Sabin Manuilă

———————— ✦ ✦ ✦ ————————

Viorel Achim

During World War II, several important Romanian intellectuals were involved in a big project of the government headed by Marshal Ion Antonescu aiming at the restoration of the Romanian borders from before 1940 and the transformation of Romania into an ethnically homogeneous country. The contemplated means were population exchanges with neighboring countries and population transfers.[1] Professors, researchers, and experts in statistics, demography, ethnography, economics, geography, history, and others areas contributed, through their research and work in specific fields, to the substantiation of various aspects of the project.

The aspects relating to population—primarily the Romanian population of the country and ethnic Romanians from abroad, but also the ethnic minorities living in the territory of Romania—were the most important in this effort. These preoccupations can be defined as pertaining to ethnopolitics, although in that time this term was not used in Romania. The term "population policy," then preferred by Romanians despite its larger meaning, also covered what today is usually called ethnopolitics.

One of the scholars who played a central role in this project was Sabin Manuilă (1894–1964), who served as the general director of the Central Institute of Statistics (Institutul Central de Statistică, ICS) between 1937 and 1947. The institute reported directly to the Council of Ministers Presidency (in fact, to Antonescu himself) and played a great role in substantiating the government's decisions. The collaboration of Manuilă and his institute from 1940 to 1944 with German scholars and some German institutions is the topic this chapter seeks to highlight.

Notes for this chapter begin on page 151.

The term "collaboration" is used here without the negative tinge that usually clings to the word when it comes to World War II. This is because, during those years, Manuilă and other Romanian scholars collaborated not just with the Germans but with the Anglo-Americans as well. Since Romania was at war with Great Britain and the United States, the contacts with these countries were naturally few and hard to establish, but they existed nevertheless. As will be shown in this chapter, in those years there was an exchange of maps with the Germans; at the same time the Romanians transmitted to London materials to be used for the elaboration of the Western plans for postwar restructuring of Eastern Europe.[2]

At the same time, it should be pointed out that Manuilă's and others' involvement in this project of the Antonescu government must not be rigidly linked to their political beliefs. Many Romanian intellectuals directly or indirectly supported the Antonescu government not because they loved totalitarian regimes, but because they felt only Antonescu would be capable of keeping order in the country and perhaps also of regaining its lost territories. Many of these scholars were trained in the Western tradition and held democratic convictions. Manuilă, despite his antiminority opinions, was perceived by many contemporaries, both before and after the war, as a democrat. In 1944 he became a leading member of the National Peasant Party. In the wake of Romania's turnaround on 23 August 1944, no one accused Manuilă of collaborating with the Antonescu regime. He kept his previous position as general director of the Central Institute of Statistics and joined the Sănătescu-Rădescu government as subsecretary of state with the Council of Ministers Presidency from October 1944 to 6 March 1945. Manuilă's task was to project a "reorganization of the State." The communists then forced Manuilă to resign from the institute in August 1947. No one reproached him for his wartime activity. Instead, he was accused of maintaining relations with the Americans (chiefly, though not only, with U.S. academics).[3] In these circumstances, Manuilă fled the country in 1948 and settled in the United States.

Sabin Manuilă's Activity in Ethnopolitics

Manuilă's papers, which were published for the most part in the 1930s and 1940s, make up a relatively rich corpus of works.[4] Some of them have been reprinted in recent years, and a few studies have appeared dealing with Manuilă's activity as a whole or in some specific areas.[5]

His first contributions dealt with social medicine and social hygiene. Trained as a physician—he studied medicine in Budapest from 1912 to 1919, and spent a year (1925/26) as a Rockefeller Foundation fellow at the Public Health School at Johns Hopkins University in Baltimore—Manuilă is considered the chief organizer of scientific statistics in Romania. His main contributions, however, related to demography, particularly ethnic demography. He concerned himself with ethnodemographic prognosis, a subject that failed to attract much interest in the late 1920s. His studies on the ethnic composition of Transylvania and the prospects of ethnodemographic relations in that province were significant in content and exemplary in their method. Manuilă documented the tendency of the Romanian population to experience more rapid demographic growth compared to ethnic minorities as a result of greater fertility, and also studied the romanianization of the towns, a process occurring through in-migrations at a time when Romanians preponderated in the rural hinterland.

Manuilă played an important role in introducing the idea of population exchanges, first to Romanian intellectual circles and then, in the summer of 1940, to the Romanian government agenda. Population exchanges with neighboring countries were mentioned in his writings as early as 1929.[6] In the summer of 1940 Manuilă engaged in documenting the Transylvanian "problem." That August he was part of the Romanian delegation sent first to the Romanian-Hungarian negotiations that were held in Turnu Severin, then to the second Vienna Award on 30 August 1940, at which the foreign ministers of Germany and Italy ruled in Hungary's favor. It was he who proposed a population exchange between Romania and Hungary, accompanied by a territorial adjustment.

From then on, Manuilă focused on the ethnic data of Romania not only to prove that ethnic Romanians were the majority of the population in the surrendered territories (besides northern Transylvania, which had been ceded to Hungary, they included Bessarabia and Northern Bukovina, which the Soviet Union had occupied since late June 1940), but also with an eye to a future ethnic homogenization of the country. Concerning the ethnic situation of various provinces, he wrote several studies, some of which were published in those years,[7] while others remained unpublished.

Under General (later Marshal) Ion Antonescu's government, Manuilă started to work on a population politics of the Romanian state, the core element of which was ethnic homogenization. Because his position at the top of the Central Institute of Statistics carried a lot of weight, Manuilă became an important person in the government's policymaking. The leading expert in population politics, he can safely be described as the gray eminence behind the ethnopolitics of the government. He not only developed the theory of ethnic homogenization, but was also directly involved in shaping Romania's state policy in this area. Marshal Antonescu and other high-ranking officials would consult with him on every population policy issue. While they did not always take his advice, he usually succeeded in bringing them round to his views.[8]

Sabin Manuilă was also involved in preparing the documentary material sustaining the borders of Romania in anticipation of the peace conference to be held. Manuilă worked in the Ethnic and Statistical Section of the Peace Bureau (Biroul Păcii), which was set up in June 1942 at the Ministry of Foreign Affairs in Bucharest, for exactly this purpose.[9] In 1940/41,

Manuilă elaborated several works on projects concerning the ethnic homogenization of the country. Destined for Antonescu, they were for the most part entitled *Population Policy*.[10] The most important of them was a project for population exchanges included in a memorandum to Antonescu of 15 October 1941.[11] It provided for exchanges of populations with neighboring countries (Hungary, Yugoslavia, Bulgaria, Ukraine in the USSR), which could involve territorial adjustments, depending on the numbers of people transferred in and out of the country. Ethnic Germans and Turks were to be repatriated, while the Jews and Gypsies, who lacked states of their own, were to be "transferred unilaterally"—a project that materialized as the partial deportation of both communities to Transnistria, the Soviet territory between the Dniester and the Bug rivers. These deportations resulted in the death of approximately 100,000 deportees and of even more Ukrainian Jews that lived in the region.[12] This constituted the Romanian segment of the Holocaust.

Manuilă's project was the first material to give the Antonescu government a plan of action in population politics. Strictly speaking, the government never turned it into an official program; nor did they ever adopt any such program, for that matter. Nevertheless, from 1941 to 1944, Romania's policy with respect to the ethnic minorities belonging to its neighbors and to its own ethnic Romanians living in neighboring states was largely consistent with Manuilă's ideas.

The government's steps in this area were as a rule preceded by statistical, economic, and other studies and reports supplied by Manuilă's institute. Some of the studies that referred to the Jews, including some that paved the way for anti-Jewish measures, have been already published and are a good indication of the important part the institute and Manuilă played in shaping government policy.[13]

Sabin Manuilă's Collaboration with German Scholars

Manuilă's wartime contacts with a number of German scholars should not be viewed from the sole perspective of his competence and interest in demography and ethnopolitics, but also from that of the special position the Central Institute of Statistics held in Romania at the time. Romania had no structure that could compare—in terms of organization, personnel, and so on—to Germany's vast network of bodies and institutions that were responsible for population policy. As was mentioned earlier, the idea of an ethnopolitical approach did not emerge in Romania until 1940. Aside from being Romania's chief expert in ethnopolitics, Manuilă had gathered at the institute almost all of the handful of other scholars who dealt or were beginning to deal with the issue. The ICS Office for Studies, which in 1941 hired many young researchers from the disbanded, well-known Romanian Social Institute (headed by Dimitrie Gusti), worked extensively on ethnopolitics. Manuilă's chief co-worker, Anton Golopenția, served as director of the office.

An interest in ethnopolitics also developed at the Ministry of Foreign Affairs, where a number of projects targeting specific regions or population groups (i.e., minority groups in Romania or ethnic Romanian groups in neighboring countries) were elaborated. These projects, which were actually built on ethnodemographic and other ICS-supplied data, worked out various aspects of the overall policy, such as international justifications for the planned population transfers.

Still, the ICS was the main center for ethnopolitical studies and the only one to which the Germans and other foreigners were given access. The institute employed various experts whose activities ranged from thorough scientific studies to development of propaganda material in diverse areas—statistics, demography, economics, history, geography, etc. Given this vast array of tasks, which in Germany were carried out by many different entities, the institute was an attractive resource to anybody who took interest in Romania.

Of course, the ICS was not the sole Romanian institution taken into consideration by German scientists. They and their institutions had contacts in the Romanian universities, the Romanian Academy, and other institutes. The Deutsches Wissenschaftliches Institut (German Cultural Institute) in Bucharest, headed by the romanist Ernst Gamillscheg (a member of the Westdeutsche Forschungsgemeinschaft or West German Research Society) was very active in promoting German-Romanian scientific contacts. Also, the research institutes of the German Ethnic Group in Romania (Deutsche Volksgruppe in Rumänien) were subordinated to the Southeast German Society in Vienna. But for the interests in the field of ethnopolitics, the ICS was the most important.[14]

Evidence of Manuilă's contacts with the Germans can now be found in but a few documents, as very little of the ICS archive for 1940–1944 is still available. This particular archive was destroyed in 1948/49 to wipe out the traces not only of the census but also of a sociological survey of the Romanians living east of the Dniester and Bug rivers in the Soviet Union. An ICS team headed by Golopenția had conducted the survey in 1942/43, when the Romanian government was laying the groundwork for the repatriation of those communities.[15] The Sabin Manuilă Collection in the Romanian National Archives currently contains the remains of that archive, including many Manuilă papers, most of them unpublished and virtually unknown, as well as a few of his letters. Other materials concerning him are kept at the Romanian Intelligence Service Archive. Unfortunately, access to this archive is restricted. Yet we do have materials in other archives and collections—papers of different types Manuilă sent to various institutions, official correspondence with those institutions, letters from or about him—that are illustrative of Manuilă's and the institute's contacts with the Germans.[16]

While the hard evidence available to us may be lacking, the ICS un-doubtedly had many contacts with the Germans during that period:

- Romania was an ally of Germany. Militarily and economically it was Germany's most important partner in Eastern and Southeastern Europe, so academics traveled frequently between the two countries.
- Several fellow workers of Manuilă's institute had contacts with Germany. Anton Golopenția, director of the ICS Office for Studies, was one of them. In the period from 1933 to 1936, he studied in Berlin, Leipzig, and Hamburg, earning his doctoral degree in Leipzig with a thesis entitled *Die Information der Staatsführung und die überlieferte Soziologie* (Supplying information to state leaders and traditional sociology) under the supervision of Hans Freyer.
- On their visits to Bucharest, German scientists, particularly those who were interested in Romanian statistics and ethnopolitics, but others too, would rarely fail to make at least a formal call at the ICS. These visits are mentioned in the institute's documents, but also in the reports of the Ministry of Foreign Affairs, which usually organized these visits. Among the best-noted guests were Hans Platzer, vice-chairman of the Statistical Institute of the Reich, who visited the ICS at the head of a delegation in September 1941,[17] the geographer Hugo Hassinger, who visited the ICS and met with Manuilă and Golopenția in April 1942,[18] as well as Friedrich Burgdörfer and Wilfried Krallert, to whom I will refer below.
- Identically, scientists of the ICS made informing visits to Germany. Between 7 February and 10 August 1943, the general subdirector of the institute, C. G. Georgescu, made a study trip to Switzerland, Italy, Germany, and Slovakia. In Germany he visited the Statistical Institute of Bavaria (Munich), the Statistical Office of Munich, the Statistical Institute of the Reich (Berlin), and Statistischer Zentralausschuss (Berlin).[19]
- In 1941, the ICS was ready to send 20 delegates to the congress of the German Statistical Society and of the Society of the Communal Statisticians called at Vienna for 1–7 September 1941, but the congress was postponed.[20]
- An exchange of published as well as unpublished materials was maintained between the ICS and various, especially Vienna-located, German institutions.

It is thus reasonable to conclude that the ICS was the Germans' primary source of statistical and demographic data on Romania, while the Romanians drew on the ICS for information on some German projects concerning Romania and Southeastern Europe.

Restructured by Manuilă and provided with first-rate experts, the ICS had developed into a flagship institution, and the government liked to present it as such.[21] But this characterization seems trivial compared to what I think were the truly significant aspects of this relation, as the following sections will demonstrate.

Friedrich Burgdörfer's Participation in the Romanian Census of April 1941

The Bavarian Statistical Office's chairman Friedrich Burgdörfer—"Germany's greatest demographer," as Manuilă portrayed him[22]—was invited as an observer to the Romanian general census of 6 April 1941. He was in Romania from 31 March to 11 April 1941. During that visit he went to the ICS and talked with Manuilă on the census preparations and methodology. Accompanied by A. Golopenția, he made a six-day field trip, most of it spent in regions with multiethnic populations, to see how the census was carried out. On 11 April he had an audience with Marshal Antonescu.

Burgdörfer published an account of the 1941 Romanian census in *Allgemeines Statistisches Archiv* (1941/42),[23] in which he praised the method the Romanian statisticians had used and estimated it ensured an accurate count in terms of ethnic origin, religion, and language. He also expressed a special concern about the identification of the Jews and the Gypsies.[24] In his report he did not fail to mention that the Jewish question had come up at his meeting with Antonescu (p. 318). Burgdörfer wrote that in Romania the Jewish problem is "of painful importance" (ibid.). As for the Gypsies, he depicted them as a "problem of capital importance to Romania" (p. 319). The Antonescu government had not yet zeroed in on the Gypsies and would not take any steps against them until May 1942. As is known, some of them, the Gypsies who were considered to be "problems," would later be deported to Transnistria. Burgdörfer's emphasis on this population was probably intended as a suggestion to the Romanians.

Alessandro Molinari, director of the Statistical Institute of Italy, also participated in the census as an observer. Buttingha Wichers, subdirector of the Permanent Office of the International Institute of Statistics, was also invited, but could not participate. By inviting leading statisticians from the two countries that seemed poised to dictate Europe's fate, Manuilă intended to prove that the Romanian census was properly designed and carried out. The 1941 census was a giant, extremely complex operation that involved huge effort, for in Manuilă and Marshal Antonescu's views, it was supposed to guide the population politics of the Romanian state. The ICS published provisional results of the census in 1944.[25]

The Germans showed great interest in the census of April 1941, as well as in the regional censuses and inventories made later. H. Platzer, mentioned above, visited the ICS in September 1941 just to inform himself about the processing of the census. From Bucharest he traveled to Czernovitz (Romanian: Cernăuți), where he visited the headquarters of the

project of inventorying the population and goods in Northern Bukovina
and Bessarabia, territories recently liberated by Romanian troops, an operation then in progress. This complex inventory was personally conducted
by Sabin Manuilă.

Sabin Manuilă's Contributions to *Deutsches Archiv für Landes- und Volksforschung* and the Controversy over the Number of the Jews in Romania

A Manuilă article called *Das Judenproblem in Rumänien zahlenmäßig gesehen*[26]
appeared in *Deutsches Archiv für Landes- und Volksforschung* in 1941. As shown
in an editorial note, it came as a response to two other articles the journal had
published in 1939: one by Wilfried Krallert, concerning the Romanian census of 1930,[27] and another by Hans Bobek reviewing the book of Peter
Heinz Seraphim, *Das Judentum im osteuropäischen Raum* (Essen, 1938).[28]

Manuilă's article was actually conceived as a reply to speculations on
the strength of the Jewish population in Romania. According to the 1930
census he had supervised, 728,115 persons identified themselves as ethnic
Jews; 518,754 declared Yiddish to be their mother tongue; and 756,930
were of Mosaic religion. In the circumstances of the resurgence of the anti-
Semitism in the late 1930s, some far-right circles were putting the total
number of the Jews at 1 million, 2 million, or even 2.5 million. The latter
numbers had been adopted in German literature as well. Manuilă's response in *Deutsches Archiv* described the criteria on which the census had
been based and showed that in 1930 Romania's Jewish population truly
numbered around 800,000.

He went on to explain that the Jewish problem in Romania lay in the
economic power of that minority, most of whose members were involved
in trade, industries, and liberal professions, rather than in their numbers.
As Manuilă put it, "die jüdische Frage in Rumänien ein *qualitatives* und
kein quantitatives Problem ist" (emphasis added).[29]

Manuilă had already pressed this point and even gone into more detail
on previous occasions, including an ample lecture he gave at a meeting of
the Historical Section of the Romanian Academy on 24 February 1939
about the ethnic structure of Romania based on the results of the 1930 census. There, too, he tackled the number of the Jews in an attempt to end the
dispute on this topic. Just as in his German article, he argued that "the
problem of the ethnic Jewish group is not a matter of numbers, but rather
a serious economic and social problem arising from *the function the Jews are
playing in our country's every sort of manifestation*" (emphasis in original).[30]

Manuilă also took up the topic of the number of the Jews in Romania
during the talks he had with Burgdörfer in Bucharest in April 1941. The
German statistician eventually accepted in his article that the number
reported by the 1930 census was the right one:

Following the documented conversations I had with Dr. Manuilă and his coworkers, I came to the conclusion that these estimates [i.e., putting the numbers of the Jewish population at 1 or 2 million] cannot be sustained and there is no reason to doubt the results provided by Romanian statistics.... The results of the 1930 census ... reflect to some extent the real number of the Jews in Romania. At the worst, this can be considered a minimum number to which an extra number of, say, 10 or 20 percent, representing the Jews that are not of Mosaic religion, should be added.[31]

From these two papers one can see that Manuilă's anti-Semitism was economic rather than racial. In this he differs from other Romanian scientists of the time, who spoke of the Jews as a "racial threat." As I have already mentioned, in his project of ethnic cleansing from October 1941 Manuilă advocated the "unilateral transfer" over the border of the Jews and Gypsies. Arguments of a racial nature appear in a few of Manuilă's texts from 1940/41 when it comes to the Gypsies. Certainly, Manuilă's eclectic thought was influenced to some extent by the eugenicists.[32]

Sabin Manuilă's Collaboration with Wilfried Krallert

Wilfried Krallert[33] was the director of Publications Office Vienna *(Publikationsstelle Wien)*, an organization that focused on Romania and Hungary.[34] It is uncertain how far back the contacts between Manuilă and Krallert went. They certainly met during the second Vienna Award (August 1940), where the former was an expert with the Romanian delegation and the latter also served as an expert. An ethnic map by Krallert—in fact, only an extract from it representing the ethnic German groups—was used in drawing the border between Romania and Hungary.[35]

During a trip to Romania in June 1941, Krallert visited the Central Institute of Statistics and talked with Manuilă, who made a mention of their meeting in a report to Marshal Antonescu of 7 June 1941.[36] On this occasion Krallert presented the institute with the ethnic map of Greater Romania (44 map sheets), scale 1:200,000, drawn by the Publications Office Vienna. The institute got five copies as part of an exchange of maps, and the General Staff of the Army received ten other copies. Krallert also visited the ICS on 19 November 1941 and 20 February 1942.[37]

Both Manuilă and Krallert and their institutions collaborated well with one another, according to Manuilă's reports. In one such report of 20 November 1941, Manuilă informed Antonescu at length about the German scholar and his contacts with the ICS. "Dr. Krallert has *a relation of collaboration and mutual favors with our Institute*," Manuilă said and underscored, continuing:

The Institute has been of help by informing him on the latest Romanian publications and sending him copies as well as various statistical data he has requested. In return for our favors that have allowed him to become a perfect source of information for the German Foreign Ministry with regard to Romania's geographical and political concerns, Mr. Krallert has done us many good turns, providing us some unpublished results of the 1931 Yugoslavian census as well as copies of some rare maps and texts held by the German libraries. To the Institute our relation with Mr. Krallert is a valuable documentation source regarding Germany."[38]

The same report listed the projects and missions in which Krallert had been or was still involved:

- Krallert's preoccupation for gathering ethnic data from censuses that were conducted in Southeast European countries, and his visits to the institutes of statistics and geography operating in the capitals of those countries;
- His 1939 report on the Romanian census, which Manuilă described as a "most complimentary presentation of the method used in the 1930 Romanian census";
- The task Krallert had been assigned in 1939 by the German Foreign Ministry to map the ethnic results of the 1930 census broken down by villages, how the drawings were proceeding, and the dates of their appearance;
- Krallert's appointment to the top of the Südostdeutsche Forschungs-gemeinschaft (Southeast German Research Society);
- His initiation, in this capacity, of a study on the hungarianization of the Germans (*Schwaben*) living in Satmar and Banat and on their regermanization under the Romanian administration;[39]
- His supervision of *Volkstum im Südosten*, a Vienna-based periodical that, Manuilă said, "systematically refuted the Hungarian case for a Hungarian hegemony over Southeastern Europe or for Hungary's posturing as a mediator between the Reich and the Southeast European countries. Mr. Krallert firmly sided with the Romanians in the ethnic map controversy stirred up by the Hungarian publicists";
- Krallert's work, after the beginning of the war on Yugoslavia, on the German teams gathering statistical and geographical material, and his seizure, in this capacity, of the material of the Yugoslavian Institute of Statistics and Geography in Belgrade;
- His recent appointment to head "an operation to gather geographical and statistical material as well as documents for a future White Paper covering the entire USSR territory captured from the Soviets";
- And finally that "according to our findings, the German Foreign Ministry is instructing every official that is being sent to Romania on matters of statistics and political literature to contact Mr. Krallert beforehand." (Manuilă naturally judged by his own experience of the German visitors to the ICS.)

Manuilă obviously knew Krallert fairly well, which seems to indicate a close collaboration, and since he was even informed of the German's secret missions, some mutual trust must have developed between the two of them.

Manuilă hoped that by supplying ethnic, demographic, and other data to the Germans he would convince them the Romanian side was right on Transylvania. And in his view, Krallert's ethnic map of Romania proved that this goal had been attained.[40] This map was so significant to him not only because it showed the real ethnic composition of northern Transylvania and therefore the unfairness of the Vienna solution, but also because the Romanian side could rely on it as evidence in support of its case. Manuilă alluded to this advantage in a special report to Antonescu on this map: "The interest and importance of this map lie, on the one hand, in its being made by the German Government, so it can easily be cited in any talks with this government concerning the detached territories; on the other hand, the data supplied by the Romanian census have been preferred over the results of the Hungarian censuses."[41] There is no way to check whether Krallert told the truth when he assured Manuilă the ethnic map of Greater Romania had not been handed to anyone else abroad and had been denied to Hungary, which had asked for it repeatedly.[42]

For Manuilă, the ethnic map elaborated by Krallert's team was very important. Until that moment no detailed ethnic map of Romania had existed. The results of the 1930 census were published in 1938, but the Romanians had not yet succeeded in drawing up an ethnic map that illustrated these new data. Such a map was indispensable for ICS studies, as well as for the plans of ethnic and territorial changes the Romanians were working on. In late 1941 a team of the Geographical Society started work on an ethnic map of Romania under the guidance of the geographer Vintilă Mihăilescu. The map, which would not be finished and printed until the end of the war, would be used at the Peace Conference in Paris in 1946.[43] In the meantime, Krallert's map made up for this lack. Since it noted the ethnic situation as was recorded in the 1930 census data, it was convenient for the Romanians and was largely used in certain government institutions in Bucharest. Up to the end of the war, the Romanians also had at their disposal for their studies and plans another German map: the ethnographic map of Romania by Paul Langhans. This map was printed in 1939 but had ben recalled by the German authorities at the request of the Hungarian government. These two German maps served as cartographical support for the population exchange projects elaborated by the Antonescu government.

The older and newer foreign maps that Krallert procured, in copy form, from the German libraries for Manuilă—as is apparent from the archival material mentioned above—concerned the territory of not only Greater Romania, but the neighboring countries as well. Because—as the Romanians believed—there were no accurate ethnographic maps of these countries, this deficiency was remedied with foreign maps. Manuilă was of the opinion that the Bucharest government's standpoint on the Romanian population in these countries could be supported very well by means of the foreign maps.[44]

It is worth noting that during that period the ICS too was working on an ethnic map of Romania based on the 1930 census data and including drawings for every county. The document was made under Manuilă's supervision. Meanwhile, controversy over ethnographic maps of Transylvania had broken out between Romania and Hungary: each side would publish maps of its own that sparked an outcry from the other side. In their publications in foreign languages the Romanians and the Hungarians accused each other of tendentiousness.[45] The dispute even reached Wilfried Krallert's periodical, *Volkstum im Südosten*, which in 1941 published an article by Josef Reissner called *The argument or battle between Hungary's and Romania's ethnographic maps* (in German). As mentioned earlier, Manuilă regarded this article as favorable to the Romanian side.[46]

The various cartographic efforts above referred to the ethnic situation of Romania based on the 1930 census. The German experts praised both the manner in which the Romanians carried out this project and the volumes containing the census data, published by the ICS. Krallert deemed the census to be "an exceptional scientific achievement in the field of statistics."[47] There were several other panegyrics of this kind.[48]

With Antonescu's approval, the ICS also supplied data to Krallert on the Romanian census of April 1941. (These were provisional data, of course, since the first partial results of this census were not published until 1944.) In 1943, relying on these data, Publications Office Vienna put out a study for inside use, entitled *Bevölkerungszählung in Rumänien 1941*.[49] The relation worked both ways: Krallert-supplied data on the Yugoslavian census of 1931 were used by the Romanian experts to prepare several studies on the ethnic Romanians living in Yugoslavia and on the Yugoslavian provinces of Banat and Timok, which were home to a numerous Romanian population.

This information exchange with the Germans, however, was confined to the Romanian censuses of 1930 and 1941. The results of another census that was conducted under Manuilă's direct supervision in Bessarabia and Northern Bukovina in the fall of 1941 were not disclosed to the Germans. They remained classified, due partly to the deportation of the Jews from these two provinces and partly to a planned ethnic mass restructuring of those areas by transferring their Ukrainian and Russian population east of the Dniester and bringing in ethnic Romanians from the Soviet territories.[50] Yet Krallert did manage to get data on the population of these provinces from intelligence sources. The German scholar was afraid the Romanians would refuse to collaborate with him in the future if they found out.[51]

Remarks

The facts outlined in this chapter are, I think, the most important aspects of the Romanian-German wartime contacts concerning ethnopolitics. Since my sources were confined to the Romanian archives, I have mostly looked at these contacts from a Romanian perspective; factoring in the conclusions of researches in neighboring states would complicate the picture considerably. This ethnopolitical collaboration between two countries bound by a close political and military alliance remains an interesting, even challenging, subject for historians.

Notes

1. For this project of the Antonescu government, see Viorel Achim, "Schimbul de populaţie în viziunea lui Sabin Manuilă" (The Population exchange in Sabin Manuilă's views), *Revista istorică* 13, nos. 5–6 (2002): 133–150. Some data are also in Mariana Hausleitner, "Auf dem Weg zur 'Ethnokratie.' Rumänien in den Jahren des Zweiten Weltkrieges," in *Kooperation und Verbrechen. Formen der "Kollaboration" im östlichen Europa 1939–1945*, ed. Babette Quinkert, Christoph Dieckmann, and Tatjana Tönsmeyer (Göttingen, 2003), 78–112.
2. In November 1943, Vasile Stoica, the first plenipotentiary minister at the Ministry of Foreign Affairs and the President of the Commission for Co-ordination of the Works of Preparation of the Documentation concerning the International Position, Rights and Interests of Romania, sent to Great Britain, with the help of a Romanian diplomat in Ankara, a parcel of maps concerning the ethnic situation of Romania. Arhiva Naţională Istorică Centrală (ANIC), fond Vasile Stoica, dosar II/203.
3. This was an old accusation. Radu Lecca, the government official in charge of the Jewish problem, suspected Manuilă of working for U.S. espionage: Radu Lecca, *Eu i-am salvat pe evreii din România* (It's me who saved the Jews from Romania), ed. Alexandru V. Diţă (Bucharest, 1994), 235, 285–286. According to Lecca (ibid., 286), the German ambassador to Bucharest during the war, Manfred von Killinger, also suspected Manuilă and reported him to Marshal Antonescu.
4. Some of Sabin Manuilă's publications: "Evoluţia demografică a oraşelor şi minorităţilor etnice din Transilvania" (The demographical evolution of towns and ethnic minorities in Transilvania), *Arhiva pentru Ştiinţa şi Reforma Socială* 8, nos. 1–3 (1929): 91–212; "România şi revizionismul. Consideraţii etnografice şi demografice" (Romania and revisionism: Ethnographic and demographic considerations), *Arhiva pentru Ştiinţa şi Reforma Socială* 12, nos. 1–2 (1934): 55–82; "Le développement des centres urbains en Transylvanie," *Revue de Transylvanie* 1, no. 4 (1934/35): 445–460; *Populaţia României* (The population of Romania) (Bucharest, 1937) (with D. C. Georgescu); *Aspects démographiques de la Transylvanie* (Bucharest, 1938); *Etude ethnographique sur la population de la Roumanie/Ethnological survey of the population of Romania* (Bucharest, 1938); "Consideraţii asupra prezentării grafice a etnografiei României" (Considerations on the graphic representation of Romania's ethnography), *Analele Academiei Române*, Memoriile Secţiunii Istorice, series III, vol. 21 (1939): 357–371; *The Population of Dobrogea* (Bucharest, 1940); *Studiu etnografic asupra populaţiei României* (Ethnographic survey of the population of Romania) (Bucharest, 1940); *Structure et évolution de la population rurale*. With the abridged English version (Bucharest, 1940). See also the titles in footnotes 7 and 26. Part of

Manuilă's oeuvre was reprinted in Sabin Manuilă, *Studies on the Historical Demography of Romania/Études sur la démographie historique de la Roumanie*, ed. Sorina Bolovan and Ioan Bolovan (Cluj-Napoca, 1992).

5. For Sabin Manuilă's life and work, especially in the field of demography, see Sorina Bolovan and Ioan Bolovan, "Introduction," in Manuilă, *Studies*, 7–17; Sorina Bolovan, "Sabin Manuilă's Contribution to the Research of Urban Population of Romania," *Transylvanian Review* 1, no. 1 (1992): 56–64; Louis Roman, "Sabin Manuilă et la démographie historique," *Transylvanian Review* 3, no. 1 (1994): 47–68; Roman, "Demografia istorică în opera lui Sabin Manuilă" (Historical demography in the works of Sabin Manuilă), in *Sabin Manuilă. Istorie și demografie. Studii privind societatea românească între secolele XVI—XX* (Sabin Manuilă. History and demography. Studies on Romanian society in the 16th–20th centuries), ed. S. Bolovan and I. Bolovan (Cluj-Napoca, 1995), 26–40; Vladimir Trebici, "Dr. Sabin Manuilă, organizatorul statisticii științifice în România" (Dr. Sabin Manuilă, the organizer of scientific statistics in Romania), in *Sabin Manuilă. Istorie și demografie*, 7–25; Gheorghe Buzatu, "Noi informații privind viața și opera lui Sabin Manuilă" (New information concerning the life and work of Sabin Manuilă), in *Sabin Manuilă. Istorie și demografie*, 41–55; Sorina Bolovan and Ioan Bolovan, "Problemele demografice ale Transilvaniei între știință și politică (1920–1945). Studiu de caz" (Transylvania's demographic problems between science and politics, 1920–1945. A case study), in *Transilvania între medieval și modern* (Transylvania between Medieval and Modern), ed. Camil Mureșan (Cluj-Napoca, 1996), 119–131; Achim, "Schimbul de populație." See also the title in footnote 11.

6. For Manuilă's preoccupation with population exchange, see Achim, "Schimbul de populație."

7. See especially Sabin Manuilă, *Die Folgen der Teilung Siebenbürgens in demographischer Hinsicht* (Bucharest, 1943); English version: *The Vienna Award and Its Demographical Consequences* (Bucharest, 1945); republished in Manuilă, *Studies*, 135–165.

8. At a cabinet meeting of 16 November 1943, Antonescu berated Manuilă for overlooking his desire that residents of Northern Bukovina should be counted as Romanians if their ancestors had been Romanians, even though they no longer spoke Romanian but Ukrainian at home. Manuilă, who had conducted the census, had put them down as Ukrainians. Commenting on this, Antonescu exclaimed: "Such is the policy of Mr. Sabin Manuilă, who once said to me we'd lost our case in Northern Bukovina and we'd better have the courage to acknowledge it. I then retorted to him: You may have lost your case, but I haven't, nor has the Romanian nation. As far as we're concerned, even if we lost it in the past, we can still win it back today." ANIC, fond Președinția Consiliului de Miniștri—Cabinet (PCM-Cabinet), dosar 375/1943, f. 357.

9. For a few data on this body, see Ion Ardeleanu, "Biroul Păcii: proiecte privind soluționarea problemei frontierelor României și realizarea unor bune relații în Balcani (1942–1943)" (The Peace Bureau: Projects concerning the solution to the border issues of Romania and the establishment of good relations in the Balkans, 1942–1943), *Europa XXI* 1–2 (1992/93): 128–132.

10. For survey of some of these works, see Achim, "Schimbul de populație," 140ff.

11. For this project, see Viorel Achim, "The Romanian Population Exchange Project Elaborated by Sabin Manuilă in October 1941," *Annali dell'Istituto storico italo-germanico in Trento* 27 (2001): 593–617; Achim, "Schimbul de populație," 141ff.

12. The number of persons who were murdered or who died in Transnistria under Romanian administration is disputed. See, more recently, Jean Ancel, *Transnistria, 1941–1942: The Romanian Mass Murder Campaigns*, 3 vols. (Jerusalem, 2003), 1:509ff.

13. *Evreii din România între anii 1940–1944* (The Jews in Romania between 1940 and 1944), 2, *Problema evreiască în stenogramele Consiliului de Miniștri* (The Jewish question in the shorthand records of the Council of Ministers), ed. Lya Benjamin (Bucharest, 1996), 72–85, 107–113, 124–125.

14. See Frank-Rutger Hausmann's contribution in this volume.

15. See Anton Golopenția, *Ultima carte* (The last book), ed. Sanda Golopenția (Bucharest, 2001), 487–488, 547.

16. A Sabin Manuilă Collection is also to be found at Stanford University's Hoover Institution Archives. A Romanian researcher who took no particular interest in Manuilă's work on population politics happened to take a look at this collection fifteen years ago. Part of it, namely Box 24, was due for declassification on 1 August 1988 (Buzatu, "Noi informații," 42), but I don't know whether anyone has since been curious to find out what was in there. It might have had to do precisely with population politics, but this is just a guess.

17. *Cronicarul Institutului Central de Statistică*, no. 1 (1 August 1942): 24.

18. ANIC, fond Sabin Manuilă, dosar X/206. See also *Cronicarul Institutului Central de Statistică*, no. 1, 25; Michael Fahlbusch, *Wissenschaft im Dienst der nationalsozialistischen Politik? Die "Volksdeutschen Forschungsgemeinschaften" von 1931–1945* (Baden-Baden, 1999), 651–652.

19. *Cronicarul Institutului Central de Statistică*, no. 2 (31 December 1943): 20–21.

20. *Cronicarul Institutului Central de Statistică*, no. 1, 25.

21. This happened, for example, when the foreign media correspondents to Bucharest toured the institute on 27 March 1942. D. C. Georgescu, P. Vlad, and A. Golopenția spoke on ICS activity on that occasion. *Cronicarul Institutului Central de Statistică*, no. 1, 25.

22. In a report to the Minister of Foreign Affairs from 15 July 1942: Arhiva Ministerului Afacerilor Externe, Fond 71/Germania, dosar 89, f. 120.

23. Friedrich Burgdörfer, "Die rumänische Volkszählung," *Allgemeines Statistisches Archiv*, Bd. 30, Heft III (1941/1942): 302–322; Romanian translation: "Recensământul general al României din 1941. Dare de seamă," *Analele Institutului Statistic al României* 1 (1942): 323–337.

24. Chapter 9 of the report bears the title "Remarks concerning the Jewish and the Gypsy problem" (Burgdörfer, "Die rumänische Volkszählung," 317–320).

25. *Recensământul populației României dela 6 aprilie 1941. Date sumare provizorii* (The Census of the population of Romania of 6 April 1941. Summary provisional data) (Bucharest, 1944).

26. Sabin Manuilă, "Das Judenproblem in Rumänien zahlenmäßig gesehen," *Deutsches Archiv für Landes- und Volksforschung* 5 (1941): 603–613. Brief considerations on this article appear in Fahlbusch, *Wissenschaft*, 638; Michael Fahlbusch, "Politische Beratung in der NS-Volkstumspolitik: Südostdeutsche Forschungsgemeinschaft Wien," *Annali dell'Istituto storico italo-germanico in Trento* 27 (2001): 486.

27. Wilfried Krallert, "Geschichte und Methode der Bevölkerungszählungen im Südosten. 1. Rumänien. Mit besonderer Rücksichtnahme auf die Zählung des Jahres 1930 und ihre Veröffentlichung," *Deutsches Archiv für Landes- und Volksforschung* 3 (1939): 489–508.

28. Hans Bobek, "Das Judentum im osteuropäischen Raum. Betrachtungen zu dem gleichnamigen Werk von P. H. Seraphim," *Deutsches Archiv für Landes- und Volksforschung* 3 (1939): 697–706.

29. Manuilă, "Das Judenproblem," 608.

30. Manuilă, "Considerații asupra prezentării grafice," 365.

31. Burgdörfer, "Die rumänische Volkszählung," 318.

32. See Viorel Achim, *Țiganii în istoria României* (The Gypsies in the history of Romania) (Bucharest, 1998), 137; Maria Bucur, *Eugenics and Modernization in Interwar Romania* (Pittsburgh, 2002), 146–147.

33. The existence of some contacts between S. Manuilă and W. Krallert is mentioned in Fahlbusch, "Politische Beratung," 486–487.

34. For Publications Office Vienna, see Fahlbusch, *Wissenschaft*, 628–642; Fahlbusch, "Politische Beratung," 481–490, and his contribution in this volume.

35. See Fahlbusch, *Wissenschaft*, 634.

36. ANIC, fond PCM-Cabinet, dosar 381/1942, f. 350 bis.

37. *Cronicarul Institutului Central de Statistică*, no. 1, 24–25.

38. ANIC, fond PCM-Cabinet, dosar 560/1942, f. 16-16 bis.

39. This research was finalized in a work elaborated by Marie Luise Thomé from Publikationsstelle Wien, but published under a pseudonym: Sepp Pfeiffer, *Zur Geschichte der Magyarisierung des Sathmarer Deutschtums* (Leipzig, 1941).

40. *Volkstumskarte von Rumänien* von Wilfried Krallert (1941), auf Grund der Ergebnisse der amtlichen rumänischen Zählung über die Volkszugehörigkeit von 1930 (Recensământul general al populației României 1930, Vol. II, Bukarest 1938) (dargestellt auf den Blättern der Generalkarte von Mitteleuropa), 44 Blätter im Maßstab 1:200.000.

41. ANIC, fond PCM-Cabinet, dosar 381/1941, f. 350 bis.

42. Ibid., dosar 560/1942, f. 16.

43. *Carte ethnique de la Roumanie d'après le recensement roumain de l'anné 1930* par Vintilă Mihăilescu, professeur a l'Université de Bucarest. Echelle de 1:200.000 (Bucharest, n.d.).

44. From a memorandum Manuilă sent to Marshal Antonescu on 9 April 1943: "[B]ecause of the lack of honest ethnographic maps in the neighboring countries, we don't know the situation of Romaniandom [*Românism*] in these countries…. Nevertheless, Romaniandom constituted a reality so manifest that, despite all tendencies of falsification, Romaniandom appears massively in the course of the nineteenth and twentieth centuries. For these reasons the Romanian thesis can be supported very well with a complete collection of foreign ethnographic maps, drawn up even without the aid of the Romanian science." (ANIC, fond Președinția Consiliului de Miniștri (PCM), dosar 1246/1943, f. 2).

45. An ICS file containing materials concerning the Romanian-Hungarian dispute over the ethnic maps: ANIC, fond PCM, dosar 1246/1943.

46. Manuilă made this judgement also in the memorandum of 9 April 1943: ibid., f. 3.

47. Krallert, "Geschichte und Methode," 504.

48. Egon Lendl, "Das letzte rumänische Volkszählungswerk. Statistische Unterlagen einer politischen Streitfrage—Erste Zählung nach neuen Grundsätzen," *Südost-Echo* 10, no. 32 (Vienna, 9 August 1940). A survey of the two papers of Krallert and Lendl, in Anton Golopenția, "Recensământul românesc din 1930 văzut de statisticieni germani" (The Romanian census of 1930 seen by German statisticians), *Excelsior* 6, no. 17 (1941); republished in *Recensământul României din 1941. Lămurirea opiniei publice. Proclamații și apeluri. Studii, articole, reportaje, umor. Insigne, medalii, afișe* (Romania's census of 1941. Explanation to the public opinion. Proclamations and appeals. Studies, articles, reports, humor. Badges, medals, posters) (Bucharest, 1941), 235–239.

49. Fahlbusch, *Wissenschaft*, 637.

50. On the Romanian plans for Bessarabia and Bukovina, see Viorel Achim, "Proiectul guvernului de la București vizând schimbul de populație româno-ruso-ucrainean (1943)" (The Project of the government in Bucharest concerning the Romanian-Russian-Ukrainian population exchange [1943]), *Revista istorică* 11, nos. 5–6 (2000): 395–421.

51. Fahlbusch, *Wissenschaft*, 637–638.

Chapter 8

PALATINES ALL OVER THE WORLD
Fritz Braun, a German Emigration Researcher in
National Socialist Population Policy

✦ ✦ ✦

Wolfgang Freund

Do you know your family tree? Are you interested in your family's history? Does your family have German origins, especially Palatine origins? If so, you might be in contact with the German genealogists and migration researchers who know best the local and regional history of those who left Germany in the last two centuries to start their lives over in North America. Many of those who left the Palatinate in southwestern Germany for the New World went to Pennsylvania, where genealogical interest is quite strong today. That state's genealogists often ask their Palatine colleagues for help in tracing family histories to their German beginnings.

Perhaps the most eminent of these Palatine migration researchers was Fritz Braun, Ph.D. (1905–1976), of Kaiserslautern in the Palatinate. In the 1950s and 1960s, he headed the Palatine documentation and research center on migration history, the Heimatstelle Pfalz (Home Center Palatinate), the nucleus for today's Institut für pfälzische Geschichte und Volkskunde (Institute for Palatine History and Folklife Studies)[1] in Kaiserslautern. At the Heimatstelle Pfalz Braun recorded about three hundred thousand Palatine migrations on card files. Because of his intensive research on Palatines who had emigrated to North America, he kept up good relations with American genealogists, many of whom visited him in Kaiserslautern; he often is cited in American family histories.[2] Besides these genealogical contacts Braun developed a partnership between Lancaster County, Pennsylvania, and the district of Kaiserslautern. He was many times honored for his work on the migration history of the Palatines, and in 1973 was awarded the Order of the Federal Republic of Germany. He also was honored for his studies on the family histories of Americans: in 1958 he was given the Freedom of Frederick, Maryland, and in 1976 he became an honorary member of the Pennsylvania German Society.[3] What most of his genealogist friends and correspondents on both shores of the Atlantic ignored was that Fritz Braun received his first important awards not in the 1950s, but in the 1930s under the regime of Adolf Hitler. For example, the revisionist Volksbund für das Deutschtum im Ausland (League for Germans Abroad, VDA) had awarded Braun the Great Silver Badge of Honor "For Work on Germandom." In addition, the Nationalsozialisti-scher Deutscher Studentenbund (National Socialist German Students League, NSDStB) honored his political engagement with Silver Badge of Honor number 338.[4]

This chapter will uncover the intriguing twentieth-century history of Palatine emigration research and its political implications, especially during the Third Reich. A short overview of the current state of research on Nazi migration history reveals that much work is still to be done. True, some studies have been done on the national socialist institutions connected to migration research, such as Stuttgart's Deutsches Ausland-Institut (German Foreign Institute, DAI).[5] In addition, there is some new light being shed on the Third Reich's migration research from essays on the *Volksdeutsche Forschungsgemeinschaften* (ethnic German research societies, VFG), as well as on North American migration research, particularly by the Übersee-Forschungsgemeinschaft (Overseas Research Society).[6] A few Palatine emigration studies were also introduced by brief descriptions of the history of migration research in Germany, including some lines on its Nazi history.[7] However, neither scholars of German and Palatine emigration research nor genealogists have ever investigated the history of their own discipline under National Socialism.[8]

Braun's prewar career was closely connected to Nazi cultural institutions in Josef Bürckel's *Gau* (National Socialist Party district). Bürckel was *Gauleiter* (party district head) of the *Gau* Palatinate, to which he annexed both the Saarland in 1935 and the former French department of the Moselle in 1940. Therefore, his *Gau*—and all of its institutions—often changed its name: to the Saar-Palatinate in 1936 and to the Westmark (Western Marches) in 1941. Fritz (actually Philipp Peter Friedrich) Braun was born on 11 March 1905 in Metz, in the part of the Lorraine that from 1871 to 1918 was annexed by the German Empire. After World War I, he and his family were no longer able to stay in Lorraine, now recuperated by France, and decided to move to Germany. After his graduation from high school, Braun studied natural sciences at the universities of Heidelberg, Munich, and Bonn, where he received his Ph.D. in 1933. From 1934 to 1935 he was an assistant at the Institut für geschichtliche Landeskunde der Rheinlande (Institute for Historical Regional Studies of the Rhineland) at the University of Bonn, the center of Western German ethnic studies. Braun made a career in the fields of ethnic politics and of research on German populations in foreign countries. His personal experiences as a youth might have had something to do with this. From 1933 to 1936 he was the Saar expert at the Reich's direction for the German student body. Probably in these years he became a member of the NSDStB. From 1933 to 1935 he headed the department for Germandom near the border and in other foreign countries of the professors' association of the University of Bonn. Braun was a protégé of Kurt Kölsch, the regional head of cultural affairs in the NSDAP. Having headed up of the VDA's Saar department since 1934, Braun took over as the regional VDA manager when the Saarland was annexed to the Palatinate in 1935.[9] He kept this office until July 1936. During the same period he was an expert consultant in the regional NSDAP's department for border and foreign countries. After already holding offices in the NSDAP, he joined the party in March 1936.[10]

From July 1936 to spring 1945 Braun was secretary of the association Mittelstelle Saarpfalz "Landsleute drinnen und draußen" (Saar-Palatinate Mediation Center "Countrymen Inside and Outside").[11] Following the example of other regional emigration research centers in Germany, created as of 1934 primarily under the auspices of the VDA,[12] the *Gau's* Nazi cultural organizations founded the Mittelstelle Saarpfalz in Kaiserslautern in June 1936. Its purpose was to do research on the regional migration history and to serve as an interface between the region's inhabitants and the descendants of the historically emigrated. Kölsch had no problem pushing through Braun's candidacy to head the Mittelstelle.[13] Thus, Braun became one of the Saarland's rare academics who took an overall leading role in the *Gau*. He became not only head of the Mittelstelle, but at the same time head of the migration research department in the Saarpfälzisches Institut für Landes- und Volksforschung (Saar-Palatine Institute for Research on Region and People) in Kaiserslautern.[14] Although the Mittelstelle moved into the Saarpfälzisches Institut, it remained an organizationally, legally, and scientifically independent association. Aside from the scientific institute, it became the *Gau's* most important research institution. Whereas during World War II the Saarpfälzisches Institut lost almost all its researchers to the military, the Mittelstelle, which was financed by local and regional authorities,[15] managed to extend its resources and to profit from the institute's empty rooms.[16] From the end of the 1930s on the VDA and the DAI bore considerable shares of the costs.[17]

The Mittelstelle had the task of determining the Saar-Palatine population share given over time to Germandom abroad. Then it was to document the great successes that Palatine descendants had achieved all over the world. It also established direct links to Germans abroad,[18] especially to the descendants of German emigrants who lived in the Balkans or in North America.[19] In cooperation with local and national Nazi authorities, Braun established a central card file which intended to secure the names of "all the Saar-Palatines living abroad."[20] By the mid 1940s the archives of the Mittelstelle had registered almost one hundred thousand migration cases.[21] The Mittelstelle was proud of its "extensive kinship card file, which (was) rarely found anywhere else in Germany."[22] The bridge to the "outpost of Germandom" was provided by an annual *Heimatbrief* (Letter from Home). The *Letter from Home*, also sent by other Nazi emigration research centers, served as propaganda to create a common German ethnic consciousness among other countries' ethnic Germans. Every year ten thousand copies of the Saar-Palatine *Letter from Home* were delivered free to German households abroad.[23] The Mittelstelle could not complain of a shortage of personnel, not even during World War II.[24] In summer 1939 the German American Friedrich Schlenz arrived, collaborating at least until the middle of 1942. He replaced Braun, in his absence, in the Mittelstelle in Kaiserslautern. During the first half of the 1920s, Schlenz had emigrated to the United States, been naturalized, and done work for Germandom in the National Socialist "German American Bund," which cooperated with the DAI.[25]

In the Nazi period, historiography of German emigration and contact with descendants of former emigrants fulfilled several political functions. On a foreign policy level, research on family, kinship, and ancestors' ties established social contacts. Through political propaganda this research forged a bond between the German Reich and German descendants abroad, whose numbers were ever increasing through continuous research. All "German born men" should be brought back "into the great German people family": "The way goes from the family to the people, to the ethnic community." The German people became a protective super-family:[26] "All German emigration research and tribal centered ethnic care lead always to the idea of the Pan-German family." Blood metaphors were readily stressed.[27] In the Nazi blood concept, family and people flowed into the same riverbed. Considering this "blood anchoring in the family community the most profound link ... to the construction and the revival of the community of all Germans," the Mittelstelle also reestablished and broadened the familial, communal, and compatriotic ties between the Saar-Palatinate and the descendants of emigrants.[28] At the level of interior policy, the demonstration of historical mass emigration from Germany supported the thesis of a "people without space" and psychologically prepared Germans for an aggressive expansion. German megalomania was enforced by crediting international accomplishments of German descendants to the account of German cultural creativity. The German people's ground was increased manifold by the addition of foreign German properties. The idea of a people whose fighting outpost emigrants had over centuries defended their language and tradition against alien ethnicities, strengthened the concept of cultural and racial superiority to provide a mental armament for German society. In light of National Socialism regarding emigration as a detrimental "blood-letting of the German people's body,"[29] Braun had to ask the public for understanding for the harsh historical situation of emigrants. Their descendants had even maintained their traditions and their "boundless love for their ancestral people."

Braun felt that Germany had forgotten its bonds to Germandom abroad, until the "school of Adolf Hitler" taught all Germans "to follow the ways of our people abroad with an inner willingness." That is why the Mittelstelle saw itself as in the service of the whole nation.[30]

Each summer from 1934 to 1937 Braun guided group trips to visit the descendants of southwestern German emigrants in Yugoslavia, the so-called Batschka-Palatines. With around one hundred seventy thousand persons of German origin before World War II, the Batschka was one of the largest ethnic German colonies in the Balkans.[31] Braun's Batschka trips were taken to commemorate the 150-years anniversaries of the founding of colonial villages. These "days of ethnic experience" cultivated relations between Palatines, Palatine authorities, and Yugoslavian citizens of German origin. It also strengthened the ethnic consciousness of both sides.[32] For its second trip in August 1935 the Palatinate brought along a thirsty visitor in the person of Gauleiter Bürckel, obviously enjoying the celebrations of Novi Vrbas: "We, the leaving Palatines, have only the one need to come back to you each year and to call you to us."[33] The climax of the last Batschka trip in 1937 was the erection of a colonist statue in Novi Vrbas, a gift to all Batschka Germans of the "original home."[34] The trips had the desired political effect: The familiarity of the Batschka-Palatines with the Reich grew, and admiring ethnic Germans turned into propagandists of Nazi Germany.[35]

As negotiated by the DAI, the German Reich's railroads gave preferential reductions for most ethnic Germans from spring 1931 on. The offer was used, and Bürckel's recall into the *Gau* followed in 1935.[36] Invited by the Saar-Palatinate's VDA, groups of Batschka-Palatines began arriving to visit the land left by their ancestors one and a half centuries earlier. Besides the return to the family roots, sightseeing of the Saar-Palatinate's social and cultural institutions was on the agenda; foreign citizens of German descent could "convince themselves of their original home's new spirit and new work." Thus did National Socialism abuse the emotionally moving moment of personal family history in a treacherous manner, cultivating it with the aim of families' political indoctrination in the service of the German Reich's foreign interests.[37]

In spite of these mutual visits the *Gau*'s public did not pay much attention to its Palatines abroad. Indeed, Braun had to stir up public opinion, inviting local historians to include the history of the colonists in Saar-Palatine village books.[38] Representatives of the most important Saar-Palatine cultural institutions planned a "World Meeting of the Saar-Palatines," to take place in mid 1940 over several weeks in the whole *Gau* area. Braun expected five to ten thousand visitors from Germany, Europe, and overseas. Once again, family and Reich were to overlap: the cultural and political arrangement of the World Meeting should give "the compatriots an extensive image of the strong forces of the new Germany." Time was also allotted to guests for visiting "their closer home" and their relatives. The

Gauleiter would give a political speech, the Saar-Palatine social scientists had to speak about emigration, and a conference for the researchers of family and kinship researchers was also planned.[39] But the World Meeting was not held: not only did the *Gau*'s public lack understanding of the relationship between native and foreign Germandom; the event's organizers lacked sufficient financing. German war preparations and the aggravation of the international situation as of autumn 1938 excluded any further thought of the World Meeting.[40]

During the first half of the twentieth century, the VDA represented the interests of border and foreign Germandom. After World War I, it supported the establishment of a German irredenta in the lost territories and propagated the idea of a community of all ethnic Germans that would transcend borders between classes and states. In 1933 the VDA was integrated into the Nazi regime. In the mid 1930s disagreements arose between the National Socialist Party and the head of the VDA, Hans Steinacher, who was not willing to give up border German territories just to fulfil Hitler's foreign policy stratagem. Having relieved Steinacher of his duties in 1937, the SS's Volksdeutsche Mittelstelle (VoMi) took over the management of the VDA. From that point on the SS would continually interfere in VDA affairs. During World War II, the VDA and SS together proceeded in registering, resettling, or expelling ethnic Germans and foreign ethnicities in the conquered territories.[41]

Another German research institution that was responsible for Germandom abroad was the DAI in Stuttgart. At the end of the 1930s, the DAI profited from the VDA's management crisis, gaining control over the foreign German research centers that depended on its Hauptabteilung Wanderungsforschung und Sippenkunde (Main Department of Migration Research and Kinship Studies). In 1940, twenty-nine of these regional research centers had ninety-five affiliated collaborators, half of them academics.[42] The research centers were uniformly oriented and served the DAI as intermediaries to regional Nazi leaders. Formally, the Mittelstelle Saarpfalz stayed independent. But from December 1938 on, its council was stacked with DAI representatives and the Mittelstelle brought its research into line with the head office for kinship in Stuttgart. Its foreign work followed DAI rules.[43]

The DAI's main kinship studies department (Hauptabteilung Sippenkunde) combined scientific research with practical tasks. It investigated the emigration of Germans to other countries and their further migrations abroad, recorded the names of emigrated fellow countrymen and their descendants, and established relationships to Germany and its regions. The foreign German contacts nurtured by the Hauptabteilung and its research centers paid off at the beginning of World War II.[44] As the Reich's supervisory authority, the SS's VoMi was put over the Hauptabteilung Sippenkunde and constantly assigned it special tasks. The growing political signification of the research centers from the beginning of the war on warranted increasing VoMi intervention in their supervision. In 1943 the VoMi gained direct control of the regional research centers in order to use the German minorities as a political mass against their native countries.⁴⁵

Inside the DAI's Hauptabteilung Sippenkunde, Braun's Mittelstelle closely cooperated with the Hauptstelle für die Sippenkunde des Deutschtums im Ausland (Main Office for Studies on the Kinship of Germandom Abroad), which was in charge of the foreign Germans' certificates of Aryan descent.⁴⁶ Work with foreign Germans carried out Hitler's imperialist orders and gave him a hand in preparing for Nazi military aggression.⁴⁷ In addition, new tasks developed in the Mittelstelle Saarpfalz as of 1938: "With the present political conditions, the mass emigrations of the eighteenth century to the South East [of Europe] and overseas and of the nineteenth century to overseas are of particular importance," Braun hinted.⁴⁸ The Germans of Czechoslovakia had demonstrated this kind of "particular importance." Brought into action for the expansionist policy of the Nazi regime, a politicized ethnic German group could subvert a foreign state from the inside.⁴⁹

A further purpose of the migration research in the coming war was to supply the German invasion and occupation machinery with data about usable men and women in enemy countries. Being the only institution in the Reich in 1939 to have at its disposal a great number of foreign German names and addresses, the DAI received "special orders" to establish at once a central card file of "Germans abroad ready for action," which was obtained from the address card files of the over 110,000 *Letters from Home* subscribers. The central card file distinguished the foreign Germans as citizens of the Reich and ethnic Germans, the "German-conscious," or those alienated from Germandom.⁵⁰ Data on the German Americans were similarly ascertained. The Hauptabteilung Sippenkunde demanded from its research centers the names, addresses, and professions of North American celebrities of German origin. Stuttgart was interested in whether a given German American was ready for action, whether he enjoyed public influence and whether he was active in ethnic German undertakings. The most important indicator was whether he was a convinced confessor of *völkisch* ideology in the spirit of the National Socialism. The DAI's aim was to install a network of intermediaries and a permanent intelligence service in North America. At the beginning of 1939 the Hauptabteilung sent a collaborator into the research centers dealing with the United States. The Mittelstelle Saarpfalz and its well organized and movable card file left an excellent impression.⁵¹ In the end, though, the DAI's attempts to use the ten thousand German Americans gathered in its central card file to enhance the goals of the German Reich failed, mainly because of the lack of a unified Germandom organization in the United States.⁵²

Immediately after the German attack on Poland, the DAI requested and received all card files with foreign addresses from its research centers. In Kaiserslautern, Schlenz drew up a register of those "ethnic companions" in

Poland who had reacted positively to the *Letter from Home* and who were considered "reliable." Without the detour via Stuttgart, Schlenz sent the first register of Poles of German origin directly to Breslau in Silesia near the Polish border, where the list was obviously used by the German occupation administration in Poland.[53] DAI representatives personally reviewed the Polish card file in Kaiserslautern and took to Stuttgart "another stock of Polish addresses." In this way the DAI's "central card file of Germandom abroad" increased; by the beginning of 1942 it numbered one hundred twenty thousand addresses. The German occupation administrations needed these names of local residents whom they could use for the Nazi exploitation policy. The logistical knowledge about foreign German settlements at last came to be of service to the planning staffs of the SS and other German administrations engaged in the implantation of German colonists and the germanization of the annexed and occupied territories.[54]

In the West, the German military successes changed the political frontiers beginning in mid 1940, when Luxemburg and parts of Eastern France were annexed de facto into the German Reich. The French Department of Moselle fell to Bürckel, who expelled almost one hundred thousand French-speaking people from the Lorraine and all the Jews from his *Gau*. From 1942 on, remaining Lorraine men were forced into the Wehrmacht. To support the attempts at germanization Bürckel founded new research institutions in Metz, the capital of the department; notably, a new scientific institute, the Lothringisches Institut für Landes- und Volksforschung (Lorraine Institute for Research on Region and People), as well as a branch of Kaiserslautern's Mittelstelle, which became the Mittelstelle Westmark (Western Marches Mediation Center).

The Mittelstelle in Metz was built up in the house of the Deutsche Volksgemeinschaft (German People's Community, DVG), the implanted Nazi collective movement.[55] German ethnic policy demands required close cooperation between the Mittelstelle and the party's headquarters in Lorraine. With his removal to Metz, Braun garnered more and more authority in annexation tasks and made practical use of migration research and ethnic German work for the benefit of Nazi expulsion and germanization policy.

It was also in 1940 that the region's Nazi Party established an office for emigration research and repaid Braun's long years of ethnic activity with a public post. Furthermore, Bürckel intended to make Braun, who spoke French, the commissariat director of the departmental archives in Metz.[56] But the Reich's Commissioner for the Protection of the Archives opposed the appointment. Instead Braun became the collaborator of Rembert Ramsauer, the researcher at the Lothringisches Institut who was in charge of the return of cultural assets from western France to Lorraine. On several business trips to western France, always accompanied by the SS's Security Service, Ramsauer and Braun brought back cultural goods and archives that had been evacuated from the Moselle at the beginning of the war.[57]

Braun's main occupation in annexed Lorraine remained the ethnic work, which he required to go "hand in hand with the political instruction." The purpose of his ethnic work was to cultivate in the Westmark population "pride in the greatness and performance of its own people." In the Saar-Palatinate his work found fertile ground. The population was very much interested in ethnic German questions and kept up relations to Germandom abroad, Braun said. The Saar-Palatines possessed a "natural ethnic sense" and showed "an absolutely irreproachable attitude" on ethnic questions. Their discrimination against prisoners of war and foreign compulsory workers made this visible. Nevertheless, the influence of "an occidental way of thinking" and of "plutocrat propaganda" impeded ethnic work in the Lorraine part of the *Gau*, Braun declared. Rumors pouring in from Nancy in the occupied territories of France hindered the development of a racist ethnic sense. Braun repeatedly reprimanded the Lorraine people's conduct regarding prisoners of war.[58] Besides the employment of foreign German speakers in Lorraine,[59] Braun's ethnic work concentrated on the proliferation of propaganda materials. For example, his own little book of implanted colonists' letters, *Wir schaffen im Glauben an Deutschland* (We Are Working in the Faith in Germany), and the book *Unser aller Führer* (The Führer of Us All) were distributed by the hundreds of thousands, reaching almost every household in Lorraine.[60]

The greatest target for Braun's ethnic work was the high proportion, in industrial regions in the Lorraine, of foreign workers and especially of notoriously anti-German Poles. The French government of the interwar period was suspected of having pushed ahead with "the planned foreign infiltration of the industrial region by workers from the four corners of the earth."[61] The non-German-speaking industrial workers were spared from the first massive expulsions of autumn 1940, because the German war economy could not allow itself a loss of production in the Lorraine iron and steel industry.[62] To lower the social position of the foreign workers further and to smother any communication between them and their ethnic German co-workers, Braun trained camp leaders of the Deutsche Arbeitsfront (German Labor Front, DAF) in racist treatment of foreign workers.[63] In autumn 1941 Braun took over the task of *Gau* representative for the SS's Völkische Schutzarbeit (Ethnic Protection Work). In this connection he used the infrastructure of regional Nazi organizations and of the Westmark VDA. He installed ethnic experts in Lorraine districts from the DVG's district units and appointed all twenty-seven VDA district heads representatives of the Völkische Schutzarbeit.[64]

The SS's VoMi needed data about the non-German workers in Lorraine in order to prepare their deportation and their substitution with foreign German implanted colonists. Braun had to record the number of foreign workers and of German workers with foreign nationalities. Immediately after having received all of Braun's surveys in February 1942, the VoMi started segregation by issuing color-coded passports to ethnic Germans and foreigners.[65] Braun subordinated his experience in ethnic German contact care to the services of the SS and made an effective contribution to the continuing expulsions of "foreigners" from the Moselle.

In the course of the general *Entwelschung* (extermination of Latin culture and language), the German civil government in the Lorraine pushed forward the germanization of the Lorraine's Christian and family names. In 1942 the plan of the Nazi regime to press the men of the de facto annexed territories into the Wehrmacht accelerated the germanization of the names. Section 2 of the "Ordinance on German Name Giving in Lorraine" of 29 August 1942 fixed the German spelling of romanized names on the basis of a name index "which according to folkloristic and linguistic principles was drawn up by the Gau's Training Office of the Gauleitung Westmark of the NSDAP."[66]

Indeed, Bürckel's administration had carried out the germanization of French family names by academics. In the spring of 1941 Braun was recruited to this task by the *Gau*'s training office. He convoked a "working conference for the germanization of the Lorraine's family names" in the Palatine wine-growing village St. Johann on 24 March 1941. Attending were experts in onomastics, Germanists, teachers, genealogists and kinship researchers, collaborators in ethnic German work and in the SS's Völkische Schutzarbeit, local VDA representatives, one head of the NSDAP's regional Race Political Office, and one judge at the racial court for genetic public health; some of them were members of the Nazi Party or the regional Reich Propaganda Office.[67] Having germanized half of them, Braun counted his names before they were hatched: "I am very content with the outcome of our work and the Lorraine people can be pleased too."[68] After a month, the conference dispersed. Braun alone took over the continuing organization and as a precautionary measure expanded the research to cover the whole *Gau*. He contemplated also the germanization of foreign sounding names in the Saarland and the Palatinate. On 30 January 1942 he reported to the *Gauleiter* "that the germanization of the foreign family names of Lorraine and also of the old-Gau is in the final stages."[69] Braun's efforts resulted in a 43-page "Index of First Names with Devices for Their Germanization" and over 330 pages devoted to a list of family names in their former French and new German spellings partly typed in double columns.[70] However, the germanization of the foreign names in the "old-*Gau*" was shelved. Citizens of the Reich who took their residence in the annexed territories, too, were exempted from germanization of their names.[71] Not so the people of Lorraine. They all had to accept the German names chosen by Braun and his collaborators.

It was not only in Western Germany and in Eastern France that Braun's migration research supported the expulsion of non-German ethnic groups. The Mittelstelle Westmark was also involved in the criminal settlement and extermination policy in occupied Poland.[72] In March 1941 a letter from Lublin in the General Government in Poland arrived at the Mittelstelle. An acquaintance from Braun's migration research, the former Vienna Hof-kammer archivist, Franz Stanglica, described his duties in Poland:

> In the meantime I was ordered from the army hereto by the Reichsführer-SS and I am doing my service as an SS-Sturmmann in the Ethnic Political Depart-ment of the SS- and Police Leader in the Lublin District. My task is really great and might have similarities with the task of Mr. Ph.D. Braun in Alsace [*sic*]. My tasks are among others: resettlement of Germans, Poles and Jews, winning back of German blooded, still racially pure, but polonized men, institution of an eth-nic German library in Lublin, looking after the ethnic Germans in our district, tracking down long-lost German blood in the Polish villages and returning it to Germandom and so on. My chief is SS-Brigadeführer Globocnik, who as the representative of the Reichskommissar für die Festigung deutschen Volkstums [Reich Commissioner for Strengthening Germandom, RKF] is charged with these tasks. These are rewarding but difficult tasks in this dreadful Poland.[73]

In the 1930s the historian Stanglica, author of a history of emigration from Lorraine to Southeast Europe, collaborator of the "Research Department on the Jewish Question" at Walter Frank's Reich Institute for the History of the New Germany, member of the NSDAP and of the SS, had put up at the Vienna Hofkammer Archives a card file of eighty thousand German emigrants to Southeast Europe, that was used by Wilfried Krallert and the Südostdeutsche Forschungsgemeinschaft (Southeast German Research Society) to prepare and carry through the Nazi ethnic policy in the Balkans.[74] About the beginning of 1941 the Ethnic Political Department at the staff of Odilo Globocnik in the Lublin district hired Stanglica as an expert for Ger-man migration history. He became the "planner in chief" for regional and environmental planning in the Lublin district.[75] Stanglica drew the RKF office's attention to Poles of German stock in Lublin's Zamosc subdistrict.

Braun remembered his historical research on the Palatines who had moved into the Lublin area in the late eighteenth century and offered the Lublin SS- and Police Leader his help in looking for their descendants.[76] Braun's offer was welcomed. The SS's objective in the Lublin area was a giant germanization project in the General Government of Poland, a purely German settlement liaison between the Baltics and Transylvania that Himm-ler and Globocnik populated with the Poles of German origin living in the area.[77] In fact, by order of Himmler all polonized Germans living in the General Government were concentrated in the Lublin area. In the first half of 1941, twenty-five thousand ethnic Germans were distributed among twelve newly formed "Palatine villages" in the Zamosc subdistrict.[78]

The colonization of Germans and ethnic Germans was only one side of the coin of Braun's emigration research in Poland, and even this side was criminal, resulting as of 1942 in the deportation into the Lublin district of Lorraine people deemed "racially valuable or racially beyond doubt" but "politically intolerable."[79] The other side of the coin ran dark with the blood of the expelled and exterminated non-German population of the colonization area. In German-occupied Eastern Europe, the "resettlement of Jews" referred to in Stanglica's letter of 1941 meant mass murder. Approximately fifty thousand Jews were killed in Stanglica's planning area.[80] In the "Reinhard Operation" Globocnik ordered the indiscriminate murder of over one hundred seventy-five thousand Jews–men, women, and children–in his extermination camps.[81] Property stolen from the victims was sold to the German colonists in the Zamosc subdistrict.[82]

By the beginning of 1942 Stanglica made no mention of the "resettlement" of Jews. They all were dead. Instead he hinted at the practice of expulsion of Poles: "I am in active ethnic policy, often with the weapon in my hand."[83] A German soldier in a conquered enemy land certainly bore arms, a fact the officer Braun knew well. If Stanglica specifically stated this commonplace, it is because he used the weapon for killing. Braun did not burden himself by trying to illumine the background of Stanglica's hints. Surely he noted that the Zamosc population selections that arose from his emigration research meant expulsion for most Poles and all Jews. But where they were sent simply was not his problem. Even the VoMi collaborator Braun probably lacked a vivid idea of the cruel reality in the Zamosc subdistrict: Between November 1942 and August 1943, one hundred thousand Poles were selected and deported. Families of German stock or families able to be germanized were spared, but Polish families were torn apart. Children together with elderly Poles were abandoned to death by starvation in so-called retirement villages. Poles able to work were deported into the East or into the interior of Germany. A final selected group, which the Germans estimated to be one-fifth of the Zamosc Poles, was sent to certain death at the Auschwitz concentration camp. Knowing what lay in store, the Polish peasants took up armed resistance.[84] In the Zamosc subdistrict, the attempts at germanization led to a debacle. Deportations of Polish peasants led to a lack of crucial manpower and in turn a shortage of agricultural products. Himmler had to stop the operation.[85]

Braun did not worry about the miserable fate of the expelled. On the contrary, he was pleased that his research results had gained importance in this way and were directly of service to the "ethnic purpose."[86] In 1942 the so-called pass through the Einwandererzentrale Litzmannstadt (Lódz Immigration Center in Poland, EWZ) started to select the seven to eight thousand Poles of German stock from the Zamosc subdistrict, taking advantage of the know-how of Palatine emigrant research: "Is there any possibility of determining how strong the German blood share of these villages is and how much strange blood came into it in the past?"[87] Braun, who meanwhile had a better understanding of the Lublin district's German administration than some German planning experts in the General Government, referred EWZ to the "comrade Stanglica" on the Lublin RKF staff.[88]

The collaboration between the Lublin SS and Police Leader and the foreign German institutions in the Westmark developed into a "close comradeship." The Ethnic Political Department of the Lublin SS and Police

Leader wanted to study Germandom in the district so as to determine and regermanize the polonized Germans who had remained "racially pure."[89] In February 1941, a VoMi representative asked the Mittelstelle Westmark for help in regermanizing the population of German origin in its district. Their Catholic religion had made their adaptation to their Polish vicinity easier for the Palatine colonists. By the nineteenth century they had acquired the Polish language and married Poles. The Lublin Ethnic Political Department sought all data about the Palatine emigrants, including *Letters from Home* and propaganda booklets to instruct them.

The Nazi regermanization policy was supported from the Westmark both scientifically, by the described provision of fundamental kinship group information used for the murderous population selection, and practically, by social services for the construction of German cultural institutions in the annexed and occupied territories. The VDA found sponsors from the Reich for the German annexation authorities.[90] In the spring of 1941 the Westmark VDA association was assigned the sponsorship not only for the Poles of Palatine origin in the Lublin subdistricts of Zamosc and Bilgoraj, but also for the subdistricts of Kutno and Lentschütz in the annexed Wartheland, the *Gau* under the brutal Gauleiter Arthur Greiser.[91]

To give the "fellow countrymen" in Poland a picture of the "original home," the Mittelstelle Westmark sent slide shows, literature, and mural decorations from its region to the East, particularly to a training hostel newly established in Zamosc for continuation of professional education and for recuperation.[92] Since "particularly the folk song from the original home rings out the soul and the strongest side of the memory of lost traditions," the Westmark sent recordings and Palatine song books into the subdistricts of Zamosc, Kutno, and Lentschütz.[93] From autumn 1941 on each issue of the *Colonists' Letters* in Zamosc brought contributions on the "original home of our German descendants." Braun's *Letters from Home* sent the necessary materials.[94] Braun personally suggested improvements to the *Colonists' Letters*, recommending articles on the Westmark's landscape, men, and performances.[95] Until he was called to arms in the spring of 1942,[96] the Westmark VDA deputy president Braun was kept well informed about the correspondence with the German authorities in Poland, and on many points he was consulted by the VDA's central management.[97]

From April 1942 on Braun again served as an officer in the Wehrmacht.[98] The *Gau*'s migration research, and also the *Gau*'s ethnic policy had to go without him. As Braun remained ever silent about his deeds during World War II, we have no knowledge of whether he resumed his military service to remove himself from the *Gau*'s affairs, or whether he would have preferred to dwell on his political tasks in the Westmark. Anyhow, after 1945 he pursued Palatine emigration research[99] and gained international reputation. He refounded the Mittelstelle, now called Heimatstelle Pfalz, which he headed until 1970. As before 1945 the Heimatstelle Pfalz saw itself as a "meeting place for all Palatines 'inside and outside'" and kept on sending ten thousand copies annually of *Letter from Home* to eighty-four countries all over the world.[100] Braun became one of the most influential academics in Kaiserslautern's Institut für pfälzische Geschichte und Volkskunde. When he died in Kaiserslautern on 26 July 1976, most Palatines had long forgotten or repressed, or even just left behind, the memory of Braun's political, scientific, and folkloric way, the career that had led him from revisionist political research on populations of German origin at the German borders and abroad, to active and conscious furthering of the fascist annexation and occupation policy in Eastern France and the racist segregation policy in Poland. Clearly, in these countries Braun's work had a practical political result in determining Nazi population policy. His work helped to decide who would stay and who would be driven from his farm and home, from his friends and family; sometimes even who would live and die. This part of Braun's career was less influential, and remains less visible, in other luckier countries, like the United States, whose population did not have to suffer from German invasion, and whose Palatines were not forced to receive preferential treatment.

Notes

I would like to thank my friend and colleague Ronald Lyndaker (Nancy, France) for his meticulous work correcting this essay and improving its style.

1. "Institute for Palatine History and Folklife Studies," in *Pfälzer in Amerika/Palatines in America*, ed. Roland Paul (Kaiserslautern, 1995), 247–249.
2. http://www.genealogy.org/~yoder/YNL/vol05.html; www.intersurf.com/~rcollins/ crum.html; harbaugh.uoregon.edu/History/WHH%20on%20Harbaugh%20History, %202000.pdf, all consulted on 7 February 2003.
3. Publications on Braun's biography: Karl Scherer, "Dr. Fritz Braun zum Gedächtnis," in *Pfälzer—Palatines: Beiträge zur pfälzischen Ein- und Auswanderung sowie zur Volkskunde und Mundartforschung der Pfalz und der Zielländer pfälzischer Auswanderer im 18. und 19. Jahrhundert*, ed. Karl Scherer (Kaiserslautern, 1981), 7–9; *Das große Pfalzbuch*, ed. Karl-Friedrich Geißler, Jürgen Müller, and Roland Paul, 7th rev. ed. (Landau, 1995), 553; Viktor Carl, *Lexikon der Pfälzer Persönlichkeiten*, pref. Helmut Kohl (Edenkoben, 1995), 75–76. For the period before 1945 these titles are not very instructive.
4. BArch, ZA VI 404, A. 8: Questionnaire Braun on 11 November 1940, cf. personnel department to the Reich's Propaganda Ministry (RMVP) on 3 January 1941; cf. Bayerisches Hauptstaatsarchiv, Munich (BayHStA), MK 15553: Bavarian Ministry for Cultural Affairs (BayKM) to Governmental President of Palatinate (Regpräs.) on 23 March 1940(a).
5. Ernst Ritter, *Das Deutsche Ausland-Institut in Stuttgart 1917–1945: Ein Beispiel deutscher Volkstumsarbeit zwischen den Weltkriegen* (Wiesbaden, 1976), henceforth abbreviated as *DAI*; Cornelia Wilhelm, *Bewegung oder Verein? Nationalsozialistische Volkstumspolitik in den USA* (Stuttgart, 1998), 120, 125–126.
6. Michael Fahlbusch, *Wissenschaft im Dienst der nationalsozialistischen Politik? Die "Volksdeutschen Forschungsgemeinschaften" von 1931–1945* (Baden-Baden, 1999), 41–43.

7. Joachim Heinz, *"Bleibe im Lande und nähre dich redlich!" Zur Geschichte der pfälzischen Auswanderung vom Ende des 17. bis zum Ausgang des 19. Jahrhunderts* (Kaiserslautern, 1989), 7.

8. Connections between the Pennsylvania German "dialectical renaissance" in the 1930s and the Nazi foreign culture policy were not researched by Don Yoder, "The Dialect Church Service in the Pennsylvania German Culture," in *Pfälzer—Palatines*, ed. Scherer, 352; Don Yoder, "Die Pennsylvania-Deutschen: Eine dreihundertjährige Identitätskrise," in *Amerika und die Deutschen: Bestandsaufnahme einer 300jährigen Geschichte*, ed. Frank Trommler (Opladen, 1986), 78–79. It would be telling to clarify the relationship between increasing popular German interest in genealogy and the Nazi demand for an Aryan family tree.

9. Historisches Museum der Pfalz, Speyer (HMP), G/Vbv., VDA: Kölsch, circular to VDA district heads on 17 April 1935.

10. On Braun's prewar career: BArch, ZA VI 404, A. 8: Questionnaire Braun on 11 November 1940, personnel department to RMVP on 3 January 1941; Berlin Document Center in the BArch (BDC), Braun: NSDAP-member-no. 6 922 619. BayHStA, MK 15553: BayKM to Regpräs. on 23 March 1940(a).

11. BArch, ZA VI 404, A. 8: Questionnaire Braun on 11 November 1940.

12. Cf. Ritter, *DAI*, 69.

13. Landesarchiv Speyer (LASp), H 3/8009, f. 23: Karl Heinrich Roth(-Lutra), minutes on 2 June 1936.

14. HMP, G/Vbv.: Mittelstelle Saarpfalz's foundation meeting on 20 June 1936; register of the official members of the Association (on 20 June 1936); BayHStA, MK 15552: Roth(-Lutra), minutes of the Pfälzische Gesellschaft zur Förderung der Wissenschaften (PGFW) on 15 October 1936.

15. BArch, R57neu/550: Braun to (Hermann) Maurer on 27 May 1938; HMP, G/Vbv., VDA: confirmation on Emrich on February 1938. Stadtarchiv Kaiserslautern (StdAKl), AIII, 303/8d: NSDAP Office for Municipal Policy to mayor of Kaiserslautern on 15 March 1938; mayor's order on 26 April 1939.

16. BayHStA, MK 15552: minutes on 2 June 1936; cf. Hermann Emrich, memorandum on the PGFW (approx. April 1937), S. 4–5; Meyer, audit of the PGFW on 13 November 1937, S. 15; cf. LASp, H 21/449: (report of 1945–1946 on the) Westmark-Institut. BayHStA, MK 15552: (Roth-Lutra u.) Emrich, minutes of the PGFW on 22 June 1937, S. 16. HMP, G/Jahresrechnungen: estimate of the PGFW for 1944, titel 16: division of the rent for the Institute's rooms.

17. BAKo, R57neu/550: Braun to DAI-Hauptstelle Sippenkunde (DAI-HS) on 20 March 1939; subsidy requirements of the Kaiserslautern Research Center; cf. Manfred Grisebach and Scheerer (DAI administration department) to Braun on 1 June 1939; Gr(isebach) and K(eller) to the DAI cashdesk on 15 March 1941; cf. Maurer and Keller, receipt on 25 September 1939.

18. HMP, G/Institutssitzungen: Emrich, "Wissenschaftliche Arbeit im Gau," *NSZ Rheinfront* (1 April 1937).

19. HMP, G/Institutsitzungen: Emrich, Saarpfälzisches Institut: Task and Work (7); cf. Roland Paul, "Auswanderung aus der Pfalz vom 17. bis zum 20. Jahrhundert," in *Das große Pfalzbuch*, ed. Geißler et al., 98–110.

20. Fritz Braun, "Landsleute drinnen und draußen, Mittelstelle Saarpfalz, Kaiserslautern," *Abhandlungen zur saarpfälzischen Landes- und Volksforschung* 1 (1937): 270–271; cf. Braun, "Landsleute drinnen und draußen: Mittelstelle Saarpfalz," *Unsere Heimat: Blätter für saarländisch-pfälzisches Volkstum* (1936/37): 30–31; cf. LASp, H 3/8009, f. 33: (Braun) "'Landsleute drinnen und draußen': Die Aufgaben der Mittelstelle Saarpfalz," *NAZ 263* (10 November 1936).

21. Scherer, "Braun," 7–8. The card file was lost at the end of World War II.

22. HMP, G/Sach 1943–44: Christmann to the Metz Municipal Library on 27 January 1944.

23. StdAKl, AIII, 303/8d: NS-Office to mayor on 15 March 1938; cf. Fritz Braun, "Landsleute drinnen und draußen, Mittelstelle Saarpfalz, Kaiserslautern," *Saarpfälzische Abhandlungen zur Landes- und Volksforschung* 2 (1938): 478–479; cf. BAKo, R57neu/550: Schlenz to Mittelstelle on 26 June 1940; cf. Ritter, *DAI*, 79–80.

24. BAKo, R57neu/550: Braun to Maurer on 27 May 1938; cf. Archives départementales de la Moselle, Saint-Julien-lès-Metz (ADM), 1W234: Braun to Schwar(t)z on 23 March 1941, Schlenz to Waldenmaier on 16 April 1942; cf. ADM, 1W98: Braun to Exterior Office Metz on 30 October 1941; "Mitarbeiter des 5. Bandes der Westmärkischen Abhandlungen," *Westmärkische Abhandlungen zur Landes- und Volksforschung* 5 (1941/42): 400; HMP, G/Besprechungsbelege, Mitarbeiter: Kirschner to Dittler on 2 February 1942.

25. Friedrich Schlenz, born approx. 1890: BAKo, R57neu/550: Grisebach, Grisebach, trip Kaiserslautern 17–20 September 1939; Schlenz to Maurer on 8 September and 13 October 1939; BAKo, R57neu/626: DAI-HS-Sachgebiete, Index of the Research Centers on 1 April 1941; ADM, 1W234: Schlenz to Braun on 18 November 1941, Schlenz to Waldenmaier on 8 June 1942; cf. Wilhelm, *Bewegung oder Verein?* 115–159, 291–292; cf. Bruce F. Ashkenas, "A Legacy of Hatred: The Records of a Nazi Organization in America," *Prologue* 17 (1985): 99; cf. Arthur L. Smith, Jr., *The Deutschtum of Nazi Germany and the United States* (The Hague, 1965), 63–64, 91–113, 117–151; cf. Ritter, *DAI*, 101, 119–120; cf. Hans-Adolf Jacobsen, *Nationalsozialistische Außenpolitik 1933–1938* (Frankfurt am Main, 1968), 528–549.

26. August Rupp, "Die größere Volksgemeinschaft," *Unsere Heimat: Blätter für saarpfälzisches Volkstum* (1937/38): 75; cf. Wilhelm Groos, "Auslanddeutschtum und Familiengeschichte," in *Hermann Blumenau: Jahrbuch des Volksbundes für das Deutschtum im Ausland* (no ed.) (Berlin, 1937), 71; cf. John Hutchinson and Anthony D. Smith, "Introduction," in *Ethnicity*, ed. John Hutchinson and Anthony D. Smith (Oxford, 1996), 7; cf. Donald L. Horowitz, *Ethnic Groups in Conflict* (Berkeley, 1985), 184; cf. Ritter, *DAI*, 50–51. Karl von Möller, "Liebe Landsleute drinnen und draußen!" *Unsere Heimat* (1937/38): 76–77, sent a letter to the "Great Mother Saar-Palatinate."

27. Ludwig Weinkauff, "Jahrestagung des Deutschen Ausland-Instituts in Stuttgart," *Die Westmark* 5 (1937/38): 622; cf. Fritz Braun, whose "Im Blutstrom Deines Volkes," *Heimatbrief aus der Westmark* 4 (1942): 9–10 worked itself up into a real "blood"frenzy.

28. Cf. Fritz Braun, "1. Arbeitsbericht der Mittelstelle Saarpfalz in Kaiserslautern von der Gründung am 15. Oktober 1936 bis zum 1. April 1938," *Unsere Heimat* (1937/38): 258.

29. Ritter, *DAI*, 101; cf. J. H. Kell, A. Jakob, "Die Auswanderungen aus den Bürgermeistereien Haustadt und Hilbringen im 19. Jahrhundert," *Saarpfälzische Abhandlungen zur Landes- und Volksforschung* 2 (1938): 435.

30. Braun, "1. Arbeitsbericht," 257–258.

31. Hans-Ulrich Wehler, *Nationalitätenpolitik in Jugoslawien: Die deutsche Minderheit 1918–1978* (Göttingen, 1980), 14–15, uses the nationalities' statistics from the last prewar Yugoslav census, but indicates the problems of getting evidence of an ethnic affiliation; cf. 28. Wehler's interpretation of the documents was critized by Fahlbusch, *Wissenschaft*, 657.

32. StdAKl, AIII, 303/8d: Prof. Grewenig (Ludwigshafen, team for the preparation of the Batschka trip) to mayor Weisbrod on 1 August 1934; Richard Ledermann, *Die Batschkareise: Poetisches Tagebuch* (Novi Vrbas, 1936), 8; cf. Fritz Braun, "Treu der Heimat—treu dem Volk," *Unsere Heimat: Blätter für saarländisch-pfälzisches Volkstum* (1936/37): 34.

33. Cited by Fritz Braun, "Batschkafahrt 1937," *Unsere Heimat* (1936/37), 355, cf. 353; cf. Landesarchiv Saarbrücken (LASb), SM 45: Braun to Keuth on 24 June 1935. Cf. StdAKl, AII, 312: VDA-Saarpfalz: Batschka-trip 28 July–20 August 1936; cf. Wilhelm Wüst, *Wir fahren in die Batschka* (Saarbrücken [1938]).

34. Braun, "Batschkafahrt 1937," 354; Kreisarchiv Saarlouis (KrASls), IF14: Braun, circular on 25 June 1937; cf. VDA-Saarpfalz's booklet "Batschkafahrt 1937." Cf. StdAKl, AIII, 303/8d: VDA-Saarpfalz to mayor of Kaiserslautern, received on 28 June 1937: invitation to the Batschka-trip 1937.

35. Archives des Affaires Etrangères Paris, Allemagne 757, f. 104–107: Adrien Thierry (French envoy in Romania) to foreign ministry Paris on 11 May 1939.

36. Ritter, *DAI*, 50: reduction of 25 percent, from summer 1934 on of 50 percent. StdAKl, AIII, 303/8e: newspaper clippings of the Palatinate trip of Batschka-Palatines in mid August 1933; Braun, "Treu," 35, cf. 33.
37. Braun, "Batschkafahrt 1937," 356. Cf. StdAKl, AIII, 303/8d: "Empfang der Batschka-Pfälzer," *Pfälzische Presse* 121, no. 226 (28 August 1937).
38. Braun, "1. Arbeitsbericht," 258; cf. BayHStA, MK 15552: appendix 1 to the PGFW's minutes on 30 June 1938, (S. 2).
39. HMP, G/Vbv.: meeting to prepare the World Meeting of 16 May 1938 (20 May 1938).
40. BayHStA, MK 15553: (Braun) Tasks of the Mittelstelle (winter 1938/39); BAKo, R57neu/550: Braun to DAI-HS on 11 May 1939.
41. Hans Steinacher, *Bundesleiter des VDA 1933–1937: Erinnerungen und Dokumente*, ed. Hans-Adolf Jacobsen (Boppard, 1970), 120–121, 449–451; Hans-Adolf Jacobsen, "Hans Steinacher: Eine biographische Skizze," ibid., xi–xxxiii; Kurt Poßekel, "Verein für das Deutschtum im Ausland (VDA) 1881–1945," in *Lexikon zur Parteiengeschichte: Die bürgerlichen und kleinbürgerlichen Parteien und Verbände in Deutschland (1789–1945)*, ed. Dieter Fricke (Cologne, 1986), 4:282–297.
42. Wilhelm Kohlhaas, *Chronik der Stadt Stuttgart 1918–1933* (Stuttgart [approx. 1965]), 260–262; Ritter, *DAI*, 59, 69, 128–129; Robert Ernst, *Rechenschaftsbericht eines Elsässers*, 2nd ed. (Berlin, 1955), 190–191, cf. 194–195.
43. BAKo, R57neu/550: Grisebach and Keller to Mittelstelle on 11 November 1940; Kölsch/Braun and Csaki, cooperation treaty between the Saarpfälzische Mittelstelle and the DAI on 12–18 December 1938.
44. BAKo, R57neu/1986: Grisebach, report of the HS 1 September 1939–31 December 1940; cf. BAKo, R57neu/626: Forkmann (HS-central card files), HS-card files on 9 June 1942.
45. Michael G. Esch, *"Gesunde Verhältnisse": Deutsche und polnische Bevölkerungspolitik in Ostmitteleuropa 1939–1950* (Marburg, 1998), 30; cf. Ritter, *DAI*, 69.
46. BAKo, R57neu/626: DAI-HS-Sachgebiete, register from 1 April 1941; Forkmann, HS-card files on 9 June 1942; Ritter, *DAI*, 45–46, 68, 84–85; cf. Fritz Braun, "Sippenkartei des Außendeutschtums," *Jahrbuch des Deutschen Ausland-Instituts zur Wanderungsforschung und Sippenkunde* 6 (1941/42): 258–262.
47. Ernst, *Rechenschaftsbericht*, 199–200.
48. BayHStA, MK 15553: (Braun) Tasks of the Mittelstelle: "Bei den augenblicklichen Gegebenheiten der politischen Verhältnisse wird den Massenauswanderungen im 18. Jahrhundert nach dem Südosten und nach Übersee und im 19. Jahrhundert nach Übersee besondere Bedeutung beigemessen."
49. Jacobsen, *NS-Außenpolitik*, 443–444; Jörg K. Hoensch, "Hitlers 'Neue Ordnung Europas': Grenzveränderungen, Staatsneugründungen, nationale Diskriminierung," in *Der nationalsozialistische Krieg*, ed. Norbert Frei, Hermann Kling (Frankfurt am Main, 1990), 249. Cf. Bernd-Jürgen Wendt, *Großdeutschland: Außenpolitik und Kriegsvorbereitung des Hitler-Regimes*, 2nd ed. (Munich, 1993), 147, 153, cf. 151–155, cf. 167–173; cf. Dieter Wolfanger, "Populist und Machtpolitiker: Josef Bürckel: Vom Gauleiter der Pfalz zum Chef der Zivilverwaltung in Lothringen," in *Die Pfalz unterm Hakenkreuz: Eine deutsche Provinz während der nationalsozialistischen Terrorherrschaft*, ed. Gerhard Nestler and Hannes Ziegler (Landau, 1993), 71; Karl Heinz Roth, "Krieg vor dem Krieg: Die Annexion Österreichs und die Zerschlagung der Tschechoslowakei 1938/39," *1999* 16, no. 1 (2001): 28–48.
50. BAKo, R57neu/1986: Grisebach, HS report 1 September 1939–31 December 1940.
51. BAKo, R57neu/550: draft of a research centers's form to the DAI-HS; Katharina Reimann, visitation of the research center Saarpfalz on 6 February 1939 to seize materials for the American German central card file; cf. Wilhelm, *Bewegung oder Verein?* 125, cf. 147, 151; cf. Ritter, *DAI*, 81.
52. Smith, *Deutschtum*, 46.
53. BAKo, R57neu/550: Schlenz to Ernst Boehlich (Breslau, Schweidnitzer Stadtgraben 23) on 8 September 1939.

54. BAKo, R57neu/550: Grisebach, trip to Kaiserslautern 17–20 September 1939. The High Command of the Wehrmacht ordered ethnographical maps from the DAI; Ritter, *DAI*, 146–147.
55. ADM, 1W239/Mappe "Saarpfälzische Abhandlungen Bd. IV": Haufen Edition Society to Braun on 30 December 1941; BayHStA, MK 15553: BayKM to Regpräs. on 23 March 1940(a).
56. BayHStA, MK 15553, file Braun: NSDAP-Munich on 5 October 1939, BayKM to Regpräs. on 23 March 1940, cf. Regpräs. to BayKM on 11 March 1940; cf. BArch, ZA VI 404, A. 8: Questionnaire Braun on 11 November 1940; ADM, 1W1: Barth to Hofmann on 2 July 1940.
57. ADM, 1W106, Fahrtenberichte: trip's report (13–21 August 1940); trip's report (28 November–10 December 1940); 1W204, Ramsauer: personal file from 28 October 1940; cf. BArch, R21/10599, f. 7: proof of the archives evacuated from Alsace and Lorraine to the interior of France (beginning of 1941).
58. ADM, 1W211: B(raun), (1st) and 2nd report on the ethnic work (no dates).
59. ADM, 1W234: VDA-Westmark to Braun on 8 February 1941; 2W63/3, f. 2: DAF-Saarpfalz to Braun on 28 March 1941; ADM, 1W211: B(raun), 2nd report.
60. Fritz Braun, ed., *Wir schaffen im Glauben an Deutschland: Umsiedler aus dem Osten schreiben an ihre westmärkische Heimat* (Kaiserslautern, 1941); HMP, G/Besprechungsbelege, Christmann allg.: Christmann to Braun on 26 November 1941; cf. ADM, 1W234: Schlenz to Braun on 18 November 1941; ADM, 1W234: Uhrig to VDA-Management on 29 October 1941, cf. Braun to Holl on 17 November 1941.
61. Kurt Kölsch, "Der Sprachenkampf in der Westmark (Schluss)," *Die Westmark* 10 (1942/43): 351; cf. ADM, 1W211: Braun, (1st) report; cf. Adolf Blind, "Struktur und Entwicklung der Bevölkerung Lothringens," *Westmärkische Abhandlungen zur Landes- und Volksforschung* 4 (1940): 100–102.
62. Uwe Mai, "Volkstumspolitik in Lothringen," in *Heimatbewegung und NS-Kulturpolitik in Hessen, Pfalz, Elsaß und Lothringen: Dokumentation eines Seminars*, ed. Förderverein Projekt Osthofen (Osthofen, 1999), 130.
63. ADM, 1W211: B(raun), 2nd report.
64. ADM, 2W63/2, f. 37, 32–34, 24: ADM, 2W63/2,: SS-Obersturmführer Weber to Braun on 1 November and 8 December 1941, Braun to Völkische Schutzarbeit on 5 December 1941, Braun's notice for a telegram to Weber on 9 December 1941, Braun to Völkische Schutzarbeit on 12 February 1942; ADM, 1W211: B(raun), (1st) report; cf. 2nd report; cf. ADM, 1W234: W(aldenmaier) to Holl on 6 March 1942; cf. ADM, 2W63/2, f. 19: Braun to NSDAP-Frankenthal on 26 February 1942; cf. Valdis O. Lumans, *Himmler's Auxiliaries: The Volksdeutsche Mittelstelle and the German National Minorities of Europe, 1933–1945* (Chapel Hill, 1993).
65. ADM, 2W63/2, f. 31, 24, 21–22: Braun to Völkische Schutzarbeit on 20 December 1941, on 12 and 26 February 1942; cf. f. 23: Braun to VDA-Westmark on 26 February 1942.
66. Archives municipales de Sarreguemines, Hiegel/Lorraine, folder "Evénements politique 1942": *Verordnungsblatt für Lothringen* no. 36 (3 September 1942): 422: Ordinance on German Name Giving in Lorraine on 29 August 1942; cf. BABL, R43II/1339a, f. 124: ordinances for the germanization of names in Lorraine on 28 September and on 17 December 1940; cf. Dieter Wolfanger, "Die nationalsozialistische Politik in Lothringen (1940–1945)," (Ph.D. diss., University of the Saarland, 1976), 101–103, henceforth abbreviated as "NS-Politik in Lothringen"; cf. Henri Hiegel, "La germanisation et la nazification de la vie culturelle du département de la Moselle sous l'occupation allemande de 1940 à 1944," *Mémoires de l'Académie Nationale de Metz* 11, no. 6 (1983): 102–103.
67. ADM, 1W237: postcard from Birkweiler at the Weinstraße with the attendance list of the work conference 24 March–24 April 1941 in St. Johann near Albersweiler; ADM, 2W1233: *Propaganda!* 5; ADM, 2W63, f. 19: Braun to NSDAP-Kreisleitung Frankenthal on 26 February 1942; Mr. Hans-Walter Herrmann to the author on 14 April 1999.
68. ADM, 1W234: Braun to Schwar(t)z on 11 April 1941.

69. ADM, 1W220: B(raun) to Civil Government in Lorraine on 30 January 1942. Cf. Philipp Fuchs, "Zur Frage der Familiennamen in Lothringen: Verwelschung und Entwelschung," *Westmärkische Abhandlungen zur Landes- und Volksforschung* 5 (1941/42): 327; cf. Hiegel, "La germanisation," 102.
70. ADM, 1W220.
71. BABL, R43II/1339a, f. 169: Chief of the Reich's Chancellery, notice on 4 March 1943; cf. f. 171–172: Wilhelm Frick to Civil Government in Alsace on 10 March 1943.
72. Ernst Christmann, "Bericht über die Arbeit des Westmark-Instituts für Landes- und Volksforschung in Kaiserslautern für die Zeit vom 1. Juli 1942 bis 30. Juni 1943," *Westmärkische Abhandlungen zur Landes- und Volksforschung* 5 (1941/42): 397.
73. ADM, 1W234: Stanglica to Mittelstelle on 12 March 1941: "Ich bin unterdessen auf Befehl des Reichsführers-SS von der Truppe hierher abkommandiert worden und mache als SS-Sturmmann der Waffen-SS hier im volkspolitischen Referat des SS- und Polizeiführers im Distrikt Lublin Dienst. Meine Aufgabe ist ganz gross und dürfte vielleicht ähnlich sein, wie die des Herrn Dr. Braun im Elsass [*sic*]. Zu meinen Aufgaben gehören: Umsiedlung von Deutschen, Polen und Juden, Rückgewinnung deutschblütiger, reinrassig deutsch gebliebener, aber polonisierter Menschen, Einrichtung einer volksdeutschen Bibliothek in Lublin, Betreuung der Volksdeutschen im hiesigen Di(s)-trikt, Aufspürung verschollenen deutschen Blutes auf den polnischen Dörfern und Rückführung zum Deutschtum usw. Mein Chef ist SS-Brigadeführer Globocnik, dem als Beauftragten des Reichskommissars zur Festigung deutschen Volkstums diese Aufgaben zugewiesen sind. Es sind dankbare aber schwierige Aufgaben in diesem scheusslichen Polen."
74. BDC, Stanglica (1907–1946); BDC-SSO, Stanglica. Hofkammer-Archives, Vienna; Archivverhandlungen, Zl. 261/1938: J(osef) K(allbrunner) to (Wilhelm Grau) on 4 March 1938; Stanglica, balancing of the financial year 1937/38 on 4 March 1938. Friedrich Walter, "Das Wiener Hofkammerarchiv," *Inventare österreichischer Archive* 7: *Inventar des Wiener Hofkammerarchivs* (Vienna, 1951), xxxv; Leo Santifaller, *Das Institut für Österreichische Geschichtsforschung: Festgabe zur Feier des zweihundertjährigen Bestandes des Wiener Haus-, Hof- und Staatsarchivs* (Vienna, 1950), 148, 151; Patricia von Papen, "'Scholarly' Antisemitism During the Third Reich: The Reichsinstitut's Research on the 'Jewish Question' 1935–1945" (Ph.D. diss., Columbia University, 1999), 11–13; Wolfgang Leesch, *Die deutschen Archivare 1500–1945*, Bd. 2: *Biographisches Lexikon* (Munich, 1992), 586; Fahlbusch, *Wissenschaft*, 247–297; Franz Stanglica, *Die Auswanderung der Lothringer in das Banat und die Batschka im 18. Jahrhundert* (Frankfurt am Main, 1934).
75. BABL, R69/132, f. 28–29: Gradmann, The Germandom in the Zamosc Area on 19 March 1942; ADM, 1W234: Stanglica to Mittelstelle on 12 March 1941; Götz Aly und Susanne Heim, *Vordenker der Vernichtung: Auschwitz und die deutschen Pläne für eine neue europäische Ordnung* (Frankfurt am Main, 1992), 432–440.
76. BABL, R69/132, f. 12: R. Foerth, notice to the EWZ's head on 17 February 1942.
77. Czeslaw Madajczyk, *Die Okkupationspolitik Nazideutschlands in Polen 1939–1945* (Berlin, 1987), 422; BABL, R69/132, f. 20v and 19v: Lothar von Seltmann, "Pfälzersiedlungen im Zamoscer Kreis," *Volkstum im Südosten* (October 1941): 180, 182–183.
78. ADM, 1W234: Uhrig to Emrich on 9 August 1941, 1.
79. Eberhard Jäckel, *Frankreich in Hitlers Europa: Die deutsche Frankreichpolitik im Zweiten Weltkrieg* (Stuttgart, 1966), 318; cf. Wolfanger, "NS-Politik in Lothringen," 174.
80. Madajczyk, *Okkupationspolitik*, 422.
81. Hermann Weiß, "Globocnik, Odilo," in *Biographisches Lexikon zum Dritten Reich*, ed. Hermann Weiß, 2nd ed. (Frankfurt am Main, 1998), 148–149; Esch, "Gesunde Verhältnisse," 43–45; Dieter Pohl, *Von der "Judenpolitik" zum Judenmord: Der Distrikt Lublin des Generalgouvernements 1939–1944* (Bern, 1993), 183; Bruno Wasser, "Die 'Germanisierung' im Distrikt Lublin als Generalprobe und erste Realisierungsphase des 'Generalplans Ost,'" in *Der "Generalplan Ost": Hauptlinien der nationalsozialistischen Planungs- und Vernichtungspolitik*, ed. Mechtild Rössler and Sabine Schleiermacher (Berlin, 1993), 271–293;

Dirk Jachomowski, *Die Umsiedlung der Bessarabien-, Bukowina- und Dobrudschadeutschen: Von der Volksgruppe in Rumänien zur "Siedlungsbrücke" an der Reichsgrenze* (Munich, 1984), 194–197.

82. Bruno Wasser, *Himmlers Raumplanung im Osten: Der Generalplan Ost in Polen 1940–1944* (Basel, Berlin, and Boston, 1993), passim.

83. ADM, 1W234: Stanglica to Braun on 15 January 1942: "Ich bin in aktiver Volkspolitik, oft auch mit der Waffe in der Hand, tätig."

84. Madajczyk, *Okkupationspolitik*, 119–121, 422–424; Edouard Conte and Cornelia Essner, *La quête de la race: Une anthropologie du nazisme* (Paris, 1995), 265–344.

85. Jachomowski, *Umsiedlung*, 196–197; Madajczyk, *Die Okkupationspolitik*, 120–121; Esch, *"Gesunde Verhältnisse,"* 45; Weiß, "Globocnik," 148–149; Pohl, *"Judenpolitik,"* 183.

86. ADM, 1W234: Braun to Stanglica on 29 January 1942.

87. ADM, 2W63/4, Germanisation, f. 16: Gradmann (to the DAI), copy fr. 27 February 1942: "Kann festgestellt werden, wie stark der deutsche Blutsanteil dieser Dörfer ist und wie weit im Laufe der Jahrzehnte fremder Blutsanteil hinzugekommen ist"? Cf. f. 15: Kloß to Braun on 27 February 1942. The operation was managed by SS-Untersturmführer Wilhelm Gradmann who also came from the DAI. Karl Heinz Roth, "'Generalplan Ost'—'Gesamtplan Ost': Forschungsstand, Quellenprobleme, neue Ergebnisse," in *Der "Generalplan Ost,"* ed. Rössler et al., 89, cf. 55; cf. Karl Heinz Roth, "Heydrichs Professor: Historiographie des 'Volkstums' und der Massenvernichtungen: Der Fall Hans Joachim Beyer," in *Geschichtsschreibung als Legitimationswissenschaft 1918–1945*, ed. Peter Schöttler (Frankfurt am Main, 1997), 269; cf. Fahlbusch, *Wissenschaft*, 115.

88. ADM, 2W63/4, Germanisation, f. 13: Braun to DAI on 5 March 1942.

89. ADM, 1W234: Hauptgefolgschaftsführer Lothar von Seltmann to Mittelstelle on 12 February 1941; cf. BABL, R69/132, f. 11–12: R. Foerth, notice to the EWZ's head on 17 February 1942.

90. ADM, 1W234: Bruno Hübler to Braun on 13 May 1941, Tasks of Sponsorship.

91. ADM, 1W234: Stanglica to Mittelstelle on 15 May 1941; Uhrig to Eckelmann on 9 August 1941 (S. 1). Cf. Hermann Weiß, "Greiser, Arthur," *Biographisches Lexikon zum Dritten Reich*, 160–162; Volker Rieß, "Wartheland, Reichsgau," in *Enzyklopädie des Nationalsozialismus*, ed. Wolfgang Benz, Hermann Graml, and Hermann Weiß, 2nd ed. (Munich, 1998), 797–798.

92. ADM, 1W234: Uhrig to Hillebrand on 22 August 1941, S. 2, Uhrig to Seltmann on 12 August 1941, cf. Uhrig to Braun on 28 July 1941, 12 August, 24 November, and 10 December 1941; cf. Uhrig to Eckelmann on 24 November 1941.

93. ADM, 1W234: Uhrig to Eckelmann on 9 August 1941 (S. 1–2), Uhrig to VDA-Hauptabt. Patenschaftsarbeit on 29 October 1941.

94. ADM, 1W234: Bargel to Braun on 1 November 1941.

95. ADM, 1W234: Braun to SSPF Distrikt Lublin on 25 July 1941.

96. ADM, 2W63/4, Germanisation, f. 13: Braun to DAI on 5 March 1942.

97. ADM, 1W234, passim.

98. BArch, ZA VI 404, A. 8, PA Braun, Referent Saarpfalz; cf. Trampler to RMVP on 27 March 1942.

99. Mr. Hans-Walter Herrmann to the author on 14 September 1996.

100. Jürgen Keddigkeit, "Institut für pfälzische Geschichte und Volkskunde in Kaiserslautern," in *Das Landesarchiv Speyer: Festschrift zur Übergabe des Neubaues*, ed. Karl Heinz Debus (Koblenz, 1987), 251–253, quotation 253; cf. Paul, "Auswanderung," 110.

Chapter 9

GERMAN *WESTFORSCHUNG*, 1918 TO THE PRESENT
The Case of Franz Petri, 1903–1993

✦ ✦ ✦

Hans Derks

It has been just a few years since the concept of German *Westforschung* was revived in ongoing debates about the role of scholars before, during, and after World War II.[1] An entire library has become available relating to the study of German *Ostforschung* and this *Ostforschung* itself.[2] Today one can perceive competing schools in this research, which is partly based on different geographical orientations. In several respects this *Ostforschung* research is comparable to the recent Polish work on *Westforschung* by scholars like Jan M. Piskorski of Poznań.[3] It comes as no surprise that recently someone proposed to organize a colloquium under the title "French *Ostforschung* and German *Westforschung*" to suggest their interchangeability as well as their differences in approach.

Whatever the geographical focus of the research on *Ostforschung* as a largely German affair, the study of *Westforschung* as a new broad, fascinating, and complex field will always have a close relationship with its "eastern counterpart." Still, the obvious question of why it took so long for the studies of German *Westforschung* to start is in need of an answer albeit a complex one.

Part of the explanation is to be found in the commonplace notion that "the East" is associated with "evil" and "the West" with "good." And indeed, the seriousness of the German war crimes in "the East" had no parallel in "the West." But is it not equally true that a substantial part of the victims lived in "the East" and that the perpetrators came from "the West," while the first (and for many people, the main) liberators arrived from "the East"? Another part of the explanation is, therefore, that the study of something like "the Western origins of the Eastern conquest"

Notes for this chapter begin on page 193.

was taboo as long as the Cold War propaganda was in need of an "Eastern Evil Empire." Now the study of the case of *Westforschung* is freed from this ideological obstacle.

The following chapter will show the motivations for the actions of numerous German scholars and other *Westforscher* up to and in the period from 1933 to 1945 and describe how, in principle and practice, the services rendered to the German conquerors were the same as in the *Ostforschung*. As will be discussed, *Westforschung* as such was reintroduced by "Bonn" soon after the war through, for instance, the so-called *Kulturraumforschung*. Its main actors always vigorously denied that they themselves or the institutions in which they worked had done anything wrong during the war: meanwhile, they wielded decisive influence over West German postwar historiography.[4] Important as well is that substantial support came from Belgian and Dutch historians, linguists, and other researchers. Besides this, one gets the strong impression that the so-called *Abendland* elements of *Westforschung* united the Catholic Adenauer government and the Roman Catholic universities in specific aims; their medievalists play(ed) therefore a pivotal role in its development.

The life and times of one of the main *Westforscher*, the medievalist Franz Petri, who worked in the highest echelon of the military occupation administration in Belgium, is the example I will use to clarify the context of *Westforschung* from 1918 to the present. Although Petri (and his supporters) saw himself as an innocent, hardworking scholar, it is quite easy to show how he tried to execute aims of the SS in Belgium, acted as one of its sponsors, and propagated racism and anti-Semitism. This fundamental change of perspective means that large parts of the (military) history—to mention only the obvious discipline—of Belgium and the Netherlands and consequently of Germany must be rewritten.

This became possible after highly revealing new archival material was discovered and discussed in the first general overview of *Westforschung*.[5] Besides this and contrary to most *Ostforschung* research, the present *Westforschung* covers several disciplines and their interrelationship: history, geography, *Volkskunde* (which is actually quite different from anything like folklore),[6] linguistics, biology (in particular physical anthropology, which before and during the war was identical to *Rassenkunde*). Before I deal with the story of Franz Petri and his career from 1918 to the present, a few words must be said about the new field of historical research.

Defining *Westforschung*

Because the research and publications about *Westforschung* have only just set in, we are in a good position to clarify its aims in comparison with (German) *Ostforschung* and its present study.[7] Nowadays, the latter mainly discusses the German population policy in East-Central Europe from 1939 to 1945 under which millions of Jews, Poles, Russians, and others were murdered. Scholars of socioeconomic history, geography, agricultural sciences, demography, and the like aimed not only at the military-political expansion of the Third Reich but also at complete and radical reshaping of the (conquered) societies, including drastic changes in the population density and composition, as Christian Gerlach's work has demonstrated anew.[8]

However, with the addition of *Westforschung* the scope is considerably widened, and it seems more necessary than ever to replace in all respects a strict German outlook with a European one, in order to compare the many kinds of perpetrators and victims, the several often contradicting occupation policies, the forms of collaboration and protests, the science policies, and so on.

The question of how to define *Westforschung*, or who implemented the concept and why, can be answered briefly and unsatisfactorily as follows. Generally, *Westforschung* supported the Western expansion of Germany, the Third Reich, and the Federal Republic of Germany with scholarship to make the people believe in and/or execute this expansion. These (pseudo-)scientific works were produced in medieval history, linguistics, geography, *Volkskunde*, physical anthropology, *Rassenkunde*, and other disciplines.

A clear statement appears, for example, in Franz Petri's *Zweiter Bericht* (Second Report) of 1940. As *Kulturpapst* in the German occupation administration in Belgium, he planned the germanization of this country and its universities by installing certain German professors "in harmony with the methods used by German *Kulturpolitik* in the Danube and Balkan countries." Furthermore, Petri states that at the Flemish University of Ghent, "the German forces [*Kräfte*] will be employed in the areas of prehistory [*Vorgeschichte*], Germanic languages and literature [*Germanistik*], geography, history and *Volkskunde*. Among them is the well-known champion of folk-oriented Westforschung [*volkswissenschaftlich vertieft*], the director of the Institut für geschichtliche Landeskunde der Rheinlande [Institute for Regional Studies] in Bonn, Professor Steinbach."[9]

The three "countries" of (Weimar) Germany, the Third Reich, and the FRG must be mentioned because directly after the end of World War I, *Westforschung* was started at the University of Bonn, and after World War II, the universities of Münster, Bonn, Cologne, and Frankfurt, as well as specific research institutes, explicitly began with *Westforschung*.[10] Hermann Aubin, Franz Steinbach, Franz Petri, and others reorganized and reinstitutionalized their scholarly territory in 1949 in order to work in what was called the Working Group of West German Research on Region and People (Arbeitsgemeinschaft für westdeutsche Landes- und Volksforschung, AWLV). The AWLV explicitly referred to "the old well-tried principles of the West German Research Society [Rheinischen, later Westdeutsche, Forschungsgemeinschaft]," and it boldly claimed a realm that extended over "Southwest Germany, the middle and lower Rhine, the adjacent Hessen, Westphalia and the northern German coastal area as suitable to Westforschung. In the framework of the present possibilities and with an aim suitable for the present European requirements, [it will] reinstate the former scientific relationships beyond the Western borders."[11]

In Westforschung, "Western" connoted the Scandinavian countries, the Netherlands, Belgium, Luxemburg, and (northern) France. In other words, "the West" meant the northern part of continental Western Europe and excluded Spain and the United Kingdom, never mind the United States. In prewar Germany, and certainly since 1933, the term "Western" was often used in a pejorative sense, particularly in racist discourse. A "Western race" roughly equaled a Mediterranean type of people that lagged far behind a "Nordic race": the former people allegedly did not like to work, had less Geist, produced fewer men of genius. It was cruel in a different way from the "Nordic race," said to enjoy teasing in a sadistic way, unlike the "Nordic Roheit," which remained "sachlich und anständig."[12]

The meaning of "West" in Westforschung can be grasped, furthermore, in one of the aims of the German Kulturpolitik that Petri implemented in Belgium: "The currently still dominant Western, in particular French, influence has to be replaced by a clear orientation toward Germany, and the country within the borders of the German sphere of influence has to be guarded in a cultural-political sense against the European West."[13]

The concept of a Westforschung with the above characteristics has its own historical background. Just as Ostforschung as such cannot do without the medieval German Eastern colonization and its legitimation or the "Mitteleuropa" concept of Friedrich Naumann and others,[14] Westforschung cannot do without the medieval empire of Charlemagne (768–814) and its legitimating function. The First Reich concept was coined around this Charles the Great and the centralizing European policy of Charles V (1500–1558), both of whom were not only more Catholic than the Pope, but ruled with an iron fist and genocidal practices. Their reigns were used long after 1945 in the Abendland ideology as a "glorious" frame of reference.[15] Nor can Westforschung do without the strongest possible duality between German and Romance peoples, not only in a linguistic sense but also in the realms of culture, politics and ethnicity.[16]

The heartland here is not "Mitteleuropa" but the Moselle-Meuse-Rhine region with its adjacent districts in France, Belgium, Luxemburg, and the Netherlands. Often this heartland is called "Niederrhein." Here, they say, Charlemagne had his strongholds in Aix-la-Chapelle, Cologne, and Dutch Nijmegen. A bit later the central and, apparently, "Nordic" lands of the so-called Mittelreich were located here, as was the northern center of political Roman Catholicism's worldly and cultural hegemony.

Within a Pan-Germanic framework, however, the concepts "Mitteleuropa" and "Mittelreich" had different legitimating functions. The former legitimated German hegemony or imperialism over historical and actual foreign countries. The latter had to legitimate first and foremost its own

Germanic and German descent, a basic element of German imperialism including "Mitteleuropa," "the East," or the world. Had not Charlemagne tried to conquer the East as well? Was not Germania to be seen as the "Grenzmark," the stronghold at the border of Christian civilization? All this kind of "argumentation" led the first leaders of the West German Research Society, the medievalist Hermann Aubin and his successor Franz Steinbach, to see *Westforschung* as the foundation of *Ostforschung*. In particular, Aubin, who stayed in Breslau during the war, played an important double role, influencing both *Westforschung* and, later, *Ostforschung* when the *Westforschung* method, *Kulturraumforschung*, became a model for research in the East.[17]

Several kinds of *Westforschung* can be discerned, each relating to a given occupied country and Germany (Dutch *Westforschung*, etc.). The same is true for the several disciplines (historical *Westforschung*, etc.) and for the different functional views (political, cultural, etc.).

Only by combining these and other characteristics, such as the religious allegiance of participants, is it possible to come up with a reliable profile of the "parties" involved in *Westforschung*. For instance, within Dutch historiography or linguistics from before World War II up to today, one can detect how and why Dutch *Westforscher*, German *Westforscher*, and German *Westforscher* of Dutch nationality (those Dutchmen who collaborated in every respect with Germans) worked side by side or against each other. Furthermore, the antagonisms between Roman Catholicism and Lutheran Protestantism, with their highly complex infrastructure and different political support for Nazism and Fascism, are of the utmost importance in understanding the orientations within *Westforschung*. It is along these lines, for instance, that an explanation can be found for the enmity between the "Protestant SS" and its *Ahnenerbe*, and the religious *Volkskunde* of the Catholics, notwithstanding the fact that both factions planned and undertook nearly the same *Volkskunde* activities.[18]

Most of these characteristics of *Westforschung* can now be demonstrated in a short sketch of the prewar, wartime, and postwar political activism and scholarly work of a remarkable man, the medievalist Franz Petri, who during his long and busy life apparently never questioned the political or scholarly relevancy of his rigid points of view, his *Westforschung* or *Kulturraumforschung*.

The Prewar Period to 1940

Petri was born on 22 February 1903, in the small town of Wolfenbüttel, southeast of Hanover, and raised in the Lutheran Protestant faith within a middle-class clerical environment. His father died a year later and his mother in 1919, so the orphan had to take care of himself and apparently succeeded quite well. He managed to study medieval history in Berlin, finishing in 1925. At that time he still lived in a Christian spirit and was a member of several Christian youth clubs, which all had a conservative and nationalistic outlook.

From the next year onward, however, starting with a two-year scholarship at the Institut für Grenz- und Auslandsdeutschtum in Marburg, he quickly found the themes with which he would work and the political creeds that would inspire him for the rest of his life. His cooperation with Franz Steinbach and the Institut für geschichtliche Landeskunde der Rheinlande in Bonn was particularly decisive.

This institute had been established in 1921 by "Berlin," the Rhineland authorities, the historian Hermann Aubin (1885–1969), and the linguist Theodor Frings (1886–1968). Among the staff members it was Franz Steinbach (1895–1964) who became Aubin's successor after Aubin and Frings went to the East (Breslau, Leipzig) to develop and sustain *Ostforschung*. Their institute had a number of assignments concerning the districts along the border with France, Belgium, Luxemburg, and the Netherlands: pedagogical-propagandistic work geared to the Rhenish population, political work including *Abwehr* (intelligence) for "Berlin," and scientific work, mostly in medieval history, for everybody else. They arranged numerous conferences with academics from abroad and from Germany, so as to infiltrate their networks, making them collaborators in their "Western" variant of the German cause. From the beginning their motivation was clear: to help undo "Versailles" and develop a new German national spirit, i.e., an identity, by appealing to the old Germanic medieval history of the Rhineland and adjacent regions.

Around 1931 Petri jumped on this bandwagon and formed with Aubin, Frings, and Steinbach the nucleus of the historical *Westforschung*, which survived as such long after the death of its founders. Around them an extensive network of scholars from several disciplines, (radical) right-wing politicians, and civil and religious authorities was established from the local to the national level. From 1931 the so-called West German Research Society (WFG) formed an important part of this network; the WFG was in turn incorporated into an (inter)national network of such research societies.[19]

In a political sense, there was practically no other choice for these groups but to rally around the radical right, which for a man like Steinbach and many others in the Rhineland was not at odds with their Roman Catholicism. On the contrary, they all had been right-wing conservatives before 1933 and quickly enlisted in the SA, NSDAP, or SS thereafter. They also worked for particular border districts providing information, propaganda materials, or direct action support. Steinbach and Aubin, for instance, activated irredentist movements in the Saarland and Alsace-Lorraine.[20]

Petri also made contact with the noisy supporters of the Flemish (Autonomy) Movement who lived in Cologne. From about 1935 to 1939 he not only was a historian at the university, but served as director of the

German-Dutch Institute and assisted in the establishment of the Deutsch-Vlämische Arbeitsgemeinschaft (DeVlag), wrote articles in its journal, and spoke at the Flemish activists' political meetings, making them collaborators and defenders of the German interests in Belgium, France, and the Netherlands.

Whatever their political choice or area of political work, scholars like Steinbach, Petri, Aubin, and Frings also produced scholarly work that was closely related to their other tasks. In Petri's case this involved studies on the so-called language border (*Sprachgrenze*) between Germany and France (1934). In this genre he wrote his most important work, *Germanisches Volkserbe in Wallonien und Nordfrankreich* (1937).[21] For these studies, he lived in Belgium for several years and started sympathizing with the strong supporters of Flemish autonomy known as "flamingants." Thanks to his work with DeVlag, Petri became a true flamingant; still, his political ideology was clearly National Socialist.

He and his compatriots, however, also had a scholarly ideology (for some people a contradiction in terms). The basis for this was laid in his Marburg years under the influence of J. W. Mannhardt. In a publication about Germans abroad (*Deutschtum im Ausland*) Petri asked:

> [W]hich of the great forms of Germanship should determine the starting point of [our] work: the German State, the Soil of the German People [*Volksboden*] or the whole of the German People [*deutsche Gesamtvolk*].... If the German State is the starting point, the scene of German History is minimalized more and more.... If one starts with the [*Volksboden*], i.e. the united living space of the Germans,... one sees a serious and continuous interest in the actions of Germans in their history [*viel größere Beharrung für den Schauplatz deutscher Geschichte*].... But [the starting point] must be the *deutsche Gesamtvolk*, it must be the history of the German People and not only in its State and on its Living Soil, but also outside these in the dispersion all over the world.[22]

To choose between exactly these three alternatives is in itself a typical characteristic of German conservatives, but Petri's answer in 1925 belonged to the standard expressions of the more radical right-wingers.

A few years later he wrote about the need to "create a real history of the People [*Volksgeschichte*]," in which *Volk* must be at the very center and base of the narrative, analyses, and concepts. Through his cooperation with Aubin, Steinbach and many others also adopted his *Volk* racist connotations. Studies in thus field, he learned in Bonn, had to be done in cooperation with several other disciplines, in particular with the geography of dialects, toponymic studies (*Namenkunde*), physical anthropology, and the German type of folklore (*Volkskunde*). In Bonn these came to be combined in what was called *Kulturraumforschung*, the historical study of cultural characteristics in a specific region. Such regions were often called a "historical landscape" (*Geschichtslandschaft*), "landscape" being conceptualized in a German organic way.

Special attention was devoted to borders, where two or more cultures and "races" would come into conflict; here the Germans could demonstrate their true Germanic power in a provocative way[23] while the political validity of their claims was tested. Aubin, Frings, and especially Steinbach had invested much work in the study of the language boundary (*Sprachgrenze*) between Germans and Roman(ic)s. This boundary was supposed to run from the area of Geneva, through Basel, the French city of Metz, the city of Luxemburg, between Liège and Maastricht, and then westward via Brussels to the Belgian coast.

Before the *Westforscher* at University of Bonn adopted this language boundary, it was common wisdom that it amounted to a separation between the early Germanic and Romance tribal settlements. Steinbach, however, denied this in 1926. He advanced the thesis that this boundary was the result, the "sediment" of long-lasting cultural conflicts between Germanic and Romance tribes: it is the final line of retreat of the Germanic withdrawal (*Rückzugslinie des Germanischen*) arrived at in the late Frankish history.[24] Whatever the historical truth, one thing is certain about this language boundary: it became a centerpiece of historical *Westforschung*.

It was Franz Petri who argued that if there was a withdrawal to this boundary, then there must also have been an ultimate settlement area somewhere to the south. Indeed, in the thousand-plus pages of his *Germanisches Volkserbe*, he indicated a Frankish settlement area that extended in the west to Brittany, in the south to the Loire River, and in the east from the Moselle, Meuse, and Marne region all the way up to the Teutoburger Wald in Westphalia. Petri called this whole eastern region the core of Frankish culture (*Kerngebiet der fränkischen Kultur*), and it has remained so for *Westforscher* in this area and its adjacent countries.[25] The space allowed here does not permit discussion of this book or the many contradictory reactions that it provoked.[26]

More importantly, Petri was not very original; his contention was just more of the same of what Steinbach, Frings, or Walter von Wartburg had already argued. Steinbach saw his chance and extended Petri's arguments[27] so that his book could be better used in the German's propaganda battle to legitimate the German claim that up to the Loire, France had "in fact" a German heritage. Also, Petri stressed, like all *Westforscher* that his work on the old European history served present political aims. To indicate this, he claimed that his work was actual. In Petri's case it was even said that Adolf Hitler himself had read *Germanisches Volkserbe* in one night from cover to cover![28]

The goal of *Westforschung*, i.e., the German political claim to French territory, turned out to be a double-edged sword: the "fact" of the partly ethnic, historical, linguistic, geographic, *volkskundliche* "equality" between Germany and France, between the German's and the French, was translated into a threat of military conquest as well as an offer of "Let's join together, because we are somehow Brüder." Beethoven's "Ninth" was never played so often.[29]

It was the three million French-speaking Walloons in Belgium who would experience what it meant to be confronted with a double-edged sword after Petri and the German army invaded Belgium in May 1940. He was brought quickly up the career ladder, over his compatriot and boss Steinbach, as a reward for his work as a dedicated *Westforschung* fighter. However, he proved very able to veil the German threat with a friendly handshake. Even his theory concerning the Germanic basis of old Francia supported this ambiguity.

A look at the map of the Walloon provinces provides two answers to an obvious question: How does one explain the Romanic-Walloon wedge between two Germanic areas? If one stresses "racial" equality, then it is not a wedge at all, whereby it might be concluded that the Walloons are more or less Germanic (*Mischlinge,* in the lingo of the day). However, if the Steinbach-Petri thesis concerning the *Rückzugsgebiet* was interpreted to mean that the Walloon provinces were the result of the last "Romanic attack" on surrendering Germanic tribes, then the Walloons were the heirs of the sworn enemy. During the war a solution was concocted that—if there had been enough time to execute it—would have meant the end of the Walloon provinces. Petri was among the core decision-makers.

A *Kulturpapst* in Brussels

The director of the Zentrum für Niederlande Studien, Horst Lademacher, a successor to Franz Petri, stated in his necrology for Petri in 1993 that he also had strong views on this highly complex task.[30] At the very beginning of his Belgian career, Petri wanted nothing less than to prepare "a fundamental renewal of the countries" culture and to realize already this renewal's main items. With this it should be possible to enlarge and enhance the community with Germany based on the folk and natural solidarity and imperial tradition and necessity."[31] Lademacher's piece is misleading.[32] In fact, Petri was a highly motivated conqueror in Belgium who formulated the aims of the SS in their earliest stages.

Petri was on the relatively small staff of the German military government, where he was given the task of controlling every aspect or activity that could be called *Kultur* on behalf of the Führer. He and his colleague Werner Reese—until the middle of 1941, when Reese died—had to manage everything from primary education to universities, film to theater, religion to art, including a large part of what was called cultural or ethno-policy (*Volkstumspolitik*). This ethno-policy dealt with the acute linguistic and ethnic antagonisms among the Flemings, the Walloons, and a small minority of German speakers in Belgium. Very few members of the staff could speak the languages reasonably well or were experts in the "Flemish Question." The result was that Petri practically had absolute power in all these matters of *Kultur*.

Petri's aims were realized slowly but in a determined fashion, first in the background and more or less in competition with the war aims of the Wehrmacht, i.e., of its representatives at the top of the military government: von Falkenhausen, Reeder (Petri's boss in Belgium), and others. Later, as Himmler personally joined the battle against Reeder, the aims of the SS and Petri's role in realizing them became much clearer. When Belgium was liberated in August 1944, the SS had just gained total victory over Reeder. With respect to Lademacher's arguments, here are further details.

Lademacher's interpretation starts by reducing the role of the German military government "as a one hundred per cent supervision administration [*Aufsichtsverwaltung*], which has to consolidate or repair things which are in order and to continue with economic life rather than to pursue some political goals [*nicht irgendwelche politischen Lösungen anzustreben*]. Whatever the political differences within this government, it did not act in a way that aimed at future political reconstruction and did not go beyond the general maintenance of the communication with Germany." His next assertion concerns the typical role the SS played in Belgium: "the military government continuously had to counterbalance a growing number of SS and NSDAP institutions that made attempts at interfering [*hineinzuregieren*]." Lademacher's last contention reveals that the sinister plans of the SS resulted "in the incorporation of Belgium into a Grossgermanisches Reich while the country is divided in two departments [*Reichsgaue*] ... all this is based on DeVlag, transformed in a National-Socialist sense, and the Algemene SS-Vlaanderen [the general SS organization in Flanders]."

What is the conclusion reached from these statements? They are interconnected because Lademacher's central thesis is that Petri belonged to the military government, which was nothing but a kind of innocent traffic controller that continuously had to fight against the SS; therefore, Petri did nothing but his duty, and had nothing to do with the SS. In this time of conflicts, "Petri acted as an admonisher [*Mahner*] as well as a responsible scholar defending the historical truth who did not manipulate developments if others made such demands [*wenn andere solche Forderung erhoben*]."[33]

The serious downsizing of Petri's position of power by mitigating the role of the German military government ignores its war crimes and its assistance in rounding up Belgian Jews and others, as well as the obvious and crucial support needed to conquer a peaceful country and withstand all the consequences. Cynically, Petri wrote in his *Zweiter Bericht*, for instance, of the Germans' second destruction of the famous library at the University of Louvain (the first time was in World War I): there was now the chance to replace several million books with the superior German cultural products. He had apparently organized a spectacular, large military transport of Germanic books, journals, and encyclopedias (he proudly mentioned titles) in order to show how helpful the Germans could be.

In painting the German military occupation as something like an innocent, humanitarian, attractive affair, Lademacher only repeats what Petri trumpeted after the war. Petri even referred to a doctoral thesis by one of his pupils, Mathias Haupt, who concluded with the help of Petri's personal archive that "it is without any doubt that notwithstanding some conflicts the military staff ... succeeded ... in realizing and sustaining an acceptable relationship with the Belgian General Secretaries as leaders of the bureaucracies and with the population. Therefore, serious military resistance did not occur in Belgium."[34] Neither the many hundreds of Belgian resistance fighters who were shot by this very military staff, nor the Belgian resistance organizations that had learned their lessons from the first German occupation in 1914–1918, counted for Petri or his pupils. Haupt did not use Petri's archive to disclose the facts.[35]

Franz Petri and Anti-Semitism

Time and again people have stressed the strong religious attitudes of Franz Petri as proof of his innocence. The frequently repeated "argument" by scholars like Lademacher, however, comes from Petri himself as he answered a critic, the Dutch historian Ivo Schöffer: "That we in Belgium in the military government chiefly stood with our back against the wall and fought against the SS, DeVlag (which was dominated by the SS) and their opinions is a fact which is rather unknown to Schöffer."[36]

In the light of what was said above about Petri's involvement in DeVlag before the war, what he wrote here was dubious in 1956, and so it was when Lademacher wrote nearly 40 years later. Before I comment further on Petri's thoughts and behavior during the war, another bold and curious statement of 1962 should be mentioned. Petri wrote that the military government "was without any doubt relatively the best German occupation bureaucracy during the Second World War ... it was its duty to act within the framework of Hitler's ... fundamental directives ... its competence was slowly eroded [*durchlöchert und ausgehöhlt*] by all kinds of SS and party institutions. In particular, the latter are responsible for ... the repression and cruelties ... in Belgium ... especially the deportation of the Jews."[37]

It has to be clarified that all these quotations, written over a long period, are interchangeable, having the same tune by only one composer. Now that sources like Petri's *Zweiter Bericht* can be studied, this fairy tale with a real happy ending (after the war Petri was awarded one medal or honor after another by the Belgian and Dutch authorities and prime ministers) crumbles, and there remains a repellent story.

Apart from what was said above about Petri's position on the staff of the military government, the best demonstration of the staff's importance is that he was able to wage a personal war against the Belgian Cardinal van Roey, who was no less important than the Belgian king. But here we shall stress what Petri wrote about DeVlag, the Jews, and the aims of the *Westforschung* in his *Zweiter Bericht*.

In this internal report one never reads any criticism of the SS-dominated DeVlag. On the contrary, DeVlag is discussed in a very positive and exclusive way. For instance: "In relation to the Cultural Councils [*Kulturräten*] and other personalities like … the Flemish leader of DeVlag, J. van de Wiele/Antwerp, the basic principles of an organic organization of the Flemish artistic and cultural community are already discussed and developed months before they are tested at local levels." Or: "The practical work of DeVlag tries to enhance in many young local groups in the country which form in several respects the lively nucleus of the Flemish cultural organizations, the deployment [*Einsatz*] of German forces [*Kräfte*]."[38]

At least two conclusions can be drawn with respect to DeVlag: in their postwar statements Petri, Lademacher, and others spread much disinformation: and by the beginning of the occupation, Petri was already a rather staunch defender of the SS-dominated DeVlag.[39] This second conclusion is important not only in the evaluation of the *Westforschung* or Petri's biography, but also for many other reasons such as, for instance, the need to rewrite a substantial part of the Belgian war-history books on which Petri stamped his views.[40] I shall return to this question below.

Next there is Petri's statement that it was not the military government but the SS that persecuted the Jews. The *Zweiter Bericht* also provides the necessary background information in this respect. Here, Petri thinks it "quite appropriate (that) Jews remain locked out from the artists" corporation [*Künstlerverband*]."[41] He ordered that eighty to hundred university professors be dismissed because they had supported anti-German protests before the war; included were "the ones who must be disqualified because of their Jewish descent."[42] Later in his *Zweiter Bericht* Petri announced that universities and other institutions of higher learning "which are supported with Jewish money and subventions of the French Ministry of Foreign Affairs" be closed immediately.[43] This was a few months after Petri arrived in Belgium.

The conclusion seems unequivocal: contrary to Petri's postwar lip service, the military government, too, persecuted the Jews, while Petri was its handyman in cultural matters. We now turn directly to the relationship between the aims of *Westforschung* and Petri's behavior during the war.

SS *Westforschung* and the Walloon Country

If he wanted to, a man of Petri's background and position was able to fight a very personal war in Belgium. That Petri wanted this can be deduced from the aims of *Westforschung* as circumscribed in his *Zweiter Bericht*: to abolish the "Western orientation" of the Flemish and Walloon people; to "germanize" science and its institutions over the long run; to realize the flamingant goals that were formulated in his prewar political life; to provide his old German and Flemish friends like Steinbach, van Roosbroeck,

Cyriel Verschaeve, and DeVlag members with lucrative jobs; to transform into practice the demands formulated in his *Habilitationsschrift* concerning the *Sprachgrenze* such as, for instance, support for the ethnic Germans in Arel and Luxemburg.

Therefore, in these years Petri's personal stand and position as a scholar match to a very large degree *Westforschung*'s interests, which were in turn instruments in the general Western expansion of the Third Reich. This is demonstrated, for example, in the following statement (1940): "In this country along the border of the Germanic and Romanic world, one special scholarly discipline must be boosted, which is uniquely derived from the spirit of the New Germany while, till now, it is purposefully disregarded at the Belgian universities: this is *Volksforschung*. For this study the establishment of professorships in *Rassenkunde* and prehistory [*Vorgeschichte*] is an urgent task. This must be accompanied by a fundamental reform of prehistoric research in Belgium, in which the rich Nordic and Germanic tradition has been systematically studied only in small part."[44]

Here, personal interest, *Westforschung*'s ideals, and ideology coalesced with the research program of the SS-Ahnenerbe. As such, it does not prove that Petri was anything like an "SS-mole" within the Wehrmacht government. Much stronger proof appears in the following years. In 1943, Petri published two articles remarkable in form and content.[45] Both appeared in the prestigious journal *Westland*, a most typical *Westforschung* journal issued in The Hague by the Dutch Reichskommissar Arthur Seyss-Inquart with the subtitle "Journal for landscape, history and culture along the Rhine, Moselle, Meuse and Scheldt." It was lavishly illustrated and beautifully printed, with articles written by scholarly, military, and political authorities.[46] Apart from the fact that Seyss-Inquart was also an honorary SS officer, the editors were all high-ranking SS officers and mostly members of the SS-Ahnenerbe. The strict propaganda articles and many of the pictures were part of SS propaganda, while all articles had to support the *Großgermanische Reichsgedanke* of the SS rather than the earlier ideological stand of so-called Pan-Netherlands Thought (*Großniederländische Gedanke*). The least one can say of the scholarly writers is that they all belonged to the inner circle of *Westforschung* and most were also longtime members of the SS-Ahnenerbe, like Petri's colleague, the prehistorian Walther von Stokar. Of course, publishing in the German language in *Westland* in the core zone of *Westforschung*, the Niederrhein, heralded the commitment of the SS to this zone after several years of work in the backwoods of the Third Reich.

Another noteworthy fact was that Petri's position was apparently so important that the highest officials in Berlin paid him tribute. One of these, the Ahnenerbe-Reichsgeschäftsführer Wolfram Sievers, kept an interesting diary. After a visit to Seyss-Inquart in The Hague on 15 April 1943, where he apparently had a car-meeting with SS-Hauptsturmführer Dr. Schneider, at that time the highest-ranked Ahnenerbe man in the Netherlands,[47] he wrote the next day in a business-like manner but also very tellingly: "9h12 Departure from The Hague …; 13h45 Arrival in Brussels; 15h–16h in the office of the commander of the Wehrmacht a conference with Oberkriegsverwaltungsrat Professor Dr. Petri and Kriegsverwaltungsrat Professor Dr. Rosemann, in particular about the cooperation concerning prehistorical security measures [*Sicherungsmassnahmen*]; 16h30 on to Waterloo."[48]

At this point, Wolfram Sievers had reached the zenith of his power. From this visit to Waterloo until his ultimate encounter with the hangman, it was only a few years of struggle against an inevitable defeat. Petri also stood at the height of his power; only fifteen months were left before he would steal away to the *Heimat*, where he soon started a new honorable life. Then, in April 1943, Petri was not only busy with his reconstruction of the Belgian *Kultur* but with the *Arbeitseinsatz* of the Belgian students as well. He combined theory with practice with great ease.

In this room at the top, one spoke what Victor Klemperer later would call the *lingua tertii imperii*. These people talked about the practice of what Petri had formulated as early as 1940. The looting of valuable prehistoric artifacts from Belgium should not be overlooked.[49] Illustrative of their mindset is the case of one typical *Westforscher*, the prehistorian Professor Walther von Stokar of the University of Cologne. He cooperated energetically with Sievers and Schneider in 1943. This prehistorian did indeed do some of the usual digging work in the Netherlands. However, he was also very busy "borrowing" specific medical instruments from the University of Leiden to enable Sievers to undertake all sorts of experiments in concentration camps.[50]

Turning to the content of Petri's articles in *Westland*, in particular the first one, a short programmatic text concerning the origin of the Walloons, he professes that "scientific pronouncements about these things [Petri meant his own theory of the *Germanische Volkserbe*, which, according to him, could be developed further] … shall find their proof in the study of the racial anthropological pictures [*rassenbiologischen Aufnahmen*] which are being made at the moment in the Walloon provinces on the initiative of the Reichsführer-SS."[51] One hagiographer was eager to stress that "Petri did not rally to the SS planning experts."[52] Still, Petri's racism came to the fore in all its boldness in this article.

It was also important for other reasons, for which some background information will be helpful. *Ostforschung* had earned a nasty image mainly because of its help in the planning and execution of the so-called population *Umsiedlungen*. This typical example of SS camouflage language refers to the compulsory transfer of many millions of East European families, which is in turn connected to the death of millions of Jews, Romany, and Slavs. Yet *Westforschung* did not acquire a similar stigma. Was this so because the Germans merely "visited" their so-called *Brüdervölker* in the West? These were said to be people with more or less the same ethnic constitution and *Kultur*, who lived during long periods of their history within a Germanic *Lebensraum* or under a German political umbrella. The sturdy, blond Dutch polder-farmers who had managed to conquer a large colonial empire were beloved by the "Protestant SS." The Flemish farmers were "racially pure" too; to be sure, their colonial empire has been established by their cruel kings, but they were beloved by their Rhenish Catholic *Brüder*. From an SS point of view, this latter quality did not confer advantage, as was demonstrated when the Catholic Steinbach did not get the position that was given to the Protestant Petri, even though objectively Steinbach had the better credentials.[53]

The Walloons, on the other hand, had virtually nothing that was attractive to either the Protestant SS or the Rhenish Catholics: they spoke French (and that a dialect that some derided as only French slang); their mountainous country lacked a large agricultural base with farmers' conservative religious traditions; theirs is typically an urban and industrial (coal and steel) polity with sharp class conflicts and large areligious groups like communists and socialists. In addition, on linguistic or cultural maps it seemed clear that historically the Walloon provinces had driven a Romanic-French wedge between two Germanic entities. Could this war provide the latter with the opportunity to connect?

For all of these reasons "the Walloon provinces" and their three million people formed a large problem for the authorities. Only the highest German authorities knew the solution: *Umsiedlung*, for instance to the East as far as the *Generalgouvernement* in Poland. The main argument in favor of this was a racist one: Were the Walloons *Untermenschen* or not? Accordingly, Himmler's "racial anthropological pictures," to which Petri referred, were quite decisive regarding the life and death of most Walloons.[54]

In this fundamental debate Petri occupied the key position: as top *Westforscher* he was the expert in Flemish-Wallonian questions; as *Oberkriegsverwaltungsrat* he was one of the most senior bureaucrats; and as "Superflamingant" he was strongly motivated to side with the Flemish. As a scholar, he supported the threat as well as the handshake option indicated earlier. At that time, he could not escape the consequences of his SS allegiance, but he still made a crucial decision: in the *Westland* article, he asked what the "limited problem of the descent of a few million people [*begrenzten Frage nach der Abstammung von ein paar Millionen Menschen*]" meant compared with the "fundamental decision of what will be the development of the Abendland." In this way, one slides from planner (*Vordenker*) to collaborator.[55]

Petri's career can be followed in great detail because incriminating archival material was saved thanks to research into the *faites et gestes* of Hermann Roloff, Seyss-Inquart's chief staff member for national and regional planning. After many SS intrigues from the middle of 1942 onward, Roloff became the pivot in the so-called Hollandplan.[56] This was a regional development plan to construct the West-Central part of a grid on the European continent in which each region found its proper place with its own economic, cultural, and ethnic qualities. In this plan Niederrhein stretched from Cologne to the north and west as far as Rotterdam and Antwerp. A spectacular infrastructure would be constructed with the brand-new Albert Canal from Maastricht to Antwerp as a southern axis.

It was Oberkriegsverwaltungsrat Franz Petri who cooperated with Roloff in this mega-project, working out proposals, with some other Belgian and German experts. The "armchair scholar" who was, in fact, the Belgian *Kulturpapst*, and had already had much experience with the *Arbeitseinsatz*, now became a planner of a new *Lebensraum* as well. This planning project on a West European scale was based on the following argument concerning the Walloon provinces.

This part of Belgium was meant, of course, to become a district (*Gau*) in the Grossgermanisches Reich. Problem one: In a "racially pure" Reich there was no place for the Walloon "*Mischlinge*." Problem two: What to do with the very important Walloon industrial potential? The answer: Nothing, for a brand-new infrastructure was to come between Rhineland-Westphalia and the Dutch delta, ignoring the Walloon provinces. Therefore, Wallonia's large industrial complexes, the basis of its existence, were to be taken away and resettled (*umsiedeln*) to the north. The Walloon provinces were to be transformed into a *Grenzmark* as in the Middle Ages, i.e., an area with large agricultural enterprises and a strong military devoted to defending the Reich against a possible French attack.

Time was running out for Petri, but on paper he and his colleagues had already wiped out the Walloon provinces. The fate of the Walloons within this framework remains unknown. Since these plans and their far-reaching consequences were discussed before Petri published his *Westland* article, one has to read between the lines to understand their implications. For example, the meaning of his "limited problem of the descent of a few million people" could be a veiled reference to murder.

A Proper Scholarly Life after 1945

The return to the destroyed *Heimat* must have been traumatic for Petri. In the first few months, the 41-year-old historian apparently wanted to compensate for this by showing an extreme form of "hand wringing." For a while he stayed in a detention camp for interrogation by the British, where he became a convert to a democrat in true medieval style; he even started to preach, while presenting himself as a humble servant in a hospital. Meanwhile, he compared his relatively luxurious detention camp with nothing less than a Nazi concentration camp.[57] In short, Petri contrived to demonstrate another side to his character: his ability to turn himself into the most peaceful, unassuming, suffering person on earth. It was a side that he showed preferably to foreigners who might accuse him of something.

It is also remarkable that Petri tried to reproduce exactly the social circumstances of his life after 1918: again he joined conservative Christian movements that advocated a spiritual renewal, the origins of which they found in early medieval times. These "restoration" movements spread rapidly as they got all the help they needed from the Adenauer government and the Roman Catholic authorities. This led to the apotheosis of the Karl der Grosse festivals in the early 1950s, again in the principal role of the Savior of the *Abendland* but this time fighting against the "Red Menace."[58] Aubin, Steinbach, and Petri were the main writers of this extreme restoration movement. Aubin was moreover an adviser-ideologue to Franz-Joseph Strauss, the controversial Minister of Defense in the Federal Republic.[59]

This restoration movement can be explained only in part by reference to Cold War "necessities."[60] To a large extent it was a genuine reaction of German conservatives who remained in power thanks to the absence of a strong opposition. Also in play were the frailty of democratic ideas and practices in all institutions, and the difficult digestion of war trauma. Cold War ideology and practice legitimated everything.

This was true in the German Democratic Republic as well. Take, for instance, the *faites et gestes* of the linguist Theodor Frings, who invented and led the historical *Westforschung* with Aubin from 1918 onward and supported *Ostforschung*.[61] He did not leave the Soviet sector in 1945, nor later the GDR, and became a highly important and honored scholar there by continuing to publish his original ideas and theories without changing a word. Nor did he abandon his personal "good old boys" networks in West Germany, Belgium, and the Netherlands.

Between Petri's detour into detention and crocodile tears and the Karl der Grosse apotheosis, the already mentioned restoration of *Westforschung* in the Arbeitsgemeinschaft für westdeutsche Landes- und Volksforschung took place, while the former West German Research Society and Steinbach's Institut für geschichtliche Landeskunde der Rheinlande in Bonn were reestablished in all of their former glory. All of these institutions, with their obscure connections and branches, were manned by members of the "good old boys" club and drew their staff from there or other "reliable" quarters. In addition, they were boasted to eminence by the establishment of the capital of the Federal Republic in Bonn, the capital city of German *Westforschung*.

It is nearly impossible to underestimate the influence of these institutions (often operating separately from but attached to university, while not subject to any public control) within the government bureaucracy, which led to funding of their numerous new branches, international conferences with prospective foreign and German clients, and expensive series of books and journals as an excellent means to attract foreign academics.[62]

For a short time it seemed that Petri would be able to return to the university because of opposition at the University of Cologne (led by Professor

Peter Rassow), but the help of Franz Steinbach, Hermann Aubin, Theodor Mayer, Hermann Heimpel, Secretary of State Franz Thedieck (a former member of the Belgian military occupation administration), and many others was enough to give him a fresh start. Scholars like Aubin, Steinbach, and Gerhard Ritter defended Petri with the argument that he had not been a National Socialist.[63] However, in his written defense against Rassow from October 1945, Petri demonstrated his short memory and started a postwar life full of disinformation with often remarkable results.

It was no longer a white lie when he suggested that during the war he had opposed attempts to misuse his *Germanisches Volkserbe*, while he apparently believed his writings were not fundamentally wrong. He also denied his contacts with Gantois, the priest who headed the French-Flemish collaborators' movement.[64] Furthermore, he promoted the theory that the military government had done a good job in Belgium, but, alas, the SS and many others had thwarted his cultural policy and his work for the *Arbeitseinsatz*. In particular, he now stressed his serious difficulties with DeVlag and the SS in the Walloon provinces. This argumentation served as Petri's life story during the rest of his life.

To sustain his personal legend, Petri was backed by a substantial number of persons with more or less the same professional problems.[65] They enabled him to aspire to gain recognition for the scholarly part of his life in the service of *Westforschung*, even in the former conquered countries.[66]

Worst, his pugnacious nature would engage him in a lifelong battle against attempts to undermine his and Steinbach's theory of the *Sprachgrenze*. He was apparently convinced that this centerpiece of historical *Westforschung* and of the legitimation of German claims to Western territories had to remain intact after 1945.

Several publications by Petri were issued (often with testimonies from friends, preferably from Belgium and the Netherlands); in numerous conference lectures Petri, Steinbach, a client abroad, or a pupil from one of their institutes in Münster, Bonn, or elsewhere proved how right in some or all of its aspects this theory was.[67] Convincing non-German historians of his political innocence became his quest (and that of *Westforschung* in general).

The crème de la crème of the Dutch and Belgian medievalists (and of some other fields), alongside representatives of other relevant *Westforschung* disciplines like linguistics and *Volkskunde*, flocked to Aubin's, Petri's, and Steinbach's conferences from the late 1950s onward, published in their works, became members of their societies.[68] In my book I detail how all this dramatically affected the historiography of Belgium and the Netherlands, as may be seen in the official new fifteen-volume *Algemene Geschiedenis der Nederlanden* (*NAGN*). This is particularly true if compared with the first edition published directly after the war (*AGN*), with its very sharp criticism of *Westforschung* by Charles Verlinden and Bernhard Slicher van Bath. Significantly, the many writings of the latter, a world-famous medievalist pitted during and after the war against the *Westforschung* of Geyl, Petri, Reese, and others, were ignored.[69]

It is no surprise from his war experiences that another part of Petri's work after the war and subsequently another part of *Westforschung* involved urban and regional planning (*Raumplanung* in Germany; also *Raumforschung*). In March 1949 Steinbach organized a position for Petri as manager of an Institut für Raumforschung in Bonn, in which capacity he would reorganize the West German Research Society.[70] This was followed by comparable jobs in Münster, where he worked for the Province of Westphalia and cooperated in a project that Aubin had started in 1929 as a form of "historical *Kulturraumforschung.*" In fact, it dealt with classic *Westforschung* subject: historical-political analysis of the province Nordrhein-Westfalen and its German and international borders. Before the war, Aubin and his scholars had published several volumes in the series, which Aubin continued until 1996 in cooperation with Petri.

Both used their newly gained position of power for many purposes, including developing another classic *Westforschung* theme: racial studies. They wanted to "invent" a typical "Westphalian Race" (*Westfälischer Rassetypus*). In pursuit of this aim and against a small and desperate public opposition, they cooperated over many years with former top Nazi anthropologists such as Egon Freiherr von Eickstedt, Otmar Freiherr von Verschuer, and Ilse Schwidetzky. Their "racial research" was also supported by the University of Münster. In 1967 Petri combined the "results" with the original "*Volkstums*" ideas from before the war.

Petri's star radiated ever brighter within and outside the Federal Republic. He achieved a position quite comparable to the one he had held in the Belgian military occupation administration. He was celebrated with several *Festschriften* and other publications in his honor, and was awarded numerous medals in Germany, Belgium, and the Netherlands. He became the embodiment of *Westforschung* and of the *Vergangenheitspolitik*. The question remains whether *Westforschung* disappeared with his death in 1993.

Notes

I thank Michael Fahlbusch for his stimulating comments and Alison Fisher for correcting my English.

1. See Michael Fahlbusch, *Wissenschaft im Dienst der nationalsozialistischen Politik? Die "Volksdeutschen Forschungsgemeinschaften" von 1931–1945* (Baden-Baden, 1999), with an excellent chapter on the Westdeutsche Forschungsgemeinschaft: 350–440 and 506–512, 691–728. See also Peter Schöttler, "Die historische 'Westforschung' zwischen 'Abwehrkampf' und territorialer Offensive," in *Geschichtsschreibung als Legitimationswissenschaft 1918–1945,* ed. Peter Schöttler (Frankfurt am Main, 1997).

2. It does not make very good reading but it is, of course, indispensable to differentiate between *Ost-* and *Westforschung* themselves and the present study of these phenomena in particular, because there are persons and institutions that are doing genuine *Westforschung* at present.

3. Jan M. Piskorski et al., eds., *"Deutsche Ostforschung" und "polnische Westforschung" im Spannungsfeld von Wissenschaft und Politik* (Osnabrück, 2002). For the simplistic equation Deutsche *Ostforschung* = Polish *Westforschung*, see Manfred Grässlin, "Was kostet eine Krone? Ein deutsch-polnisches Kolloquium zum Akt von Gnesen," *Frankfurter Allgemeine Zeitung*, 22 Febuary 2000, or "Widerstreitende Historiographien. Ostmitteleuropas Konfliktgeschichte, Tagung des Herder Instituts, Marburg," *AHF-Information 28*, 17 May 2000. Piskorski works within a Polish tradition of criticizing the partisan *Ostkunde* in the schools of the Federal Republic in which, for instance, the longing for a lost *Heimat* predominated. See Waclaw Sobanski, *School Textbooks in the German Federal Republic* (Warszawa, 1962), 76–113.

4. Those who now (re)read the critical comments of George Iggers on Winfried Schulze's, "German Historiography from the 1930s to the 1950s," in *Paths of Continuity: Central European Historiography from the 1930s to the 1950s*, ed. Hartmut Lehmann and James van Horn Melton (Cambridge, 1994), 43–47, will experience how far this influence extended even in the most liberal form of German historiography. No one in this important anthology had written yet about *Westforschung* and its many peculiar problems, while Schulze apparently learned nothing from Iggers's comments when he was directly confronted with its existence. See my review in Winfried Schulze and Gerhard Otto Oexle, eds., "Deutsche Historiker im Nationalsozialismus," *German History* 19 (2001): 122–126.

5. Hans Derks, *Deutsche Westforschung. Ideologie und Praxis im 20. Jahrhundert* (Leipzig, 2001). The Franz Petri story told in this essay is only part of what is written about in this book. Petri's historical analyses for other than the Frankish period remain untouched, as does a large part of the organizational work to propagate *Westforschung* or *Kulturraumforschung*. In this contribution my notes must be minimal. Only where I quote or have to elaborate on something will I give a reference.

6. It is necessary to use here *Volkskunde*, because we are dealing with a specific German activity and discipline with a mainly Nazi background, as is explained in Derks, *Deutsche Westforschung*, 71–85, in my conference contribution "Volk und Volkskunde in der Westforschung," in *Regionalisierungen im Vergleich*, University of Leipzig, December 2001, and in my book *Volk ohne Sprache und andere Kapitel aus der Westforschung* (forthcoming, 2005, chap. 3).

7. For earlier kinds of *Ostforschung* (the study of the German *Ostkolonisation* in the Middle Ages, etc.), see Michael Burleigh, *Germany Turns Eastwards: A Study of Ostforschung in the Third Reich* (Cambridge, 1988), 22ff., and the definition given by Wolfgang Wippermann in *Enzyklopaedie des Nationalsozialismus*, ed. Wolfgang Benz et al. (Stuttgart, 1997), 632.

8. Christian Gerlach, Kalkulierte Morde. Die deutsche Wirtschafts- und Vernichtungspolitik in Weissrussland 1941 bis 1944 (Hamburg, 1999), 11–35 and 1126–1162; the whole spectrum of perpetrators and victims came to the fore as demonstrated, for instance, in chaps. 8 and 10.

9. Quoted in Derks, *Deutsche Westforschung*, 265.

10. See the previous paragraph.

11. Quoted in Derks, *Deutsche Westforschung*, 208–209.

12. Cornelia Schmitz-Berning, *Vokabular des Nationalsozialismus* (Berlin, New York, 2000), 694ff.

13. Quoted in ibid., 258.

14. Sven Papcke and Werner Weidenfeld, eds., *Traumland Mittelauropa? Beiträge zu einer aktuellen Kontroverse* (Darmstadt, 1988); Hans Ester, Hans Hecker, and Erika Poettgens, eds., *Deutschland, aber wo liegt es? Deutschland und Mitteleuropa. Analysen und historische Dokumente* (Amsterdam and Atlanta, Ga., 1993).

15. Derks, *Deutsche Westforschung*, 233–247.

16. Ibid., 62–71.

17. Discussions about these views raged among prewar medievalists, and only the German ones, in particular, Henri Pirenne in Belgium and Johan Huizinga in the Netherlands, were involved. The only one during the war who openly analyzed and protested against the falsification of medieval history by the Bonner Schule (such as Aubin, Steinbach, Petri, and Reese) was the Dutch medievalist Bernhard Slicher van Bath. His work, therefore, became one of the main sources of criticism of *Westforschung* in my *Deutsche Westforschung*.

18. For elements of this antagonism, see Derks, *Deutsche Westforschung*, 84–92 and below.

19. Michael Fahlbusch, *Wissenschaft im Dienst*, and his contribution to this volume.

20. See the excellent study by Wolfgang Freund, *Volk, Reich und Westgrenze: Wissenschaften und Politik in der Pfalz, im Saarland und im annektierten Lothringen 1925–1945* (Ph.D. diss., University of Saarbrücken, 2001), 507. It is the first detailed study on the effects of *Westforschung* at the local level, the work of the WFG, and the formation of the so-called Westmark.

21. This very large *Habilitationsschrift* was completed in May 1935 and defended under the title *Die fränkische Siedlung in Frankreich und den Niederlanden und die Bildung der germanisch-französischen Sprachgrenze. Volkstum, Staat und Nation an der deutschen Westgrenze*. The new title was evidence of the politicized scholarly work.

22. Quoted in Karl Ditt, "Die Kulturraumforschung zwischen Wissenschaft und Politik. Das Beispiel Franz Petri (1903–1993)," *Westfälische Forschungen* 46 (1996): 82n32.

23. An example of this kind of provocation in the borderlands between Liège and Maastricht can be found in *Deutschland-Berichte der Sozialdemokratischen Partei Deutschlands (SOPADE)* (Frankfurt am Main, 1989; reprint), vol. 6 [1939], 592–596.

24. Franz Steinbach, *Studien zur westdeutschen Stammes- und Volksgeschichte* (Jena, 1926).

25. See last paragraph.

26. For its shaky archaeological basis, its racist nonsense borrowed from Nazi Germany's top *Rassenkundler* Egon Freiherr von Eickstedt, or its linguistic brainwaves borrowed from Frings and others, see Derks, *Deutsche Westforschung*, 32–40, 61n30, 62–71, 110n53, 136–140.

27. See Ditt, "Die Kulturraumforschung," 89.

28. Schöttler, Die historische "Westforschung," 220.

29. The fact that a short time later the Germans occupied France only up to the Loire cannot be considered strange in the light of the *Westforschung* debate that followed the publication of *Germanisches Volkserbe*. These *Westforschung* points of view and tactics concerning France were not very new. In 1897, the Pan-German Fritz Bley had already written in an anti-French tract: "The German hand has five fingers: the Flemish, the Boer, the Dutch, the High Germans and the Low Germans, but the German hand can mass together and hit hard if fury shall make it tremble. And where it hits, grass will never come upright again." Quoted by B. Doncker, "Les prétentions allemandes sur les Pays-Bas français," in *De Franse Nederlanden/Les Pays Bas Français. Jaarboek Stichting Ons Erfdeel* (Rekkem, 1976), 33. This is an interesting yearbook for Petri's biography as well, thanks to other contributions: an article by the Belgian Petri supporter Maurits Gysseling on the language boundary (71–85) and the testament of the priest Gantois (207–225). Together with the priest Cyriel Verschaeve, spiritual leader of the Flemish Movement, Gantois, leader of the French-Flemish Movement, collaborated with the Germans, particularly due to Petri's personal involvement.

30. The complicated history of the German occupation of Belgium cannot be told here. Instead, I will use the recent defense of Petri by one of his successors, the historian Horst Lademacher.

31. Franz Petri and Werner Reese, *Zweiter Bericht über Tätigkeit und Arbeitsziele der Militärverwaltung in Belgien auf dem Gebiet der Kultur*, Brussels, 15 November 1940 (hereafter *Zweiter Bericht*). This is a mimeographed internal report. See Derks, *Deutsche Westforschung*, 104ff. Translations in English of German texts are always difficult. In his own words, Petri saw as his double task "eine Neuordnung des kulturellen Lebens im Lande

allmählich vorzubereiten und in wesentlichen Punkten durchzuführen und damit zugleich die Gemeinschaft mit Deutschland auf Grund der völkischen und natürlichen Verbundenheit und der reichspolitischen Tradition und Notwendigkeit auszubauen." It is, for example, difficult to translate *völkisch*, which has not only political or sociological but also racial, yet nearly no "ethnic," connotations. *Reichspolitisch* has a specific meaning for a scholar like Petri, as indicated in the first paragraph.

32. Horst Lademacher, "Franz Petri zum Gedächtnis," *Rheinische Vierteljahrsblätter* 57 (1993): vii–xix.

33. All citations: ibid., 12.

34. Matthias Haupt, *Der "Arbeitseinsatz" der belgischen Bevölkerung während des Zweiten Weltkrieges* (Ph.D. diss., University of Bonn, 1970), 219. Derks, *Deutsche Westforschung*, 111n55. Even at the start of Haupt's book (17), suggestions already appear that had to be proved, such as: "The deviating (from the SS opinion of the military government, which was determined by political as well as humanitarian arguments, could be often realized." Petri must have been a man who believed in his German mission. After the war, he was also involved in cleaning up German behavior from World War I.

35. A recent book about the Belgian resistance describes not only the harsh hangman's work of the SS and its top Jew hunter, Kurt Asche, but also the cowardly behavior of the military government, which did not lift a finger to prevent the pogroms: Marion Schreiber, *Stille Rebellen* (Berlin, 2000). It remains a fact that the remarkably low percentage of Belgian Jewish victims (43 percent versus 75 percent in Holland) is also a result of an effective non-Jewish resistance and of a Jewish resistance that was unknown in the Netherlands.

36. Quoted in Derks, *Deutsche Westforschung*, 111. Apart from what is said in the text about this Petri statement, it is an impertinent utterance as well, because Petri was reacting to Schöffer's doctoral dissertation on the National Socialist historiography, in which enough information about DeVlag and Petri himself was given to make this statement ambiguous. In addition, given the highly distorted personal relationship between Petri and Schöffer, Petri's attack was simply in bad taste. Ivo Schöffer, *Het nationaal-socialistische beeld van de geschiedenis der Nederlande* (Arnhem, Amsterdam, and Utrecht, 1956, 1965, 1978). See Derks, *Deutsche Westforschung*, 109–112.

37. Quoted in Derks, *Deutsche Westforschung*, 112.

38. Quoted in ibid., 106, including note 44. In ibid., 256–275, main extracts of this *Zweiter Bericht* are reproduced together with other documents relating to Franz Petri.

39. The effects of Petri's aggressive whitewashing activities among historians are devastating and astonishing. In Derks, *Deutsche Westforschung*, I tell at length the tragic histories of the Dutch historians Pieter Geyl and Ivo Schöffer and their relationship with Petri. Even today, most of Petri's Dutch and Belgian colleagues believe(d) and defended him or his spokesmen (Lademacher in Germany and Draye in Belgium) without hesitation, including very critical and otherwise competent scholars such as the Belgians A. de Jonghe and B. de Wever and the Dutch Hermann von der Dunk. The last did this recently and rather boldly. After he had received evidence to the contrary, he still declared that Lademacher had "distanced himself silently" from Petri (*NRC-Handelsblad*, 23 November 2001, in a review of Lademacher's new book *Der europäische Nordwesten*). Most typical is that Petri was invited to write his own history in many lemmas of the official Flemish encyclopedia, the *Encyclopedie van de Vlaamse Beweging*, ed. J. Deleu et al. (Tielt and Utrecht, 1973), even in the new 1999 edition, although less extensively. His Belgian friend, the Germanist Henri Draye, even wrote Petri's biography in this encyclopedia full of disinformation. In 1982 Petri reported to the historian de Jonghe that he had not immediately received his professor title at the University of Cologne in 1941 because he did not support the SS-dominated DeVlag. This is mentioned in Ditt, "Die Kulturraumforschung," 130, note 217. Although he provides us with a great deal of interesting data, Ditt himself sustained this image in this 100-page hagiography of Petri. Ditt was apparently laboring under the influence of his mother, who was a lifelong assistant to Petri.

40. In particular, thanks to the voluminous work of A. A. De Jonghe, "De strijd Himmler-Reeder om de benoeming van de HSSPF te Brussel (1942–44)," in *Bijdragen tot de Geschiedenis van de Tweede Wereldoorlog* (1974–1984), about the military government versus the SS controversy, which gave this historiography its pretty black-and-white scheme, with all of its consequences for political or scholarly careers. In this view, Eggert Reeder, the German "President" of Belgium and Petri's only Belgian boss, was a strong defender of the harshest *competitor* of DeVlag-SS, namely, the collaborating VNV (the Vlaams Nationaal Verbond). Now that the proof can be found that Petri was something like an "SS-mole," this whole view must be revised: the stronger the substantiation of this suspicion, the earlier this revision must be made.

41. Quoted in Derks, *Deutsche Westforschung*, 112, 260. The same held for Freemasons.

42. Quoted in ibid., 112, 263.

43. Quoted in ibid., 112.

44. Quoted in ibid., 113, 114, 263. By *Volksforschung* Petri does not mean *Volkskunde*, the German kind of folklore studies, but those disciplines that formed the very basis of his *Habilitationsschrift* on "the border between the Germanic and Romanic world." See also his declaration of 1925 about *Volksgeschichte* quoted in an earlier paragraph.

45. They are nearly completely reproduced in Derks, *Deutsche Westforschung*, 267–275.

46. This journal, *Westland. Blätter für Landschaft, Geschichte und Kultur am Rhein, Mosel, Maas und Schelde*, appeared in 1943 and 1944 with 4 issues each year. In this prestigious *Westforschung* journal, the relation with "the East" ("*Nach Ostland wollen wir fahren*"; *Ostarbeit*, etc.) was an often repeated theme based on the underlying thought that "here in the West live the people of our Nordic race who are obliged to develop the barbaric East." There was also another *Westland*, a cultural literary monthly for Flanders issued from the middle of 1942 till August 1944 by the collaborating Vlaams Nationaal Verbond. It was infiltrated and taken over by DeVlag at the beginning of 1943.

47. This is the same Schneider who after the war managed to become a vice-chancellor of the University of Aachen, one of the typical *Westforschung* institutions, and therefore a Petri colleague. The only (!) thing he had to do was change his name to Schwerte. See Helmut König et al., *Vertuschte Vergangenheit. Der Fall Schwerte und die NS—Vergangenheit der deutschen Hochschulen* (Munich, 1997).

48. Quoted in Derks, *Deutsche Westforschung*, 115.

49. For the nasty background of the word *Sicherungsmassnahmen,* see Schmitz-Berning, *Vokabular des National-Sozialismus*, 571ff.

50. See Gjalt Zondergeld, "Hans Ernst Schneider und seine Bedeutung für das SS-Ahnenerbe," in König et al., *Vertuschte Vergangenheit*, 29ff., for Sievers's and Rascher's experiments in Dachau; Derks, *Deutsche Westforschung*, 91n13. For von Stokar, see also Gerhard Hirschfeld, "Die nationalsozialistische Neuordnung Europas und die 'Germanisierung' der westeuropäischen Universitäten," in König et al., *Vertuschte Vergangenheit*, 90–93, 101. For the relationship between *Westforschung* and the theft of culturally valuable artifacts in these years, see Freund, *Volk, Reich und Westgrenze*, 304ff., 346ff.

51. Quoted in Derks, *Deutsche Westforschung*, 116, 268.

52. Ditt, "Die Kulturraumforschung," 131.

53. Fahlbusch, *Wissenschaft im Dienst*, 355ff.

54. It is well known how after the war the tensions between the Flemish and Walloons increased to such a degree that Belgium had to be split up into several parts. For the history of the conflicts, see Kas Deprez and Louis Vos, eds., *Nationalism in Belgium: Shifting Identities, 1780–1995* (London and New York, 1998). It is a pity that the voice of the Catholic University of Louvain fully dominates in this book.

55. Quoted in Derks, *Deutsche Westforschung*, 117, 268. The original: "Man erkannte sehr bald, dass hier außer der begrenzten Frage nach der Abstammung von ein paar Millionen Menschen grundsätzliche Seiten der abendländische Entwicklung zur Entscheidung stehen." In this *Westland* essay many other questions are discussed, but it would take up too much space to talk about them here.

56. See the detailed description of intrigues and plans in Derks, *Deutsche Westforschung*, 195–205.
57. Ditt, "Die Kulturraumforschung," 153ff.
58. Derks, *Deutsche Westforschung*, 208–216.
59. Ibid., 214.
60. See Jeffrey Herf, *Divided Memory: The Nazi Past in the Two Germanys* (Cambridge, Mass., 1997). Thomas Banchoff, *The German Problem Transformed: Institutions, Politics, and Foreign Policy, 1945–1995* (Ann Arbor, 1999) has a more optimistic view because he only looks at the foreign policy, i.e., the problem of the *Westbindung*, without analyzing its dialectical relationship with internal developments such as the apparently unstoppable rise of neo-Nazism.
61. For Theodor Frings, see Derks, *Deutsche Westforschung*, 53–60, 66ff., 119ff., 224ff.
62. Such a book series is, for example, *Städteforschung*, published by Petri *after* he retired in 1968, by a top *Ostforscher* such as Emil Meynen or Heinz Stoob; these expensive and lavishly illustrated books, mostly full of *Kulturraumforschungs* products, are still in print. The international conferences of the historical *Westforscher*, their purpose, subjects, attendants, etc., before, during, and after the war are well known, thanks to new research by Fahlbusch, *Wissenschaft im Dienst*, 380ff.; Schöttler, "Die historische Westforschung," 232ff. and Derks, *Deutsche Westforschung*, 220ff. Comparison teaches much about the uninterrupted continuity in this field of the historical branch of *Westforschung*.
63. Ditt, "Die Kulturraumforschung," 133.
64. See note 29; Derks, *Deutsche Westforschung*, 106n45; and Ditt, "Die Kulturraumforschung," 132.
65. When Petri retired, he was a "big gun" again in the Rhineland and Niederrhein. He therefore easily managed to assign his many jobs only to "reliable" successors. Thus, the medievalist Edith Ennen, Steinbach's war assistant, received a lucrative job in Bonn; the historian Heinz Stoob, Aubin's pupil, and Stoob's own "pupil," Horst Lademacher, were similarly rewarded in Münster. Petri had already demonstrated this charitable attitude in wartime Belgium with his DeVlag friends. It became an infectious trend: Ennen nominated, in turn, "her" Franz Irsigler; Matthias Zender, the Steinbach *Volkskundler*, "his" Georg Wiegelmann, and so forth.
66. See note 39 on well-known Belgian and Dutch historians.
67. Publishers of the historical *Westforscher* mostly were Böhlau (Cologne, Vienna) and the Wissenschaftliche Buchgesellschaft (Darmstadt). The latter was directed by Ernst Anrich, a typical *Westforscher* (who published in 1940 a history of the *Westgrenze*) and a fanatical member of the "old comrades club," who rallied even to the neo-Nazistic NPD. A most typical example of Petri's *oratios pro domo* is his nearly 700-page reader: Franz Petri, ed., *Siedlung, Sprache und Bevölkerungsstruktur im Frankenreich* (Darmstadt, 1973). Apart from his own contributions and commentaries, he published here a plethora of (neo-)Nazistic writers such as Steinbach, Frings, von Wartburg, Draye, Bach, and Zeiss, along with too naive protégés such as Werner (who worked together with Zeiss), Gysseling, and Niermeyer. In a book review of two short pages, Petri himself tries to damage (54–55) his strongest opponent from before the war, Ernst Gamillscheg, who at the end of his life published a new view on the *Sprachgrenze* problem. His strongest opponent from after the war, the Belgian historian Charles Verlinden, is treated in an only slightly warmer manner, who in a review (485–489) is confronted time and again with "Steinbach und ich" and threatened with new publications (*Gegenpublikation*) by Werner, Petri, and others. For Verlinden, see Derks, *Deutsche Westforschung*, 254ff. For the Nazi and *Westforschung* backgrounds of prehistorians such as Zeiss and Werner, and for their "Bonner Schule" (Aubin-Petri-Steinbach) connections, see the excellent essay by Hubert Fehr, "Hans Zeiss, Joachim Werner und die archäologischen Forschungen zur Merowingerzeit," in *Eine hervorragend nationale Wissenschaft. Deutsche Prähistoriker zwischen 1900 und 1995*, ed. Heiko Steuer (Berlin and New York, 2001), 311–417, esp. 359ff; see also the essay by Laurent Olivier in this book.

68. In Belgium, it was/is in particular historians, linguists, and other experts from the University of Ghent (Gysseling, Verhulst) and the Roman Catholic University of Louvain (Draye, etc.), and in the Netherlands from the Roman Catholic University of Nijmegen (Post) and the University of Utrecht (Geyl, Alberts) including specific institutes such as the Meertens Institute for Volkskunde in Amsterdam, who were, became, or are now active supporters of *Westforschung*. For instance, leaders of the last institute such as Jan de Vries and Pieter Meertens were *Westforscher* from about 1930 onward and strong SS supporters during the war. After the war, Meertens and other representatives of this institute had a close relationship with "Bonn," "Münster," and "Frings." Derks, *Deutsche Westforschung*, passim.

69. Ibid., 250–255.

70. For the following, see Ditt, "Die Kulturraumforschung," 136, 141ff.

Chapter 10

OTTO SCHEEL

National Liberal, Nordic Prophet

✦ ✦ ✦

Eric Kurlander

Born in 1876 to a modest, middle-class family of Danish-evangelical extraction, Otto Scheel would go on to become one of Germany's greatest Protestant theologians and a leading National Liberal politician. But raised in
the border region of Tondern, Schleswig-Holstein, Scheel also developed
an extraordinary devotion to ancestral hearth and home (*Heimat*). This
love for his native "blood and soil" would lead Scheel, despite his liberal
pedigree, to become an ardent supporter of Nordic racial superiority and
Pan-German *völkisch* nationalism. Later forced to endure the national
embarrassment of the Versailles Treaty and the vicissitudes of Weimar
republicanism, Scheel's career culminated, not in an unconditional endorsement of liberal democracy, but in an open embrace of Hitler and National
Socialism. Though ignored by most historians, Scheel's equally *völkisch*
and liberal past therefore provides an indispensable case study in the profound ideological contradictions that impressed German politics and society during the first half of the twentieth century.

Otto Scheel's adolescent *Ideenwelt* could not have been more conducive
to inculcating *völkisch* ideologies of "blood and soil" (*Blut und Boden*). He
came of age during the last decade of the nineteenth century, a period of
profound social and political change across Germany, characterized in
particular by the rise of a virulent Pan-German nationalism and right-
wing anti-Semitism.[1] At the same time traditional German provincialism
(or what I prefer to call particularism) remained a powerful cultural force
in the young Reich, often superseding national goals on the local level.[2]
Following the historian Peter Wulf, it is clear that in Schleswig-Holstein
"regional particularities … played a special political role in relation to the
Empire." In fact, well before 1890, the province had developed a "local

Notes for this chapter begin on page 209.

and racially conscious thinking" that worked "to create a certain degree of common political views" among regional liberals.[3] Certainly, nowhere else in the Reich did a racialist-inflected, particularist consciousness impress local liberal politics to the degree that it did in Schleswig-Holstein. The province was home, after all, to some of the greatest *völkisch* demagogues of the twentieth century, many of whom had personal or political ties to either the left-leaning Progressives or the somewhat more conservative National Liberal Party (NLP). No Schleswig-Holsteiner better exemplified the contradictions between liberal reform and racist exclusion than the Hadersleben-born cultural critic Julius Langbehn. His most famous work, *Rembrandt als Erzieher*, presented one of the earliest and most articulate examples of German *völkisch* ideology, glorifying the renowned Dutch painter as an ideal exponent of a putative Nordic racial and cultural superiority. Yet Langbehn, like many of his *völkisch* contemporaries, was for much of his young adulthood a supporter of bourgeois liberalism and democratic reform, only moving into the explicitly right-wing, *völkisch* social camp during the turbulent 1890s.[4] Another of Scheel's Schleswig-Holstein compatriots, the social critic and publicist Adolf Bartels, believed in creating a "German form of democracy" while simultaneously making clear his disdain for those liberals who failed to recognize the principle of race in German politics, culture, and aesthetics.[5] Perhaps the contemporary most similar to Scheel in political temperament and career path was the erstwhile liberal and future Nazi Reichstag representative, Count Ernst von Reventlow. Once a progressive social reformer who had written for the, in his own words, "Jewish liberal" *Berliner Tageblatt*, Reventlow eventually insinuated himself into the right-wing German-Social movement near the middle of the Wilhelmine epoch, convinced that the struggle for German national superiority and racial purity should supersede any idealistic flirtation with "Western" liberal democracy.[6]

Summed up in the ubiquitous Low German *Stichwort* "Schleswig-Holstein, Up Ewig Ungedeelt" or "undivided for eternity," Schleswig-Holsteiners' nationalist antipathies toward the Danes were not always compatible with a Pan-Germanic belief in the superiority of all Nordic peoples. Liberal uncertainty about how to treat a racially pure but politically and culturally hostile minority did not prevent discriminatory government policies, often relegating the hundred thousand Danish speakers in German North Schleswig to a second-class status. But provincial liberals remained equally ambivalent toward the political, administrative, and cultural incursions of "half-slavic" Prussia.[7] Hence, there bubbled beneath the surface of anti-Danish policies in Schleswig-Holstein a powerful feeling of Nordic racial solidarity that viewed Danes as well as Schleswig-Holsteiners as superior to West Prussians, Saxons, Silesians, or any other racially mixed Germanic "tribes [*Stämme*]."[8] However, when thrust into the crucible of popular interest group politics, colonial rivalries, and minority unrest during the second half of the 1890s, this fervent *völkisch* particularism showed itself to be eminently compatible with a Pan-Germanic *völkisch* nationalism. So-called patriotic (*vaterländische*) military and naval associations proliferated at this time, spearheaded by the infamous Navy League (Flottenverein), and followed closely behind by the Pan-German League (Alldeutscher Verband). Regular visits by the Kaiser, parades celebrating military virtues, and Kiel's position as the centerpoint of German Great Power politics all contributed to a new "sea-colored nationalism" that fit nicely within the arc of German imperialism and *Weltpolitik*. Indeed, Schleswig-Holstein's predominantly left liberal parties countered the intense rural nationalism and anti-Semitism of right-wing Conservatives, not by invoking cosmopolitan values, but by propagating their own peculiar brand of bourgeois-liberal imperialism. Nowhere else in Germany, in any case, was liberal participation in radical nationalist pressure groups stronger than in Schleswig-Holstein.[9]

Weaned on this unique political culture of fervent *völkisch* nationalism and particularism, the precocious Scheel entered the University of Kiel in the mid 1890s. Educated at Halle as well as Kiel, Scheel rapidly completed his dissertation, *Die Anschauung Augustins uber Christi Person und Werk*, in 1900, receiving his doctoral degree within weeks of his twenty-fourth birthday. In the same year he took a position as *Privatdozent* at Kiel.[10] Scheel was made *Titularprofessor* of religion shortly thereafter, and accepted the more prestigious position of Professor of Church History at the University of Tübingen in 1906. Obviously brilliant, Scheel had become an established professor at the nearly unprecedented age of twenty-nine.[11] Early in his career, there is little evidence to suggest that Scheel had a taste for politics or public life, preferring to focus his energies on his first passion, the origins of the Lutheran faith. Scheel quickly established a reputation as a noted authority on the works of the great Carthaginian philosopher and theologian Saint Augustine.[12] The young professor soon began a lifelong love affair with Martin Luther as well, moving seamlessly from ancient Rome to Early Modern Europe and building an impressive body of historical work, increasingly political, social, and contemporary in tone.[13]

While at Kiel, the young Scheel seems to have first developed a nose for German national (*Deutschnationale*) and liberal politics. Schleswig-Holstein's liberal parties had suffered unprecedented losses to the Socialists in the elections of June 1903. The patriotic Scheel was deeply affected. Responding to the liberals' failure to fend off the "unpatriotic [*vaterlandlose*]" and "godless [*gottlose*]" SPD, at the age of twenty-seven Scheel delivered a well-received speech at the annual festival of Schleswig-Holstein's Evangelical Association (Evangelische Bund). Titled *Wie erhalten wir das geistige Erbe der Reformation in dem Kampfen der Gegenwart?* Scheel's peroration indicated a budding enthusiasm for National Liberal politics and a firm belief in the need to bring a dynamic, patriotic Lutheranism into German public life.[14] The speech is likewise remarkable for its open anticlericalism, aimed at the "un-German [*undeutsch*]" Catholic Center Party, along with Scheel's apparent willingness to defend Germany's national "mission" to the detriment of liberal-democratic constitutional reform.[15]

Disgusted by the putative lack of patriotism and flirtation with the left that defined the liberal election campaign of 1903, Scheel supported the turn toward a more "national," often *völkisch*, politics. This new strategy was greatly assisted by the 1904–1906 Herero uprisings in German West Africa, as well as the escalating colonial conflict with France in Morocco during the same period. This rise in popular national feeling eventually pushed the liberals toward a parliamentary coalition (*Sammlung*) with conservatives and anti-Semites, endorsing a nationalist gospel of blood and soil directly opposed to the "rootless" internationalism of the Catholics and Socialists. These tensions came to a head in autumn 1906. Although additional funds for the German armies in West Africa were approved by a large minority of Progressives, National Liberals, conservatives and anti-Semites, the bill was narrowly defeated by a coalition of Socialists, Catholics and minority parties. Unable to achieve his "national majority," Chancellor Bernhard von Bülow boldly dissolved the Reichstag and called for new elections. The national parties would finally face down the "enemies of Empire."[16]

Fueled by this nationalist hysteria, a new working relationship developed among the liberal parties in Schleswig-Holstein, a marriage of convenience based on the need to serve the fatherland.[17] The liberal election platform ("any splintering of votes means a weakening of the national interest") and demands for national solidarity over economic special interest (particularly "in the Nordmark," where "only a united German race could defeat its enemies") reflected a shift in party fortunes that eerily foreshadowed the postwar epoch, when liberals and conservatives would again come together in a series of desperate attempts to destroy the international left and assuage the *völkisch* national right.[18] In January 1907 this *bürgerlich* coalition helped the Progressives and National Liberals garner seven of Schleswig-Holstein's ten Reichstag seats, their best provincial showing in nearly two decades. For Scheel and many other liberals, the returns wholly validated Bülow's nationalist *Sammlungspolitik*.

Yet the resulting Bülow Bloc was rife with contradictions. While NLP leaders like Scheel and Schifferer defended nationalism as the only basis on which to hold the disparate liberal ranks together, Schleswig-Holstein Progressives like Johannes Leonhart and Walther Schücking warned that *Sammlungspolitik* would tear both liberalism and the Reich apart by once again privileging national aggrandizement over social and political reform.[19] Indeed, many liberals were wary of ethnic minorities, civil rights, and universal suffrage. But when the conservatives refused to support tax reforms that virtually all liberals agreed were necessary to keep pace with French, British, and Russian rearmament, the liberal-conservative *Sammlung* lost its raison d'être. Importantly, however, when the liberal coalition with the nationalist right dissipated in 1909, Scheel continued to nurture ties with right-wing *völkisch* intellectuals. If his academic circle included nominally liberal colleagues such as Ernst Troeltsch and Kiel's own Otto Baumgarten, by the eve of World War I these ranks also attracted devout nationalist conservatives like Adolf von Harnack and Friedrich Michael Schiele.[20]

Nevertheless, increasing tensions between Germany and the Entente presented the German liberals with a real dilemma. Unlike conservatives, for whom Germany's increasing diplomatic isolation and the ensuing world war was a perfect excuse to postpone much-needed reforms, many *völkisch* liberals were challenged by the outbreak of war to reconcile their indiscriminate nationalism with the humanist foundations of classical liberalism. Like his notable contemporaries, Scheel faced a stark decision: to support Pan-German annexationism at any cost, or to ally with the progressive lobby in the Reichstag in the interest of peace and domestic political reform.[21] As Jeffrey Verhey reminds us, German war enthusiasm was largely bourgeois in tone. It was the liberals as much as any other single party who endorsed this exaggerated patriotic feeling.[22] Scheel was not alone in his bellicose demands for territorial annexations and a "victorious peace [*Siegfrieden*]." But the carnage of the Marne and the Somme exercised a great influence on Germany's liberal elites, many of whom began to realize that annexation of Belgium or Kurland was hardly worth bleeding Germany white. Faced with mounting casualties and declining military prospects, Scheel followed Gustav Stresemann, his pragmatic party leader, into the so-called peace camp, opting for, in Scheel's words, the "supranational and non-materialist … qualities that were bequeathed to us by Martin Luther [*übernationalen und überweltlichen Güter … die uns durch Martin Luther beschert wurden*]."[23] Eventually, Scheel rejected the unyielding, Pan-German views of his colleagues Schiele, Schifferer, and Traub, determining in July 1917 to back the Reichstag's Peace Resolution (*Friedensresolution*) of the majority parties, liberals, Catholics, and Socialists. But Scheel's *Vernunftpazifismus* did not mean that he relinquished any underlying *völkisch* convictions. He merely realized, like Stresemann before him, that a negotiated peace based on the Wilsonian principle of self-determination might preserve more hard-won, racially Germanic territory than an increasingly costly, drawn-out military conflict.[24]

Following the November Revolution and the devastating political and economic burdens dictated by the Treaty of Versailles, a disillusioned Scheel plunged himself into the debate surrounding the fate of North Schleswig.[25] Despite his permanent position in Tübingen, Scheel became a founding member of the German national Schleswig-Holsteiner Bund (SHB), winning a reputation as one of the leading instigators of anti-Danish assemblies in the province.[26] For Scheel, the question was not merely one of defending territory, but also the Germanic traditions, which were threatened by the Danes' love of French and Anglo-Saxon culture.[27] When the Versailles plebiscites ended with North Schleswig's cession to Denmark in April 1920, Scheel began to contemplate a permanent return to the *Grenzgebiet* in order to serve the cause of Nordic German *Volkstum* directly. Three years later, intent on developing a closer relationship between the SHB and local *völkisch* groups of all political inclinations, Scheel secured a position as Professor of Church History at the University of Kiel.[28] Committed to Germany's rebirth and wholly disgusted by the course of Weimar politics, Scheel's days of poring over Latin manuscripts in search of hidden religious truths had ended. During the last three decades of his life, Scheel's best known publications would concern not theology but history, culture, and politics, namely, the history of Schleswig-Holstein, the culture of Nordic-Germanic peoples, and the politics of German racial and territorial expansion.[29]

Scheel's *völkisch* obsessions were not confined to the *Nordseeraum*. Already elected president of the rabidly nationalist Schleswig-Holsteiner Bund, Scheel soon joined the Baltische Kommission for the preservation of German *Volkstum* in the East as well.[30] At a time when even the left-wing Democrats (Deutsche Demokratische Partei or DDP) admonished their voters to teach a German child "from what race he descends [*welcher Rasse er entstammt*]," Scheel's provincial roots, *völkisch* proclivities, and unparalleled *Bildung* were greatly prized by both liberal parties. Not surprisingly, the renowned academic rejected the too "cosmopolitan" (read "Jewish") DDP, to which many former National Liberals belonged, becoming instead a fixture at local political assemblies of the right liberal German People's Party (Deutsch Volkspartei or DVP).[31] Led by Stresemann, the DVP maintained pretensions to classical liberalism, and Scheel himself insisted that the regional People's Party support "a liberal ruling of minority questions in Schleswig-Holstein, that secured for the Danish minority the preservation of its ethnicity."[32] But Scheel and his provincial colleagues had very specific views about what constituted "the true Danish minority [*der echten dänischen Minderheit*]," joining the right-wing German National People's Party (DNVP) in a demagogic attempt to quash any legislation that supported cultural tolerance or Danish self-administration.[33] In fact, Scheel rose to the top of the Schleswig-Holstein liberal ranks, alongside fellow SHB members and future Nazis Christian Tränckner (DDP), Wilhelm Iversen (DVP), and Hinrich Lohse (Schleswig-Holsteinsche Landespartei), precisely because of his devotion to *völkisch*, not liberal, principles. As chairman of the German University Association (Deutschen Hochschulverbandes) Scheel only "permitted the right of political engagement to those professors who shared his conservative-nationalist viewpoint," admonishing colleagues not to attend a speech by the cosmopolitan, Jewish philosopher Theodor Lessing, "in order to avoid, in the holy service of Nation and public opinion ... anything which could call forth the appearance of worthlessness and unconscionable, literary superficiality [*gewissenlosen Literatentums*]."[34] And in a speech that would have rivaled any of Heinrich Himmler's in its medieval, *Ur*-Germanic mysticism,

Scheel declared at the Berlin Student Conference in 1925, "Our universities [*hohen Schulen*] are also Germany's grail castles [*Gralsburgen Deutschlands*]; our academic youth the guardians of the holy grail of German greatness and power."[35]

Of course, Scheel and his *völkisch* liberal colleagues were considerably more enthusiastic about a rapprochement with the Danes than other Reich minorities. At least the Danes, unlike the Poles, Czechs, Wendisch, or Jews, were a kindred Nordic race. As such, they represented an indispensable component of Schleswig-Holstein's "combined West Germanic and North Germanic culture [*westgermanischer und nordgermansicher Gesamtkultur*]."[36] Scheel's firm belief in racial pseudo science was hardly unique among contemporary liberals, but it did help lay the groundwork for the Nordic anthropology propagated by the local Nazi Party.[37] Indeed, by the end of the 1920s, Scheel enjoyed an international reputation as one of Northern Germany's chief *völkisch* ideologues, co-authoring the *Deutsch-Nordische Zeitschrift* with his fellow liberal, the Pan-German annexationist Anton Schifferer.[38]

In the last years before Hitler's *Machtergreifung*, Scheel occupied himself with two main activities: he worked behind the scenes to establish closer ties between the liberal parties in Schleswig-Holstein and "apolitical" nationalist groups in Eastern and Southern Germany (e.g., the Deutsche Schutzbund and the Deutsch-Österreichischen Arbeitsgemeinschaft); at the same time, Scheel became increasingly visible as a *völkisch* publicist.[39] In collaboration with his DVP colleague at the University of Kiel, Carl Petersen, Scheel composed a magnificent tome of *völkisch Wissenschaft*, the *Handwörterbuch des Grenz- und Auslanddeutschtums*. A paean to German nationality and racial science, Scheel's massive work promised "an overview of all branches of the German ethnicity, on a scientific basis, for the practical use of all professional classes [*eine Übersicht aller Zweige des Deutschtums auf wissenschaftlicher Grundlage für den praktischen Gebrauch aller Berufsstände*]." In the interest of the "struggle for self-preservation [*Selbsterhaltungskampf des deutschen Volkstums*] of German ethnicity abroad," this work would inspire Germans throughout "the old and new border regions of the German fatherland ... to strengthen the consciousness of community of fate and spirit among all Germans."[40] Like many liberal nationalists, Scheel chose Hindenburg over Hitler in the Reich presidential election of April 1932. But this hardly constituted a vote of confidence for the Republic. By this time Scheel agreed with his DVP colleague Kurt Maeder that, for all the Nazis' radicalism and violence, a "true liberal" should "receive joyously Hitler's great, national assemblies," concluding, "Within the realm of national goals there existed only the difference that we were a reform party, and they [the Nazis] a revolutionary party."[41] As if to prove Maeder's point, within weeks of the Nazi seizure of power, Scheel had abandoned liberalism for the NSDAP, "the greatest movement of our time, the most powerful and widespread since the Reformation; it will bring us political and spiritual rejuvenation and it will create for us the pre-condition for a new and happy efflorescence of German life."[42]

A Hitler enthusiast without reservation, Scheel put his considerable talents at the service of the Nazi regime. In 1934 he published a lavish study of Bismarck's role in fashioning the Second Reich, *Bismarcks Wille zu Deutschland in den Friedensschlüssen 1866*. Scheel followed this up with a hackneyed piece of racialist hagiography honoring Martin Luther as the mystical embodiment of the German *Volk*. Both works were thinly veiled encomiums to Adolf Hitler, alluding to him as not only Bismarck's equal as a statesman, but Luther's peer in all matters spiritual and cultural.[43] Contrary to the faltering passion of many Nazi fellow travelers, who soon realized that the Führer was no Bismarck, Scheel's enthusiasm for the Nazi regime only increased over time. In 1938, as Hitler picked up his anti-Semitic campaign and rode roughshod over Austrian and Czechoslovakian sovereignty, Scheel volunteered to represent the regime at the Internationalen Historikertag in Zürich. In front of a largely foreign audience, most of whom were critical of the Third Reich, Scheel defended Hitler and his repudiation of bourgeois liberalism and Christian morality. Invoking Luther's call for a "blessed hero [*gesunder Held*]" to save the German people, Scheel referred to Hitler as a "man of miracles [*Wundermann*]" who would "tear down all that was rotten and create a new law [*das morsch Gewordene niederzureißen und neues Recht schaffen*]." Subsequently praised by Josef Goebbels in the *Völkischer Beobachter* as one of Germany's great "wandering scholars," Scheel became a regular on the party lecture circuit, delivering nationalist speeches at rallies, military encampments, and armaments factories across Germany, working to raise morale for the coming struggle with the Reich's enemies.[44] Employing history for political and military ends, Scheel spent the early years of the war publishing numerous, quasi-academic books and articles on the superiority of the Nordic race.[45] It is important to emphasize that many liberals who supported Nazi policies in the early 1930s—Hjalmar Schacht, Gertrud Bäumer, and Werner von Rheinbaben most prominent among them—encountered serious self-doubt by the end of the decade.[46] Scheel experienced no such pangs of conscience. He was a Nazi by conviction, so much so that in 1940 even Nazi Party officials had to restrain the newly elected president of the German Cultural Institute (Deutsche Wissenschaftliche Institut, DWI) in Copenhagen from making outrageous territorial demands on the still nominally independent Danish government.[47]

During World War II, Scheel's aggressive lobbying on behalf of the Third Reich was accompanied by all kinds of *völkisch* pseudo history, including a rather subjective account of the rise and fall of British sea power, *Aufsteig und Niedergang der englischen See- und Weltmacht*. Warning the British that their Empire was about to collapse, Scheel's work concluded with a for the time typically ahistorical but politically popular invocation of pan-Germanic *völkisch* tradition: "The German people of the world, descendants of Germanic seafarers, inheritors of German strength on the sea, will again become wedded to the sea [*Das deutsche Weltvolk, Nachfahre germanischer Seevölker, Erbe deutscher Kraft auf der See, wird sich ihm wieder vermählen*].[48] As the war took a turn for the worse, however, Scheel stepped down as president of the DWI, returning to Kiel to look after his beloved family, hearth, and home. This return would be unfortunately brief. In 1944, Scheel's house, along with many of his papers, was destroyed in an Allied bombing raid. His life's work literally lying in ashes, Scheel journeyed to Copenhagen at the behest of the *Reichsbevollmächtige* in Denmark, the Gestapo leader Dr. Werner Best. Nearing seventy years of age, with the glorious Nordic world he knew crumbling around him, Scheel delivered one last, stirring speech, demanding all Germanic peoples, Danes and Germans alike, to defend their race and honor to the last drop of blood.[49] Sensing few signs of Nordic brotherhood among the largely anti-Nazi Danish people, Scheel spent the final months of the war calling for a more brutal Nazi assimilation of Scandinavia and bitterly lamenting the Dane's foolhardy insistence on outdated liberal values: "Only a new North European generation will be open to fruitful conversation [*Erst eine neue nordeuropäischer Generation wird für eine fruchtbare Aussprache zu haben sein*].... Only by German victory as well will the intellectual world of the North, which opened itself in the nineteenth century to Anglo-Saxon liberalism and Semitic democracy, be inspired and also find the strength to transform [*Erst der deutsche Sieg wird auch die geistige Welt des Nordens, die im 19. Jh. ganz dem angelsächsischen Liberalismus und der semitischen Demokratie sich öffnete, zu wandeln berufen sein und auch die Kraft besitzen*]."[50] With these lines, rife with eschatological racism, anti-Semitism, and the complete repudiation of pestilent "Anglo-Saxon liberalism," Scheel closed the book on World War II.

Like a great many contemporary academics, Scheel was never condemned for his intellectual complicity in National Socialism. Despite an active, fervent, unwavering support for the Nazi regime, the resilient Scheel emerged from the ruins of the Third Reich as the éminence grise of Schleswig-Holstein's political and academic elite, lauded by his colleagues as a Nordic prophet, a "loyal native son [*treuer Sohn Ihrer Heimat*]," a "good Schleswig-Holsteiner," and "an upright German [*ein aufrechter Deutscher*]."[51] Although he published little during the last few years of his life, Scheel received much praise for the "scholarly" work he had produced before 1945, culminating in the 1952 *Festschrift für Otto Scheel: Beiträge zur deutschen und nordischen Geschichte*. Authored by well-known academics and local politicians, the *Festschrift* glorified Nordic culture, history, and race, producing a collection of essays passionately committed to salvaging a German *Volksgemeinschaft*. Barely seven years removed from the most murderous race war in history, these essays reveal an utter lack of reflectiveness on the part of Schleswig-Holstein's intellectual elite.[52]

Hardly troubled by questions of guilt or responsibility, Otto Scheel passed away peacefully in 1954, at the age of seventy-six. He died convinced that his vast opus had contributed, in the words of his good friend and confidant, Johannes Schmidt-Wodder, to the creation of a greater "Germanic communal consciousness [*germanisches Gemeinbewußtsein*]," a sentiment of *völkisch* solidarity that might one day shape the consciousness of "every good European [*jeder guter Europäer*]."[53] Fortunately, this widespread *völkisch* ideal of racial community and "German democracy" perished with Scheel's generation, paving the way for a German liberalism divorced from the destructive myths of blood and soil.

Notes

1. For more on the rise of *völkisch* and anti-Semitic populism in this period, see in particular Richard S. Levy, *The Downfall of the Antisemitic Parties in Imperial Germany* (New Haven, 1975); Peter Pulzer, *The Rise of Political Anti-Semitism in Germany and Austria* (Cambridge, 1988); Geoff Eley, *Reshaping the German Right* (Ann Arbor, 1990).
2. The seminal work on *Heimat* as a political, social, and cultural artifact is Mack Walker's *German Home Towns* (Ithaca, 1998). Also see Celia Applegate, *A Nation of Provincials* (Berkeley, 1990).
3. Peter Wulf, *Die politische Haltung des schleswig-holsteinischen Handwerks 1928–1932* (Cologne, 1969), 148–149.
4. See Julius Langbehn, *Rembrandt als Erzieher* (Weimar, 1922).
5. See Adolf Bartels, *Der völkische Gedanke: Ein Wegweiser* (Weimar, 1923); Bartels, *Die Berechtigung des Anti-Semitismus: Ein Widerlegung der Schrift von H. von Oppeln-Bronikowski "Anti-Semitismus?"* (Leipzig, 1921); Bartels, *Rasse: Sechzehn Aufsätze zur nationale Weltanschauung* (Hamburg, 1909).
6. Graft Ernst von Reventlow, *Nationaler Sozialismus im Neuen Deutschland* (Berlin, 1933); von Reventlow, *Wertung: Die völkische Eigenart und der Internationalismus Heft 5* (Leipzig, 1910). For more on Langbehn, Bartels, and Reventlow, see Georg Mosse, *The Crisis of German Ideology: Intellectual Origins of the Third Reich* (New York, 1998); Levy, *Downfall*; Pulzer, *Rise*; Fritz Stern, *The Politics of Cultural Despair: A Study in the Rise of the Germanic Ideology* (Berkeley, 1974).
7. For more detail on the relationship between Schleswig-Holstein liberalism, the "Danish Question," and *völkisch* nationalism (particularism), see Eric Kurlander, "Multicultural and Assimilationist Models of Ethnopolitical Integration in the Context of the German Nordmark, 1890–1933," *The Global Review of Ethnopolitics* 1, no. 4 (2002): 39–53.
8. Ibid.
9. See Eley, *Reshaping*, 125. So-called patriotic organizations also began to spread, enjoying a considerable following in the 1880s, even among the working class and despite an SPD ban against such activities. This happened throughout Germany, but especially virulently in Schleswig-Holstein: "Already before the Army Association, the Navy League had nurtured Schleswig-Holstein's nationalist "armament," insofar as it helped form people's consciousness of the provincial capital Kiel as the central location of the symbol of Germany's arrival as a Great Power and of its World Policy—the navy. Behind the scenes of Imperial speeches, sailing shows, parades, flag ceremonies and displaying monuments there developed during the Wilhelmine era an elite-imperialistic, 'sea-blue' nationalism, that represented the counterpart to the 'German nationalism" of the big

Schleswig-Holstein farmers, which was forced by the Agrarian League. Rudy Rietzler, *Kampf in der Nordmark* (Neumünster, 1982), 45. For details on the rise of radical nationalist pressure groups, see Eley, *Reshaping*, 41–98.

10. Erwin L. Lueker, ed., *Lutheran Cyclopedia* (St. Louis, 1975).

11. Ibid.

12. Otto Scheel, *Die Anschauung Augustins über Christi Person und Werk unter Berücksichtigung ihrer verschiedenen Entwicklungsstufen und ihrer dogmengeschichtlichen Stellung* (Tübingen, 1901). Scheel, ed., *Augustins Enchiridion* (Tübingen, 1903).

13. Scheel, *Luthers Stellung zur Heiligen Schrift:* Vortrag/gehalten auf der 14. theologischen (2. landeskirchlich-wissenschaftlichen) Konferenz am 3. Juli 1902 in Kiel (Tübingen, 1902). Scheel, *Wie erhalten wir das geistige Erbe der Reformation in den Kämpfen der Gegenwart?* (Leipzig, 1904). Scheel, ed., *Dokumente zu Luthers Entwicklung (bis 1519)* (Tübingen, 1911). Scheel, *Die Kirche im Urchristentum* (Tübingen, 1912).

14. For more on the fraught relationship between Lutheranism, nationalism, and liberalism in this period, see Gangolf Hübinger, *Kulturprotestantismus und Politik zum Verhältnis von Liberalismus* (Tübingen, 1994).

15. *Wie erhalten wir das geistige Erbe der Reformation in dem Kämpfen der Gegenwart?* 20–27.

16. For more on the foreign policy and colonialism from 1904–1906, see Thomas Nipperdey, *Deutsche Geschichte*, 286–289, 662–668.

17. *Apenrader Tageblatt*, 28 December 1906. For a thorough analysis of the prospects and candidates in each district, see the *Schleswiger Nachrichten*, 4 and 6 January 1907.

18. In North Schleswig, economic policy became virtually an afterthought in the campaign as the "national parties," liberal and conservative, combated the Danes and Socialists, united only in their unequivocal demands for minority rights. See clippings and reports in *Landesarchiv Schleswig*, Abt. 301, 59.

19. "This was almost an obsession with ideology, with the rhetoric of patriotism, and the myth of immutable national needs. It implied that all the problems of capitalist development could be solved by firmness of the national will and the union of all classes behind nationalist slogans." Eley, *Reshaping*, 261–270; Hartwig Thieme, *Nationaler Liberalismus in der Krise: Die Nationalliberale Fraktion des Preußischen Abgeordnetenhaus 1914–1918* (Boppard, 1963), 170–212.

20. Hermann Gunkel, Otto Scheel, Friedrich Michael Schiele, and Leopold Zscharnack, eds., *Die Religion in Geschichte und Gegenwart: Handwörterbuch in Geschichte und Gegenwart* (Tübingen, 1913).

21. On the political and cultural contradictions of *völkisch* liberalism in this period, see Eric Kurlander, "The Rise of *Völkisch* Nationalism and the Decline of German Liberalism: A Comparison of Schleswig-Holstein and Silesian Political Cultures, 1912–1924," *European Review of History* 9, no. 1 (2002): 23–36.

22. See Jeffey Verhey, *The Spirit of 1914: Militarism, Myth and Mobilization in Germany* (Cambridge, 2000).

23. "Deutschlands Weltgeltung soll nicht bestehen ohne die Ehrfurcht vor dem übernationalen weltgeschichtlichen Inhalt seiner Geschichte im 16. Jahrhundert." Scheel in "Aus dem Vorwort zur ersten Auflage," *Martin Luther: Vom Katholizismus zur Reformation* (Tübingen, 1917), V-VI.

24. Exactly two weeks after the *Friedensresolution*, on 4 August, Scheel wrote, "Beim Eintritt ins vierte Kriegsjahr können nicht wohl die Ansprüche gestellt werden, die in ruhigen Jahren des Friedens erhoben werden dürfen." See Scheel, "Vorwort zur zweiten Auflage," in *Martin Luther*, VIII.

25. Manfred Jakubowski-Tiessen, "Kulturpolitik im besetzten Land. Das deutsche Wissenschaftliche Institut in Kopenhagen 1941 bis 1945," *Zeitschrift für Geschichtswissenschaft* 42, no. 2 (1994): 132.

26. See reports on Scheel's involvement in the *Erhebungsfeier* of March–April 1923, celebrating the 75th anniversary of Schleswig-Holstein's revolution against Danish rule dated 26 February, 28 February, and 4 April 1923 in *Landesarchiv Schleswig*, Abt. 309, 35266.

27. See the discussion of Danish racial miscegenation by the Schleswig-Holstein liberals Karl Strackerjan and Johannes Tiedje in Karl Strackerjan, *Nordmärkische Dänentreue* (Hadersleben, 1916).

28. At a *Reichsgründungsfeier* in 1925, he declared: "We were Germany's Marine province. The symbol of its power fluttered in the port of Kiel, which thereby approached the rank of a second Berlin." Rietzler, *Kampf*, 45. Also see *Kieler Neuste Nachrichten*, 15 December 1923.

29. See the foreword in Harald Thurau, ed., *Festschrift für Otto Scheel* (Neumünster, 1952).

30. According to French authorities, Otto Scheel numbered, "au premier rang de ceux qui travaillent pour la cause allemande dans le Slesvig rédimé.… Il est président de la ligue du Slesvig-Holstein dont les membres sont pour le plupart des nationalistes et des conservateurs prussiens qui n'ont rien oublié et presque rien appris." See folder marked "Minority questions: 'Les Minorités devant la L.D.N'" in the *Archives departementales du Bas-Rhin*: 98 AL 691. Scheel also became chairman of the *Deutsche Hochschulverband* and the *Verein für Reformationsgeschichte*, and was active in the Gesellschaft für Schleswig-Holsteinische Geschichte. See Jakubowski-Tiessen, "Kulturpolitik im besetzten Land" *Zeitschrift für Geschichtswissenschaft* 42, no. 2 (1994): 132. Also see Broder Schwensen, *Der Schleswig-Holsteiner-Bund 1919–1933: Ein Beitrag zur Geschichte der nationalpolitischen Verbände im deutsch-dänischen Grenzland* (Frankfurt am Main, 1993), 370–373.

31. *Kieler Zeitung*, 27 and 30 April 1924. Also see Rietzler, *Kampf*, 341.

32. See speech by Scheel, 25 October 1925; letters and press clippings, 13, 15, and 19 February 1926, in NL Ludwig Ahlmann, *Landesbibliothek Kiel*: Cc, 19.

33. In his speech of 25 October 1925, Scheel continued by noting that the other bourgeois parties had decided to support the Socialists and Center Party on this issue: "[S]odass nur die DVP und die DNVP auf ihren Beschlüssen für 1925 beharrten und die von der Regierung vorgeschlagene Regelung verwarfen.… Der geschäftsführende Ausschuss verwirft die getroffene Regelung, die weder dem Willen der überwiegenden Mehrheit der SHen Bevölkerung noch der Stellungnahme der S(chleswig-)H(olsteinisch)en Parteien entspricht."

34. Rietzler, *Kampf*, 341.

35. Ibid.

36. In a 1925 address, Scheel's colleague Anton Schifferer argued that the Nordmark was different from the Rheinland or Ostmark because there persisted in the latter two areas a conflict between the German race and incursions of Latin and Slavic races. While in the Nordmark there prevailed a "1000-jährigen Auseinandersetzung zwischen westgermanischer und nordgermanischer Kultur " that only Schleswig-Holstein, due to "seiner Geschichte und der Eigenart seines Volkstums im Rahmen deutscher Gesamtkultur," could resolve. Anton Schifferer, *Deutsche Kulturarbeit in Schleswig-Holstein: Vortrag gehalten am 22. Juni 1925 auf dem Bierabend bei dem Herrn Reichsbankpräsidenten Dr. Schacht* (Berlin, 1925), 3–16. Also see Pastor Johannes Schmidt-Wodder, "On the Meaning of *Deutschtum*" in Jahresschrift 1929, folder *Verband der Vereine Heimattreue deutscher Nordschleswigs e.V. Kiel. Landesarchiv Schleswig*, Abt. 309, 35298. Scheel's successor as chairman of the SHB, the DVP's Wilhelm Iversen, called for a "national organism, born of the power which unfolds from race and soil,'" uniting all "Lower German regions" and awakening the forces that "slumbered in the race." Many Nazis "swore" themselves to Iversen because of his impeccable *völkisch* credentials, "Führer qualities," and "Nordic-Germanic" views. Schwensen, *Bund*, 370–373, 403–404.

37. The historian Bröder Schwensen is therefore accurate in his claim that Scheel's "*neue Richtung*" toward Scandinavia failed at this time due to the "considerable opposition of right-wing groups," such as the Prussian conservatives in the Schleswig-Holsteiner Bund. But he is deliberately ambiguous in not emphasizing the degree to which the radical *völkisch* "right" and the incipient National Socialist movement approved of closer ties with their equally "Nordic" Danish neighbors. Schwensen, *Bund*, 319–325.

38. See folder marked "Minority questions: 'Les Minorités devant la L.D.N,'" in *Archives departementales du Bas-Rhin*: 98 AL 691. Also see Dähnhardt, Petersen, Röer, and Scheel, eds., *Festgabe Anton Fischerer zum 60. Geburtstag* (Breslau, 1931).
39. See reports by the German Protection Association (Schutzbund), joined by many Schleswig-Holstein liberals, from 22 February 1931, 20 September 1931, 30 March 1933. *Panstwowe Archivuum Wroclawiu* (Polish State Archive, Wroclaw): K 792, *Acta betr. Deutsche Schutzbund-Briefe*.
40. Carl Petersen and Otto Scheel, *Handwörterbuch des Grenz- und Auslanddeutschtums* (Breslau, 1932). Review to be found in *Acta betr. Deutsche Schutzbund-Briefe, Panstwowe Archivuum Wroclawiu*: Widzial Samorzadowy, Prowincji Slaskiej, K 792.
41. Article by Kurt Maeder, 23 April 1933, in BArch, R 45 II, 48.
42. *Landesarchiv Schleswig*, Abt. 399, 71 as quoted in Jakubowski-Tiessen, "Kulturpolitik im besetzten Land," *Zeitschrift für Geschichtswissenschaft* 42, no. 2 (1994): 132. Scheel accepted the logic of DVP leader Kurt Maeder, who called joining the NSDAP "kein feindseliger Akt. Denn welches Mitglied der Deutschen Volkspartei sollte nicht den nationalen Grosstagen der Führer der Nationalsozialisten begeistert anerkennen? … wir haben nun einmal dem nationalen auch ein liberales Herz in uns. Und dieses kann nicht ganz zu schlagen aufhören." Article by Kurt Maeder, 23 April 1933. BArch, R 45 II, 48. Also see official DVP declaration of 10 May 1933, "Ausgehend von der Grundeinstellung der Partei, immer im Dienste des Vaterlandes zu stehen, wünsche die DVP aus ganzem Herzen den Bestrebungen der Regierung des Reichskanzlers Adolf Hitler vollen Erfolg…. Tätige Mithilfe werde von jedem Anhänger der Partei gefordert." NL Zapf, BArch, N 1227, 1.
43. Scheel, *Bismarcks Wille zu Deutschland in den Friedensschlüssen 1866* (Breslau, 1934); Scheel, *Evangelium, Kirche und Volk bei Luther* (Leipzig, 1934).
44. See Jakubowski-Tiessen, "Kulturpolitik im besetzten Land," 133; Scheel, *Der Volksgedanke bei Luther*, 1940. Also see Scheel, *Handwörterbuch des Grenz- und Auslanddeutschtums* (Breslau, 1936).
45. See, for example, Otto Scheel, *Die Wikinger: Aufbruch des Nordens* (Stuttgart, 1938), or the journal *Die Nordische Welt* Jg. 1939–1940.
46. On Schacht, see John Weitz, *Hitler's Banker* (Boston, 1997); Schacht, *76 Jahre meines Lebens* (London, 1955); on Bäumer, see Angelika Schaser, *Helene Lange und Gertrud Bäumer: Eine politische Lebensgemeinschaft* (Cologne, 2000); Werner Huber, *Gertrud Bäumer: Eine politische Biographie* (Ausgburg, 1970); on Rheinbaben, see Werner von Rheinbaben, *Kaiser, Kanzler, Präsidenten: Erinnerungen* (Mainz, 1968); Rheinbaben, *Um ein neues Europa: Tatsachen und Problem* (Berlin, 1939).
47. Also see Jakubowski-Tiessen, "Kulturpolitik im besetzten Land," 134.
48. Scheel, *Aufstieg und Niedergang der englischen See- und Weltmacht* (Flensburg, 1940).
49. Jakubowski-Tiessen, "Kulturpolitik im besetzten Land," 138; Vorwort in Thurau, *Festschrift*.
50. Scheel to Matthes, 28 February 1944, in *Landesarchiv Schleswig*: Abt. 399, 67 (Kt. 18), quoted in Jakubowski-Tiessen, "Kulturpolitik im besetzten Land," *Zeitschrift für Geschichtswissenschaft* 42, no. 2 (1994): 138.
51. "Sie haben uns das Gemeinsame des Germanischen gelehrt, vor dem das Trennende der Gegenwart und Vergangenheit, schon um der Zukunft willen, zurücktreten müsse…. Als treuer Sohn Ihrer Heimat waren Sie stets ein guter Schleswig-Holsteiner, ein aufrechter Deutscher, der frühzeitig die Forderung nach einem vereinten Europa erhob." Vorwort in Thurau, *Festschrift*.
52. Ibid.
53. Johannes Schmidt-Wodder, "Mein erstes Auftreten im dänischen Reichstag," in Thurau, *Festschrift*.

Chapter 11

THE "THIRD FRONT"
German Cultural Policy in
Occupied Europe, 1940–1945

✦ ✦ ✦

Frank-Rutger Hausmann

The State of Research

It has taken almost half a century for researchers of different backgrounds
to engage in intensive research on the role of art and culture in the Third
Reich. The primary historiography of this era narrowly focused on personal history, lavishing attention on even the most insignificant events.
Until recently, this has been called into question only by historical studies
with a social bent, focusing on mentality. Besides a considerable body of
Holocaust research, there also exist now important studies on party and
organizational history, and on the role played by law, medicine, art, theology, natural sciences, technology, and the representatives of these disciplines. There are even studies on the institution of the university and on
the conduct of faculty.

Less is known about the importance of the humanities and the arts
and their use to strengthen the ruling ideology. There is certainly a cor-
relation between the hesitancy of research into these topics and the fact
that academic research into historically orientated disciplines often
affects prominent representatives in these fields whose disciples and
"academic grandchildren" hold influential positions in the academic
structure and are not particularly interested in a reappraisal of this period.
Appropriate reconstruction work is also difficult because relatively few
coherent archival resources exist. It will still take some time for a body of
facts to be constructed from complementary details in the daily press,
journals, personal papers, private letters, and memoirs.[1]

This chapter deals not with a single discipline, university, institute, or
researcher's oeuvre, but with the totality of the German academic institutes

called *Deutsche (Wissenschaftliche) Institute* (DWI, DI; German cultural institutes) as intermediaries of German culture during World War II.[2] They formed an integrated system and were one of the many crucial Nazi "networks" that boomed especially during the war. "Network" refers to the state-ordered integration of normally independently functioning academic institutions that for political reasons coordinated their activities and used their power to enhance the political influence of Nazi Germany.[3] At regular intervals the heads of the participating establishments were called to conferences, mainly in the capital, in order to update and optimize their research objectives. Whereas some of these network systems in the fields of technology, medicine, and the natural sciences had been practiced even before the Third Reich, the integration of such diverse disciplines as the humanities and the arts was an invention of the Nazi academic administration. The reconstruction of such networks proves to be very enlightening with regard to the subordinate role the Nazis had originally given to the arts and humanities. After all, the "litterae" did not want to take second place to the "arma," especially after the outbreak of war. The arts and humanities also wanted to be *kämpfende Wissenschaften* (fighting disciplines) and wanted to "do their bit" toward final victory.[4] As mentioned before, the concentration of historical accounts dealing with diplomatic and military events of the Nazi period can easily give the wrong impression that academic and cultural life was irrelevant during times of war or had even stopped altogether. The exact opposite was the case; it flourished as never before. This (pseudo) blossoming continued even when the war began to claim its increasingly relentless toll, attested in the numerous obituaries of academics and artists who either had fallen in combat or were killed in bombing raids as well as items on the destruction of university buildings, libraries, museums, publishing houses, theaters, concert halls, and other installations.

The Nazis considered individual research obsolete, running counter to the principles of the racially defined national community, and therefore not really compatible with the basic principles of the Nazi state. Under their aegis, research was supposed to be undertaken in collaboration with academic and other institutions, and especially in study groups, operational centers, and camps that could not and would not try to defy their military mentors or martial intentions. In light of these considerations, interdisciplinary research institutions based on the Nazi model were created. To this day, much of Germany's top research is still practiced in this way, though free of the ideological demands of the Nazis and without the hierarchical internal structure of a Führer principle. Since the 1960s, interconnected academic systems have been developed that pay tribute to a multidisciplinary idea. This poses the question of whether the Nazi tendency toward modernization was also realized in the field of academic research.

These remarks aim to explain the position that institution of the DWI held in the academic enterprises of the Third Reich and to clarify at the same time the "network" character of all DWIs. All in all, about sixteen DWIs were established in European capitals during the course of the war, as well as an indeterminate number of subsidiaries in the provinces.[5] The first institute of this type was established in Bucharest on 6 April 1940; the last, on 20 June 1944 in Tirana. Even as late as 18 February 1945 a new branch of the Venice DWI was to have been opened in Milan.

The fact that some countries did not receive a DWI is indicative of their importance in the Nazi scheme. The Netherlands and Norway, for example, were originally considered as DWI sites, but Himmler reserved the right to "supervise" their cultural needs for himself and for his genealogical Ahnenerbe e.V. SS project. This was done with the aim of creating in the future a greater pan-Germanic Reich that would incorporate these two countries as equal partners. For different reasons no DWIs were established in neutral Ireland or neutral Switzerland. Ireland, which in April 1938 had signed the Anglo-Irish Agreement, removing the tensions that had existed with Great Britain since independence, was considered too difficult a location for the work of a DWI (which depended on an indispensable continuous communication) because of the crushing Anglo-American air and sea superiority across the Atlantic. The small Republic also did not want to provoke its neighbor and former colonial masters by tolerating a DWI. Switzerland, meanwhile, clearly counted as part of a German-speaking academic community rooted in identical traditions, so that the representation of German academic research in its territory seemed superfluous.

A special case was Italy, with its many German academic institutions,[6] where only at the beginning of 1944, six months after the "about-face" of Marshal Badoglio and the creation of the Repubblica Sociale Italiana, was a cultural institute opened in Venice. The established institutions dealing with history, history of art, and archaeology were mainly situated in Rome, close to the Allied power structure, and as the front drew closer, it was decided to transfer the papers, books, and the rest of the inventory to Northern Italy, which was still firmly in the hands of the German Army and was therefore a safer place. They found an interim shelter at the German Institute (DI) in Venice, or rather at its subsidiary in Milan, and were put to use again, unless they had been taken back to the Reich.

Attempts to establish a DWI in Turkey were defeated by the united opposition of mainly Jewish emigrants led by the scholar of Romance languages Erich Auerbach, who had been exiled from Marburg. As Poland had become the *Generalgouvernement* and Czechoslovakia the "Protectorate," and the independent state of Slovakia, Ukraine, and other large parts of the Soviet Union had been absorbed into so-called *Reichskommissariate*, their populations had been relocated, oppressed, and if not murdered outright, condemned to a slave-like existence; thus these areas were naturally not in need of a DWI. There is evidence that there were attempts to establish DWIs overseas, for example, in Japan and Latin

America. There existed even before 1933 so-called exchange offices in countries like Argentina and Chile, and probably in other Latin American countries with large German colonies. We know most about the German-Chilean Cultural Institute (Instituto Cultural Germano-Chileno de Santiago) in Santiago, Chile. It published its own journal, *Academia Spiritus, Publicación del Instituto Cultural Germano-Chileno*, which clearly documents the diverse activities the institute was involved in.[7] These "offices" were similar to European DWIs, but the great distances and the superior air and sea power of the Allies made close contact with German academic institutions overseas difficult. The Munich Germanist Herbert Cysarz was chosen by the Reichsministerium für Erziehung, Wissenschaft und Volksbildung (REM) to replace the jurist Otto Koellreutter as head of the Japanese-German Cultural Institute in Tokyo. Cysarz was willing in principle, but because of the war situation, he asked to delay the journey several times, and in the end, it never took place.

The European DWIs were continuously expanded. In 1940 three were opened (Bucharest, Paris,[8] Sofia); in 1941 five more were added (Budapest, Belgrade, Copenhagen,[9] Madrid, Athens); in 1942 one (Brussels);[10] in 1943 four (Helsinki, Stockholm, Agram/Zagreb, Preßburg/Bratislava, and in 1944 three more (Lisbon, Venice, Tirana). Ambassador Franz Alfred Six, who was later in charge of the DWIs, stated that in 1944 he was responsible for over 293 employees; it is unclear whether this number also included all the branches.[11]

The DWIs were supposed to be long-term institutions whose costs would not diminish over time because after the war was won, scientific and academic activities would increase and be put on a much broader basis. Considering that the material costs were between RM 50,000 and RM 150,000 per year, depending on the size of a DWI, a median value can be estimated at around RM 1 million per year. It seems reasonable to posit a similar sum to cover the salaries from director down to receptionist and porter. Assuming only ten DWIs in operation, this would mean a further RM 1 million, to which fairly substantial costs for stipends, entertainment, and other extras must be added. Putting these at another RM 500,000 brings the total amount to around RM 2.5 million for the upkeep of all the DWIs, which translates by today's standards into roughly USD 10–15 million per year. This was not an exorbitant amount in wartime, considering that the total war debt of the German Reich was as high as RM 400 billion. But because at least half of this amount had to be found in foreign currency that was hard to come by, it nevertheless constituted an item in the national budget that had to be taken seriously. Not only did the item take effect in 1943, when the construction phase for the DWIs was essentially completed, but funding was provided as early as 1940, since several of the institutes started operating up to a year and a half before their official opening.

The "Cultural Policy" of the Third Reich and the Founding of the DWIs

At the time of the NSDAP's seizure of power there was no unified Nazi concept of academic policy in place, nor was there a clear plan for a systematic foreign cultural policy. This changed only after Hitler's groundbreaking speech at the Nuremberg Party Congress of 1937, the so-called Workers' Congress (Parteitag der Arbeit), when on 7 September he pointed to the active cultural policies of, particularly, the French and British, and then demanded a similar concentration of all academic and cultural forces for Germany.[12] In large part, he was reacting to the neglect of cultural propaganda before and during World War I, which in hindsight was another factor held responsible for Germany's defeat. Never again should the cultural and propagandistic initiative be left to Germany's potential enemies. Here, Hitler was either motivated by the trauma he experienced in World War I, or he was already thinking of the coming war.[13]

After Nazi power had been internally consolidated, territorial expansion under the guise of Germany's "higher mission" was planned from 1937 on. This "mission" included "German" literature, music, art, theater, film, and philosophy, as well as the theoretical sciences, that had been "cleansed" of all foreign elements. The idea of separating propaganda from cultural policy, as practiced in the Weimar Republic, was abandoned.[14] In 1936 the cultural section of the Ministry of Foreign Affairs (Kulturabteilung des Auswärtigen Amtes) was renamed Department for Cultural Affairs (Kulturpolitische Abteilung).

Only under Joachim Ribbentrop, who became foreign secretary in 1938, were new concepts developed to intensify the politicization of the Department for Cultural Affairs. At a conference in September 1942 the director of this department, Ambassador Fritz von Twardowski, summarized the findings of these studies by stating that "cultural policy means the conscious effort of all intellectual forces of the German nation to influence the intellectual strata of other nations and thereby gain academic superiority in Europe."[15] However, this planned influencing precluded the use of daily propaganda, because National Socialism saw itself as a "German" movement that had to remain inaccessible to its neighbors, unless they were true Germanic brothers. Academic achievement that was closely linked to the ideas and values, respected worldwide, of Humboldt University, was now to be replaced by propaganda. Initially, nothing happened. Only after the outbreak of war, was it realized that a cultural-political department attached to individual legations or embassies would not be sufficient. Rather, centralized institutions had to be established in the neutral, friendly, and conquered countries in order to familiarize the local elite with the German point of view. Through this approach, it was felt, intellectual and cultural leaders should feel tied to Germany and its culture, thereby multiplying and disseminating these ideas.

Originally, the initiative for the creation of the DWIs came from civil servants of the Foreign Ministry, or rather from the Ministerium für Erziehung, Wissenschaft und Volksbildung (REM or Ministry of Education, Science and Public Instruction),[16] which employed the required specialists. Though their ministers were kept informed, they had very little interest in these academic institutes. In the final structure of the DWI, internationally renowned professors from different disciplines were to be the representatives, organizers, and promoters of a "German academic and cultural policy" in foreign capitals. Upon the assumption of office, they were promised that they would be able to continue their academic work freely and without interference. These promises, made by various ministerial departments in Berlin responsible for DWIs, must be seen in the light of the general academic and cultural policy of the Nazis. Although even at this point the Nazis spoke of "academic freedom," they meant by this an academic culture that had been "cleansed" and "freed" of all Jewish and Western influences and was based on national and racist (*völkisch*) ideas; in other words, a "German science." However, the renunciation of the use of NS-propaganda was paramount in order not to doom this cultural political work to failure from the beginning. Science and culture had to appear objective; propaganda as party-political and purpose-oriented. Antiliberal, anti-Marxist, and anti-Semitic convictions were allowed to bear on the work of the institutes only in that academics or artists of Jewish descent, or those expressly professed to be Liberals or Socialists, could not be mentioned and certainly could not be invited. In only a few cases did this procedure meet with any opposition in the host countries. Repression in the cultural sector, a result of the enactment in 1933–1935 of the new racial and civil service laws, was rarely touched upon by the German side, and attempts were made to hide behind the kudos of internationally renowned "German" representatives of culture. As can be seen from other sources, the DWIs were also used to search out Jewish emigrants in order to isolate them internationally. It cannot be ascertained how much the staff of these institutes knew about extermination campaigns, although these were highly visible in the Balkans.[17]

Even before the war, and in some cases before 1933, most European countries had had German visiting professors as well as German-funded and German-founded research institutes. At the very least, they had DAAD offices and German (or Goethe) Institutes that were often still in existence. Therefore, it seemed appropriate to absorb them into the new type of institute.[18] The DWIs now being established had at least three departments: one for academic studies and organization (often under the joint leadership of a director and general secretary), one for academic exchanges and one for language studies.[19] These were headed by a president, normally a tenured university professor, whose special subject was of particular interest to the host country.

The office of president combined administrative, academic, and representative duties in an almost ideal fashion. It was well paid, offered excellent working conditions for personal research, was interesting and varied, and protected its holder from dreary and life-threatening military service. The status of *Reichsprofessor*, someone who was directly answerable to the REM, guaranteed independence. Usually, this office was also combined with a visiting professorship at the university of the city in which the DWI was located. On the one hand, using academics in this way was supposed to strengthen the role the university played in the political and cultural aspects of this foreign service, and on the other hand, it was supposed to force the professors to make their highly specialized research work accessible to a lay audience. In general, it was felt that academics should be viewed not just as researchers, but also as cultural facilitators and scientific managers. Scholars in the field of Romance languages were sent to countries speaking a Romance language (Karl Epting to Paris, Theodor Heinermann and Karl Vossler to Madrid, Walter Mönch to Brussels, Harri Meier to Lisbon, Ernst Gamillscheg to Bucharest), while an expert in Slavonic studies was dispatched to the Balkans (Alois Schmaus[20] to Belgrade), and a historian with experience in Nordic history to Denmark (Gustav Adolf Scheel). A Germanist and expert in Nordic studies was appointed as his successor (Otto Höfler), and for Finland a scholar in Finno-Ugric studies was chosen (Hans Grellmann). An exception was made for Budapest, where the sociologist Hans Freyer was sent. Other exceptions were Agram (Croatian: Zagreb) and Preßburg (Slovakian: Bratislava), which appointed jurists and former university rectors (Gustav Adolf Walz of Breslau, later Cologne and Munich, and Wilhelm Saure of Prague) as presidents. The same applied to Stockholm, which was led by an expert on soil and plant nutrition (Fritz Giesecke).

Even the directors who acted as deputies to the presidents and academic department managers were supposed to be professors or at least lecturers; most of them were Germanists. The most famous directors were in Athens (Rudolf Fahrner, who was also a well-known specialist in old and modern Greek literature) and Bucharest (Hermann Schneider, old and modern Germanist, who after the war became the first rector of the University of Tübingen). In Lisbon the director was the Germanist Wolfgang Kayser, who for his Portuguese students there wrote a bestseller, entitled *Das sprachliche Kunstwerk* (Analysis and interpretation of literary texts), which was used for generations to come to introduce students of literary studies and comparative literature to this discipline.[21]

But there were exceptions even to this rule based on the roles the Nazis assigned to different countries to fit in with their political concepts. For instance, in Zagreb the Viennese agricultural economist and specialist in pricing policy, Max Stadler, served as director in charge of bringing the Croatian economy into line, alongside Walz, a specialist in national and international law. He kept up close contact with the Deutsch-Kroatische

Handelskammer (DHK; German-Croatian Chamber of Commerce) as well as with the Südosteuropa-Gesellschaft (SOEG; Southeastern European Association) in Vienna, an institution that had been founded at the instigation of Baldur von Schirach to coordinate Eastern studies and research with the long-term objective of taking over the Balkans and simultaneously exploiting their economy.[22] In Paris we find Karl Heinz Bremer[23] second-in-command, who had a doctorate in history, was a specialist in international law and an expert in Romance languages. His main function was to monitor French writers, who would either be persuaded to collaborate with the Germans or if they refused, silenced. Helmut Bauersfeld, a specialist in Celtic studies and active SS officer who had been working abroad for the SS for many years, worked behind the scenes in Stockholm. In Brussels, Wolfgang Krönig held the director's office. A well-known art historian and Rubens specialist, Krönig was well respected in Belgium because of his in-depth knowledge of Flemish art.

Even the personnel appointments of the DWIs, which attest to their heterogeneity, reflected the mostly correct political assessments made of the host countries and ostensibly took their interests into consideration. Long-time party members or leaders with close connections to the SS were only employed in places where active resistance against German interests was expected, or where the German point of view was to be imposed without too much consideration.

DWI operations varied widely depending on whether the institute was located in an occupied country, a country only nominally independent, or a neutral country; in other words, on whether the aim was to foster collaboration, exploitation, or *Gleichschaltung* (bringing into line), or to deepen a partnership based on almost equal rights. In this, close proximity to Germany, as well as the overall war situation at the time the institution opened, played an important role. As an example, Portugal and Spain, and with some limitations also Sweden and Finland, could feel relatively safe from the German war machinery and accordingly were able to act in a confident manner; they could even impose limitations on German planning. Interestingly enough, both the military government and the DWIs abstained from massive indoctrination in occupied countries like Belgium, Denmark, France, Greece, and Serbia due to the slow but steady growth of resistance groups. Those parts of the elite that had succumbed to Nazi ideology even before the war did not have to be convinced, but with all other groups one had to proceed carefully, in order to eventually achieve a transformation of their reserve into a pro-German commitment, or at least into neutral tolerance. The German cultural administration showed its truest face in the Fascist and pro-Fascist satellite states (Albania, Italy, Croatia, Serbia, Slovakia). This was the case for Albania and Serbia only after Italy had been removed from the axis and its system of occupation had been dismantled. The other German allies, countries such as Bulgaria, Romania, and Hungary that were ruled by authoritarian regimes and that until 1944 had their political future closely linked to that of Germany, formed the last group. Their pro-German elite had partly studied in Germany, admired both the country and the people, and had been blinded by the early military successes. Here German cultural propaganda had the function of tempting, imploring, or even threatening, depending on which pro- or anti-German faction held the balance of power. Traditionally trained philologists were therefore not suitable for the office of president, especially in the Balkans. Where such scholars did direct a DWI, as in Belgrade (Alois Schmaus) and Sofia (Herbert Duda), the DWI played no real role in public life. But where men like Rudolf Fahrner (Athens), Hans Freyer (Budapest), Ernst Gamillscheg (Bucharest), or Karl Epting (Paris) presided—men who were scholars, cultural managers, and diplomats all in one—their leadership greatly enhanced the attraction and prestige of those institutes.

The Humanities Department was always the most important in the DWI, because it was responsible for the exchange of professors and the planning and organization of exhibitions, concerts, and book fairs. Second in status was the Academic Department, which organized the exchange of students, teachers, and members of trade unions (*Deutsche Arbeitsfront*), apprentices and school children, and so on. To a large extent, it took over the duties of the Deutsche Akademische Austauschdienst (DAAD; German Academic Exchange Office) and the Alexander von Humboldt Foundation (which under Franz Alfred Six was later renamed Deutsches Studienwerk für Ausländer). Both these institutions still operated under their original names in cities without DWIs, for example, in Rome. The third DWI department, the Language Department, oversaw all of the German studies lectorates in different countries and organized the language courses that the DWI offered in a country's capital city. If this city had a university, as was mostly the case, the director was also given a university appointment as lecturer in German. It was impressed upon these lecturers that they should see themselves not only as guardians of German culture, but also as champions of a new greater European order.[24]

Occasionally, there was a separate fourth department, the Literature Department, which was responsible for the translation and bibliographical registration of important German books into the language of the host country and vice versa. This department was also in charge of publishing every journal or book series that was edited by a DWI. Of course, the library could not include every academic German publication, but was expected to buy primarily such books as were needed by local scholars who were working on particular research projects. Most new publications were accessioned. In addition to this, the library was supposed to carry the most important German classics and magazines, as well as all Nazi legislation and regulations. The latter were kept together in so-called information libraries, which were supervised by the Ministry for Propaganda. These libraries also collected recordings of German music and German recording artists, as well as readings of the classics and speech specimens for language courses. Also photos of German university towns, landscapes, and works of art were collected and could be lent out.

In individual cases, further departments were planned, for example, for archaeology, archive studies, forestry, geology, history of art, agriculture, medicine, law, technology, and economics. This was to be done according to the needs of a given country. Unique was the Arctic Department of the DWI in Copenhagen, run by Hans Frebold, a well-known paleontologist, geologist, and glaciologist, who had led several successful expeditions to Spitzbergen and Greenland. He was the only member of the institute who successfully cooperated with northern colleagues because his research was above suspicion, and he was also able to reconnect with former contacts. The most curious plan was to attach an Enology Department to the DI in Bordeaux, to be run by a representative of the German wine trade in collaboration with a lecturer. Under pressure from Rosenberg, a few institutes were supposed to include departments for Jewish or Freemason affairs, especially in places where there was a significant Jewish population. However, this project did not come to anything.

The DI in Paris had a unique status because its head, Karl Epting, enjoyed a special relationship of trust with the ambassador Otto Abetz[25] and for a while had been leading both the DI and the Cultural Department of the embassy. The two knew each other through joint German-French cultural work in the early 1930s in the Sohlberg circle. They were both still influenced by the desire for rapprochement that had peaked during the late Weimar Republic. Now their cooperation was to be continued under very different circumstances and with very different means.[26] Epting was very well funded, and in addition to basically equipping four departments, he was able to add three more for history of art, archival studies, forestry, and earth sciences. It is fair to say that the Paris institute was the prototype of a DWI, and in a practical sense Abetz, Epting, and Bremer were the spiritual fathers of this institution. On the one hand, they wanted to turn the Paris DI into a meeting place for collaboration. On the other, they wanted to change it into a platform for a new direction for local scholarship in the tradition of French studies in German language and literature. Their early success—an audience of 300 to 400 listeners at lectures, 500 to 1,000 concert-goers, and over 5,000 applicants for the language courses, a number that rose to 12,000 in 1942—seemed to prove this concept right. If one wants to know which personalities were constant visitors to the German Institute in Paris, one only has to read the memoirs of Epting's wife, Alice Kullmann-Epting, a woman of German descent from Geneva.[27] She gives a vivid picture of the rich cultural life that blossomed then, even though she glorifies the period. The opening of the exhibition of the complete works of the sculptor Arno Breker, which Epting organized in the Orangery of the Paris Tuileries, is a particularly good illustration of the bridging function that collaboration could have been used for, had it lasted: it was attended by the top functionaries of the Vichy government,[28] and while Albert Speer and Hermann Göring did not attend the private viewing for security reasons, but visited the exhibit at night, Prime Minister Pierre Laval was present. Minister of Culture Abel Bonnard gave the opening speech. Marshall Petain acknowledged the magnificent catalog, published by Flammarion, with a handwritten thank-you note.

Although the other DWIs, which were not nearly as well funded as Paris, operated in principle in a similar way, one must look at each individual institute in its local context when making comparisons, bearing in mind that Paris was in a special position. Just as in the case of the Paris DI, they were given representative buildings, usually in vacated embassies of occupied countries that had lost their independence. In Paris, Brussels, and Bucharest they were the Polish embassies, in Athens it was the Yugoslav embassy, and in Madrid at first, the Czech embassy. In Paris, the center of the Czech residents was also used to house the Art History Department. Additionally, they searched for other representative rental properties. Erecting new buildings on newly state-owned property could not be considered because of the weakened foreign exchange situation caused by the war. In addition to offices and libraries, each DWI had a special hall for lectures, concerts, and receptions that could accommodate at least 150 people.

In accordance with the polycratic system at the time, the DWIs came under the jurisdiction of several ministries and other authorities. The elected scientists were administered by the REM (Ministry of Education), the lecturers by the Deutsche Akademie (German Academy), which in turn was jointly governed by the Ministry for Foreign Affairs and the Ministry of Propaganda in accordance with a decree by Hitler dated 15 November 1941.[29] The Exchange Department again came under the Ministry for Foreign Affairs, which until the end of the Third Reich was in overall charge of the DWIs and also administered the funds. Locally, the cultural officer at the German embassy or legation was the contact person for the DWI. Using the leadership principle, the position of the DWI president was strengthened because several ministries and institutions were involved in the DWIs.

Only once did a German minister participate in the opening ceremonies of a DWI, and that was Minister of Education Bernhard Rust, in October 1940 in Sofia. Ribbentrop considered it beneath himself to attend such a ceremony; it was sufficient for him to graciously give permission for the formation of individual institutes. In the end, cultural policy was not that important to the Nazis, therefore the representation was left to the lower echelons of permanent and assistant secretaries.

Due to the personnel reshuffle after the fall in February 1943 of Permanent Secretary Martin Luther, who had attempted to overthrow Ribbentrop by having him declared mentally ill and unable to work, the Cultural Department came under the leadership of SS and later brigade leader Franz Alfred Six. Six was also Dean of the Auslandswissenschaftliche

Fakultät (DAWF; Faculty for the Study of Foreign Affairs) at the Friedrich-Wilhelms-University in Berlin and director of the attached Deutsches Auslandswissenschaftliches Institut (DAWI; German Institute for the study of Foreign Affairs). He joined the Ministry of Foreign Affairs with the rank of ambassador and on 1 February 1944 took control of all the DWIs, which as a formality had each previously been assigned to the university from which the president had been elected. Six launched into a busy traveling and visiting schedule that took him to several DWIs. First and foremost, he pushed ahead with the formation of institutes in those European countries that had none. He was personally present at the opening ceremonies in Zagreb (German: Agram) on 23 September 1943, in Bratislava (Preßburg) on 18 November 1943, Lisbon on 21 January 1944, and Venice on 17 February 1944. He visited most of the other institutes at least once. The institutes in Helsinki, Stockholm, Tirana, and Milan were established through his initiatives. It is surprising that despite the slavophobia of the Nazis, the DWIs in Agram, Belgrade, and Preßburg were always showcased and their importance for Germany stressed. It was also thanks to Six that those institutes that had hitherto been independent now fell under the influence of the SS in an unstoppable way; by this time they had definitely lost their innocuousness. As an example, Otto Höfler, who replaced Otto Scheel in 1943 in Copenhagen, was the ideal candidate for the SS, since he had written expert opinions for them and lectured at their training camps.[30] During Höfler's reign, the language courses of the Copenhagen DWI were used as training events for Danish Gestapo agents. President Giesecke in Stockholm, as Sturmbannführer (stormtrooper) and training leader, belonged to the Rasse- und Siedlungshauptamt (SS Race and Settlement Main Office). His deputy Bauersfeld was exposed as a Gestapo agent in 1944 and expelled. In May 1944 the DWI in Budapest functioned as a coordinating point for the Reichssicherheitshauptamt (RSHA; Reich Security Main Office). In Venice, where the DWI was led by Six's friend SS-Hauptsturmführer Albert Prinzing, SS-Obergruppenführer Karl Wolff was a frequent visitor. Since July 1944, Wolff, in his capacity as authorized representative general of the army, had supervised Mussolini's government in Salò. Preßburg President Saure was also SS-Oberführer in the Rasse- und Siedlungshauptamt. According to eyewitnesses, SS informers operated under false names in other DWIs.

The Academic Activities of the DWIs

At this point, questions must be asked about the academic quality and dignity of the DWIs, the influence they had on their host countries and, in the widest sense, the role played by the academics who were employed by them. First it has to be said that only about half of all DWIs really functioned. If one looks at foreign cultural policy in its most important phase during the war, one can see that it ran parallel to the stages of political-military history: the propagandistic early phase of stock-taking and the assigning of guilt for the outbreak of war (1939–1940) was followed by the victory phase (1940–1942) and then by the retreat phase (1942–1945). The DWIs were established in phases two and three. In the victory phase, the Ministry for Foreign Affairs dominated and tried with the help of science, art, and culture to ensure German influence on the foreign elite, who in the face of the French and their own defeat, and the early victories of the Wehrmacht in the East, had dismissed any thoughts of revenge. They were willing to accommodate the Germans, if not out of conviction then out of prudence. In the last phase, dominated by Six, the appeals for the survival of Western civilization eclipsed all other motives. According to Six, the Greater German Reich fought on all fronts for European culture and civilization against the "Anglo-American plutocrats" or the "Bolshe-vik subhumans" (Untermenschen). Instead of Großraum (Greater Germany) they talked about a new Europe, but this European ideology was in no way supposed to detract from the German plans for domination. With his tireless rallying calls, Six tried to give the illusion of a final German victory, in order to keep a hold over the other countries. But this was merely tilting at windmills. The DWIs that were established during this final phase in Preßburg (Bratislava), Tirana, Venice, and Milan could barely get off the ground in light of the emerging German military defeat. The ephemeral governments with whom the institutes were accredited either had no backing in the general population and therefore supplied no audience, or the administrations were in a state of dissolution due to combat or partisan activities. That meant that the institutes had a maximum of four years, but mostly only two years, to become established and to find a normal working rhythm.

Keeping this in mind, their publications were indeed impressive. The series volumes—sixty volumes in all—that were published in Belgrade, Brussels, Bucharest, Copenhagen, Lisbon, Paris, Sofia, and Stockholm covered all subjects from the humanities to the sciences, including law and medicine. The Paris and Stockholm institutes covered the widest spectrum. Several of the institutes also published journals (Agram/Zagreb, Lisbon, Madrid, Paris [and its branch in Besançon], Sofia, and Venice). These journals printed the lectures that had been given at the institutes by visiting scholars in the language of the country, as well as contributions by local academics in German, including reviews and bibliographical material. If one excludes the Paris journal Vierteljahresschrift des Deutschen Instituts Deutschland-Frankreich, all the other journals were free of Nazi propaganda. This was partly due to the fact that in Lisbon and Venice only one issue appeared, and in Madrid the journals contained only bibliographical information.

All DWIs invited well-known German artists, actors, writers, and scholars, and also sent foreign colleagues to Germany. The cultural and academic tourism that took place, which can now no longer be reconstructed in detail because each year hundreds of people participated, was of considerable proportions. These travel activities did not slow down in any way during the war; on the contrary, they were strongly encouraged and were seen as an integral part of collaboration and international cooperation. During the academic year 1940/41 over 400 foreign scholars visited Germany. In addition, 5,000 students went under the auspices of the Deutsche Studienwerk für Ausländer, the former Alexander von Humboldt Institute, which in some cases awarded grants. On the other hand, 700 German academics were invited to give lectures or readings or as visiting professors, mainly to Rome, Sofia, Budapest, Bucharest, and Preßburg. The DWIs also arranged for 200 foreign laymen to be sent to Germany; however, the number of foreigners who lectured or performed at DWIs is unknown. During the academic year 1942/43, 900 German scholars gave lectures in other countries, and 700 foreign scholars lectured in Germany.

The REM argued that one should not retaliate against the defeated countries by socially excluding their scholars in the way that they had excluded Germans after 1918. Because the most decisive weapon for Germany in the contest between nations was practical achievement, the Reich wanted to align itself primarily with countries that acknowledged a common European destiny and were willing to "fight the threatening anarchy of Bolshevism and the British-American threat of restriction of the European continent."[31] But foreign top scholars and researchers avoided accepting German invitations or canceled at the last minute. The fear of being accused of collaboration by the international community, and therefore of being compromised, was too great. This even applied to the friendly Italians and Spaniards. Even after the outbreak of war, the international organizations for geographers, philosophers, artists, specialists in oriental studies, and so on were still in existence, however hard the Germans tried to replace them with new German-run organizations and to attract foreign academic participation.

Meanwhile, German research results (in nuclear physics, vitamin or hormone research, tropical medicine) could not be shared with foreigners at congresses in Germany; this had to be done either at, or by, the DWIs. But the reception remained one-sided and only rarely led to an exchange, which was true of the influence of the DWIs as a whole. In this respect, the conference of German and Hungarian nuclear physicists held in Budapest from 30 November to 4 December 1942, which was attended on the German side by Max Planck, Werner Heisenberg,[32] and Carl Friedrich von Weizsäcker, was a rare exception.[33] A similar precursory meeting had taken place in Copenhagen in the spring of 1941.[34] The programs run from October 1940 to July 1943 by the Paris DI, which have been preserved and which list 109 lectures aimed at the French public, document that almost all of the German intellectual elite appeared in Paris: Friedrich Sieburg, Anton Zischka, Erich Edwin Dwinger, Georg Britting, Ina Seidel, Heinrich

Ritter von Srbik, Ottmar von Verschuer, Carl Schmitt, Leonardo Conti, Eugen Fischer, Hans-Georg Gadamer, and Erich Rothacker. Although the scientists, with the exception of the race researchers, always considered themselves apolitical, the same could not be said, even at that time, of the humanities scholars. The Leipzig philosopher Hans-Georg Gadamer, who traveled through Portugal between 12 March and 4 April 1944 giving lectures in Lisbon as well as Coimbra in German and French, reported extensively on his travels. He was under no illusion that he was being used by the Nazi state as an advertisement, but he justified himself thus: "I was fully aware that one was being misused for foreign propaganda, for which very often a politically spotless person was just right…, but I feel that I was right in thinking that among the audience there were some people who could abstract from all the circumstances and ulterior motives, and just saw the science. The res publica literarum exists whatever one says."[35] Whether this excuse is valid remains an open question.[36] Budapest DWI President Freyer,[37] who at first had welcomed the Nazi take-over, was quickly disillusioned and had turned away from the Nazis to accept a visiting professorship in Hungary. He had established the Budapest DWI together with his assistant Helmut Schelsky, who in his memoirs asserts that Freyer never had any contact with the SS or the official NSDAP bureaucrats, and that he always acted in a conciliatory and even-handed manner. However, this version is contradicted by other witnesses. It is said, for instance, that shortly after the attack on the Soviet Union, Freyer negotiated with the representatives of the ethnic Germans in Hungary to establish a volunteer unit.[38]

This raises the question, therefore, as to how much the institutes' leaders were aware of being instrumentalized by the Nazis. The DWI presidents held quasi-diplomatic status and were seen as representatives of the German Reich, considering that they were unable to avoid the Nazi communiqués and their entanglement with the expansionist objectives of the Nazi regime and that therefore they became Nazi functionaries, whether they were party members or not. They could hardly have had any illusions about their involvement in a system that they had served for either material or idealistic reasons. At least once a year they were asked to attend a meeting in Berlin where the latest guidelines for Nazi cultural and academic policies were impressed upon them. They were also obliged to send reports on a regular basis, which forced them to constantly evaluate and quantify their work.

However, as the case of Athens DWI President Rudolf Fahrner shows, a courageous president shielded by NS institutions had the ability to thwart the intentions of the NS regime. Rudolf Fahrner, a disciple of Stefan George, belonged to the circle of friends around Claus Graf Schenk von Stauffenberg, and advised and helped him with formulating memoranda to be used just before and after the putsch planned for 20 July 1944.[39] Alois Schmaus in Belgrade, who was married to a Serbian woman

and sympathized with the cause of her defeated and oppressed countrymen, was later also able to claim that he had supported Serbian interests as
much as he was able to. This was recognized by Yugoslavia after the war.
All other presidents contributed to a greater or lesser degree to increasing
German prestige, and thereby helped prolong the unlawful regime.

The amazing political importance of the DWIs can be assessed by the
choice of speakers who were invited repeatedly to visit them. They consisted mainly of academics whose research supported the expansionist
policies of the Nazis and who could prove to be politically useful and sup-
portive in preparing for the new European order. Among them were the
professor of national and international law Carl Schmitt, and the economic
geographer and development planner Hugo Hassinger. Both scholars left
behind extensive travel reports. Schmitt visited Paris in October 1941;
Budapest in May 1942 and again in November 1943; Bucharest in February
1943; Madrid in June 1943 and again in May–June 1944, when he also visited Lisbon. Because these visits were always arranged by the local DWI or
DI, he gave at least one of his important lectures on *Großraum* (Greater
Germany) and the New European Order, on the differences between land
and sea powers (the United States and England on the one hand, and Germany together with Italy on the other); on the role of civil law in France; or
on the changes in German administrative law. His lectures, which he
delivered in German, French, or Spanish, were attended by many personalities favorably disposed toward the Germans, from the ranks of politics,
diplomacy, administration, science, culture, and art, in addition to the
impressive number of about 100–200 students. We have an accurate picture of this, thanks to Schmitt's detailed reports. The lectures were preceded by refreshments in the best local houses or followed by banquets
where, according to Schmitt, all participants conversed in a friendly and
open manner and showed their complete willingness to adopt German
viewpoints. The "crown jurist" of the Third Reich, a title Schmitt liked to
give himself, was received at his various travel destinations by the ministers of culture or the vice prime ministers of the host countries. He had the
impression that his discussion partners, who had mostly been educated in
France, or French Switzerland, whether they were Romanians, Spaniards,
Portuguese, or Hungarians, now saw the Germans as the only possible
allies in the battle against the universally hated Bolsheviks. They also saw
Germany as their strongest economic partner. The fact that jurists had a
major influence in the countries German guests visited, was seen as proof
of a strong potential for closer academic collaboration.[40]

Hugo Hassinger, in his capacity as representative of the newly founded
German Geographical Society undertook an orientation tour of Southeastern Europe in April–May 1942, which brought him to Greece, Croatia, Bulgaria, Romania, Hungary, and Slovakia.[41] In agreement with several Reich
authorities, the geography society was supposed to convene three international congresses in 1941/42 that would deal in turn with Northern,

Southwestern, and Southeastern Europe, and to which scholars from the involved northern countries, as well as from Spain, Italy, and the Balkans, were to be invited. These were also the three regions in which DWIs were being established. According to the expansionist *Großraum* plans conceptualized by the Nazis, the neutral, allied, or occupied countries within these regions were to remain independent entities. How this concept was going to work in detail can be gathered from Hassinger's lectures, which radiated an immense political force, although on a superficial reading of the text they seem innocuous. According to this scenario, countries like Slovakia, Hungary, Bulgaria, Romania, Yugoslavia, Albania, and Greece would fall under the German cultural sphere of influence, which was evident from the enclaves of a German population in most of the cited countries. Once Southeastern Europe had been freed of disruptive foreign influences,[42] Germany had to help these countries to establish a new order of regional development. This should include an exchange of populations and a strong protection of minorities. These countries should supply Germany with agricultural products, mineral resources, and other raw materials and receive industrial goods in return. Even if Germany were to regain colonies, which was likely in the foreseeable future, its economic interests in the region of Southeastern Europe would remain.

With the help of the DWIs, Hassinger met important contact people from universities and ministries during his visits. Among them were geographers, geologists, environmental and land planners, statisticians, demographers, and experts in administration who could be considered well disposed toward Germany and who could prove helpful in the implementation of the newly planned expansionist order by supplying essential locally obtained information. Whenever he met with representatives of the German minority, he did it unobtrusively or in secret. But it is quite clear from his report what the object of these talks was.[43]

All DWIs in the East (Agram/Zagreb, Athens, Belgrade, Budapest, Bucharest, and Sofia, and later also Preßburg/Bratislava and Tirana) belonged to an association of German scientific Eastern and Southeastern institutes that were founded shortly after the attack on the Soviet Union under the conceptual leadership of the Breslau Eastern European institute, run by the economist and settlement expert Hans-Jürgen Seraphim. Altogether, 36 different institutions (this number rose at later congresses to over 50) in Berlin, Breslau, Danzig, Kiel, Königsberg, Cracow, Leipzig, Leoben, Munich, Prague, and Vienna were supposed to jointly focus and concentrate on the great objectives "which through the military, political, and economic development in the East as a whole constitute the future task of German scholarship."[44] Topics to be explored were: the nation; state and economy in Europe; Greater Germany and Eastern Europe; the legal relationship between nation, state, ethnic groups, and minorities since Versailles; economic nationality struggle; structure and current situation of the population; German nationality law; the "Jewish Question"; problems of aryanization; problems of national law in the Generalgouvernement and the Protectorate of Bohemia and Moravia; the situation in the Central Southeastern European greater economic region.

It is documented that the DWI presidents Fahrner, Freyer, Duda, Gamillscheg, Reichenkron, and Schmaus participated in the inaugural meeting of all Eastern and Southeastern institutes in Breslau (25–27 September 1941) in preparation for individual research projects. Therefore, they had to be aware of what was expected of them. The procedure of this meeting was determined by senior civil servant Scurla of the REM, who made the political priorities very clear. A protocol of the preparatory meeting discusses the plans for a follow-up meeting of the "Southeastern group" in February 1942 in Vienna under the aegis of rector Kurt Knoll of the Hochschule für Welthandel (Academy for World Trade).[45] After an evaluation of academic facilities and possible job projects had taken place in Breslau, a special meeting on economics and law was to be planned in Vienna to discuss future projects by individual entrepreneurs or entrepreneurial groups with a view to Großraumwirtschaft (Greater European economic planning) and to solving practical questions of coordinating trade and economic law.

Although the DWIs in Western Europe did not belong to such a network, they too had nationwide and cross-professional organizations. The Romance presidents and directors Epting and Bremer (both Paris), Heinermann (Madrid), Mönch (Brussels), and Vossler (president-elect of the Madrid DWI), but also Gamillscheg and Reichenkron, as well as Höfler (later president in Copenhagen) and Schmaus (president in Belgrade), contributed to the so-called intellectual war effort of the humanities (Kriegseinsatz der Geisteswissenschaften).[46] This was to be achieved by publishing a gigantic series entitled "The German Humanities" with the purpose of breaking French and English intellectual superiority, for even Vichy France successfully continued to publicize French culture abroad after the French defeat. Epting's deputy Bremer, in his capacity as former assistant to REM representative Paul Ritterbusch, head of the so-called intellectual war effort, was for a while general secretary in charge of this Kriegseinsatz, and he tried to put his stamp on these publications. One aim of the series was to prove that even Romance cultural achievements can be traced back to Germanic influence. The battle against French principles of civilization and English ideology of humanitarianism was expressly one of the tasks of the DWIs.

However, the DWIs were only small players in the big schemes of the "Führer almighty." For Hitler, such collaboration was only a means to an end. Goebbels, the trusted voice of his master, made this quite clear with regard to the defeat of France. During the war, on 26 April 1942, he came to the conclusion that this "macabre and hedonist French nation is not worth anything anymore" and "no achievements of any consequence can be expected of her for the development of a new Europe." It was true that

Vichy was willing to stand by Germany "if we were to offer them an acceptable peace now. This the Führer does not want, and rightly so. One should not play one's trump card too early. Most importantly, it is necessary to bring the war against France to a historic conclusion. We therefore have to eliminate the military and political power of France once and for all from future power dynamics. If the French only knew what the Führer will one day demand of them they would most likely be thunderstruck. It is, therefore, better to keep these things quiet for the time being and to exploit the French attentism as much as possible. Idle talk about collaboration is only intended for the moment."[47] What was said here about France surely also applied to all other countries to which Hitler allotted a certain amount of autonomy, as long as it fitted into his plans for world conquest. In light of this fact there was very little independence left for national scholarship. Researchers had to subordinate themselves and learn from Germany.

State Secretary Werner Zschintzsch had said at the opening of the DWI in Budapest: "The right that we claim as the highest national right for us, we will grant to all other nations; we are of the opinion that every self-confident nation that does not want to subject itself to foreign intellectual infiltration has the right, even the duty in the face of its history, to follow its own form of political and intellectual perception."[48] In practice, however, the work of the DWIs repudiates this claim. In the occupied, allied, and neutral countries the DWIs were as a rule actively involved in demonstrating the successes and superiority of German culture and science. The preserved lectures by guest speakers, for instance, document the fact that even scholars who were committed to nonpartisan scholarship, such as Vossler, Rothacker, or Gadamer, overaccentuated the Germanic influence on foreign cultures. Zschintzsch's words possibly reflect the early National Socialist concept advocating "a healthy system of nation states on the basis of historic and present achievements that were not born out of imperial ideas but out of a national principle."[49] This was a constructive and forward-looking vision that was very soon displaced by Hitler's and the SS's nihilistic concept of Eastern Europe.

So what was the actual return on the activities of the DWIs in the host countries? It can be said across the board that the attraction of these establishments lasted only as long as a German victory and therefore a long-lasting German occupation was expected. The countries took the German occupation the hardest were those whose people had time-tested democratic or liberal traditions, such as the Danes, for example, who with a few exceptions did not want to know anything about National Socialism. The Danish historians who influenced public opinion showed total solidarity with their Norwegian colleagues, acted with hostility toward the German occupiers, and characterized German science as "devilish." The French were also largely resistant to German culture and science. One should not be misled by the relatively high number of visitors to the Paris DI and its outposts: though there was an initial willingness to collaborate, a long-term promotion of German culture proved impossible. The broad-based interest in Germany, born more out of opportunism than affinity, withered and was soon supplanted by the same unchanging circle of diehards who visited the DI, and even they did this more out of calculation than conviction.

The Inglorious End of the DWIs

At the beginning of 1944, the impending dismantling of the DWIs and thereby of the foreign cultural activities of Nazi Germany became apparent. The institutes in the neutral countries (Portugal, Spain, Sweden) were active until capitulation and were only closed after that. Those in Italy, Croatia, Slovakia, and Hungary were able to continue their work until the beginning of 1945, whereas the institutes in Belgrade, Brussels, Bucharest, Helsinki, Paris, Sofia, and Tirana had to be abandoned in the summer and fall of 1944, because of the advance of the Allied and Soviet armies. However, Franz Alfred Six kept alive the fiction that this was only a temporary disruption of the work, and as late as 18 December 1944 he summoned the DWI presidents to Berlin in order to assign new tasks to them. Seven of them actually appeared (Epting, Fahrner, Gamillscheg, Höfler, Mönch, Saure, and Schmaus). Clearly, at this meeting the prevailing mood was one not so much of disaster but rather of departure. Mönch was supposed to look after Flemish and Walloon collaborators in the Göttingen-Hildesheim area, Epting to attend to around 10,000 French intellectuals who were dispersed throughout the Reich as prisoners of war, forced laborers, and refugees. Gamillscheg was to take care of the Romanian "national government" (exile government) of Horia Sima in Vienna and Berlin, which combined the remains of the Fascist Iron Guard. Residing in the same Hotel Imperial in Vienna where Gamillscheg had taken up his work, Alois Schmaus took care of a small group of Serbs friendly to Germany. Six allowed himself to be guided by his "werewolf" mentality, which did not consider surrender.[50]

To prevent any papers or files from falling into "enemy hands," they were either burned or sent to the Reich for storage. All DWIs together owned 300,000 books, 20,000 records, and a similar number of photos of German landscapes, cities, and monuments, not to mention sumptuous furniture, paintings, and other decorative equipment. Hardly anything has survived. Possibly, one can still find remnants in the U.S. Library of Congress, to which some parts were moved, or in the libraries of the cities where DWIs were located, as is the case in Copenhagen. Otherwise, only institute publications, monographs, anthologies, and journal volumes (altogether eighty titles) survive to serve as testimony.

The history of the DWIs can be read as a parable of German academic scholarship in the NS-state. Well-known scholars allowed themselves to advocate a cultural policy, maybe not fully aware of the full consequences of its intentions, but certainly aware of the aims from the beginning. At great material and idealistic cost, the elite of the subjugated and neutral countries of Europe, as well as Germany's allies, had to be convinced of the superiority of German scholarship, science, culture, and art and, thereby politically tied to the ruling superpower in Europe, i.e., Germany. Everyone who accepted a leading position as a DWI president, director, or department head was motivated by a mixture of duty, idealism, vanity, and conviction. The early successes of the DWIs between the middle of 1941 and beginning/middle of 1944 were indeed quite formidable, and of course many staff members were also motivated by more honorable aims such as international understanding. However, for the responsible people in the Ministry of Foreign Affairs, Ministry of Education, Ministry for Propaganda, and other appropriate ministries, this was only a pretext for consolidating German hegemony and keeping, or rather making, their neighbors dependent. Their intellectual potential and material resources were first to be made available to, and then to serve, German scholarship and the German national economy.

Notes

1. See the survey in Frank-Rutger Hausmann and Elisabeth Müller-Luckner, eds., *Die Rolle der Geisteswissenschaften im Dritten Reich 1933–1945* (Munich, 2002).
2. All existing DWIs are described in Frank-Rutger Hausmann, *"Auch im Krieg schweigen die Musen nicht." Die Deutschen Wissenschaftlichen Institute im Zweiten Weltkrieg*, 2nd ed. (Göttingen, 2002).
3. Frank-Rutger Hausmann, *"Termitenwahn*—Die Bedeutung der Gemeinschaftsforschung für die NS-Wissenschaft," in *Semantischer Umbau der Geisteswissenschaften nach 1933 und 1945*, ed. Georg Bollenbeck and Clemens Knobloch (Heidelberg, 2001), 58–79.
4. Jan-Pieter Barbian, *"Kulturwerte im Zeitkampf.* Die Kulturabkommen des 'Dritten Reiches' als Instrumente nationalsozialistischer Außenpolitik," *Archiv für Kulturgeschichte* 74 (1992): 415–459.
5. See the presentation of Klaus Popa, "Das 'Deutsche Wissenschaftliche Institut' (DWI) Zweigstelle Hermannstadt und ihr Leiter Hermann Roth," *Halbjahresschrift für südosteuropäische Geschichte, Literatur und Politik*, vol. 2 (2002).
6. Andrea Hoffend, *Zwischen Kultur-Achse und Kulturkampf. Die Beziehungen zwischen "Drittem Reich" und faschistischem Italien in den Bereichen Medien, Kunst, Wissenschaft und Rassenfragen* (Frankfurt am Main, 1998).
7. Víctor Farías, *Los nazis en Chile* (Barcelona, 2000), 345–359.
8. For more details, see Eckard Michels, *Das Deutsche Institut in Paris 1940–1944. Ein Beitrag zu den deutsch-französischen Kulturbeziehungen und zur auswärtigen Kulturpolitik des Dritten Reiches* (Stuttgart, 1993).
9. Manfred Jakubowski-Tiessen, "Kulturpolitik im besetzten Land. Das Deutsche Wissenschaftliche Institut in Kopenhagen 1941 bis 1945," *Zeitschrift für Geschichtswissenschaft* 42, no. 2 (1994): 129–138.
10. Frank-Rutger Hausmann, "Das Deutsche (Wissenschaftliche) Institut in Brüssel (1941– 1944)," in *Griff nach dem Westen. Die "Westforschung" der völkisch-nationalen Wissenschaften*

zum nordwesteuropäischen Raum (1919–1960), ed. Burkhard Dietz, Helmut Gabel, Ulrich Tiedau, vol. 2 (Münster, New York, Munich, and Berlin, 2003), 907–294.

11. Lutz Hachmeister, *Der Gegnerforscher. Die Karriere des SS-Führers Franz Alfred Six* (Munich, 1998).

12. Herbert Scurla, "Die französischen Kulturinstitute im Ausland. Ein Beitrag zur französischen Kulturpropaganda," *Zeitschrift für Politik* 31, no. 2 (1941): 139–159.

13. Herbert Scurla, *Die Dritte Front. Geistige Grundlagen des Propagandakrieges der Westmächte* (Berlin, 1940), summarizes all relevant concepts.

14. Jesús de la Hera Martínez, *La política cultural de Alemania en España en el período de entreguerras* (Madrid, 2000), 292ff.; *Ein Institut und sein General. Wilhelm Faupel und das Ibero-Amerikanische Institut in der Zeit des Nationalsozialismus*, ed. Reinhard Lier, Günther Maihold, and Günter Vollmer (Frankfurt am Main, 2003).

15. BArch, R 51/62, "Bericht über die Tagung der Präsidenten der Kulturinstitute des Auswärtigen Amtes vom 28. und 29. September 1942."

16. Michael Grüttner, *Biographisches Lexikon zur nationalsozialistischen Wissenschaftspolitik* (Heidelberg, 2004).

17. Walter Manoschek, "Serbien ist judenfrei." *Militärische Besatzungspolitik und Judenvernichtung in Serbien 1941/42* (Munich, 1993), 33ff.; Ilse Schmidt, *Die Mitläuferin. Erinnerungen einer Wehrmachtsangehörigen* (Berlin, 1999).

18. Volkhard Laitenberger, *Akademischer Austausch und Auswärtige Kulturpolitik (Der Deutsche Akademische Austauschdienst, DAAD, 1923–1945)* (Göttingen, 1978), 90ff., 135ff.

19. Further information can be found in Dirk Scholten, *Sprachvermittlungspolitik des nationalsozialistischen Deutschlands* (Frankfurt am Main, 2000).

20. Helmut W. Schaller, "Alois Schmaus (1901–1970). Zum 100. Geburtstag des Slawisten und Balkanologen," *Zeitschrift für Balkanologie* 37, no. 2 (2001): 189–217.

21. Teresa Seruya, "Wolfgang Kayser in Portugal. Zu einem wichtigen Kapitel der portugiesischen Germanistik," in *Zur Geschichte und Problematik der Nationalphilologien in Europa*, ed. Frank Fürbeth et al. (Tübingen, 1999), 715–725.

22. Dietrich Orlow, *The Nazis in the Balkans: A Case Study of Totalitarian Politics* (Pittsburgh, 1968), 24ff., 57ff., 88ff., 189ff.; in addition, Vienna, ÖStA ARW 04R008, Kästen 56–60.

23. Frank-Rutger Hausmann, "Karl Heinz Bremer et Henry de Montherlant," *lendemains* 25, no. 100 (2000): 97–121.

24. Walter Kunze, "Die Spracharbeit der Deutschen Akademie," *Jahrbuch der deutschen Sprache* 2 (1944): 135–142.

25. Barbara Lambauer, *Otto Abetz et les Français ou l'envers de la Collaboration* (Paris, 2001).

26. Barbara Unteutsch, *Vom Sohlbergkreis zur Gruppe Collaboration. Ein Beitrag zur Geschichte der deutsch-französischen Beziehungen anhand der Cahiers Franco-Allemands/Deutsch-Französische Monatshefte, 1931–1944* (Münster, 1987).

27. Alice Epting-Kullmann, *Pariser Begegnungen* (Hänner ü. Säckingen, 1972); Epting-Kullmann, *Zwischen Paris und Fluorn. Erinnerungen aus den Jahren 1944–1945* (Burg Stettenfels b. Heilbronn a.N., 1958).

28. Laurence Bertrand Dorléac, *Histoire de l'art. Paris 1940–1944. Ordre national, traditions et modernités* (Paris, 1986), 91–99; Dorléac, *L'art de la défaite 1940–1944* (Paris, 1993), 83–106.

29. Edgar Harvolk, *Eichenzweig und Hakenkreuz. Die Deutsche Akademie in München (1924–1962) und ihre volkskundliche Sektion* (Munich, 1990), 128–129.

30. Harm-Peer Zimmermann, "Vom Schlaf der Vernunft. Deutsche Volkskunde an der Kieler Universität 1933 bis 1945," in *Uni-Formierung des Geistes. Universität Kiel im Nationalsozialismus*, ed. Hans-Werner Prahl (Brodersdorf, 1995), 171–274.

31. Herbert Scurla, "Wissenschaft und Ausland im Kriege," *Geist der Zeit* 20 (1942): 225–234.

32. Mark Walker, *Nazi Science: Myth, Truth, and the German Atomic Bomb* (New York and London, 1995), 153–181.

33. BArch R 4901/3025 (W 6), Nr. 4 (Tagung des DWI Budapest, 1.–2. December 1942).

34. Otto Gerhard Oexle, *Hahn, Heisenberg und die anderen. Anmerkungen zu 'Kopenhagen,' 'Farm Hall' und Göttingen* (Berlin, 2003).

35. Hans-Georg Gadamer, *Philosophische Lehrjahre. Eine Rückschau* (Frankfurt am Main, 1977), 69.
36. Frank-Rutger Hausmann, "Unwahrheit als Methode? Zu Hans-Georg Gadamers Publikationen im 'Dritten Reich,'" *Internationale Zeitschrift für Philosophie* 1 (2001): 33–54.
37. Jerry Z. Muller, *The Other God That Failed: Hans Freyer and the Deradicalization of German Conservatism* (Princeton, 1987).
38. Helmut Schelsky, *Rückblicke eines Antisoziologen* (Opladen, 1981), 151.
39. Eberhard Zeller, *Der Geist der Freiheit. Der zwanzigste Juli* (Berlin, Darmstadt, and Vienna, 1965), 239ff., 267ff., 362ff., 518ff.
40. Christian Tilitzki, "Die Vortragsreisen Carl Schmitts während des Zweiten Weltkrieges," *Schmittiana* 6 (1998): 191–270.
41. BArch R 4901/2819, f. 257–281, Bericht über die in der Zeit vom 10.–27. April 1942 nach Griechenland, Bulgarien, Serbien, Ungarn, Kroatien und vom 7.–9. Mai 1942 nach der Slowakei ausgeführten Studienreise(n).
42. Franz Thierfelder, *Der Balkan als kulturpolitisches Kraftfeld. Zwischenstaatliche Propaganda und geistiger Austausch in Südosteuropa* (Berlin, 1940); Hermann Neubacher, *Sonderauftrag Südost 1940–1945. Bericht eines fliegenden Diplomaten* (Göttingen, 1956).
43. "My aim is to outline a preliminary national development plan for the settlement of the Danube region, so that we can be scientifically prepared for such an undertaking, provided there is adequate political strength. A prerequisite for this, is an accurate registration of the ethnic population, including the groups affiliated by blood but no longer by language, and their biological, economic, and social condition. This should also include studies about the regional structure of the settlement area and its geographical development for transportation. Ideally the market areas of the German settlement centers should also be transformed into German population areas, by resettling dispersed and isolated German groups who are threatened by being economically dependent on central foreign-language locations" (Hassinger, BArch R 4901/2819, f. 273).
44. *Tagung deutscher wissenschaftlicher Ost- und Südostinstitute Breslau 25. bis 27. September 1941* (Breslau, 1942), 3 (no author indicated).
45. Vienna, UA NL Hassinger Inv. 131, Kasten 18. As for Knoll, see Frank-Rutger Hausmann, *Anglistik und Amerikanistik im "Dritten Reich"* (Frankfurt am Main, 2003), 286–293.
46. Frank-Rutger Hausmann, *"Vom Strudel der Ereignisse verschlungen." Deutsche Romanistik im "Dritten Reich"* (Frankfurt am Main, 2000), 393–616; Hausmann, *"Deutsche Geisteswissenschaft" im Zweiten Weltkrieg. Die "Aktion Ritterbusch" (1940–1945)*, 2nd ed. (Dresden and Munich, 2002).
47. Citation from the Goebbels diaries in Lothar Gruchmann, *Nationalsozialistische Großraumordnung. Die Konstruktion einer deutschen 'Monroe Doktrin'* (Stuttgart, 1962), 79.
48. Speech reprinted in *Ungarn* 2 (1941): 139.
49. *Ungarn* 2 (1941): 139.
50. Politisches Archiv des Auswärtigen Amts Berlin, R 64302, Niederschrift über die Tagung der Präsidenten der Deutschen Wissenschaftlichen Institute im Ausland am 18. Dezember 1944.

Chapter 12

"RICHTUNG HALTEN"
Hans Rothfels and Neoconservative Historiography on Both Sides of the Atlantic

+ + +

Karl Heinz Roth

During the course of 1946, the surviving members of the former Königs-berg historians' group, who had fled that year to West Germany, ap-proached their mentor Hans Rothfels, who was then living and teaching in the United States. They wrote remorseful and even guilt-ridden letters. Would their professor, who had lost his chair in the summer of 1934 and the European continent just before the outbreak of war, be interested in renewing the contacts between them? Would he be angry with them and ask embarrassing questions about their conduct during the prewar years when he was being marginalized? Or would he have questions about their involvement in the murderous policies in Eastern Europe after the assault on Poland? The latest studies on the postwar careers of the Königsberg Rothfels circle[1] show us that such misgivings were unfounded. With a generous gesture Rothfels made such concerns redundant. He stood be-hind his former students without reservation and without being asked; he also shielded them, now with the authority of an American citizen. He even shared their feelings of guilt. "Was it not the Nazis who had with diabolical skill infiltrated everything that was 'real and genuine,'" he wrote to Reinhard Wittram when discussing the fate of the Baltic Ger-mans: "to some extent 'we' helped them with this, and I don't exclude myself, in order to exploit and explode it from the inside."[2]

This was a remarkable statement. From his American perspective, Rothfels saw himself and his kind as facilitators who had made it possible for the Nazis to adopt his doctrines on the political concept of history, to "exploit" "real" questions of nationality, and, finally, to bring them to

---

Notes for this chapter begin on page 253.

explosive conclusion. Such insights were no longer mentioned in subsequent correspondence, and the awareness of joint responsibility led in the end to a strategy of reciprocal silence that was respected for decades even by the "grandchildren."

Only half a century later did these problems become subjects for discussion again. However, to this day, no one has postulated a shared responsibility in the early Nazi years as clearly as Rothfels did himself.[3] By now, there is a general consensus on the role that Rothfels's students, especially Werner Conze and Theodor Schieder, played during the Third Reich and the early years of the Federal Republic. However, in the debate about their charismatic teacher, who in his third creative period became West Germany's leading political historian, opinions and findings are more divided than ever. Critical assessments of his paradigms and practices relating to his political concept of history during the early Königsberg years from 1926 to 1934[4] are now being confronted with attempts at rehabilitation that point to a more recent political instrumentalization.[5] A heated controversy is now raging regarding the interpretation of a radio lecture given between 1930 and 1933[6] that Rothfels updated and changed several times.

I have stated elsewhere why I consider such a narrow focus of the debate problematic, especially when analyzing a huge and wide-ranging body of work spanning several epochs and two continents.[7] In this contribution, I would like to focus on three especially problematic and unresolved aspects of the Rothfels biography, using as a starting point my knowledge about Rothfels's epoch-spanning activities: first, the analysis of his radicalized period between 1930/31 and 1935/36, which related to his political concept of history; second, an assessment of the events that occurred between his dismissal from the Königsberg chair and his departure for England in the summer of 1939; third, his opinion on topics concerning the political concept of history in England and the United States and their influence on historiography in the young Federal Republic.

Did Rothfels Ever Have Fascist Leanings?

The well-informed among us have known for a long time that Rothfels was sharply criticized by some contemporary historians. Wolfgang (later George Wolfgang F.) Hallgarten, the socialist-pacifist historian of imperialism that was rooted in the economics of armament, came from a family of German-Jewish bankers and was exiled in 1936 by the Nazis.[8] As an academic outsider he remained a lifelong enemy of Rothfels, a holder of an academic chair who had also been stigmatized as a Jew by the Nazis.[9] Hallgarten's criticism of Rothfels's exaggerated national conservative disposition as a Bismarck admirer, and later a proponent of the Cold War, was only surpassed[10] by that of the Marxist historiographer Eckart Kehr, who died in the United States in 1933.[11] In a seminar held by Bernadotte Schmitt in Chicago, Kehr characterized the Königsberg professor as the first German historian in modern history who managed to openly combine, in his 1932 lecture on Bismarck's *Ostpolitik*, the ideas of the neo-Rankian historiography of the Meinecke school with the nationalism of the political right. When confronted with the facts about the severe disruptions and hardships that the young Central and Eastern European nation-states had suffered in recent years, Rothfels made an astonishing proposal: He wanted a return to authoritarian and patriarchic regimes that would preserve a "Baltic-German upper class ruling over the many Eastern nations."[12] According to Kehr, this choice of a "dictatorship of the barons" was based on an attempt to create a new fascist interpretation of history, and never before had "German historiography of the political far right expressed itself so clearly."

Was this judgement justified? At the historians' conference in Göttingen in 1932, had Rothfels in his famous lecture[13] advocated fascist leanings for the "guild"?

The fact that Kehr in the same breath advocated the nationality policies of the Soviet Union as the only viable alternative for solving the—even in his opinion—by now very urgent Eastern and Central European nationality problems,[14] did considerable damage to his earlier analysis.[15] However, Kehr clearly pinpointed the crucial socioeconomic moment in Rothfels's paradigm shift, and he summarized precisely what Rothfels had only artfully hinted at in his lectures and essays.[16] Since the early 1930s, Rothfels had advocated a restoration of the patriarchal power system of the Junkers, patricians, and clerics for all of the Eastern and Central European "interim" states. The inevitable result would have been the forced recommitment of the multinational working classes of the Slavic west into serf-like working conditions –in short forcing them back into bondage. This suggestion had far-reaching political implications. The new "serfs" would be denationalized and integrated into a multiethnic federal system dependent on Germany as the central Western power and supervised by a German ruling class with historical colonial experience as well as superior competitiveness and cultural supremacy.

Kehr's diagnosis was so far correct, but this still had nothing to do with fascism, since several components were missing. What we are dealing with here, is a socioeconomic and power-political concept that was supposed to erase the East European postwar order of 1919/20 and replace it with an ill-defined phase of expansion of German supremacy. It was no more and no less. Fascism was and is, however, more than just a program that wants to revise control over border areas or display imperial power. First and foremost, it is a counterrevolutionary power model based on a relatively broadly based mass consensus working toward a dictatorial remodeling of the nation-state in order to cooperatively reconcile class differences and make fascism as expansionist as possible. Secondly, fascism radicalizes and expands the outward instruments of imperial aggression, trying to balance its economic and military weakness by exploiting nationality conflicts and by mobilizing ethnic (*völkisch*) irredentism. Thirdly, in Rothfels's time, Fascism in Germany was divided into different factions that retained their strong rivalries in the spring of 1933 after the destruction of the left and other democratic forces, despite their common strategic interests at the time of the presidential governments. Kehr's verdict on Rothfels's attempt at a new fascist interpretation of history was, therefore, premature and not sufficiently founded. This opinion would have been justified only if Kehr had been able to prove that the Königsberg professor wanted to apply (generalize) his ideas for Eastern and Central Europe to society as a whole, and that he wanted to project them onto the Weimar Republic itself. Moreover, Kehr had to prove that these visions were part of a *völkisch* nationalistic expansion program, and that they represented a specific faction of German Fascism.

However, this proof can indeed be found. Rothfels's ideas for restructuring the cooperative state and introducing subjugated employment conditions of the Baltic Junker type were not restricted to Eastern European states of mixed nationality. Rather, advocated an extension of a general political restoration model based on class, something that he had labored over since the second half of the 1920s as part of his research on the "real" intentions behind Bismarck's social policies.[17] His aim was to integrate the subordinate classes into a unified society and instill in them the state concept of "duty and achievement." This general demand for the establishment of an "internal Reich" through a new cooperative division of the populace received a remarkable boost in the early 1930s because of Rothfels's projection of an "open Eastern frontier." The "awareness that the East had its own independent responsibility for the development of the German state"[18] was applied to the entire Reich. The option of cooperative self-government by the patrician class, which was based on the model of a capitalist, Junker power system, was, furthermore, still dependent on the unconditional power of the state over individuals and classes. Rothfels combined the two models of "absolute state interventionism" and the "new order of a *völkisch* power system" by borrowing from the leaders of the conservative revolution, especially Arthur Moeller van den Bruck, Carl Schmitt, and Oswald Spengler, who were the visionaries of a "Third Reich" emerging from "Prussian Socialism."[19]

A strong willingness for political provocation was necessary for such a far-reaching rejection of the Weimar Republic to come from the mouth and pen of a well-established top civil servant. This was certainly not heard again until Papen's coup d'état of 20 July 1932, and it was one reason why Rothfels became spokesman of the young conservative counterrevolution, from 1931/32 on captivating as no one else the new up-and-coming academic generation.[20] Together with those young scholars, but also as the voice of the East Prussian ruling class, the military of the Reich, and the

Baltic irridentists, he welcomed the presidential governments (*Präsidialk-abinette*) as a "revival of the old authoritarian state." However, this could only be a "transitional phase meant to detach the state from the rule of interest groups and to enable it to absorb the national movement that is opposed to it. We hope that this takes place and that the daily sacrifices that are made are a testament to this."[21] Even as a political historian, Rothfels knew: only the fusion of this "national" mass movement with the authoritarian state would bring about the irretrievable break with Western democracies and destroy the social and political support for the Weimar compromise. Only then could the "new order" begin.

However, this historic model of justification for destroying the Weimar Republic was not enough for Rothfels. From 1932/33 on he included "all-German" and "*völkisch*" visions.[22] A new "Reich" would rise out of the ruins of Weimar, founded on two equally important pillars: the East Prussian Baltic Northeast and the Southeastern European outposts of the former multinational Habsburg Empire. The intellectual influence of the "all-German" Austrian political historian Heinrich Ritter von Srbik was clearly visible, and even in 1935 Srbik explicitly supported his congenial colleague from Königsberg.[23] After all, they modeled themselves not on Bismarck, the Prussian petty bourgeois proponent of unconditional power of the state, but rather on Metternich, the master of the European restoration in the nineteenth century. He was much nearer to their expansive visions.[24] The Rhine, Vistula, and Danube would run through the continental-European empire as "German rivers," the Western frontier would run somewhere between the North Sea and the Adriatic, and to the East an arch would be formed from Reval to Bucharest. "Central Europe," however, should form the cornerstone, including the "core of Germany" with its Eastern/Southeastern frontline delimiting the original "ethnic German territory" and its "living space" (*Lebensraum*).[25] This core was supposed to be dynamic. Fanning the flames of nationalism and border or territory conflicts supposedly helped this dynamic core legitimize regulating the ethnic mix of the Western and Eastern Slavic ethnic groups. It was also designed to create conditions for winning back the territories lost in 1919/20 and the subsequent annulment of agrarian reforms, followed by implementation of a new agrarian order.[26] Recent research correctly points out that by adopting these doctrines of ethnic segregation, Rothfels had clearly formed a bridge to National Socialism.[27] Simultaneously, this concluded a conceptual development, combining "absolute state interventionism" (*Etatismus*) with corporate power and aggressive nationalist expansionism, that had all the characteristics of a Fascist doctrine.

It is also possible to address the aspect of functionalism in fascism without difficulty, considering Rothfels's mindset between 1931/32 and 1936/37. The Königsberg professor, who was made emeritus in 1935, followed a specific trend of Fascism. He saw himself in historical terms as a mentor to the ruling classes, particularly the military class, Prussian junkers, government bureaucracy, and Protestant state church. He put his whole energy into creating a broad political base for them, in order to influence the educated bourgeoisie of the future in this direction. In this sense, he was not a National Socialist, but he did consider the alliance between the traditional elite and the NS mass movement an essential part of the coup d'état from within, and the subsequent unfolding of expansionist power. Obviously, he rejected the biological racism of this ideology, to which he and his family would soon be subjected. He also rejected the populist demagoguery that was used to curry favor with the ordinary people. But he trusted in the integration and taming of these influences as part of the process of consolidating the national uprising. This is why he voted, in the early years of the Nazi dictatorship, for a power-political compromise between the traditional elite and the leadership of the NSDAP: only the interplay of these powers would give German Fascism a chance. He did this despite the constantly increasing discrimination that he had to face.

In this vein of thought, Rothfels had much in common shared many aspects of this thinking with Franz von Papen, the failed Reichs Chancellor of the summer of 1932 and Vice Chancellor of the "government of national uprising," though Papen did not represent the Protestant educated classes but instead had formed an extreme right-wing group based on political Catholicism.[28] Rothfels and Papen expected a policy of absolute state interventionism represented by a Reichs administrator. They both also wanted to solve class conflicts through a hierarchical, corporate state system, with Rothfels favoring a capitalist, manorial Junker system and Papen an economic paternalism based on heavy industry.[29] In foreign affairs they wished for the resurrection of a multi ethnic greater Reich, emanating from "central Europe" and under German leadership.[30] The Eastern and Southeastern European nationalities were to be "restructured" and "well-ordered," but also federally integrated by a German "master race." They were to have the status of indentured workers under multinational, hierarchical employment conditions. The justification for this was racist, but contrary to the biological mythical racism of the Nazis, the federal integration model did not include "ethnic relocation." Geographic separation of the nationalities through population shifts and the creation of "ethnically pure" nation-states were not desirable because they interfered with the "central European superstructure." In Papen's and Rothfels's federal Reichs model such interference would have been considered counterproductive and was only justified when used it to "recover" the German territories that were lost in 1919/20. The ethnic groups living outside this German "culture sphere" were supposed to coexist with each other under the direction of the German ruling class, and according to their ability and the worthiness of their cultural heritage. They would participate in an ethnic hierarchical value system, regulated by the Germans with the help of a collaborating vassal class.

These were the power models that the two chief factions of German Fascism, i.e., the Prussian Protestant Junkers and the Rhenish Catholic industrialists, had in common with the leadership of the Nazi mass movements, despite their many differences. After the formation of the Hitler-Papen-Hugenberg cabinet, that initially found themselves in a confused situation concerning the policy of ethnic mix vis-à-vis the political options of the NSDAP leadership. Even now, this makes the first years of the Third Reich difficult to comprehend. In the end, the Fascist faction was ousted from its position of power by the political terrorist dynamic of the NSDAP apparatus. This tactic was accepted because of the common interest in a major arms buildup that was linked in the summer of 1934 with "cleansing" the NS mass movement of its petty bourgeois and plebeian trends, and thus safeguarding the material interests of the traditional leadership groups and putting the power alliance on a new basis. When in 1936/37 this excessive armament program caused severe internal crises,[31] even the "Central Europe" concept had to be radicalized, so that the increasingly insoluble problems could be tackled by pursuing aggressive foreign policy initiatives. In 1937, this in turn caused a further radicalization of the ethnic segregation policy (*Volkstumspolitik*). No longer would the expatriate Germans functions as a strategic bride for promoting the idea of a "Federal Reich"; instead, they would now be used as an excuse for a radical policy of aggression that compromised the medium-term "all-German options" in favor of immediate expansionist successes. In support of this aim, the first "ethnic cleansing" programs became the order of the day. In this phase, the old guard who had promoted "pan-German policies" and who had mainly been influenced by Rothfels's paradigms, were removed. The imperialist power structure of the state was no longer explained in terms of an "objective mindset" or as a "historical principle" for keeping in order and controlling "an ethnic mix," but instead was used as an exponent of blood and race.

With this, the dominant foreign policy vision of the Prussian-Protestant and the Rhenish-Catholic variant of German Fascism had run its course. Their representatives now began to feel excluded and marginalized from power and influence. Papen remained a loyal coalition partner of the NS leadership until the bitter end, even though he had been severely humiliated during the so-called Roehm revolution in July 1934 and then again in 1938, despite the contribution he had made in preparing the annexation of Austria.[32] Not so Hans Rothfels, who, after all, exceeded Papen in both professional integrity and charisma, even within his limited sphere of influence. His political marginalization was accompanied by something else: his stigmatization as a Jew. For a long time he refused to face this and in his publications continued to stress, which remained uncensored until the end of 1935, his seemingly unaffected political concept of history. In 1934, in the preface to an expanded version of his ominous lecture given in Göttingen in 1932, Rothfels expressed his conviction that "his vision of history" was and remained an indispensable ally in the "struggle for the future."[33] In another instance, he paid homage to the newly strengthened "ethnic rights" (*Volkstumsrecht*), as expressed in "the Führer's program, based on Germany's new 'philosophy of life' [*Weltanschauung*]."[34] A year later he wrote in an edition of his collected writings on Eastern topics that as a member of the generation of "the front line fighters" he still supported a program of "a fighting science" that would not only serve as a "commentary from the outpost" (*Vorpostenbericht*), but that he also had an obligation to serve as a connection between the generations. This was achieved by deploying a young team preoccupied with the responsibilities in the East.[35] It may be claimed for a very long time that Rothfels was instrumental in the creation of the Nazi concept of history.

Stages of Marginalization

After the Nazis takeover of power on 30 January 1933, Rothfels proposals for a political alliance were met with markedly different responses. Whenever someone is ostracized by an administration, envious people can be found who somehow feel shortchanged, and who feel that the erosion of a competitors legal status has not gone far enough. So it was in this case, though this was only the beginning of a series of humiliations. The first of Rothfels, trials was the enforcement of "Aryan paragraph" No. 3, the law for the "re-establishment of the civil service," dated 7 April 1933. Rothfels, who though born into a German-Jewish family of civil servants had converted to Protestantism as a student, was branded a Jew by this law. At the same time, as a highly decorated and disabled war veteran he was excluded from having to retire, a provision that was normally part of this paragraph. This exemption displeased the new rector of the University of Königsberg, the philosopher Hans Heyse, who accused his charismatic colleague of presumption in wanting to share the leadership of the Albertus University with the curator. During this first phase, Rothfels reacted to marginalization with self-confidence, because he felt it was his duty to "uphold the idea that the strong-willed and industrious German does exist (though not through a blood-line), and that the state especially needs our generation's voices of warning who are represented at this university and who stand apart from the old and new failures."[36] The students and assistants around him, as well as the Junker middle-class network, vigorously supported him in this. The university archives are full of touching declarations of solidarity and appeals from members of the Königsberg history seminars.[37] Rothfels dealt with this first attack by giving up his university functions: he resigned his seat in the academic senate, the leadership of the "committee to promote studies abroad," his membership in the "section dealing with Eastern questions," his position as liaison to the academic foreign service, and his position as "protector of the academic section of the League for Germans Abroad" (VDA).[38] Instead, he concentrated fully on his teaching and publishing activities.

At the beginning of 1934 a new witch-hunt began that added a political component to the anti-Semitic attacks. Reports by his fellow historians in the daily media about Rothfels's participation at the international historians' congress in Warsaw were full of anti-Semitic prejudice.[39] The NS chief of Danzig, Ralf von Brockhausen, declared that his departure from the Königsberg position was urgent for party-political reasons, because the hero worship that Rothfels received from the student body undermined the "consequence of the racial point of view."[40] The Prussian Ministry of Science responded at the end of March by saying that it was impossible to dismiss Rothfels, on account of his war record. They were, however, considering a transfer to another university. In early July, Brockhausen appealed again to the party leadership of the Reich, saying that it was "completely impossible to allow a person of foreign blood to teach German history to future generations of Germans."[41] This time his arguments were effective. On 11 July, Rothfels was informed that he was being transferred to another university. On 24 and 25 July, he said goodbye to his students and thanked them for having given him the chance to be part of their community in a way "that could only have been possible in very few places of German university life."[42]

During the summer vacation there were negotiations with other universities about an exchange of chairs, as well as a recommendation for Hamburg. Despite the fact that the Ministry of Science had clearly tried to help in accordance with the decision that had been made, his situation was still unclear in the autumn of 1934. The "guild" that had still been proud of him in August 1932 now did not wish to know him anymore. As one insider stated laconically a year later: "Rothfels, who only recently was seen as the man of the future, is no longer acceptable as a prominent figure despite his regard for Bismarck and despite his pioneering work in the East."[43]

Things now became difficult for Rothfels. He could only stop the increased professional marginalization by finding advocates for his historical-political concept. These advocates would also have to convince the regime that Rothfels's personal prestige and his perspective on the development of the NS dictatorship were still of importance, despite the fact of the recent erosion of his influence. What he needed was patronage. At the same time he thought it prudent to withdraw somewhat and only remain active in a secondary capacity. At the end of February 1935 he agreed in principle to accept emeritus status and to undertake unpaid research at the State Library of Berlin dealing with the projects of the North East Ethnic German Research Society (NOFG).[44] He insisted on one condition to which he held even when it threatened to derail the whole arrangement: He insisted on continuing to teach as professor emeritus at the University of Berlin, though on a smaller scale. He considered his reduced status as temporary and would not accept any changes to his professional legal standing that might reduce his income in the event of his reinstatement as full professor. In addition, he stressed his accomplishments in the field of scientific and human education during his eight and a half years at the frontier University of Königsberg, and he declared that the "continuation of this work, even on a smaller scale, would still substantially serve German interests, especially in the Eastern parts of Germany."[45] These arguments could only come from someone who considered the waning of influence of his long-advocated concept of history as temporary, and who was convinced that some balance could be achieved within the Fascist power alliance that would assure him a comeback.

However, a number of experts in the Ministry of Science had a different opinion. They could sense Rothfels's ulterior motivation, and this reduced their willingness to compromise to nil. The fact that Rothfels was "non-Aryan" played only a minor part in the ensuing discussions. What counted now was an assessment, mainly based on reports from the rector of the University of Königsberg, that Rothfels was rallying "reactionary forces" around him. "Reactionary centers have recently increased considerably, therefore National Socialism can only rely on upcoming generations of young people," reported the consultant responsible for higher education at the Ministry of Science to his superior.[46] Under no circumstances should Rothfels be allowed to return to teaching. He considered Rothfels a particularly "dangerous" individual, because he represented an undesirable wing of German Fascism and therefore stood in the way of consolidating the exclusive power of the NSDAP.

Rothfels, however, was intelligent enough to correctly interpret the growing delay in the decision regarding his future career. He now brought into play Joachim von Ribbentrop, who at that time was head of the "department" named after him and representative of the Reich's government for disarmament questions.[47] In the early 1930s, Ribbentrop, in his capacity as representative of the Berlin gentlemen's club, had forged a connection between the Prussian-Junker-Protestant wing and the National Socialist wing of German Fascism. He knew Rothfels as an activist of the "young Prussian movement" that was integrated into the network of national and gentlemen's clubs. Ribbentrop also launched a "relief action" for Rothfels as part of his recent and current efforts to appease British conservatives in the face of increasingly massive German rearmament. In those circles Rothfels was well known and also well liked because of his affinity with the conservative federal views of Lord Acton.[48] After several telephone calls, he informed Ribbentrop on 23 February 1935 about the state of his negotiations with the Ministry of Science, and asked him to once again intervene by asking Minister Bernhard Rust to grant permission for some limited teaching.[49] Two days later, Ribbentrop wrote to Rust recommending that the compromise package should include permission to lecture and asked him "to conclude this matter in accordance with my wishes and for the good of our foreign policy."[50]

Initially, the officials at the Ministry of Science were powerless in the face of such recommendations. Nevertheless, they did not want to give in completely. They tried to mobilize an opponent of standing equal to Ribbentrop's, NSDAP Reichs leader Alfred Rosenberg, but he seemed to show no interest in the case. On 21 March, Rothfels received his retirement notice in connection with the future research project at the Prussian State Library in Berlin. In addition, a cover letter informed him that the move to Berlin would not be an obstacle to the future resumption of his teaching position.[51] However, this was only half of what Rothfels had expected. He immediately pressed for the limited teaching permission that was normally granted to retired professors. Again he turned to Ribbentrop, who then became very outspoken and forthright with the Ministry: the teaching permission for Rothfels was indeed very important for "foreign policy reasons" because this was the "only demonstration of gratitude" that his foreign discussion partners, who were well disposed toward Germany, had asked for.[52] On 20 August 1935, after a several months-long tug of war, Rothfels was finally granted a teaching assignment of up to three hours a week at the University of Berlin in conjunction with his research assignment on the East Prussian reformer Theodor von Schön.

Whether Rothfels actually started his lectures on Theodor von Schön at the beginning of the winter semester of 1935/36 is not known, because permission was withdrawn again on 12 November 1935.[53] On 16 December, his forcible retirement followed. His income as professor emeritus did protect him and his family materially to some extent, but nothing could stop the complete exclusion from his profession. Up to that point, Albert Brackmann, the éminence grise of the Prussian archive system and of the NOFG,[54] had protected this most influential exponent of Eastern studies, allowing Rothfels to continue his research. But this too came to an end on 2 May 1936. Rothfels was just able to finish his work on the activities of Theodor von Schön and to prepare it for printing. It was the last publication to appear before his emigration from Germany.[55]

The next phase in his social decline was enforced through the regulations and decrees of the Nuremberg race laws of September 1935. In the face of this, all previous protection failed. The only way that Rothfels was able to escape his final exclusion from scientific and publishing work was through emigration. His only prior option had been to ensure, with the help of his protection network, that the new anti-Semitic state laws would not be applied to him. Hoping for the latter in December 1935, he applied to the Reichs- and Prussian Ministry of Interior to be granted special civil rights in accordance with the law that allowed for such exceptions in a few rare cases.[56] A renewed tug of war ensued, repeating the same positions. The head of the East Prussian government supported his application because Rothfels "belonged to that band of men who had with great courage and energy worked for Germany's national and political interests in the East." As a publicist and lecturer he had, in the "cause of enlightened instruction on border policies," substantially contributed to the success of "the defensive fight against our opponents from the East in the last years of the *Systemzeit*." Especially "his actions in defense of the severely threatened German cultural interest in the Baltic states and Poland" had been of the "greatest importance." For this reason, his case, "like no other, falls into the category of the legally allowed exemption from the stipulated regulations governing Jews and non-Aryans regarding state civil rights."[57] Even Ribbentrop, who meanwhile had been appointed ambassador to London, spoke out again and asked for an exemption from the regulations for Rothfels, "who lost a leg in the war and who was awarded the iron cross first class [E.K.I.].[58] Prof. R. has definitely served the national interest before the seizure of power and has excellent connections to English sources, such as T. P. Conwell-Evans who is well disposed towards Germany and who promotes German-English understanding."[59] In June 1936, an assistant secretary in the Ministry of Interior finally weighed the pros and cons between supporters and opponents: Ribbentrop and the East Prussian chairman of the regional council were opposed by the decisive "nay" of the responsible Nazi Party district leader. All other reports contained strong contradictions. Therefore, "the case for an exemption" had not been made and the application was "hereby rejected."[60] After this, another three months elapsed before Secretary of the Interior Wilhelm Stuckart informed Rothfels on 12 September 1936 of his rejection—without formality and without explanation. From the distributed copies of this letter that were sent in advance, it is apparent that three key ministries and the head of the army had all been involved in the Rothfels case.[61]

The career of political historian Hans Rothfels was hereby further restricted. He was allowed to keep his title and salary and was able to travel abroad; even the result of his latest research was still published in 1937 as a book. However, the exclusion from his profession was irrevocable. On account of his achievements as an intellectual front fighter in the "radical change of the nation," he had hoped for a personal rehabilitation until the fall of 1936, and he had wanted to be of further service to the Nazi regime. But now he was definitely marginalized. It was a very bitter pill for him and his family; meanwhile, he had to confront still further humiliations and struggles for survival.

Starting in the late fall of 1936, Rothfels began to look abroad. In November–December 1936 and May 1937 he made extensive visits to England[62] and started to take an interest in the history of English social policy.[63] The first result of this work was a lecture in several installments on Bismarck's social policy that he presented in Cambridge and that was published a year later in a social science journal.[64] In this lecture he toned down his former ideology considerably. He objectified his arguments and in a comparative examination he paid due homage to the British social insurance system with its detachments from the state, its self-administering tendencies, and its support by a strong trade union movement. It was quite evident that he was trying slowly "to gain a foothold in England" fully realizing that his "academic baggage carried too few ideological export articles for the Western European market."[65] His beginnings were accordingly difficult, especially as he had to compete with the intellectual anti-fascist refugees who had escaped from Germany. For Rothfels to obtain a visiting professorship was only possible if he became a "traitor to his country," in other words, he had to openly take a stand abroad against the Nazi regime. Such a break, however, was still unthinkable for Rothfels. Emigration was also out of the question for him. The only scenario he could imagine was a prolonged stay abroad with the agreement of the Nazi authorities.

This choice required Rothfels to endure further humiliations during the course of 1938. He was forced to register his financial assets, then to relinquish them, and finally to accept the discriminatory additional name of Israel. Shortly after *Kristallnacht*, he was no longer allowed to use archives and public libraries. Only when his oldest son Klaus Hermann was ex-matriculated from the University of Hamburg on 8 December 1938, and when he and the other children were prohibited from receiving any further professional education, did Rothfels stand up for his family and decide to act. On 20 February 1939 he sent his three children to England.[66] Two months later, payments to the children were stopped because money transfers abroad to children of civil servants were justified only "if a German education was ensured," something that "today could not be assumed of Jews," as the Ministry of Science wrote to the curator of the University of Königsberg.[67] At this time, Rothfels's English friends were making feverish attempts to find him a job at an English university. At the beginning of May, the Ministry of Science in a show of magnanimity agreed that "the professor [emeritus[68]] Rothfels could now have his domicile in England until the end of April 1941."

Permission for a possible move to a foreign country should be obtained in advance from the relevant German agency abroad. His pension would be "transferred in full to a foreign exchange bank into a special account for maintenance payments to the authorized drawer."[69] He was not allowed to take up a teaching position abroad, and he accepted this restriction. In August 1939, the Rothfels couple followed their children to England, and Hans Rothfels became a research fellow at St. John's College in Oxford.

The Concept of History in England and the United States and Its Repercussions on West Germany

After the outbreak of World War II, Rothfels's stay abroad turned into emigration without a foreseeable possibility of returning. His pension was stopped; contact with government authorities was cut off. Even in England things began to change. After all, Rothfels was not a refugee but a citizen of an enemy country (enemy alien) on a time-restricted visitor's visa. For a time, he was in a cleft stick. When the German army fell upon the Western European countries on 10 May 1940 and soon after encircled the British expeditionary forces in Northern France, Rothfels was interned on the Isle of Man. Now the British appeasers who had supported him suffered a political fiasco and were unable to protect him any more.[70] The only published sign of life from this dark year of 1940 was a short essay about the interaction of Germans and Soviets in the Baltics, in which he defended from a historical point of view the German hegemony over this "outpost of Western Europe and Western Christendom." He also bemoaned as a truly historical tragedy the "resettlement" of approximately 80,000 German-Baltic people into the annexed western provinces of Poland in the aftermath of the Ribbentrop-Molotov pact.[71]

We know only in rough outline what happened to Rothfels and his family during the following war years. The sources are largely silent on this matter, and Rothfels himself does not seem to have commented in any detail even to his closest students. We only know that in July 1940 Rothfels was invited as visiting professor to Brown University in Providence, Rhode Island, and that he traveled to the United States in November 1940. At Brown University he was given a "very exhausting position with a great deal of teaching that, however, saved him from the fate of the rootless, jobless emigrant."[72] It is not quite clear whether he was interned as an "enemy alien" for a second time after Germany declared war against the United States. In any event, his visiting professorship in Providence was extended several times beyond the end of the war, and in 1946 he became a U.S. citizen. During the summer semester of 1946, he received an offer from the well-known Department of History at the University of Chicago to be visiting professor of European history. There, again, he had to put favorite topics such as "nationality problems in Central Europe" on the back burner.[73] Instead, he had to fulfill his teaching obligations with lectures on the history of German foreign policy, on the Renaissance and the creation of the nation-state, on general theories of history, and on Leopold von Ranke.[74]

His lectures and seminars covered a wide spectrum but also prevented him from tackling new research projects in Chicago. This enabled him, in turn, to stay within his acquired academic territory and to remain rooted in his culture and belief system. The broad topics of his teaching may have broken down his worst ideological structures, and his dealings with some of the students on the far left[75] forced on him a certain measure of tolerance. This greatly advanced the process of deradicalization that had started in 1937/38. Rothfels returned increasingly to his neo-Rankian Prussian conservatism of the early 1920s.[76] However, this learning process did not go very far, since Rothfels became integrated into a conservative émigré network that had been developed under the protection of the president of the University of Chicago, Robert M. Hutchins. This network published its own German-language communications[77] and isolated itself from the influences of its environment.[78] Considering the views Rothfels expressed, one German-Jewish student attending his seminars could not understand why he had been forced to leave Germany at all.[79]

It was very likely due to the changing climate of the Cold War that a man of his caliber was offered in 1948, after only two years as visiting professor, the succession to the renowned historian of European history Bernadotte Schmitt. Throughout his life Schmitt had criticized the Prussian-German special path (*Sonderweg*), and he was convinced that the Wilhelminian elite was mainly responsible for World War I. His successor, however, had since the beginning of the 1920s tirelessly fought against the "war guilt lie" (*Kriegsschuldlüge*) and had advocated a revision of the postwar order of Versailles and Saint-Germain.

In 1944/45 a very different postwar order was being developed, and the emerging constellations brought the visiting professor of Providence and Chicago back to the writing desk.[80] He now openly expressed what he had been saying privately since the summer of 1941: he considered the Anglo-Saxon war alliance with the Soviet Union a catastrophe in world history. This was sufficient cause for him to "stick to his views" (*Richtung halten*) despite the initial risk, and to write against the advance of the Red Army. In July 1944 he published a long essay in the prestigious *Journal of Central European Affairs* about the history and the prospects of the Baltic Provinces.[81] The essay combined his own unchanged viewpoint regarding the "old cooperative" exemplary character of the German ruling class with a contemporary digression about developments since World War I and the turbulent events of 1939/40 in the shadow of the Ribbentrop-Molotov pact. In his view, the Estonians and Latvians were connected to the Germans by a deeply rooted tradition of "defending Western culture." Together they formed the outpost that until 1940 had prevented "the Bolshevik penetration of the periphery of Central Europe."[82] Since the 1920s, they jointly had cautiously tested a new way to solve the nationality problems, a way that deviated from the nation-state doctrines of the Western democracies and that had started to bear fruit across the continent with the creation of a European congress on minorities. The National Socialists had undermined these federalist-supranational tendencies with their concept of "ethnic purity." Ultimately, they had sacrificed them to the new German-Soviet definition of spheres of influence in Eastern Europe. The "resettlements" were followed in 1940 by Soviet occupation and in 1941 by the German counteroccupation, and now the liberation by the Red Army was imminent. What would happen afterwards had the importance of setting a new course. This matter should not be subordinated to an obligation to cooperate with the Soviets because of an alliance, Rothfels urged his readers. The Soviet nationality policies are only a façade, because the promised autonomy is always tied to a radical change in the Soviet system.

The above essay remained his only effort at political advice without having assignment during the final phase of World War II. Soon it became clear to Rothfels that time was overtaking his visions of a concept of history. Increasingly he restricted himself to bitter commentaries on the events, deflecting more and more from the fatal German responsibility, just as he had done after World War I. In his essay of July 1944 he had at least touched on the fateful role the Baltic-German irredenta had played in the East Central European power struggle. Now this was no longer a topic. From 1945 on, it was not the worsening news about the German genocide of the European Jews and the Slavic population of Eastern Europe that touched him, but the fact that the Soviets were settling in the heart of Central Europe.[83] A year later he launched his fiercest attack against the Western Allies by accusing participants in the Potsdam Conference of pushing through a postwar order that was the equivalent to a Hitlerian peace: the methods of the defeated were coloring the methods of the victors.[84] This verdict, which referred to the expulsion of Germans from Eastern Central Europe that had been sanctioned at Potsdam, also denied the legitimacy of the new borders. Just as in the years from 1932 to 1936, Rothfels was neither ready nor willing in 1946 to recognize the national integrity of the newly established Poland. Hans Rothfels was the first German historian to openly attack the new western boundaries of Poland on the Oder-Neiße line as well as the partition of East Prussia between Poland and the Soviet Union. He was also the first to equate the expulsion of Germans at the end of the war and afterward with the expulsion and genocide policies of the Nazi dictatorship.

A historian who so consistently followed the same principles was certainly welcome in West Germany. Rothfels was among the very few emigrated professors who were asked to return. He hesitated a long time before making the decision. In 1947 he rejected several offers of university appointments because he felt unsure whether he could once again achieve solidarity and connection with a disillusioned academic postwar generation.[85]

Only after the success of his first postwar study on the opposition to Hitler,[86] a very successful lecture tour, [87] and a triumphal appearance at the first postwar historians' conference, where he gave a lecture on Bismarck's position in the nineteenth century,[88] were those doubts removed. The intellectual and academic climate of restoration corresponded to his own neoconservative views. Upon taking up the chair in Tübingen in 1951, a new period of activity began for the 60-year-old Rothfels.[89] He rarely engaged in scientific research. Teaching also became increasingly secondary, even though Rothfels still very much valued the education of a distinctive body of students. Different tasks were expected of him now. Together with Gerhard Ritter, he became a prominent advocate of a new national identity[90] that skillfully tried to find a balance between the "open" Eastern borders (with the GDR and Poland) and the connection to the "Western world." As éminence grise of the appointment policy he separated the remorseless Nazis from the reformed ones. Together with his Königsberg students, he negotiated the obstacles of a ministerial documentation project on the "expulsion of Germans from Eastern-Central Europe" that threatened to confront them with their own past "policies of ethnic segregation."[91] In addition, he held a protective umbrella over them to allow them to break new ground with structural historical innovations within the framework of the Arbeitskreis für moderne Sozialgeschichte (Association for Modern Social History), and without jeopardizing their frontline anti-Marxist stance.[92] Rothfels's favorite child was now, however, contemporary history.[93] After his appointment at Tübingen, he participated in the reorganization of the controversial Munich Institut für Zeitgeschichte (Institute for Contemporary History) and supported the concealed solidarity between the institute and the history-conscious army generals of the Organisation Gehlen (German Military Secret Service). The *Vierteljahrshefte für Zeitgeschichte* (Quarterly Journal for Contemporary History) was founded and thrived under his auspices. This was the journal that set the standards for what was permissible and what was unpopular territory to be covered when researching the Nazi period. From 1960 on, Rothfels also worked as the main German editor on the *Akten zur Deutschen Auswärtigen Politik 1918–1945* (Documents on German Foreign Policy 1918–1945), an international editing project burdened by conflicts.

The end results of Rothfels's multifaceted work are mixed. On the one hand, he protected the networks of established history against neo-Nazi attempts at infiltration[94] and promoted the systematic empirical reappraisal of the political power mechanisms and institutions of the Nazi dictatorship by a new generation of researchers.[95] These historians were able to occupy key positions after proving themselves at the Institut für Zeitgeschichte. Yet these unquestionable contributions are juxtaposed with the fact that Rothfels set a trend that restricted contemporary research for decades, as critical assessment of the upper classes and military pillars of power as coalition partners of the Nazis became taboo and was obscured by myths of anti-Nazi resistance. In 1953 Rothfels prevented the publication in the *Vierteljahrshefte für Zeitgeschichte* of a previously accepted essay by George F. Hallgarten on the influence that the armament industry and the military had had on the early formation of the Nazi dictatorship.[96] With this he made a momentous decision concerning future trends. He tried to use similar tactics as the main German editor of the *Akten zur Auswärtigen Politik*:[97] It was not his task, he maintained, to illuminate the economic policies that led to the Nazi expansion. The American and British editors mistrusted him deeply.[98] Against his wishes, they insisted that the format of this reference work should go beyond conservative diplomatic history.[99] In addition, Rothfels was a poor representative of the interests of the edition and its collaborators vis-à-vis the Foreign Ministry. In May 1975, he accepted without protest the far-reaching cuts that the ministry wanted to make,[100] and finally he had the entire German editorial team against him.[101]

Hans Rothfels was a neoconservative representative of a nationalistic historiography of ideas. In his creative middle period he went beyond this scope and developed a fascist concept of history. His life's work, therefore, falls into three distinctly different parts. In the 1920s he combined his Friedrich Meineke-based neo-Rankian ideas with a determined opposition to the Weimar Republic and the European postwar order. This was followed by a middle period during which he not only criticized the existing order but also wanted to replace it with a concept of history advocating a utopian counterrevolution. Despite experiencing rapidly developing personal and anti-Semitic discrimination, he felt called upon to help shape a new, German Fascist order. His third creative period was marked by the basic condition of his emigration. This led to a deradicalization of Rothfels's thinking, but at the same time it led to his renewed opposition against the second postwar order of the twentieth century that became evident in 1944/45. As the power political processes in the following years were increasingly brought into line with his own philosophical concept of history, he did not go through a renewed phase of radicalization; rather, he made his mark as a neoconservative exponent of the Cold War. Only in his third creative period did he become the academic founder of cultural hegemony.

Notes

1. Thomas Etzemüller, *Sozialgeschichte als politische Geschichte. Werner Conze und die Neuorientierung der westdeutschen Geschichtswissenschaft nach 1945* (Munich, 2001), 44ff., 236ff.; Etzemüller, "Sozialgeschichte als politische Geschichte. Die Etablierung der Sozialgeschichte in der westdeutschen Geschichtswissenschaft," *Comparativ. Leipziger Beiträge zur Universalgeschichte und vergleichenden Gesellschaftsforschung* 12, no. 1 (2002): 12–33.
2. BArch, NL 1226 (Nachlaß Reinhard Wittram), file no. 44, Hans Rothfels to Reinhard Wittram, 25 October 1946, p. 1. The sentence cited here is grammatically incorrect and can only be understood on second reading. Its closeness to American idiom shows that for years Rothfels had mainly expressed himself in English.
3. This is even more surprising as Rothfels himself had referred to his co-responsibility during a lecture series on National Socialism in 1965 in Tübingen. He had stated that he had been "tainted for a time" by wanting to build a bridge between history and the racial theories of the National Socialists. Certainly, the "race theories" and their related ideas of a "master race" are in stark contrast to historical thinking. But there were also positive expectations attached to these ideas in the light of the historical interest being shown by the multiethnic groups of Eastern Europe. Specifically, this was the hope that "many ethnic groups could live side by side in one state or a confederation of states, while still maintaining their cultural individuality." Hans Rothfels, "Die Geschichtswissenschaft in den dreißiger Jahren," in *Deutsches Geistesleben und Nationalsozialismus. Eine Vortragsreihe der Universität Tübingen mit einem Nachwort von Hermann Diem*, ed. Andreas Flitner (Tübingen, 1965), 90–107, quot. 95.
4. Cf. Lothar Machtan, "Hans Rothfels und die Anfänge der historischen Sozialpolitikforschung in Deutschland," *IWK—Internationale wissenschaftliche Korrespondenz zur*

Geschichte der deutschen Arbeiterbewegung 28, no. 2 (1992): 161—210; Karen Schönwälder, *Historiker und Politik. Geschichtswissenschaft im Nationalsozialismus* (Frankfurt am Main 1992), 53ff.; Ingo Haar, *Historiker im Nationalsozialismus. Deutsche Geschichtswissenschaft und der 'Volkstumskampf im Osten* (Göttingen, 2000), 70ff.

5. Cf. Klaus Hornung, "Hans Rothfels und die Nationalitätenfragen in Ostmitteleuropa 1926–1934. In Erinnerung an den 12. April 1891 und an den 22. Juni 1976," in *Deutschland und seine Nachbarn—Forum für Kultur und Politik*, vol. 28, ed. Kulturstiftung der deutschen Vertriebenen (2001).

6. Heinrich August Winkler, "Hans Rothfels—Ein Lobredner Hitlers? Quellenkritische Bemerkungen zu Ingo Haars Buch 'Historiker im Nationalsozialismus,'" *Vierteljahrshefte für Zeitgeschichte* 49, no. 4 (2001): 643–652; Ingo Haar, "Quellenkritik oder Kritik der Quellen? Antwort an Heinrich August Winkler," *Vierteljahrshefte für Zeitgeschichte* 50, no. 3 (2002): 497–509. This controversy dealt with a multi-part radio lecture by Hans Rothfels that only survived in fragmentary form with the title: "The German idea of State from Frederick the Great to the present." The first handwritten draft is dated January 1930, and by January 1933 it had been updated several times. The Federal Archives and several prominent historians are at this point in agreement on dating the manuscript to the time after the Nazi takeover of power on 30 January 1933. Haar followed this interpretation in his presentation. Winkler, however, has now backdated the papers to 1930 in order to rehabilitate Rothfels as a common-sense Republican follower of Ebert and Stresemann. He accused Haar, but not the Federal Archives or the prominent historians, of having treated this source in a negligent manner. However, the truth is that Rothfels paraphrased the political development of the presidential dictatorships up to January 1933 and thereby tried to include the revisionist foreign policy of the Weimar Republic in his antidemocratic restoration model. The critical interpretation of this lecture that has prevailed up to now does not go far enough, and only partially does justice to the complex resources. However, Winkler's attempt at reinterpretation in the opposite direction lacks any basis.

7. Karl Heinz Roth, "Hans Rothfels: Geschichtspolitische Doktrinen im Wandel der Zeiten. Weimar—NS-Diktatur—Bundesrepublik," *Zeitschrift für Geschichtswissenschaft* 49, no. 12 (2001): 1061–1073.

8. Cf. Herbert A. Straus and Werner Röder, eds., *International Biographical Dictionary of Central European Emigrés 1933–1945*, vol. 2, part 1: A–K (Munich, 1983), 452–453; *Imperialismus im 20. Jahrhundert. Gedenkschrift für George W. F. Hallgarten*, ed. Joachim Radkau and Immanuel Geiss (Munich, 1976).

9. George W. F. Hallgarten, *Als die Schatten fielen. Erinnerungen vom Jahrhundertbeginn zur Jahrtausendwende* (Frankfurt am Main and Berlin, 1969), 316ff.; Hallgarten, *Das Schicksal des Imperialismus im 20. Jahrhundert. Drei Abhandlungen über Kriegsursachen in Vergangenheit und Gegenwart* (Frankfurt am Main, 1969), 69, 93ff., 104f.

10. Concerning biography and scholarship of Kehr, cf. *International Biographical Dictionary*, 609f.; Hans-Ulrich Wehler, "Einleitung," in Eckart Kehr, *Der Primat der Innenpolitik. Gesammelte Aufsätze zur preußisch-deutschen Sozialgeschichte im 19. und 20. Jahrhundert*, ed. Hans-Ulrich Wehler (Frankfurt am Main, Berlin, and Vienna, 1976), 1–29.

11. See Douglas A. Unfug, "Comment: Hans Rothfels," in *Paths of Continuity:Central European Historiography from the 1930s to the 1950s*, ed. Hartmut Lehmann and James van Horn Melton (Cambridge and New York, 1994), 137–154, esp. 149; Eckart Kehr, "Die Neuere deutsche Geschichtsschreibung," in Kehr, *Der Primat der Innenpolitik* 254–267, esp. 265f.

12. Kehr, "Neuere deutsche Geschichtsschreibung," 266.

13. The written version appeared 1933: Hans Rothfels, "Bismarck und die Nationalitätenfragen des Ostens," *Historische Zeitschrift* 147 (1933): 98–105. A year later there followed an expanded study: Hans Rothfels, *Bismarck und der Osten* (Leipzig, 1934). To get the flavor of the Göttinger Historikertag, also compare Haar, *Historiker im Nationalsozialismus*, 97ff.

14. "The initial situation is seen quite correctly, the conditions of these in-between territories cannot be sustained in the long run. But he avoids a decision by the conclusions he

draws from this, because the only real solution to the problem of having many nationalities live side by side in one state has long been provided by the Soviet Union." Kehr, *Neuere deutsche Geschichtsschreibung*, 266.

15. Kehr did not live to see the neo-imperialist change that took place in the Soviet Union in 1937/38 and the subsequent Fascist-Stalinist "solution" to the problems of the Eastern Central European "in-between" states that the Soviet Union achieved in 1939/40 by the classic method of separating the "spheres of influence." We can assume that had he been confronted with these events he would have changed his mind about suitable alternatives to Roth's restoration model.

16. Cf. the collection of the most important political speeches and essays: Hans Rothfels, *Ostraum, Preußentum und Reichsgedanke. Historische Abhandlungen, Vorträge und Reden* (Leipzig, 1935).

17. Hans Rothfels, "Bismarcks sozialpolitische Anschauungen," *Deutsche akademische Rundschau* 6, no. 16 (1925): 1ff.; Rothfels, "Zur Geschichte der Bismarckschen Innenpolitik," *Archiv für Politik und Geschichte* 7 (1926): 284–310; Rothfels, *Theodor Lohmann und die Kampfjahre der staatlichen Sozialpolitik (1871–1905)* (Berlin, 1927); Rothfels, "Bismarcks sozialpolitische Anschauungen," *Ärztliche Mitteilungen* 29 (1928): 988–991; Rothfels, *Prinzipienfragen der Bismarckschen Sozialpolitik*, Königsberger Universitätsreden, vol. 3 (Königsberg, 1929). Cf. the critical appraisal by Machtan, "Hans Rothfels und die Anfänge der historischen Sozialpolitikforschung," 176ff.

18. Rothfels, *Bismarck und der Osten*, 12.

19. The fact that Rothfels also borrowed heavily from Carl Schmitt has not received enough attention. In outlining a book project on the history of the relationship between politics and military leadership he stressed as late as October 1935 that he would follow in Carl Schmitt's footsteps as far as the nature of politics was concerned. BArch, NL 1213, 12, Hans Rothfels to Publishing House W. G. Korn in Breslau, 22 October 1935, p. 1. Cf. Concerning the ideological context of the conservative counterrevolution, see Joachim Petzold, *Konservative Theoretiker des deutschen Faschismus. Jungkonservative Ideologen in der Weimarer Republik als geistige Wegbereiter der faschistischen Diktatur* (Berlin, 1978).

20. See Haar, *Historiker im Nationalsozialismus*, 76ff., 86ff.

21. BArch, NL 1213, 12, Hans Rothfels, "Der deutsche Staatsgedanke von Friedrich dem Großen bis zur Gegenwart," radio address, no date (1931/33), P. 27 a.

22. Cf. Hans Rothfels, "Das baltische Deutschtum in Vergangenheit und Gegenwart," *Königsberger Auslandsstudien* 7 (1932): 37–61; Rothfels, "Das Problem des Nationalismus im Osten," in *Deutschland und Polen*, ed. Albert Brackmann (Munich and Berlin, 1933), 259–270; Rothfels, "Deutschland und der Donauraum," *Königsberger Allgemeine Zeitung*, 13 January 1933, Abendblatt; Rothfels, "Das Werden des Mitteleuropagedankens," in Rothfels, *Ostraum, Preußentum und Reichsgedanke*, 228–248.

23. Heinrich Ritter von Srbik, (review of) Hans Rothfels; Ostraum, Preußentum und Reichsgedanke *Deutsche Literaturzeitung* 17 (1935): 2054–2057.

24. He still professed these beliefes as late as 1948 in an article published in the United States on the 100th anniversary of the 1848 Revolution: Hans Rothfels, "1848—One Hundred Years Later," *The Journal of Modern History* 20 no. 4 (1948): 291–319, esp. 319.

25. Rothfels, "Das Werden des Mitteleuropagedankens," 230, 234f., 244; Rothfels, "Das Problem des Nationalismus im Osten," 183.

26. Cf. Hans Rothfels, "Bismarck, das Ansiedlungsgesetz und die deutsch-polnische Gegenwartslage," *Deutsche Monatshefte in Polen* 1 (1934/35): 214–218.

27. Cf. Haar, *Historiker im Nationalsozialismus*, 90ff.; Haar, "'Kämpfende Wissenschaft.' Entstehung und Niedergang der völkischen Geschichtswissenschaft im Wechsel der Systeme," in *Deutsche Historiker im Nationalsozialismus*, ed. Winfried Schulze and Otto Gerhard Oexle (Frankfurt am Main, 1999), 215–240.

28. Despite many journalistic attempts, there still does not exist a convincing critical biography of Papen. In most cases Papen is either glorified or underestimated. Compare the most recent attempt at categorizing his political thinking and behavior in Joachim

Petzold, *Franz von Papen: Ein deutsches Verhängnis* (Munich and Berlin, 1995); concerning Papen's role in preparing the Austrian Anschluss, see Franz Müller, "*Ein 'Rechtskatholik' zwischen Kreuz und Hakenkreuz. Franz von Papen als Sonderbevollmächtigter Hitlers in Wien 1934–1938"* (Frankfurt am Main et al., 1990). The following remarks incorporate the result of a study that I undertook when preparing a monograph on Papens activities as German ambassador to Turkey during World War II.

29. Franz von Papen, "An den deutschen Arbeiter," in von Papen, *Appell an das deutsche Gewissen. Reden zur nationalen Revolution* (Oldenburg and Berlin, 1933), 80–94; von Papen, *Die Unternehmerpersönlichkeit im neuen Staat* (Berlin-Charlottenburg, [1933]); Petzold, *Franz von Papen*, 42ff.

30. Cf. Hermann Graml, *Zwischen Stresemann und Hitler. Die Außenpolitik der Präsidialkabinette Brüning, Papen und Schleicher*, Schriftenreihe der Vierteljahrshefte für Zeitgeschichte, 83 (Munich, 2001): 199ff.

31. Cf. Timothy W. Mason, *Arbeiterklasse und Volksgemeinschaft. Dokumente und Materialien zur deutschen Arbeiterpolitik 1936–1939* (Opladen, 1975); Karl Heinz Roth, "Von der Rüstungskonjunktur zum Raubkrieg: Die Ursachen der deutschen Aggressionspolitik 1938/39," in *Der Krieg vor dem Krieg. Ökonomik und Politik der "friedlichen" Aggressionen Deutschlands 1938/39*, ed. Werner Röhr, Brigitte Berlekamp, and Karl Heinz Roth (Hamburg, 2001), 29–97.

32. In 1934 and 1938, colleagues from his immediate circle were murdered by SS commandos, and in both cases Papen tried unsuccessfully to get them rehabilitated. Despite this, he remained a loyal vassal of Hitler. For this, the exponents of the gradually forming conservative opposition punished him with contempt.

33. Hans Rothfels, *Bismarck und der Osten*

34. Hans Rothfels, "Selbstbestimmungsrecht und Saarabstimmung," quoted after Schönwälder, *Historiker und Politik*, 58, footnote 302.

35. Rothfels, *Ostraum, Preußentum und Reichsgedanke*, vi, x.

36. Rothfels to Siegfried A. Kaehler in April 1933, quoted after Hornung, "Hans Rothfels und die Nationalitätenfragen in Ostmitteleuropa," 15.

37. BArch, NL 1213, 20, Letter from 29 members of the Historical Institute of the University of Königsberg to Rothfels, 3 April 1933; Die Unterzeichneten des Briefes an Herrn Professor Rothfels: An die Deutsche Studentenschaft der Albertus-Universität, Königsberg 3 April 1933.

38. BArch, NL 1213, 20, Rothfels to the chancellor of the Albertus-Universität Königsberg, 20 April 1933, and to the "Arbeitsausschuß zur Förderung des Auslandsstudiums an der Albertus-Universität," 6 May 1933.

39. Ibid., "Der Jude Rothfels," *Prager Mittag*, 12 February 1934; letter from J. Pfitzner, Prague, to Rothfels, 28 February 1934.

40. Cited after Hans Mommsen, "Hans Rothfels," in *Deutsche Historiker*, vol. 9 (Göttingen, 1982), 138.

41. Cited after Machtan, "Hans Rothfels und die Anfänge der historischen Sozialpolitikforschung," 169, footnote 39.

42. BArch, NL 1213, 142, Hans Rothfels, "Abschiedsworte im Zusammensein mit dem Seminar in Juditten," 25 July 1934. Cf. Rothfels, "Schlußworte der Bismarck-Vorlesung und der letzten Vorlesung in Königsberg überhaupt."

43. Alfred Schulz to Dr. Möller, 14 August 1935. Forschungsstelle für Zeitgeschichte, Hamburg, NL Schulz, 15–1 A 5.

44. BArch, ZB II 4548 A. 1, Professor Eckhardt, Reichs- und Preußisches Ministerium für Wissenschaft, Erziehung und Volksbildung, to Rothfels, 5 February 1935 (draft); Rothfels, Berlin, to Eckhardt, 2 February 1935.

45. Ibid., Rothfels to Eckhardt, 22 February 1935.

46. Professor Bachér, Vermerk für Ministerialrat von Kursell, 5 March 1935, P. 3 –4.

47. See Wolfgang Michalka, *Ribbentrop und die deutsche Weltpolitik 1933–1940* (Munich, 1980), 27ff.

48. John Dalberg Acton (1834–1902), from 1869 Baron Acton of Aldenham, was an influential British conservative historian who criticized the democratic nation-states and instead demanded federal multi-national state systems.
49. BArch, ZB II 4548 A.1, Rothfels to Ribbentrop, 23 February 1935.
50. Ibid., Ribbentrop to Rust, 25 February 1935.
51. Ibid., Rust, Ordinance to Rothfels, 21 March 1935 (draft); Rust, cover letter to the ordinance, 21 March 1935 (draft).
52. Ibid., Von Kursell, Notice for Minister Rust, re. Prof. Rothfels, 23 April 1935.
53. Ibid., V. (K. Theodor Vahlen), Reich Ministry for Science, Education, and Adult Education, to Rothfels, 22 November 1935 (draft, with copies for the Faculty of Philosophy and the chancellor of the University of Berlin).
54. Cf. Michael Burleigh, "Albert Brackmann (1871–1952), Ostforscher: The Years of Retirement," *Journal of Contemporary History* 23 (1988): 573–588; Haar, *Historiker im Nationalsozialismus*, 106ff.
55. Hans Rothfels, *Theodor v. Schön, Friedrich Wilhelm IV. und die Revolution von 1848*, Schriften der Königsberger Gelehrten Gesellschaft, Geisteswissenschaftliche Klasse, 13, 2 (Halle, 1937). Despite some typical weaknesses, this was, next to the Lohmann biography, one of Rothfels's most important research successes based on empirical sources.
56. The petitions date from 15 and 23 December 1935. They have not been located so far. The dates can be ascertained from the letter of State Secretary of Interior Wilhelm Stuckart to Rothfels from 9 December 1936, in which he informed Rothfels of the final rejection. The letter of rejection can be found in BArch, ZB II 4548 A.1.
57. BArch, NL 1213, 20, The Landeshauptmann of East Prussia, Dr. Blunk, to Regierungspräsident Friedrich, 7 January 1936.
58. The Iron Cross First Class was one of the most important awards for war merits.
59. BArch, ZB II 4548 A.1, Metzner, Reich Ministry for Science, Education, and Adult Education, Notice for Dept. I, 3 March 1936 (copy).
60. Ibid., Reich Ministry of Interior, Dr. Hubrich/Eder: Notice, June 1936 (copy).
61. Ibid. These were the Foreign Office, the Reich Ministry for Science, the War Ministry, and the Supreme Commander of the Wehrmacht. Cf. Stuckart to Rothfels, Subject: Reich Citizen Law and its Regulations, 12 September 1936, distribution list.
62. See the corresponding notices by Rothfels in BArch, NL 1213, 127.
63. See the corresponding excerpts, ibid., no. 99.
64. Hans Rothfels, "Bismarck's Social Policy and the Problem of State Socialism in Germany," *The Sociological Review* 30 (1938): 81–94, 288–302.
65. Siegfried A. Kaehler to Heinrich Ritter von Srbik, 18 August 1938, reproduced in Heinrich Ritter von Srbik, *Die wissenschaftliche Korrespondenz des Historikers 1912–1945*, ed. Jürgen Kämmerer (Boppard, 1988), 496f.
66. BArch, ZB II 4548 A.1, Rothfels to the trustee of the University of Königsberg, 20 February 1939.
67. Ibid., Letter from the Reich Ministry for Science to the trustee of the University of Königsberg, Subject: Zahlung von Kinderzuschlägen an den emeritierten ordentlichen Professor Dr. Rothfels, 22 April 1939.
68. Original text read "em."
69. BArch, ZB II 4548 A.1, Letter from Scurla/Harmjanz, Reich Ministry for Science, to the trustee of the University of Königsberg, 4 May 1939.
70. The same fate was also shared by Rothfels's son Klaus Hermann (born 1919), who was interned in Canada and was later able to continue his botany studies at the University of Toronto. See *International Biographic Dictionary of Central European Emigrés*, vol. 2, part L–Z (Munich, 1983), 998.
71. Hans Rothfels, "Russians and Germans in the Baltic," *Contemporary Review* 157 (1940): 320–332.
72. Wolfgang Neugebauer, "Hans Rothfels (1891–1976) in seiner Zeit," in *Die Albertus-Universität zu Königsberg und ihre Professoren* (Berlin 1995), 245–256, cited 250.

73. BArch, NL 1213, 20, Cf. William T. Hutchinson, Department of History, University of Chicago, to Rothfels, Department of History, Brown University in Providence, 28 November 1945.
74. See the corresponding documents in BArch. NL 1213, 26 and 27.
75. For example, a student wrote in a seminar paper about the Communist Manifesto that while it had had no influence on the Revolution of 1848, "Nevertheless, the Manifesto thundered in Promethean terms the doom of bourgeois society while laying down an international program of strategy and action." This observation Rothfels marked in the margin with a question mark, but he had to accept it all the same. Ira A. Glazier, "Communist Manifesto," no date, p. 1. BArch, NL 1213, 26.
76. The return to the comforting *Übervater* Leopold von Ranke becomes obvious in a very detailed lecture manuscript on Ranke. Cf. BArch, NL 1213, 26, Hans Rothfels, Ranke, esp. "2nd lecture."
77. The "Mitteilungen der Literarischen Gesellschaft," in which Rothfels regularly reported on new publications on German history, appeared in Chicago from 1944 on.
78. See Klemens von Klemperer, "Hans Rothfels (1891–1976)," in *Paths of Continuity: Central European Historiography for the 1930s to the 1950s*, ed. Hartmut Lehmann and James van Horn Melton (Cambridge and New York, 1995), 119–135, hereto 128f.
79. This refers to Georg Iggers, who in 1948 participated in two seminars by Rothfels on "Reichfreiherrn von Stein" and on the "Paulskirche." At this point, Iggers did not know that Rothfels had been stigmatized as a Jew. On the other hand, Rothfels knew that Iggers was very critical of him and rejected his thesis proposal, commenting, "[H]e has no understanding of history. He is unable to get away with this in Chicago." Oral communication by Georg Iggers to the author during a conversation in Washington, D.C., on 6 October 2001, also written communication from 22 July 2002.
80. In 1941 and 1942 Rothfels did not publish anything. In 1943 he contributed an essay on Carl von Clausewitz to an anthology on the creators of modern military strategy. In this he presented Clausewitz to the American military as a protagonist of an unconditional willingness to use state violence in order for the boundaries between politics and war—that is to say, peace and war—to become essentially bluured. Cf. Hans Rothfels, "Clausewitz," in *Makers of Modern Strategy Military Thought from Machiavelli to Hitler*, ed. Edward Mend Earle (Princeton, 1943), 93–113.
81. Hans Rothfels, "The Baltic Provinces: Some Historic Aspects and Perspectives," *Journal of Central European Affairs* 4, no. 2 (1944): 117–146.
82. Ibid., 134.
83. Hans Rothfels, "Russia and Central Europe," *Social Research* 12 (1945): 304–327.
84. Hans Rothfels, "Frontiers and Mass Migrations in Eastern Central Europe," *The Review of Politics* 8 (1946): 37–67.
85. BArch, NL 1213, 20, Rothfels to Prof. von Guttenberg, University of Erlangen, 1 June 1947.
86. Rothfels gave a lecture on this topic for the first time in 1947 in Chicago. Under the influence of the recently published book by Allen Welsh Dulles about "Germany's Underground" he expanded this into a historical study that was published in 1948 by the ultraconservative Henry Regnery company in Hinsdale, Illinoi Cf. Hans Rothfels, "Deutsche geschichtliche Literatur," *Mitteilungen der Literarischen Gesellschaft* 4 (1947): 37–44; Allen Welsh Dulles, *Germany's Underground* (New York, 1947); Hans Rothfels, *The German Opposition to Hitler: A Reappraisal* (Hinsdale, Ill., 1948); Rothfels, Review of "Allen Welsh Dulles, Germany's Underground," *Historische Zeitschrift* 169, no. 1 (1949): 133–135.
87. BArch, NL 1213, 20, Hans Rothfels, Report on Experiences as a Visiting Professor in Germany, Summer 1949, 12ff.
88. Hans Rothfels, "Bismarck und das 19. Jahrhundert," in *Schicksalswege deutscher Vergangenheit. Festschrift für Siegfried A. Kaehler* (Düsseldorf, 1950), 233–248.
89. Interestingly enough, Rothfels stipulated amongst other things that he did not have to take West German citizenship immediately. See BArch, NL 1213, 20, Rothfels to Dr. Sauer, Secretary for Culture of Württemberg-Hohenzollern, 12 November 1950. Apart

from the Tübingen chair, he retained his professorship until 1956 and remained an American citizen until 1969.

90. Cf. Christoph Cornelißen, *Gerhard Ritter. Geschichtswissenschaft und Politik im 20. Jahrhundert* (Düsseldorf, 2001).

91. Cf. Mathias Beer, "Im Spannungsfeld von Politik und Zeitgeschichte. Das Großforschungsprojekt 'Dokumentation der Vertreibung der Deutschen aus Ost-Mitteleuropa,'" *Vierteljahrshefte für Zeitgeschichte* 46 (1998) 3: 345–389; Beer, "Die Dokumentation der Vertreibung der Deutschen aus Ost-Mitteleuropa. Hintergründe—Entstehung—Ergebnis—Wirkung," *Geschichte in Wissenschaft und Unterricht* 50, no. 2 (1999): 99–117.

92. Cf. Etzemüller, *Sozialgeschichte als politische Geschichte*, 157ff., 236ff.

93. Cf. the corresponding paradigmatic article, Hans Rothfels, "Zeitgeschichte als Aufgabe," *Vierteljahrshefte für Zeitgeschichte* 1, no. 1 (1953): 1–8.

94. Cf. BArch, NL 1213, 176. This was achieved not only through an appropriate appointment policy, but also through regular observation and critical examination of neo-Nazi literature on history. For this purpose he maintained in Tübingen a special study group (in addition to his activities for the Institut für Zeitgeschichte) entitled "History from the Right," which analyzed current neo-Nazi publications on history.

95. Cf. the corresponding documentation in the Rothfels papers: BArch, NL 1213, Nos. 44, 45, 46, 47, 48, 49, 50, 51, 52.

96. According to Hallgarten, Hermann Mau from the Institut für Zeitgeschichte had accepted an article based on the Seeckt papers for the newly founded Vierteljahrshefte für Zeitgeschichte. After Mau's accidental death, however, Rothfels rejected the manuscript. Hallgarten later published the article in book form together with a second paper that had already appeared in English. See Hallgarten, *Als die Schatten fielen*, 316ff.; Hallgarten, *Hitler, Reichswehr und Industrie. Ein Beitrag zur Geschichte der Jahre 1918–33* (Frankfurt am Main, 1955).

97. Cf. the corresponding documentation of Rothfels's activities in BArch, NL 1213, 23, 41, 42, 43.

98. A deep disagreement developed particularly between Rothfels and the American chief editor (and Stresemann biographer) Hans W. Gatzke. As a student, Gatzke had emigrated from Germany in 1937. In 1944 he became an American citizen; he served in the U.S. Army until 1946 and graduated from Harvard in 1947. In 1969 he became American chief editor of the "Akten zur deutschen auswärtigen Politik." See *International Biographical Dictionary of Central European Emigrés*, vol. II, Part I: A–K, 360; Hans W. Gatzke, "The Quadripartite Project. Akten zur deutschen auswärtigen Politik 1918–1945. Experiment in International Historiography," in *Rußland, Deutschland, Amerika. Festschrift für Fritz Epstein zum 80. Geburtstag*, ed. Alexander Fischer, Günter Moltmann, and Klaus Schwabe (Wiesbaden, 1978), 333–341.

99. Bypassing the West German chief editor, Gatzke informed himself about the internal events, and this caused a massive counterreaction from Rothfels and the representatives of the Ministry for Foreign Affairs that can be felt to this day. Compare also the official account of the conflict given by the then Rothfels confidant Roland Thimme, "Das Politische Archiv des Auswärtigen Amts. Rückgabeverhandlungen und Aktenedition 1945-1995," *Vierteljahrshefte für Zeitgeschichte* 49 (2001): 317–362, esp. 349ff.

100. The Foreign Ministry demanded an extensive curtailment of foreign participation in the editing project and was no longer willing to carry the cost for Series A.

101. Even Thimme, "Das Politische Archiv des Auswärtigen Amts," 355f., recorded this fact.

Chapter 13

POLISH *MYŚL ZACHODNIA* AND GERMAN *OSTFORSCHUNG*

An Attempt at a Comparison

✦ ✦ ✦

Jan M. Piskorski

It is a generally known fact that in nineteenth-century Europe, national ideas gained currency on an unprecedented scale. Even though medievalists and modern historians justly emphasize that researchers of contemporary history sometimes simplify the issue of the formation of nations and also the matter of possible earlier conflicts influenced by national issues, there is nevertheless no doubt that these were different and less wide-ranging processes.[1]

Growing nationalism was, as is often stressed, a general European phenomenon, related to shifts that originated in the French Revolution, Herder's national-linguistic idea, and Romantic thought. The radicalization of nationalism at the end of the nineteenth and beginning of the twentieth centuries was supposedly a general phenomenon that related above all to the collapse of the existing economic and cultural model. Rapid industrialization uprooted the rural populations and threw them into the squalor of cities. Imperialism also started to grow, and, within its framework, Darwinism was transferred from biology to social development.[2]

Even if nationalism was a typical feature of Europe in the nineteenth and greater part of the twentieth centuries, there is no doubt that it was represented in a particular form in Germany's relations with its Slav neighbors, particularly with Poland. Poland had undergone its partition between three great neighbors in 1795, and for the next 120 years it was like an open wound, not only in this part of Europe. The German precept of "healthy national egoism" (*gesunder Volksegoismus*) was indeed formed during the debates on the Polish question in 1848, when even German democrats and liberals spoke clearly against the restoration of Poland in its previous form, taking the position of narrow Prussian-German national interests.[3]

Wishing to justify the partitions, which delivered a great political and ethical shock, Prussian and later German historiography made an enormous effort to prove that the Republic of Poland-Lithuania (Rzeczpospolita Obojga Narodów) did not deserve to exist: it oppressed its minorities; total chaos reigned there; it was unable to reform. In a word, it was not so much partitioned as naturally dissolving, to the advantage of the peoples that were settled on its territories. In time, already sporadically from the 1850s, but more often after the unification in 1871, in Germany the racial superiority of Germans or the Germanic peoples in general over the "incomplete" (*unvollendete*) or "immature" (*unreife*) nations of East-Central Europe was increasingly stressed. In the almost universal German understanding, the eastern part of the continent was not an independent historical actor, but merely terrain for German colonial expansion, comparable to English colonization in India or French colonization in Algeria.[4]

For the Germans, sure of their superiority and qualities, and convinced that the time of their greatness was coming, the result of World War I, particularly in the East, could not have been anything other than a shock. The fall of Tsarist Russia and the post-revolutionary chaos, the rebirth of Poland and the return of the Polish-German border to its position before the partitions, the fall of Austria-Hungary and the emergence of Czechoslovakia, the birth of the Baltic States: in all this the Germans lost their dominant position, causing them to feel deeply humiliated. Many burned with the fervid desire for revenge known as "Versailles syndrome." Even those Germans who would have been prepared to accept a new political map of Central and Eastern Europe imposed conditions on these states and nations that were difficult to accept. They demanded recognition of their leading role in the region, and even of their historical services to civilization. They demanded particular rights for their minorities without being prepared to reciprocate in this area.

In this explosive situation, this general atmosphere of danger that equally affected both the left and right, a new so-called *Volksgeschichte* (ethnic history) or *Volksforschung* (ethnic research) took shape and gained ever increasing influence over German scholars, not only historians and archeologists but also sociologists, geographers, ethnologists, anthropologists, and economists. Sometimes this outgrowth of the social sciences emerged as the so-called German *Westforschung* (Western research), directed toward the West, concretely toward the German-Belgian and German-French border, but more often it turned eastward, the focus of the so-called German *Ostforschung* (Eastern research). A particularly characteristic element of German *Volksforschung* was its rejection of the territorial state as a starting point, a task made easier as the myth of the undefeated Germany with its Prussian heart and skillful brain was destroyed with the end of the Hohenzollern dynasty. Its place was taken by the

Volk, understood to be an ethnic or racial community, which in the end means almost the same thing.

The geographers Albrecht Penck and Wilhelm Volz created the concept of *Volksboden* and *Kulturboden*, terms that—characteristically—were mostly related to East-Central and Eastern Europe. *Deutscher Volksboden* mostly meant the territories of Central and Eastern Europe that German colonists had directly reached, most usually in the course of medieval eastern colonization (*deutsche Ostkolonisation des Mittelalters*), whereas the idea of *deutscher Kulturboden* embraced the territories that remained under a significant degree of German cultural influence; the advancement of their civilization was supposedly due to this. On the basis of Penck and Volz's assertion that the right to the land of the "earliest forefathers" could not expire, German scholars laid claim to enormous territories. Volz, for example, wrote that the area up to the Vistula had been Germanic for three thousand years and that only temporarily, for a few centuries, had it been occupied by Slavs whose primitive culture, unable to survive conflict with the German colonists, was soon destroyed.[5] Medieval settlement to the east of the Elbe was treated by German researchers such as Rudolf Kötzschke and Hermann Aubin as "the regaining of the German East" (*Wiedergewinnung des deutschen Ostens*), or as a great settlement movement thanks to which the Germans "returned" to their former lands (*die grosse Volksbewegung der deutschen Rückwanderung*).[6] What is more, within the new *Volksforschung* the medieval German colonist, even if unaware of his identity and assimilated into another society, remained a member of the German national community—the *Volksgemeinschaft* or *Blutgemeinschaft*— and must have represented German national interests. It was therefore possible and indeed necessary to "regermanize" him, restoring his near-lost blood to the *Volk*. In occupied Poland this purpose was served by the complicated system of *Volkslisten*, through which various categories of German or "germanizable" populations were recorded. This affected even those individuals who did not feel German at all and saw themselves as good and loyal Poles, but in whose veins—at least according to the Security Police—the blood of German settlers flowed.[7]

It is therefore possible to agree with the assertion that German *Ostforschung* was not only an expression of German revisionism in retaliation for the changes after World War I, but also a reflection of Germany's fear of its neighbors. The problem was that its eastern neighbors, which were mostly small or at least, like Poland, medium-sized countries, were even more afraid of Germany. Furthermore, while Germany undermined the legal status of many of them, none of them questioned the need for Germany to exist. This situation resulted in an anti-German reaction in Central Europe, despite the fact that all the societies there had long been under the overwhelming influence of German culture, learning, and also historiography.

In the new Baltic countries in particular, notably in Latvia after the coup of 1935, the discipline of history rose to the status of national educator.

President Kárlis Ulmanis treated history in a purely utilitarian manner. It should legitimize the establishment of the Latvian state and—in conflict with German historiography—create a new Latvian national consciousness, within which there was no proper place for Germans. These historians took advantage of new possibilities for research, but at the same time they were forced—though without resistance—to write their works in the spirit of what Ulmanis formulated as the rules of "nationalism and truth."[8] In Lithuania, which also grappled with the German problem and the Polish question, historians sought to find in the Lithuanian past that which was Lithuanian, condemning the opinions of even their own researchers if they did not agree with the general line marked out by the majority.[9] Even in democratic Czechoslovakia history entered the service of the national idea.[10] Furthermore, the great Mircea Eliade was unable to resist not only the nationalism prevalent in that part of Europe, in this case above all in its anti-Hungarian and anti-Slav form, but even subconsciously associated himself with the biological understanding of the nation. He did praise the Roman colonization of Dacia under Trajan, and was pleased about their romanization, but immediately added that none of this had resulted in "radical changes to the ethno-cultural basis of the Dacians," which would have been—logically—a contradiction.[11]

Taking into consideration the fact that German *Ostforschung* directed its attacks largely against Poland, it is no surprise that a counter to it very quickly developed there in the form of Polish *myśl zachodnia* (Western thought). Of course, Polish *myśl zachodnia* did not suddenly appear out of nothing, but was rooted in nineteenth-century discussions on the future of a reborn Poland, including the subject of its borders. However, active development of *myśl zachodnia* only really occurred from 1918 on.[12]

Polish historiography between the world wars was greatly decentralized and—as was earlier the case—dominated by two ideas. To generalize, one camp contained those who favored the "open and tolerant" model of Jagiellonian Poland, and other camp favored a "modern" ethnic Poland, although—as Herbert Ludat wrote—"the "Jagiellonian idea" turned out to be unachievable, while the "Piasts" on their side felt disappointed."[13] The "Piasts" were mostly associated with National Democracy, while the "Jagiellonians" joined the camp around Marshal Józef Piłsudski, although many of his followers showed increasing concern about the growing authoritarianism in Poland. Furthermore, more than one of the earlier supporters of National Democracy later came close to a position similar to that of the governing Sanacja—most notably Zygmunt Wojciechowski, creator of the concept of "motherland territories," which generally referred to the area of early Piast Poland at the turn of the tenth and eleventh centuries. The backers of Jagiellonian Poland were also clearly divided into "federalists" who were open to the needs of other nations living in the Republic and "unitarianists" who demanded that Polish nationality be strengthened at the expense of others, particularly to the

East. These "Jagiellonians" were not so far removed from many "Piasts" who called for decisive anti-German moves in the West, but also Polonization efforts in the East. Wojciechowski even postulated the use of the methods that had previously been used by Prussia against Poles in Great Poland and Western Prussia against the "immature" nations in eastern Poland.

One might have thought that regaining independence after 120 years of occupation would encourage a deep revision of opinion on Polish history and the aims of historical study. However, even though these subjects were discussed, no fundamental changes occurred because Poland still found itself in much the same situation, pressed between two powerful neighbors, one of whom still burned with the desire for revenge. The other, meanwhile, wished to spread revolution across Europe and was preparing the role of another Soviet republic for Poland, which lay in its path. Despite the circumstances it was expected that doing history in Poland would now be easier, since history no longer had to play the role of the defender of national interests. The aim was to uncover the "truest truth" without deceit or platitudes, because only on truth would it be possible—as Marceli Handelsman stressed—to build a free and civic nation. The emphasis on democratization called for more concern for the history of the masses. Finally, it was felt that examples for Poland should not be sought in the "prison cells of the partitioners" but in the greatest moments of its history. The reasons for Poland's collapse and rebirth were endlessly sought, with particular attention devoted to the roles played by Poles and their neighbors.[14]

Advocates of Polish *myśl zachodnia* between the wars were mostly associated with National Democrats, or at least their opinions were related to those of the National Democrat leaders Jan Ludwik Popławski (1854–1908) and Roman Dmowski (1864–1939). Both drew attention to the multiethnicity and minimal role of the peasantry in Poland-Lithuania as reasons for its decline. According to Dmowski, who at the beginning of the twentieth century published his *Myśli nowoczesnego Polaka* (Thoughts of the Modern Pole), which became one of the most influential Polish books for the next few generations, if Poles wanted to achieve independence, they had to rid themselves of their romanticism and dreams of a multinational and multi-confessional state, and take up the position of realistic nationalism. Only in this way would they be able to cope with the growing exclusive nationalism of their neighbors, particularly the Germans, but also the Jews and the Russians. Dmowski, who was a biologist by education, introduced certain elements of Darwinism into the understanding of national struggle in which the weak and defenseless must succumb. However, he understood the struggle not as a military conflict, but as a continuous rivalry in the fields of economics and culture.

The question of how far Dmowski's opinions spread among historians, most of whom sympathized with National Democracy, remains an issue for future research. Overall it appears that—as Michael G. Müller pertinently noted—they did not abandon from the vision of a multiethnic and confessionally tolerant Poland very easily or at once.[15] In 1920 Antoni Chołoniewski wrote about the "national lunacy" that "stupefied and paralyzed contemporary man, raising instincts in him which were worthy of a wild beast." The author also called for a change in relations with Poland's eastern neighbors and the Jews, while criticizing Jewish exclusivism. He recalled Józef Piłsudski's declaration that whoever wishes independent Poland to base its power over others on the force of its bayonets "mocks the very idea of independence."[16]

The aim of German *Ostforschung* was to document "scientific" proof of Germany's right to a significant part—if not the most—of Polish territory, while at the same time Polish *myśl zachodnia* attempted to balance "scientific" defense of the status quo, which in essence would satisfy it, and "scientific" pretensions to the former Slav lands now under German rule. Some of the Polish historians who propagated *myśl zachodnia* sometimes rattled their sabers by calling—particularly in journalistic articles—for the "return" of territories up to the Elbe. It was argued that the Slavs and Poles who had lived there in former times had been only superficially germanized, so their "reslavification" should still be possible. Just as the German *Ostforscher*—who mostly did not know either Poland or Polish—were united in their hatred of "Versailles" Poland, so the Polish historians schooled in *myśl zachodnia* (a significant proportion of whom were graduates of Austrian or German universities and who were not infrequently fascinated by German culture) were held together above all by their fear of the Germans. Sometimes they even felt a certain sympathy for Slav Russia, though this never meant acknowledgement of Communism, which was completely unacceptable for any of the usually deeply religious or at least traditional Catholic Polish historians who were connected with the National Democrats.

It is possible to find many parallels between German *Ostforschung* and Polish *myśl zachodnia*, although one should also be aware of the very different scale of the two phenomena: Polish *myśl zachodnia* was really limited to Poznań, while the German *Ostforschung* was influential, finding support even in Berlin and among such historians as Albert Brackmann.[17] Furthermore, the institutions related to Polish *myśl zachodnia* continued to remain open—as Jörg Hackmann recently emphasized—informing the public of their aims and activities. They were also in conflict with the state authorities, both before and especially after World War II. Despite formal attempts at a rapprochement with the Communist authorities in the name of the Polish *raison d'état*, substantive concessions to Stalinism were minimal.[18]

This fundamentally distinguished the Polish *myśl zachodnia* from of its German equivalent, which was able during the whole interwar and postwar period to sustain friendly relations with successive governments. The majority of German *Ostforscher* wished to serve the Reich, and also the Third Reich, which however did not mean that they had an actual influence on matters of state. Not infrequently, and indeed no differently from their Polish colleagues, they felt neglected by the state. This is especially true of the months following the signature by Poland and Germany of a ten-year non-aggression pact in 1934.

A further element distinguishing German *Ostforschung* from Polish *myśl zachodnia* is a certain chronological difference. The former had flowered rapidly in the interwar period and during World War II, although it was still active throughout the entire Cold War. The latter also emerged in the interwar period, but it really gained ground only after World War II, when Polish scholars, arm in arm with the Catholic Church and the new Polish authorities, defended the Yalta Settlement. This granted Poland partial territorial compensation at the expense of Germany in exchange for the greater territories lost to the Soviet Union in the East. After 1945, however, the subject of Polish *myśl zachodnia* changed. The resettlement of the vast majority of Germans who had lived in the new western and northern territories of Poland meant that the matter of the supposedly superficially germanized autochthons was no longer addressed. Instead, the issue of colonizing in the territories gained at Yalta and Potsdam, and of turning those territories into a fully domestic region, became a priority. Despite this, the settlers from Central and Eastern Poland continued to feel like foreigners in the regions for a very long time.

On the other hand, the interdisciplinary character of German *Ostforschung* and Polish *myśl zachodnia* came to the fore, though it was sometimes more declared than real. Nevertheless, both united a wide spectrum of researchers who were interested in the past: from archeologists and historians to sociologists, ethnologists, anthropologists, geographers, and linguists. A lively discussion is currently being conducted in Germany as to whether this interdisciplinary character influenced the modernization of historical study and, if so, whether one can therefore state that the roots of modern social history in the Federal Republic of Germany can be found in *Volksforschung* and *Ostforschung*.[19]

Another element common to both German *Ostforschung* and Polish *myśl zachodnia* was a deliberate consent to embrace a certain one-sidedness in research, which often led not only to the recovery of facts about the history of one's own nation but also even to self-censorship in the name of one's national *raison d'état*. Indeed, both Germany and Poland witnessed scholarly opposition to this way of approaching the matter, although in Germany that opposition really only arose in Slavicist circles (Reinhard Trautmann and Heinrich Felix Schmid), whereas in Poland there were many more opponents of one-sidedness, active in all disciplines—a fact noted with care in Germany.

In both cases great weight was given to journalistic and propaganda activities. It is usually possible to draw a rather clear distinction between the emotional, one-sided arguments in the popular press and works that were par excellence scholarly, where it was at least attempted to weigh the arguments more carefully. German *Ostforscher* published countless pamphlets and albums; the Polish historians preferred magazines and newspapers, such as the National Democratic *Kurier Poznański*.

German *Ostforschung* also shared with Polish *myśl zachodnia* a certain obsession with the populace, a love of the common folk, a belief that only the people, or—as it was sometimes phrased in Poland—the "peasant nation," had preserved the traditional national values, which it was necessary to discover and inject into the whole population. At least in the Polish case, this "folk" obsession was indulged only by a relatively low proportion of researchers, particularly those who came close to a biological understanding of nationhood, such as Karol Stojanowski.

Last but not least, both fields shared an aversion to Jews and, even more, to "Jewish democracy," parliamentarianism, Freemasonry, and Marxism. They also partly shared a respect for authoritarian governments and the rules of leadership. It is necessary to stress, thought, that nearly all the prominent Polish National Democrats fundamentally rejected the German and often even the Italian model of the state, identifying themselves rather with the Spanish, or more frequently the Portuguese model. Also, nearly all Polish National Democrats and the researchers associated with them remained distrustful of Hitler, although—as Hannah Arendt writes— almost the whole world admired his effectiveness.[20] In East-Central Europe, fascination with the Führer, although already mixed with growing fears, was still present in 1938 and early 1939, when it appeared that Hitler had realized nearly all of the national aims of Germany, including the so-called Greater German solution of the German question. However, the greatest ideologists of National Democracy, Roman Dmowski and Jędrzej Giertych (1903–1992), stressed that the Catholic Polish nation could agree with the Hitler movement only in their common aim, the good of the nation. They rejected the National Socialist means to this end as a form of biological racism (both, meanwhile, accepted the so-called practical racism, which allowed, for example, the social isolation of a Jew who refused to assimilate), alongside eugenics, the neo-pagan movement, and the militarism and etatism of the system in which Hitler was the law. Hitler, they wrote, had so far only shown how well he could destroy; but his chaotic program did not allow for normal government, and his totalitarianism fettered freedom of thought and industry, de facto relieving people of responsibility for their own actions.[21]

Zygmunt Wojciechowski was among those who were inclined to discern "traces of a modern national thought" in the National Socialist movement. The legal historian, originally from Lviv (now in Ukraine, formerly Lwów in Poland), was one of the co-initiators of Polish *myśl zachodnia*. He believed that Hitler, as an Austrian Catholic, was breaking with Prussian tradition in Germany and would give Poland at least a little breathing space. He still accepted nearly all the Führer's decisions, including the Anschluss with Austria and even the Munich Pact. In his opinion, Hitler would play a role in Germany similar "to that of Władysław Łokietek 600 years ago," a reference to a statesman who had united the Polish Kingdom after a period of territorial fragmentation. At first, Wojciechowski even admired Hitler's anti-Jewish policy, seeing it as a good example for Poland. Later, though, the Polish historian's distrust of Hitler and his politics, indeed of his way of governing in general, grew. From then on Wojciechowski turned his gaze toward Fascist Italy, because—as Markus Krzoska writes—he indeed wanted a state that was strong but "dependent on lasting legal norms, in the tradition of Roman law."[22]

The final question concerns the extent to which *myśl zachodnia* represents a Polish variant of *Volksforschung*. The answer is not straightforward, and it will depend on the definition of *Volksforschung*. If we understand this to be merely a certain ethnocentric aberration or deviation—at least in the colloquial understanding of ethnos as a relation dependent above all on common origins—then *myśl zachodnia* is undoubtedly in this tradition, together with exclusive Zionism and many other trends in historical research in interwar Europe that led scholars to focus on traditional research into their own nation's past. If, however, we understand *Volksforschung* or *Volksgeschichte* to be, as Georg G. Iggers puts it, "a new conception of the *Volk* as a racial community,"[23] the issue becomes more complex.

Not long ago a young German historian, Markus Krzoska, in his Berlin dissertation on Zygmunt Wojciechowski, came to the conclusion that, although it is not possible to speak of a Polish *Volksforschung*, it is difficult to ignore certain parallels. Krzoska's conclusion is certainly correct if we relate it to the main thread of Polish *myśl zachodnia*, which is more concerned with a traditional nationalism directed against Germany. For Wojciechowski, as for many of his generation, the nation was indeed the greatest good, but—as Krzoska writes—it would be difficult to find "racist or even *völkisch* patterns of interpretation" in his work.[24]

A very small radical wing did exist within Polish *myśl zachodnia*, the most "classic" representative of which was the Poznań anthropologist Karol Stojanowski, clearly an outsider in this group of scholars. This wing was very close to German *Volksforschung* in its *völkisch* and racist form. Stojanowski, himself the son of a peasant from the Polish-Ukrainian border, believed that "a healthy nation can only be the peasant nation, where all of life is grounded in the peasant smallholding." Although a Catholic, Stojanowski, also followed social Darwinism, stating that only "a nation in which a continuous battle for superiority is occurring is a healthy nation and a nation on the road to God." Indeed, Stojanowski not only was a pathological anti-Semite, but above all his anti-Semitism was undoubtedly based on biological grounds, although the author—as a Catholic—had some difficulty in writing about this. Thus, Stojanowski wrote, in the tradition of National Democracy, that he rejected racism, while in fact he accepted it in its broadest sense, at least with regard to the Jews. This was, as he himself wrote, a racism limited by a religious aspect, but in truth it is difficult to discern such distinctions since he even denied the right to be Poles to Jews who had been christened for generations and assimilated into Polish culture. The "converts" and "crypto-Jews" had to be called Jews, not Poles, Stojanowski wrote in 1939, if the national movement was victorious in Poland; this would ensure that the national movement remained Polish and was not secretly undermined.[25]

German *Ostforschung*, along with German *Volksforschung* and the anti-German Polish *myśl zachodnia*, survived for decades after World War II, aided by the Cold War. Only the generation shift in the Federal Republic of Germany in the 1960s, the process of relaxation in Europe in the 1970s, and especially the fall of the Communist system and the recognition of the Polish-German border by a united Germany allowed for deeper reflection on the history of Polish-German relations. Researchers, freed from the need to defend national interests, started looking critically at the past of their own academic disciplines, which resulted in the rejection of previous tendencies. Although is regrettable that this occurred so late and only in a world reorganized by politics, it is also cheering that scholars have been able to take advantage of the opportunity that they were offered. Furthermore, at least in the case of Polish-German relations, scholarship paved the way for politics in many fields, and thus created for politics the possibility of relatively free activity after 1989.

Notes

1. This essay is based on a few of my earlier works in Polish and in German, especially on my lecture at the last German Historikertag in Halle (September 2002), "Volksgeschichte à la polonaise. Vom Polonozentrismus im Rahmen der sog. polnischen Westforschung," in *Europäische Volksgeschichten in der Zwischenkriegszeit. Eine vergleichende Bilanz*, ed. Manfred Hettling (Göttingen, 2003), 231–274. See also Piskorski, "Przeciw nacjonalizmowi w badaniach naukowych nad przeszłością stosunków polsko-niemieckich," *Przegląd Historyczny* 81 (1990): 319–324; Piskorski, "Deutsche Ostforschung und polnische Westforschung," in *Berliner Jahrbuch für osteuropäische Geschichte*, no. 1 (Festschrift Klaus Zernack) (1996): 379–389; Piskorski, "Z badań nad historiografią Europy Środkowej i Wschodniej," *Przegląd Historyczny* 91 (2000): 451–474; Piskorski, "Herbert Ludat (1910– 1993)—historyk Słowiańszczyzny Zachodniej i stosunków polsko-niemieckich," in *Herbert Ludat, Słowianie—Niemcy—Europa. Wybór prac*, trans. and ed. Jan M. Piskorski (Marburg, 2000), 325–354; Piskorski, "Die Reichsuniversität Posen (1941–1945)," *Nationalsozialismus in den Kulturwissenschaften*, ed. Hartmut Lehmann and Otto Gerhard Oexle (Göttingen, 2004), 241–270; Piskorski in cooperation with Jörg Hackmann and Rudolf Jaworski, eds., *Deutsche Ostforschung und polnische Westforschung im Spannungsfeld von Wissenschaft und Politik. Disziplinen im Vergleich* (Osnabrück, 2002). Because all of the works mentioned above have detailed notes, in the references for the present chapter I intentionally limit myself to citing works by the authors who are directly mentioned or quoted in my essay, to other works that are truly indispensable for understanding some particular fragment of my essay, or to some of my own works wherein the reader can find a fuller version of my argumentation.

2. Benedict Anderson, *Imagined Communities: Reflection on the Origin and Spread of Nation-alism* (London, 1983); Hagen Schulze, *Staat und Nation in der europäischen Geschichte*, 2nd ed. (Munich, 1995), 126ff., 172ff.; Stefan Berger, Mark Donovan, and Kevin Passmore, eds., *Writing National Histories: Western Europe since 1800* (London, 1999); and here especially Georg G. Iggers, "Nationalism and Historiography, 1789–1996: The German Example in Historical Perspective," in Berger, Donovan, and Passmore, *Writing National Histories*, 15–29.

3. Michael G. Müller, "Wie ethnisch war die Nation? Ethnizität in polnischen und deutschen nationalen Diskursen," *Tel Aviver Jahrbuch für deutsche Geschichte* 30 (2002): 104–115.

4. Jan M. Piskorski, "O legendzie dynastycznej Hohenzollernów," *Roczniki Historyczne* 62 (1996): 127–142; Piskorski, "After Occidentalism: The Third Europe Writes Its Own History," in *Historiographical Approaches to Medieval Colonization of East Central Europe: A Comparative Analysis Against the Background of Other European Inter-ethnic Colonization Processes in the Middle Ages*, ed. Jan M. Piskorski (New York, 2002), 7–23; Piskorski, "Preussen zwischen Deutschland und Polen," in *Preußen in Ostmitteleuropa. Geschehens-geschichte und Verstehensgeschichte*, ed. Matthias Weber (Munich, 2003), 63–82.

5. Jörg Hackmann, "Volks- und Kulturbodenkonzeptionen in der deutschen Ostfor-schung und ihre Wirkungen auf die Sudetendeutsche Landeshistorie," in *Die böhmischen Länder in der deutschen Geschichtsschreibung seit dem Jahre 1848*, part 1 (Ústí nad Labem, 1996), 49–71.

6. Jan M. Piskorski, "1000 Jahre der deutsch-polnischen Grenze," *Jahrbuch für die Geschichte Mittel- und Ostdeutschlands* 44 (1995): 137.

7. Elizabeth Harvey, "Die deutsche Frau im Osten: 'Rasse,' Geschlecht und öffentlicher Raum im besetzen Polen 1940–1944," *Archiv für Sozialgeschichte* 38 (1998): 191–214, esp. 205; Carsten Klingemann, "Ostforschung und Soziologie während des Nationalsozialis-mus," in Piskorski et al., *Deutsche Ostforschung und polnische Westforschung*, 161–203.

8. Jörg Hackmann, "Contemporary Baltic History and German *Ostforschung*, 1918–1945: Images and Notions," *Journal of Baltic Studies* 30, no. 4 (1999): 322–337; Hackmann, "Ethnos oder Region? Probleme der baltischen Historiographie im 20. Jahrhundert," *Zeitschrift für Ostmitteleuropa-Forschung* 50 (2001): 531–556; Hackmann, "*Volksgeschichte* als Konzept der Geschichtswissenschaft in Osteuropa? Anmerkungen zum Vergleich von Historiographien," unpub. MS. (I want to thank the author of this article for send-ing the manuscript and for the opportunity to discuss with him some important ques-tions concerning the *Volksgeschichte*.)

9. Alvydas Nikžentaitis, "Lithuanian Settlement in East Prussia as Reflected in Lithuanian Historiography," in Piskorski, *Historiographical Approaches*, 362f.

10. Jan Patočka, *Kim są Czesi?* trans. Jacek Baluch (Kraków, 1997), 79f.

11. Mircea Eliade, *Rumuni. Zarys historii*, trans. Anna Kaźmierczak (Bydgoszcz, 1997; 1st ed., 1943), 23f., 27.

12. Rudolf Jaworski, "Die polnische Westforschung zwischen Politik und Wissenschaft," in *Polen nach dem Kommunismus*, ed. Erwin Oberländer (Stuttgart, 1993), 94–104; Jaworski, "Deutsche Ostforschung und polnische Westforschung in ihren historisch-politischen Bezügen," in Piskorski et al., *Deutsche Ostforschung*, 11–23; Roland Gehrke, *Der polnische Westgedanke bis zur Wiedererrichtung des polnischen Staates nach Ende des Ersten Welt-krieges. Genese und Begründung polnischer Gebietsansprüche gegenüber Deutschland im Zeit-alter des europäischen Nationalismus* (Marburg, 2001).

13. Herbert Ludat, "Die polnische Geschichtswissenschaft. Entwicklung und Bedeutung" (1st ed., 1939), in Ludat, *Slaven und Deutsche im Mittelalter. Ausgewählte Aufsätze zu Fra-gen ihrer politischen, sozialen und kulturellen Beziehungen* (Cologne, 1982), 174.

14. Andrzej Feliks Grabski, *Zarys historii historiografii polskiej* (Poznań, 2000), 165–184.

15. Müller, "Wie ethnisch war die Nation?"

16. Antoni Chołoniewski, *Dyalog o Polsce i "małych narodach"* (Kraków, 1920), 25, 30, 33, 47.

17. Michael Burleigh, "Albert Brackmann, Ostforscher: The Years of Retirement," in Bur-leigh, *Ethics and Extermination: Reflections on Nazi Genocide* (Cambridge, 1997), 25–36.

18. Jörg Hackmann, "Strukturen und Institutionen der polnischen Westforschung (1918–1960)," *Zeitschrift für Ostmitteleuropa-Forschung* 50 (2001): 230–255, esp. 233ff., 230, 239, 251.

19. Willi Oberkrome, *Volksgeschichte. Methodische Innovation und völkische Ideologisierung in der deutschen Geschichtswissenschaft 1918–1945* (Göttingen, 1993); Michael Fahlbusch, "Friedrich Ratzel—ein Begründer der Kulturwissenschaften?" in *Geisteshaltung und Stadtgestaltung. Referate gehalten auf dem Geographentag in Potsdam 1995*, ed. Manfred Büttner (Frankfurt am Main, 1997), 273–312; Hackmann, "Volksgeschichte."

20. Hannah Arendt, *Eichmann w Jerozolimie. Rzecz o banalności zła*, trans. Adam Szostkiewicz (Kraków, 1998), 51.

21. Albert Kotowski, *Hitlers Bewegung im Urteil der polnischen Nationaldemokratie* (Wiesbaden, 2000), 200ff. for Dmowski, 224ff. for Giertych.

22. Markus Krzoska, *Zygmunt Wojciechowski (1900–1955) als Historiker und Publizist* (Ph.D. diss., Freie Universität Berlin, 2001), 242n., 245, 254, 264 (in manuscript). The work has since been published as *Für ein Polen an Oder und Ostsee: Zygmunt Wojciechowski (1900–1955) als Historiker und Publizist* (Osnabrück, 2003).

23. Iggers, "Nationalism and Historiography," 21.

24. Krzoska, *Zygmunt Wojciechowski*, 191.

25. Karol Stojanowski, *Polsko-niemieckie zagadnienie rasy* (Katowice: Księgarnia i Drukarnia Katolicka (without year but 1939), 56n, 73n, 77.

SELECTED BIBLIOGRAPHY

+ + +

Published Sources

Akten zur deutschen auswärtigen Politik 1918–1945. Aus dem Archiv des Auswärtigen Amtes. Series E (December 1941–1945). Vol. 6 (1 May to 30 September 1943). Göttingen, 1969.

Alto Adige. Eine offiziöse italienische Tendenzschrift über Südtirol. Kritische Anmerkungen zum italienischen Faksimilewerk "Alto Adige. Alcuni documenti del passato, 3 Bände, Bergamo 1942." Ed. Franz Huter, Karl M. Mayr, Alfred Quellmalz, Josef Ringler, Walter Senn, and Otto Stolz, n.p. Innsbruck, 1943.

Aubin, Hermann. "Zu den Schriften Erich Keysers." In *Studien zur Geschichte des Preußenlandes. Festschrift für Erich Keyser zu seinem 70. Geburtstag,* ed. Ernst Bahr, 1–11. Marburg, 1963.

Bobek, Hans. "Das Judentum im osteuropäischen Raum. Betrachtungen zu dem gleichnamigen Werk von P. H. Seraphim." *Deutsches Archiv für Landes- und Volksforschung* 3 (1939): 697706.

———. "Um die deutsche Volksgrenze in den Alpen." *Deutsches Archiv für Landes- und Volksforschung* 1 (1937): 734–748.

Boehm, Max Hildebert. *Das eigenständige Volk. Grundlegung der Elemente einer europäischen Völkersoziologie.* Göttingen, 1932.

Braun, Fritz. "Im Blutstrom Deines Volkes." *Heimatbrief aus der Westmark* 4 (1942): 9–10.

———. "1. Arbeitsbericht der Mittelstelle Saarpfalz in Kaiserslautern von der Gründung am 15. Oktober 1936 bis zum 1. April 1938." *Unsere Heimat: Blätter für saarpfälzisches Volkstum* (1937/38): 257–259.

———. "Batschkafahrt 1937." *Unsere Heimat: Blätter für saarländisch-pfälzisches Volkstum* (1936/37): 353–359.

———, ed. *Wir schaffen im Glauben an Deutschland: Umsiedler aus dem Osten schreiben an ihre westmärkische Heimat.* Kaiserslautern, 1941.

Burgdörfer, Friedrich."Die rumänische Volkszählung." *Allgemeines Statistisches Archiv,* Bd. 30, Heft III (1941/42): 302–322.

Carstanjen, Helmut. *See Werner, Gerhard*

Dinklage, Karl. *Frühdeutsche Volkskultur in Kärnten und seinen Marken.* Ljubljana, 1943.

———. "Frühdeutsche Volkskulturen im Spiegel der Bodenfunde von Untersteiermark und Krain." *Mitteilungen der anthropologischen Gesellschaft Wien* 71 (1941): 235–259.

———. "Oberkrains Deutschtum im Spiegel der karolingischen Bodenfunde." *Carinthia I* 131 (1941): 360–391.

Dokumentation der Vertreibung der Deutschen. Published by the Federal Expellee Ministry [Bundesvertriebenenministerium]. Chief editor Theodor Schieder, in association [*Verbindung*] with Hans Rothfels, Peter Rassow, and Rudolf Laun, and beginning with vol. 3 also Werner Conze. 7 vols., Berlin, 1953–1960.

Generalstab des Heeres/Abteilung für Kriegskarten und Vermessungswesen, ed. *Militär-geographische Beschreibung von Jugoslawien.* Text- und Bildheft. Berlin, 1940.

Glauert, Günter. *Siedlungsgeographie von Oberkrain.* Ph.D. diss., University of Munich, 1943.

———. *Istrien: Raum, Geschichte, Bevölkerungsaufbau.* Kranj, 1943.

———. "Kulturlandschaftliche Veränderungen im Gebirgslande zwischen Drau und Sawe bis zum Beginn der deutschen Südostsiedlung." *Südost-Forschungen* 7 (1942): 9–52.

———. "Grundherrschaftsbesitz und Rodung im karantanisch-altkrainischen Grenzgebiet." *Südost-Forschungen* 5 (1940): 864–943.

———. "Ein Kärntner Grenzmarkt in den Karawanken im 17. und 18. Jahrhundert." *Südost-Forschungen* 4 (1939): 643–683.

———. "Landschaftsbild und Siedlungsgang in einem Abschnitt der südöstlichen Kalkalpen (Ostkarawanken und Steiner Alpen) und seinen Randgebieten." *Südost-Forschungen* 3 (1938): 457–524.

———. "Zur Besiedlung der Steiner Alpen und Ostkarawanken (das Gebiet Freibach, Kanker, Sann und Mieß)." *Deutsches Archiv für Landes- und Volksforschung* 1 (1937): 457–486.

———. *Die Entwicklung der Kulturlandschaft in den Steiner Alpen und Ostkarawanken.* Ph.D. diss., University of Graz, 1936.

Graber, Georg. "Volkskundliches." In *Oberkrain,* ed. Viktor Paschinger, Martin Wutte, and Georg Graber, 67–95. Kranj, 1942.

Hainzl, Sepp. "Südmärkischer Bauernwall vom Großglockner bis zur Pußta." *Odal* 8 (1939): 173–176.

Hassinger, Hugo. "Die Ostmark." *Raumforschung und Raumordnung* 2 (1938): 391–397.

Haufe, Helmut. "Zur bevölkerungsgeschichtlichen Forschung." *Archiv für Bevölkerungswissenschaft und Bevölkerungspolitik* 8 (1938): 277.

Haushofer, Karl. *Grenzen in ihrer geographischen und politischen Bedeutung.* Berlin, 1927.

Huter, Franz. "Geburtstagsansprache gehalten am 22. Mai 1946 bei der Feier der Schüler (Hermann Wopfners) im Rahmen der Universität." In *Beiträge zur Geschichte und Heimatkunde Tirols. Festschrift zu Ehren Hermann Wopfners* 1, 7–11. Innsbruck, 1947.

Ibler, Hermann. *Des Reiches Südgrenze in der Steiermark. Vergewaltigtes Selbstbestimmungsrecht.* Graz, 1940.

International Military Tribunal. *Trial of the Major War Criminals.* Nuremberg, 1947–1949 [in German].

Kaup, Ignaz. "Die Alpenbewohner im Wandel der Rassensystematik." *Zeitschrift des Deutschen Alpenvereins* 73 (1942): 31–45.

Keyser, Erich. "Die Erforschung der Bevölkerungsgeschichte." *Studium Generale* 9 (1956): 495–500.

———. "Die Historische Kommission für ost- und westpreußische Landesforschung." *Zeitschrift für Ostforschung* 1 (1952): 525–529.

———. *Die Geschichte des deutschen Weichsellandes.* Leipzig, 1939.

———. *Bevölkerungsgeschichte Deutschlands.* Leipzig, 1938. [2nd ed. Leipzig, 1941; 3rd rev. ed. Leipzig, 1943]

———. "Bevölkerungsgeschichtliche Forschungen im Staatlichen Landesmuseum für Danziger Geschichte." *Archiv für Bevölkerungswissenschaft und Bevölkerungspolitik* 8 (1938): 48f.

———. "Neue Forschungen über die Bevölkerungsgeschichte Deutschlands." *Vierteljahrschrift für Sozial- und Wirtschaftsgeschichte* 29 (1936): 45–62.

———. "Rassenforschung und Geschichtsforschung." *Archiv für Bevölkerungswissenschaft und Bevölkerungspolitik* 5 (1935): 1–8.

———. "Bevölkerungswissenschaft und Geschichtsforschung." *Archiv für Bevölkerungswissenschaft und Bevölkerungspolitik* 5 (1935): 145–161.

———. "Die Zeitalter der Bevölkerungsgeschichte Deutschlands." *Archiv für Bevölkerungswissenschaft und Bevölkerungspolitik* 4 (1934): 147–157.

———. *Die Geschichtswissenschaft, Aufbau und Aufgaben.* Munich, 1931.

———. "Die Entwicklung der landesgeschichtlichen Forschung in Ost- und Westpreußen." *Mitteilungen des Grenzmarkdienstes Posen-Westpreußen*, 14 April 1929.

Klebelsberg, Raimund von. *Innsbrucker Erinnerungen 1902–1952*. Innsbruck, 1953.

Kranzmayer, Eberhard. *Die deutschen Lehnwörter in der slowenischen Volkssprache*. Ljubljana, 1944.

———. "Der bairische Sprachraum." *Jahrbuch der deutschen Sprache* 2 (1944): 169–180.

———. *Das Volk der Friauler*. Klagenfurt, 1943.

———. "Deutsches Sprachgut jenseits der Sprachgrenze in den Alpen, mit besonderer Rücksicht auf das Rätoromanische des Grödnertales." *Deutsches Archiv für Landes- und Volksforschung* 1 (1937): 273–286.

Maier-Kaibitsch, Alois. "Reichsdeutsche Siedler in Kärnten." *Die Welt. Zeitschrift für das Deutschtum im Ausland* 10 (1933): 690–692.

Maier-Kaibitsch, Alois, and Helmut Carstanjen. "Die verstümmelten Grenzen." *Zeitschrift für Geopolitik* 8 (1931): 54–63.

Manuilă, Sabin. "Das Judenproblem in Rumänien zahlenmäßig gesehen." *Deutsches Archiv für Landes- und Volksforschung* 5 (1941): 603–613.

———. *Studies on the Historical Demography of Romania/Études sur la démographie historique de la Roumanie*. Ed. Sorina and Ioan Bolovan, 7–17. The Romanian Cultural Foundation. Cluj-Napoca, 1992.

Metz, Friedrich. "Von den Lebensgrundlagen deutschen Volkstums in Südtirol." *Zeitwende* 8 (1932): 211–219.

Neunteufl, Walter. *Die bevölkerungspolitische Lage der Steiermark im Kriege*. Graz, 1943.

———. "Blutmäßige Bevölkerungsverschiebungen im deutsch-slowenisch-madjarischen Grenzraum." *Blätter für Heimatkunde*, ed. Historischer Verein für Steiermark 4 (1939): 57–66.

Paschinger, Viktor. "Land und Wirtschaft." In *Oberkrain*, ed. Viktor Paschinger, Martin Wutte, and Georg Graber, 7–35. Kranj, 1942.

Pirchegger, Hans. "Das Volkstum der untersteirischen Städte und Märkte." *Südost-Forschungen* 1 (1936): 26–30.

Ravanelli, M(arius) W. "Die Herzogswahl im Fleimstal." *Alpenheimat. Familienkalender für Stadt und Land* (1945): 63–65.

Ritter, Gerhard. "Deutsche Geschichtswissenschaft im 20. Jahrhundert." *Geschichte in Wissenschaft und Unterricht* 1 (1950): 81–86, 129–137.

———. "Der deutsche Professor im Dritten Reich." *Die Gegenwart* 1, no. 1 (24 December 1945): 23–26.

Rothfels, Hans. "Deutsche Geschichtswissenschaft in den 30er Jahren." In *Deutsches Geistesleben und Nationalsozialismus*, ed. Andreas Flitner, 90–107. Tübingen, 1965.

———. *The German Opposition Against Hitler: A Reappraisal* (Hinsdale, Ill., 1948).

———. *Ostraum, Preußentum und Reichsgedanke. Historische Abhandlungen, Vorträge und Reden*. Leipzig, 1935.

Routil, Robert. *Völker und Rassen auf dem Boden Kärntens*. Klagenfurt, 1937.

Rudolph, Martin Viktor. *Die nordisch-germanischen Volkskräfte im südlichen Alpenraum. Ihre Entstehung und ihre Kulturzeugen in Landschaft und Siedlung*. N.p., 1944.

Sattler, Wilhelm. *Die deutsche Volksgruppe im unabhängigen Staat Kroatien. Ein Buch vom Deutschtum in Slawonien, Syrmien und Bosnien*. Graz, 1943.

———. *Die Untersteiermark. Eine Darstellung der bevölkerungspolitischen und wirtschaftlichen Grundlagen. Mit einem Beitrag von Helmut Carstanjen, einer Karte im Maßstab 1:300.000 von Walter Neunteufl sowie weiteren 15 Karten und 17 Tabellen*. Graz, 1942.

Schieder, Theodor. *Deutscher Geist und ständische Freiheit im Weichsellande. Politische Ideen und politisches Schrifttum in Westpreußen von der Lubliner Union bis zu den polnischen Teilungen (1569–1772/93)*. Königsberg, 1940.

Schmidt, Max, and Walter Neumann. "Eine Karte der steirischen Sprachgrenze." *Deutsches Archiv für Landes- und Volksforschung* 1 (1937): 720–733.

Starzacher, Karl. "Oberkrain—deutscher Kulturboden." *Deutsche Volkskunde. Vierteljahresschrift der Arbeitsgemeinschaft für deutsche Volkskunde* 5 (1943): 69–71.

Steinacher, Hans. *Bundesleiter des VDA 1933–1937: Erinnerungen und Dokumente.* Ed. Hans-Adolf Jacobsen. Boppard, 1970.

Steinbach, Franz. *Studien zur westdeutschen Stammes- und Volksgeschichte.* Jena, 1926.

Stolz, Otto. *Die Ausbreitung des Deutschtums in Südtirol im Lichte der Urkunden.* Vol. 4. Munich and Berlin, 1934.

———. "Geschichtliche Folgerungen aus Orts-, insbesondere Hofnamen im Bereiche Tirols." *Zeitschrift für Ortsnamenforschung* 7 (1931): 55–75, 152–159.

———. "Tirol als deutsche Südmark." *Mitteilungen des Deutschen und Österreichischen Alpenvereins* 51 (1925): 208–210.

Straka, Manfred. "Marburg." In *Handwörterbuch des Grenz- und Auslanddeutschtums*, vol. 3, ed. Carl Petersen, Otto Scheel, Paul Hermann Ruth, and Hans Schwalm, 476–481. Breslau, 1938.

Straka, Manfred, and Walter Neunteufl. *Die Entwicklung des Volksbekenntnisses in Kärnten nach den Ergebnissen der amtlichen Volkszählungen 1923 und 1924.* Graz, 1941.

Trampler, Kurt. "Deutsche Grenzen." *Zeitschrift für Geopolitik* 11 (1934): 15–71.

Ungern-Sternberg, Roderich v. Besprechung zu E. Keysers "Bevölkerungsgeschichte Deutschlands." 3rd ed. *Allgemeines Statistisches Archiv* 32 (1943/44): 172f.

Volz, Wilhelm, ed. *Der ostdeutsche Volksboden. Aufsätze zu den Fragen des Ostens.* Breslau, 1926.

Werner, Gerhard [pseudonym: Helmut Carstanjen]. *Sprache und Volkstum in der Untersteiermark.* Stuttgart, 1935.

Winkler, Wilhelm. *Statistisches Handbuch des gesamten Deutschtums* [Statistical Handbook of the Global Germandom]. Edited under the auspices of the Stiftung für deutsche Volks- und Kulturbodenforschung in Leipzig, in association with the Deutschen Statistischen Gesellschaft. Berlin, 1927.

Wopfner, Hermann. *Deutsche Siedlungsarbeit in Südtirol.* Innsbruck, 1926.

———. "Tirols Eroberung durch deutsche Arbeit." *Tiroler Heimat* 1 (1921): 5–38.

———. "Die Einheit Deutschtirols." In *Denkschrift des akademischen Senats der Universität Innsbruck*, 1–38. Innsbruck, 1918.

SECONDARY LITERATURE

Achim, Viorel. "The Romanian Population Exchange Project Elaborated by Sabin Manuilă in October 1941." *Annali dell'Istituto storico italo-germanico in Trento/Jahrbuch des italienisch-deutschen Instituts in Trient* 27 (2001): 593–617.

Aly, Götz. "Theodor Schieder, Werner Conze oder Die Vorstufen der physischen Vernichtung." In *Deutsche Historiker im Nationalsozialismus*, ed. Winfried Schulze and Otto Gerhard Oexle, 163–182. Frankfurt am Main, 1999.

———. "The Planning Intelligentsia and the Final Solution." In *Confronting the Nazi Past: New Debates on Modern German History*, ed. Michael Burleigh, 140–153. New York, 1996.

Aly, Götz, and Susanne Heim. *Vordenker der Vernichtung. Auschwitz und die deutschen Pläne für eine neue europäische Ordnung.* Frankfurt am Main, 1992. English: *Architects of Destruction: Auschwitz and the Logic of Destruction.* Princeton, 2002.

———. *Auschwitz und die Pläne für eine neue europäische Ordnung.* Frankfurt am Main, 1991.

Aly, Götz, and Karl Heinz Roth. *Die restlose Erfassung. Volkszählen, Identifizieren, Aussondern im Nationalsozialismus.* Berlin, 1984.

Ancel, Jean. *Transnistria, 1941–1942: The Romanian Mass Murder Campaigns.* Vol. 1. Jerusalem, 2003.

Angrick, Andrej. *Die Einsatzgruppe D. Struktur und Tätigkeiten einer mobilen Einheit der Sicherheitspolizei und des SD in der deutsch besetzten Sowjetunion.* Hamburg, 2004.

Ashkenas, Bruce F. "A Legacy of Hatred: The Records of a Nazi Organization in America." *Prologue* 17 (1985): 93–106.

Assion, Peter, and Peter Schwinn. "Migration, Politik und Volkskunde 1940/43. Zur Tätigkeit des SS-Ahnenerbes in Südtirol." *Kulturkontakt/Kulturkonflikt* 1 (1988): 221–226.

Bahr, Ernst. "Nachruf auf Erich Keyser." *Zeitschrift für Ostforschung* 17 (1968): 288–291.

Banach, Jens. *Heydrichs Elite. Das Führerkorps der Sicherheitspolizei und des SD 1936–1945.* Paderborn et al., 1996.

Beer, Mathias. "Das Großforschungsprojekt 'Dokumentation der Vertreibung der Deutschen aus Ostmitteleuropa.'" *Vierteljahreshefte für Zeitgeschichte* 3, no. 46 (1998): 345–389.

Beer, Mathias, and Gerhard Seewann, eds. *Südostforschung im Schatten des Dritten Reiches: Institutionen, Inhalte, Personen.* Munich, 2004.

Berg, Nicolas. *Der Holocaust und die westdeutschen Historiker. Erforschung und Erinnerung.* Göttingen, 2003.

Berthold, Werner. "*... großhungern und gehorchen ...*" *Zur Entwicklung und politischer Funktion des westdeutschen Imperialismus untersucht am Beispiel von Gerhard Ritter und Friedrich Meinecke.* Berlin, 1960.

Białkowski, Błażej. "Deutsche Historiker im nationalsozialistisch besetzten Posen (1939–1945)." *Inter Finitimos* 17/18 (2000): n.p.

Bockhorn, Olaf. "Wiener Volkskunde." In *Volkskunde im Nationalsozialismus*, ed. Helge Gerndt, 229–237. Munich, 1987.

———. "Volkskundliche Filme des SS-Ahnenerbes in Südtirol." In *Südtirol im Auge des Ethnographen*, ed. Reinhard Johler, Ludwig Paulmichl, and Barbara Plankensteiner, 105–135. Vienna and Lana, 1991.

Botsch, Gideon. "Geheime Ostforschung im SD. Zur Entstehungsgeschichte und Tätigkeit des Wannsee-Instituts 1935–1945." *Zeitschrift für Geschichtswissenschaft* 48, no. 6 (2000): 509–524.

Brocke, Bernhard vom. *Bevölkerungswissenschaft Quo vadis? Möglichkeiten und Probleme einer Geschichte der Bevölkerungswissenschaft in Deutschland.* Opladen, 1998.

Broszat, Martin. *Zweihundert Jahre deutsche Polenpolitik.* Frankfurt am Main, 1972.

Buchsweiler, Meir. *Volksdeutsche in der Ukraine am Vorabend und Beginn des Zweiten Weltkriegs—ein Fall doppelter Loyalität?* Gerlingen, 1984.

Burleigh, Michael. *Germany Turns Eastwards: A Study of Ostforschung in the Third Reich.* Cambridge, 1988.

———. "Albert Brackmann (1871–1952), Ostforscher: The Years of Retirement." *Journal of Contemporary History* 23 (1988): 573–588.

Carl, Viktor. *Lexikon der Pfälzer Persönlichkeiten.* Preface by Helmut Kohl. Edenkoben, 1995.

Cole, Laurence. "Fern von Europa? Zu den Eigentümlichkeiten Tiroler Geschichtsschreibung." *Geschichte und Region/Storia e regione* 5 (1996): 191–225.

Conte, Edouard, and Cornelia Essner. *La quête de la race: Une anthropologie du nazisme.* Paris, 1995.

Conze, Werner. *Polnische Nation und deutsche Politik im Ersten Weltkrieg.* Cologne and Graz, 1958.

Dachs, Herbert. *Österreichische Geschichtswissenschaft und Anschluß.* Vienna and Salzburg, 1974.

Derks, Hans. *Deutsche Westforschung. Ideologie und Praxis im 20. Jahrhundert.* Leipzig, 2001.

Ditt, Karl. "Die Kulturraumforschung zwischen Wissenschaft und Politik. Das Beispiel Franz Petri (1903–1993)." *Westfälische Forschungen* 46 (1996): 73–176.

Döscher, Hans-Jürgen. *SS und Auswärtiges Amt im Dritten Reich: Diplomatie im Schatten der "Endlösung."* Frankfurt am Main, 1991.

Ebbinghaus, Angelika, and Karl Heinz Roth. "Vorläufer des 'Generalplans Ost.' Eine Dokumentation über Theodor Schieders Polendenkschrift vom 7. Oktober 1939." *1999. Zeitschrift für Sozialgeschichte des 20. und 21. Jahrhunderts* 7 (1992): 62–94.

Eley, Geoff. *Reshaping the German Right.* Ann Arbor, 1990.

Ernst, Robert. *Rechenschaftsbericht eines Elsässers.* 2nd ed. Berlin, 1955.

Esch, Michael G. *"Gesunde Verhältnisse." Deutsche und polnische Bevölkerungspolitik in Ostmitteleuropa 1939–1950.* Marburg, 1998.

Etzemüller, Thomas. *Sozialgeschichte als politische Geschichte. Werner Conze und die Neuorientierung der westdeutschen Geschichtswissenschaft nach 1945.* Munich, 2001.

Fahlbusch, Michael. *Wissenschaft im Dienst der nationalsozialistischen Politik? Die "Volksdeutschen Forschungsgemeinschaften" von 1931–1945.* Baden-Baden, 1999.

———. "Die Alpenländische Forschungsgemeinschaft—eine Brückenbauerin des großdeutschen Gedankens?" In *Grenzraum Alpenrhein: Brücken und Barrieren 1914 bis 1938,* ed. Robert Allgäuer, 137–233. Zürich, 1999.

———. *"Wo der deutsche ... ist, ist Deutschland!" Die Stiftung für deutsche Volks- und Kulturbodenforschung in Leipzig 1920–1933.* Bochum, 1994.

Ferenc, Tone. *Quellen zur nationalsozialistischen Entnationalisierungspolitik in Slowenien 1941–1945/Viri o nacistični raznarodovalni politiki v Sloveniji 1941–1945.* Maribor, 1980.

———. *Nacistična raznarodovalna politika v Sloveniji v letih 1941–1945.* Maribor, 1968.

———. "Le système d'occupation des Nazis en Slovénie." In *Les systèmes d'occupation en Yougoslavie 1941–1945. Rapports au 3e Congrès international sur l'histoire de la Résistance européenne à Karlovy Vary, les 2–4 septembre 1963,* 47–133. Belgrade, 1963.

Fischer, Fritz. *Griff nach der Weltmacht.* Düsseldorf, 1962.

Fleischhauer, Ingeborg. *Das Dritte Reich und die Deutschen in der Sowjetunion.* Stuttgart, 1983.

Fleischhauer, Ingeborg, and Benjamin Pinkus. *Die Deutschen in der Sowjetunion: Geschichte einer nationalen Minderheit im 20. Jahrhundert.* Baden-Baden, 1987. English: *The Soviet Germans: Past and Present.* Trans. Edith Rogovin Frankel. New York, 1986.

Flügel, Axel. "Ambivalente Innovation. Anmerkungen zur Volksgeschichte." *Geschichte und Gesellschaft* 26 (2000): 653–671.

Fontana, Josef, ed. *Südtirol und der italienische Nationalismus. Entstehung und Entwicklung einer europäischen Minderheitenfrage, quellenmäßig dargestellt von Walter Freiberg* [i.e., Kurt Heinricher]. Part 1: *Darstellung.* Innsbruck, 1989.

Fritzl, Martin. *'... für Volk und Reich und deutsche Kultur.' Die 'Kärntner Wissenschaft' im Dienste des Nationalismus.* Klagenfurt, 1992.

Gehrke, Roland. *Der polnische Westgedanke bis zur Wiedererrichtung des polnischen Staates nach Ende des Ersten Weltkrieges. Genese und Begründung polnischer Gebietsansprüche gegenüber Deutschland im Zeitalter des europäischen Nationalismus.* Marburg, 2001.

Geiss, Imanuel. *Der polnische Grenzstreifen 1914–1918.* Lübeck and Hamburg, 1960.

Geißler, Karl-Friedrich, Jürgen Müller, and Roland Paul, eds. *Das große Pfalzbuch.* 7th rev. ed. Landau, 1995.

Gerlach, Christian. *Kalkulierte Morde. Die deutsche Wirtschafts- und Vernichtungspolitik in Weissrussland 1941 bis 1944.* Hamburg, 1999.

Grabski, Andrzej Feliks. *Zarys historii historiografii polskiej.* Poznań, 2000.

———. *Dzieje historiografii.* Ed. and with an introduction by Rafał Stobiecki. Poznań, 2003.

Grundmann, Karl-Heinz. *Deutschtumspolitik zur Zeit der Weimarer Republik. Eine Studie am Beispiel der deutsch-baltischen Minderheit in Estland und Lettland.* Berlin, 1975.

Haar, Ingo. *Historiker im Nationalsozialismus. Deutsche Geschichtswissenschaft und der 'Volkstumskampf' im Osten.* Göttingen, 2000.

———. "Deutsche 'Ostforschung' und Antisemitismus." *Zeitschrift für Geschichtswissenschaft* 48, no. 6 (2000): 485–508.

———. "'Ostforschung' und 'Lebensraum'-Politik im Nationalsozialismus." In *Geschichte der Kaiser-Wilhelm-Gesellschaft. Vol. 1–2,* ed. Reinhard Rürup and Wolfgang Schieder. Vol. 2: *Bestandsaufnahme und Perspektiven der Forschung,* ed. Doris Kaufmann, 437–467. Göttingen, 2000.

———. "Quellenkritik oder Kritik der Quellen." *Vierteljahrshefte für Zeitgeschichte* 50 (2002): 497–506.

———. "Der 'Generalplan Ost' als Forschungsproblem: Wissenslücken und Perspektiven." In *Wissenschaft und Wissenschaftspolitik. Bestandaufnahmen zu Formationen, Brüchen und Kontinuitäten im Deutschland des 20. Jahrhunderts,* ed. Rüdiger vom Bruch and Brigitte Kaderas, 362–368. Stuttgart, 2002.

———. "'Volksgeschichte' und Königsberger Milieu. Forschungsprogramme zwischen Weimarer Revisionspolitik und nationalsozialistischer Vernichtungsplanung." In *Nationalsozialismus in den Kulturwissenschaften*, vol. 1: *Fächer—Milieus—Karrieren*, ed. Hartmut Lehmann and Otto Gerhard Oexle, 169–210. Göttingen, 2004.

Hackmann, Jörg. "Ethnos oder Region? Probleme der baltischen Historiographie im 20. Jahrhundert." *Zeitschrift für Ostmitteleuropa-Forschung* 50 (2001): 25–63.

———. "Deutsche Ostforschung und Antisemitismus." *Zeitschrift für Geschichtswissenschaft* 48 (2000): 485–508.

———. "Contemporary Baltic History and German *Ostforschung*, 1918–1945: Images and Notions." *Journal of Baltic Studies* 30, no. 4 (1999): 531–556.

———. "'An einem neuen Anfang der Ostforschung.' Bruch und Kontinuität in der ostdeutschen Landeshistorie nach dem Zweiten Weltkrieg." *Westfälische Forschungen* 46 (1996): 232–258.

———. *Ostpreußen und Westpreußen in deutscher und polnischer Sicht. Landeshistorie als beziehungsgeschichtliches Problem.* Wiesbaden, 1996.

Hammerstein, Notker. *Die Deutsche Forschungsgemeinschaft in der Weimarer Republik und im Dritten Reich.* Munich, 1999.

Harriman, Helga H. *Slovenia under Nazi occupation, 1941–1945.* New York, 1977.

Hausmann, Frank-Rutger. *"Auch im Krieg schweigen die Musen nicht." Die Deutschen Wissenschaftlichen Institute im Zweiten Weltkrieg.* 2nd ed. Göttingen, 2002.

Heinz, Joachim. *"Bleibe im Lande und nähre dich redlich!" Zur Geschichte der pfälzischen Auswanderung vom Ende des 17. bis zum Ausgang des 19. Jahrhunderts.* Kaiserslautern, 1989.

Herb, Guntram H. *Under the Map of Germany: Nationalism and Propaganda 1918–1945.* London and New York, 1997.

Herf, Jeffrey. *Divided Memory: The Nazi Past in the Two Germanys.* Cambridge, Mass., 1997.

Heuss, Anja. *Kunst- und Kulturgutraub. Eine vergleichende Studie zur Besatzungspolitik der Nationalsozialisten in Frankreich und der Sowjetunion.* Heidelberg, 1999.

Hiegel, Henri. "La germanisation et la nazification de la vie culturelle du département de la Moselle sous l'occupation allemande de 1940 à 1944." *Mémoires de l'Académie Nationale de Metz* 11, no. 6 (1983): 99–109.

Hilberg, Raul, ed. *The Destruction of the European Jews.* Rev. ed. Vol. 1. New York and London, 1985.

Hoensch, Jörg K. "Hitlers 'Neue Ordnung Europas': Grenzveränderungen, Staatsneugründungen, nationale Diskriminierung." In *Der nationalsozialistische Krieg*, ed. Norbert Frei and Hermann Kling, 238–254. Frankfurt am Main, 1990.

Hornung, Herwig, ed. *Verzeichnis der Schriften von Eberhard Kranzmayer, als Festgabe zu seinem sechzigsten Geburtstag dargebracht von seinen Wiener Freunden und Mitarbeitern.* Vienna, 1957.

Horowitz, Donald L. *Ethnic Groups in Conflict.* Berkeley, 1985.

Hutchinson, John, and Anthony D. Smith. "Introduction." In *Ethnicity*, ed. John Hutchinson and Anthony D. Smith, 1–18. Oxford, 1996.

Iggers, Georg G. "Nationalism and Historiography, 1789–1996: The German Example in Historical Perspective." In *Writing National Histories: Western Europe since 1800*, ed. Stefan Berger, Mark Donovan, and Kevin Passmore, 15–29. London, 1999.

———. *Geschichtswissenschaft im 20. Jahrhundert. Ein kritischer Überblick im internationalen Zusammenhang.* Göttingen, 1993.

———. "Geschichtswissenschaft in Deutschland und Frankreich 1830 bis 1918 und die Rolle der Sozialgeschichte. Ein Vergleich zwischen zwei Traditionen bürgerlicher Geschichtsschreibung." In *Bürgertum im Vergleich*, vol. 3, ed. Jürgen Kocka, 175–199. Munich, 1988.

———. *New Directions in European Historiography.* Middletown, 1975.

———. *Deutsche Geschichtswissenschaft. Eine Kritik der traditionellen Geschichtsauffassung von Herder bis zur Gegenwart.* Munich, 1971.

"Institute for Palatine History and Folklife Studies." In *Pfälzer in Amerika/Palatines in America*, ed. Roland Paul, 247–279. Kaiserslautern, 1995.

Jachomowski, Dirk. *Die Umsiedlung der Bessarabien-, Bukowina- und Dobrudschadeutschen: Von der Volksgruppe in Rumänien zur "Siedlungsbrücke" an der Reichsgrenze.* Munich, 1984.

Jäckel, Eberhard. *Frankreich in Hitlers Europa: Die deutsche Frankreichpolitik im Zweiten Weltkrieg.* Stuttgart, 1966.

Jäger, Ludwig. *Seitenwechsel. Der Fall Schneider/Schwerte und die Diskretion der Germanistik.* Munich, 1998.

Jakubowski-Tiessen, Manfred. "Kulturpolitik im besetzten Land. Das Deutsche Wissenschaftliche Institut in Kopenhagen 1941 bis 1945." *Zeitschrift für Geschichtswissenschaft* 42, no. 2 (1994): 129–138.

Jaworski, Rudolf. "Die polnische Westforschung zwischen Politik und Wissenschaft." In *Polen nach dem Kommunismus*, ed. Erwin Oberländer. Stuttgart, 1993.

———. "Deutsche Ostforschung und polnische Westforschung in ihren historisch-politischen Bezügen." In *Deutsche Ostforschung und polnische Westforschung im Spannungsfeld von Wissenschaft und Politik. Disziplinen im Vergleich*, ed. Jan M. Piskorski, Jörg Hackmann, and Rudolf Jaworski, 11–24. Osnabrück and Poznań, 2000.

Johler, Reinhard. "Il concetto scientifico di 'deutsche Arbeit' e l'ergologia nell'area alpina." *Annali di San Michele. Rivista annuale del Museo degli Usi e Costumi della Gente Trentina di San Michele all'Adige* 8 (1995): 265–286.

Karner, Stefan. "Der Plan einer geschlossenen Umsiedlung der Grödner in die Steiermark 1941." *Zeitschrift des Historischen Vereins für die Steiermark* 69 (1978): 113–123.

———, ed. *Die Stabsbesprechungen der NS-Zivilverwaltung in der Untersteiermark 1941–1944.* Graz, 1996.

Kater, Michael H. *Das 'Ahnenerbe' der SS 1935–1945. Ein Beitrag zur Kulturpolitik des Dritten Reiches.* Munich, 2001.

Katz, Barry M. *Foreign Intelligence: Research and Analysis in the Office of Strategic Services 1942–1945.* Cambridge, 1989.

Keddigkeit, Jürgen. "Institut für pfälzische Geschichte und Volkskunde in Kaiserslautern." In *Das Landesarchiv Speyer: Festschrift zur Übergabe des Neubaues*, ed. Karl Heinz Debus, 251–253. Koblenz, 1987.

Kittel, Manfred. "Preußens Osten in der Zeitgeschichte. Mehr als nur eine landeshistorische Forschungslücke." *Vierteljahrshefte für Zeitgeschichte* 50 (2002): 435–463.

Klemperer, Klemens von. "Hans Rothfels (1891–1976)." In *Paths of Continuity: Central European Historiography for the 1930s to the 1950s*, ed. Hartmut Lehmann and James van Horn Melton, 119–135. Cambridge and New York, 1995.

Kleßmann, Christoph. "Osteuropaforschung und Lebensraumpolitik im Dritten Reich." In *Wissenschaft im Dritten Reich*, ed. Peter Lundgren, 350–383. Frankfurt am Main, 1985.

———. "Osteuropaforschung und Lebensraumpolitik im Dritten Reich." *Aus Politik und Zeitgeschichte* B7 (1984): n.p.

Klinkhammer, Lutz. *Zwischen Bündnis und Besatzung. Das nationalsozialistische Deutschland und die Republik von Salò 1943–1945.* Tübingen, 1993.

Köllmann, Wolfgang. "Bevölkerungsgeschichte." In *Sozialgeschichte in Deutschland*, vol. 2, ed. Wolfgang Schieder and Volker Sellin, 9–31. Göttingen, 1986.

Komjathy, Anthony, and Rebecca Stockwell. *German Minorities and the Third Reich: Ethnic Germans of East Central Europe between the Wars.* New York, 1980.

Kotowski, Albert S. *Hitlers Bewegung im Urteil der polnischen Nationaldemokratie.* Wiesbaden, 2000.

Krekeler, Norbert. *Revisionsanspruch und geheime Ostpolitik der Weimarer Republik. Die Subventionierung der deutschen Minderheiten in Polen.* Stuttgart, 1973.

Krzoska, Markus. "Nation und Volk als höchste Werte: die deutsche und die polnische Geschichtswissenschaft als Antagonisten zwischen den Weltkriegen." In *Nationalismus und nationale Identität in Ostmitteleuropa im 19. und 20. Jahrhundert*, ed. Bernard Linek and Kai Struve, 297–312. Marburg, 2000.

Lipták, Lubomir. "The Role of the German Minority in Slovakia in the Years of the Second World War." *Studia Historica Slovaca* 1 (1963): 150–178.

Lixfeld, Gisela. "Das 'Ahnenerbe' Heinrich Himmlers und die ideologisch-politische Funktion seiner Volkskunde." In *Völkische Wissenschaft: Gestalten und Tendenzen der deutschen und österreichischen Volkskunde in der ersten Hälfte des 20. Jahrhunderts*, ed. Wolfgang Jacobeit, Hannjost Lixfeld, and Olaf Bockhorn, 217–255. Vienna, 1994.

Longerich, Peter. *Propagandisten im Krieg. Die Presseabteilung des Auswärtigen Amtes unter Ribbentrop.* Munich, 1987.

Lumans, Valdis O. *Himmler's Auxiliaries: The Volksdeutsche Mittelstelle and the German National Minorities of Europe, 1933–1945.* Chapel Hill, 1993.

———. "The Ethnic German Minority of Slovakia and the Third Reich, 1938–1945." *Central European History* 15, no. 3 (1982): 266–297.

Madajczyk, Czeslaw. *Die Okkupationspolitik Nazideutschlands in Polen 1939–1945.* Berlin, 1987.

Mai, Uwe. "*Volkstumspolitik in Lothringen,*" *Heimatbewegung und NS-Kulturpolitik in Hessen, Pfalz, Elsaß und Lothringen: Dokumentation eines Seminars,* ed. Förderverein Projekt Osthofen e. V., in cooperation with the Landeszentrale für politische Bildung Rheinland-Pfalz. Osthofen, 1999.

Massin, Benoît. "Anthropologie und Humangenetik im Nationalsozialismus, oder: Wie schreiben deutsche Wissenschaftler ihre eigene Wissenschaftsgeschichte?" In *Wissenschaftlicher Rassismus: Analysen einer Kontinuität in den Human- und Naturwissenschaften,* ed. Heidrun Kaupen-Haas and Christian Saller, 12–64. Frankfurt am Main, 1999.

Melzer, Rudolf. *Erlebte Geschichte: Rückschau auf ein Menschenalter Karpatendeutschtum, Teil 2. Von 1939 bis 1945 und wie es weiterging.* Stuttgart, 1998.

Michels, Eckard. "Die deutschen Kulturinstitute im besetzten Europa." In *Kultur—Propaganda—Öffentlichkeit. Intentionen deutscher Besatzungspolitik und Reaktionen auf die Okkupation,* ed. Wolfgang Benz, Gerhard Otto, and Annabella Weismann, 11–33. Berlin, 1998.

———. *Das Deutsche Institut in Paris 1940–1944. Ein Beitrag zu den deutsch-französischen Kulturbeziehungen und zur auswärtigen Kulturpolitik des Dritten Reiches.* Stuttgart, 1993.

Mommsen, Hans. "Hans Rothfels." In *Deutsche Historiker,* vol. 9, ed. Hans-Ulrich Wehler, 127–147. Göttingen, 1982.

———. "Der faustische Pakt der Ostforschung mit dem NS-Regime." In *Deutsche Historiker im Nationalsozialismus,* ed. Winfried Schulze and Otto Gerhard Oexle, 265–273. Frankfurt am Main, 1999.

Mühle, Eduard. "Ostforschung und Nationalsozialismus. Kritische Bemerkungen zur aktuellen Forschungsdiskussion." *Zeitschrift für Ostmitteleuropa-Forschung* 50 (2000): 256–275.

Müller, Rolf Dieter. *Hitlers Ostkrieg und die deutsche Siedlungspolitik.* Frankfurt am Main, 1991.

Müller, Valerie. *Karl Theodor v. Inama-Sternegg. Ein Leben für Staat und Wissenschaft.* Innsbruck, 1976.

Neugebauer, Wolfgang. "Hans Rothfels (1891–1976) in seiner Zeit." In *Die Albertus-Universität zu Königsberg und ihre Professoren,* 245–256. Berlin, 1995.

Neumann, Wilhelm. "Martin Wutte und sein Urteil über die nationalsozialistische Slowenenpolitik in Kärnten und Krain aufgrund seiner Denkschrift vom 19. September 1943." *Carinthia I* 176 (1986): 9–40.

Oberkrome, Willi. *Volksgeschichte. Methodische Innovation und völkische Ideologisierung in der deutschen Geschichtswissenschaft 1918–1945.* Göttingen, 1993.

Oesterle, Anka. "Die volkskundlichen Forschungen des 'SS-Ahnenerbes' mit Berücksichtigung der 'Kulturkommission Südtirol.'" In *Südtirol im Auge des Ethnographen,* ed. Reinhard Johler, Ludwig Paulmichl, and Barbara Plankensteiner, 76–89. Vienna and Lana, 1991.

Olszewski, Henryk. "Die deutsche Ostforschung zwischen Wissenschaft und Politik." In *Polen nach dem Kommunismus,* ed. Erwin Oberländer, n.p. Stuttgart, 1993.

Papen, Patricia von. "'Scholarly' Antisemitism During the Third Reich: The Reichsinstitut's Research on the 'Jewish Question' 1935–1945." Ph.D. diss., Columbia University, 1999.

Pfetsch, Frank R. *Datenhandbuch zur Wissenschaftsentwicklung. Die staatliche Finanzierung der Wissenschaft in Deutschland 1850–1975*. 2nd ed. Cologne, 1985.

Regele, Ludwig Walther. "'Eindeutig rein deutsch?' Die Kommission zur Erfassung der Kulturgüter." In *Die Option. Südtirol zwischen Faschismus und Nationalsozialismus*, ed. Klaus Eisterer and Rolf Steininger, 265–274. Innsbruck, 1989.

Reitlinger, Gerald. *The SS: Alibi of a Nation, 1922–1945*. Englewood Cliffs, 1981.

Ritter, Ernst. *Das Deutsche Ausland-Institut in Stuttgart 1917–1945: Ein Beispiel deutscher Volkstumsarbeit zwischen den Weltkriegen*. Wiesbaden, 1976.

Roth, Karl Heinz. "Heydrich's Professor. Historiographie des 'Volkstums' und Massenvernichtungen: Der Fall Hans-Joachim Beyer." In *Geschichtswissenschaft als Legitimationswissenschaft 1918–1945*, ed. Peter Schöttler, 262–342. Frankfurt am Main, 1997.

Rybicka, Anetta. *Instytut Niemieckiej Pracy Wschodniej. Institut für Deutsche Ostarbeit. Kraków 1940–1945*. Warszawa, 1989.

Scherer, Anton. "Die Deutschen in der Untersteiermark, in Ober-Krain und in der Gottschee." In *Die Deutschen zwischen Karpaten und Krain*, ed. Ernst Hochberger, Anton Scherer, and Friedrich Spiegel-Schmidt, 111–156. Munich, 1994.

Schmaltz, Eric J., and Samuel D. Sinner. "The Nazi Ethnographic Research of Georg Leibbrandt and Karl Stumpp in the Ukraine, and Its North American Legacy." *Holocaust and Genocide Studies* 14, no. 1 (Spring 2000): 28–64.

Schmitz-Berning, Cornelia. *Vokabular des Nationalsozialismus*. Berlin and New York, 2000.

Schönwälder, Karen. *Historiker und Politik. Geschichtswissenschaft im Nationalsozialismus*. Frankfurt am Main, 1992.

Schöttler, Peter. "Einleitende Bemerkungen." In *Geschichtsschreibung als Legitimationswissenschaft 1918–1945*, ed. Peter Schöttler, 7–30. Frankfurt am Main, 1997.

———. "Von der rheinischen Landesgeschichte zur nazistischen Volksgeschichte oder Die 'unhörbare Stimme des Blutes.'" In *Deutsche Historiker im Nationalsozialismus*, ed. Winfried Schulze and Otto Gerhard Oexle, 89–113. Frankfurt am Main, 1999.

———. "Eine Art 'Generalplan West.' Die Stuckart-Denkschrift vom 14. Juli 1940 und die Planungen für eine neue deutsch-französische Grenze im Zweiten Weltkrieg." *Sozial.Geschichte* 18, no. 3 (2003): 83–131.

Schulze, Winfried. *Deutsche Geschichtswissenschaft nach 1945*. Munich, 1993.

Schulze, Winfried, and Otto Gerhard Oexle, eds. *Deutsche Historiker im Nationalsozialismus*. Frankfurt am Main, 1999.

Schwabe, Klaus, ed. *Gerhard Ritter, ein politischer Historiker in seinen Briefen*. Boppart am Rhein, 1984.

Schwinn, Peter. "'SS-Ahnenerbe' und 'Volkstumsarbeit' in Südtirol 1940–1943." In *Südtirol im Auge des Ethnographen*, ed. Reinhard Johler, Ludwig Paulmichl, and Barbara Plankensteiner, 91–104. Vienna and Lana, 1991.

Serejski, Marian H. *Zarys historii historiografii polskiej*. Vols. 1–2. Łódź, 1954–1956.

Siebert, Erich. *Die Rolle der Kultur- und Wissenschaftspolitik bei der Expansion des deutschen Imperialismus nach Bulgarien, Jugoslawien, Rumänien und Ungarn in den Jahren 1938–1944. Mit einem Blick auf die vom westdeutschen Imperialismus wiederaufgenommene auswärtige Kulturpolitik*. Ph.D. diss., Humboldt-University of Berlin [East], 1971.

Simpson, Christopher. *Science of Coercion: Communication Research and Psychological Warfare 1945–1960*. New York and Oxford, 1994.

Sinner, Samuel D. *The Open Wound: The Genocide of German Ethnic Minorities in Russia and the Soviet Union, 1915–1949 and Beyond/Der Genozid an Rußlanddeutschen 1915–1949*. Fargo, N.D., 2000.

Škerl, France. "Nacistične deportacije Slovencev v letu 1941." *Zgodovinski časopis* 6–7 (1952/53): 768–797.

Smit, Jan G. *Neubildung deutschen Bauerntums. Innere Kolonisation im Dritten Reich. Fallstudien Schleswig-Holstein*. Kassel, 1983.

Söllner, Alphons, ed. *Zur Archäologie der Demokratie in Deutschland. Analysen politischer Emigranten im amerikanischen Geheimdienst: 1943–1945.* Vol. 1. Frankfurt am Main, 1982.

Stobiecki, Rafał. "Between Continuity and Discontinuity: A Few Comments on the Post-war Development of Polish Historical Research." *Zeitschrift für Ostmitteleuropa-Forschung* 50 (2001): 214–229.

Stuhlpfarrer, Karl. *Die Operationszonen 'Alpenvorland' und 'Adriatisches Küstenland' 1943–1945.* Vienna, 1969.

Stuhlpfarrer, Karl, and Leopold Steurer. "Die Ossa in Österreich." In *Vom Justizpalast zum Heldenplatz. Studien und Dokumentationen 1927 bis 1938,* ed. Ludwig Jedlicka and Rudolf Neck, 35–64. Vienna, 1975.

Suppan, Arnold, ed. *Deutsche Geschichte im Osten Europas: Zwischen Adria und Karawanken.* Berlin, 1998.

Tilitzki, Christian. "Die Vortragsreisen Carl Schmitts während des Zweiten Weltkrieges." *Schmittiana* 6 (1998): 191–270.

Tomczak, Maria. "Polska myśl zachodnia." In *Polacy wobec Niemców. Z dziejów kultury politycznej Polski 1945–1989,* ed. Anna Wolff-Powęska, n.p. Poznań, 1993.

Toynbee, Arnold Joseph, and Veronica Marjorie Toynbee, eds. *Hitler's Europe.* London, New York, and Toronto, 1954.

Trampler, Kurt. "Deutsche Grenzen." *Zeitschrift für Geopolitik* 11 (1954): 15–71.

Unfug, Douglas A. "Comment: Hans Rothfels." *Paths of Continuity: Central European Historiography from the 1930s to the 1950s,* ed. Hartmut Lehmann and James van Horn Melton, 137–154. Cambridge and New York, 1994.

Volkmann, Hans-Erich. "Historiker aus politischer Leidenschaft. Hermann Aubin als Volksgeschichts-, Kulturboden- und Ostforscher" *Zeitschrift für Geschichtswissenschaft* 49, no. 1 (2001): 32–49.

Walker, Mark. *Nazi Science: Myth, Truth, and the German Atomic Bomb.* New York and London, 1995.

Wasser, Bruno. *Himmlers Raumplanung im Osten. Der Generalplan Ost in Polen 1940–1944.* Basel, Berlin, and Boston, 1993.

Weber, Wolfgang. "Völkische Tendenzen in der Geschichtswissenschaft." In *Handbuch zur "Völkischen Bewegung" 1871–1918,* ed. Uwe Puschner, Walter Schmitz, and Justus H. Ulbricht, 834–858. Munich, 1996.

Wedekind, Michael. *Nationalsozialistische Besatzungs- und Annexionspolitik in Norditalien 1943 bis 1945: Die Operationszonen 'Alpenvorland' und 'Adriatisches Küstenland.'* Munich, 2003.

———. "Tra integrazione e disgregazione: l'occupazione tedesca nelle "zone d'operazione' delle Prealpi e del Litorale Adriatico 1943–1945." *Annali dell'Istituto storico italo-germanico in Trento* 25 (1999): 239–272.

———. "'Völkische Grenzlandwissenschaft' in Tirol (1918–1945). Vom wissenschaftlichen 'Abwehrkampf' zur Flankierung der NS-Expansionspolitik." *Geschichte und Region/ Storia e regione* 5 (1996): 227–265.

Wehler, Hans-Ulrich. *Historisches Denken am Ende des 20. Jahrhunderts. 1945–2000.* Göttingen, 2001.

———. "Historiker sollten auch politisch zu den Positionen stehen, die sie in der Wissenschaft vertreten." In *Versäumte Fragen. Deutsche Historiker im Schatten des Nationalsozialismus,* ed. Rüdiger Hohls and Konrad Jarausch, 240–266. Stuttgart and Munich, 2000.

———. "Nationalsozialismus und Historiker." In *Deutsche Historiker im Nationalsozialismus,* ed. Winfried Schulze and Otto Gerhard Oexle, 306–339. Frankfurt am Main, 1999.

———. *Nationalitätenpolitik in Jugoslawien: Die deutsche Minderheit 1918–1978.* Göttingen, 1980.

Weiß, Hermann, ed. *Biographisches Lexikon zum Dritten Reich.* 2nd ed. Frankfurt am Main, 1998.

Weiß, Volkmar, and Katja Münchow. *Ortsfamilienbücher mit Standort Leipzig in Deutscher Bücherei und Deutscher Zentralstelle für Genealogie.* 2nd ed. Neustadt and Aisch, 1998.

Wendt, Bernd-Jürgen. *Großdeutschland: Außenpolitik und Kriegsvorbereitung des Hitler-Regimes*. 2nd ed. Munich, 1993.

Wilhelm, Cornelia. *Bewegung oder Verein? Nationalsozialistische Volkstumspolitik in den USA*. Stuttgart, 1998.

Wilson, Keith, ed. *Forging the Collective Memory: Government and International Historians Through Two World Wars*. Providence, R.I., and Oxford, 1996.

Winkler, Heinrich August. "Geschichtswissenschaft oder Geschichtsklitterung. Ingo Haar und Hans Rothfels. Eine Erwiderung." *Vierteljahrshefte für Zeitgeschichte* 50 (2002): 636–652.

———. "Hans Rothfels—ein Lobredner Hitlers? Quellenkritische Bemerkungen zu Ingo Haars Buch "Historiker im Nationalsozialismus.'" *Vierteljahrshefte für Zeitgeschichte* 49 (2001): 643–652.

Wolf, Ursula. *Litteris et Patriae. Das Janusgesicht der Historie*. Stuttgart, 1996.

Wolfanger, Dieter. *Die nationalsozialistische Politik in Lothringen (1940–1945)*. Saarbrücken, 1976.

———. "Populist und Machtpolitiker: Josef Bürckel: Vom Gauleiter der Pfalz zum Chef der Zivilverwaltung in Lothringen." In *Die Pfalz unterm Hakenkreuz: Eine deutsche Provinz während der nationalsozialistischen Terrorherrschaft*, ed. Gerhard Nestler and Hannes Ziegler, n.p. Landau, 1993.

Wrzesiński, Wojciech, ed. *1W stronę Odry i Bałtyku. Wybór źródeł 1795–1950*. Vols. 1–4. Wrocław, 1990/91.

Yoder, Don. "Die Pennsylvania-Deutschen: Eine dreihundertjährige Identitätskrise." In *Amerika und die Deutschen: Bestandsaufnahme einer 300jährigen Geschichte*, ed. Frank Trommler. Opladen, 1986.

Zernack, Klaus. "Schwerpunkte und Entwicklungslinien der polnischen Geschichtswissenschaft nach 1945." *Historische Zeitschrift*. Sonderheft 5. Munich, 1973.

Zierold, Kurt. *Forschungsförderung in drei Epochen. Deutsche Forschungsgemeinschaft. Geschichte—Arbeitsweise—Kommentar*. Wiesbaden, 1968.

CONTRIBUTORS

✦ ✦ ✦

Viorel Achim, Ph.D., is a Senior Researcher with the Nicolae Iorga Institute of History, in Bucharest, Romania. His main research fields include population policy in Romania during World War II and the history of the Gypsies in Southeastern Europe. He is the author of *The Gypsies in the History of Romania* (Bucharest, 1998) (with a Hungarian translation in 2001, a Bulgarian translation in 2002, and an English translation forthcoming). He has received fellowships from the Center for Advanced Central European Studies of the Europa-Universität Viadrina Frankfurt (Oder), Germany (1998/99), and the Center for Advanced Holocaust Studies of the United States Holocaust Memorial Museum in Washington, D.C. (2000, 2001).

Hans Derks received his Ph.D. in Sociology and History. He is a lecturer at several universities in the Netherlands and other countries. He gained crucial experience in sustainable development planning in African and South American countries. He specializes in ancient Greek history, modern European history, and the sociology of Max Weber.

Michael Fahlbusch received his Ph.D. in 1993 in Geography and History of Science (*Stiftung für deutsche Volks- und Kulturbodenforschung in Leipzig 1920–1931*) at Osnabrück. He has specialized in network analysis and ethnic studies and ethnic policy in the Third Reich. From 1995 to 1997, he headed a DFG research project at the University of Bonn, and in 1999 his monograph, *Wissenschaft im Dienst der nationalsozialistischen Politik? Die "Volksdeutschen Forschungsgemeinschaften" von 1931–1945,* was published. His forthcoming publication, in collaboration with Ingo Haar, is titled *Handbuch der völkischen Wissenschaften in Deutschland von 1920 bis 1960.*

Wolfgang Freund, historian, teaches nineteenth-century history in Nancy (France) at the Franco-German basic studies of the Institut d'Etudes Politiques—Sciences Po de Paris. His Ph.D. thesis, a regional history of sciences in German fascism, "Volk, Reich und Westgrenze: Wissenschaften und Politik in der Pfalz, im Saarland und im annektierten Lothringen 1925–1945" (People, Reich and Western Border: Sciences and Politics in

Palatinate, in the Saarland and in the Annexed Lorraine 1925–1945), will soon be published.

Ingo Haar received his Ph.D. in 1998 in History (*Historiker im National- sozialismus: Deutsche Geschichtswissenschaft und Volkstumskampf im Osten*) at Halle. Since 2001, he has been a contributor to the DFG-Schwerpunkt- programm *Ursprünge, Arten und Folgen des Konstrukts "Bevölkerung" vor, im und nach dem "Dritten Reich"* (Demography in the German Reich and Federal Republic of Germany).

Frank-Rutger Hausmann is a Professor of Romance Philology and Liter- ature in Freiburg, Germany. From 1982 to 1992, he was a professor at the Aachen Technical University. He specializes in the research fields of medieval literature and the Renaissance in Italy and France. He has sev- eral publications on scientific history in Third Reich.

Eric A. Kurlander received his Ph.D. from Harvard University in 2001. He is Assistant Professor of Modern European History at Stetson University in DeLand, Florida. He is the author of "The Rise of Völkisch Nationalism and the Decline of German Liberalism: A Comparison of Schleswig-Holstein and Silesian Political Cultures 1912–1924" (*European Review of History*), "Multicultural and Assimilationist Models of Ethnopolitical Integration in the Context of the German Nordmark, 1890–1933" (*The Global Review of Ethnopolitics*), and "Nationalism, Ethnic Preoccupation and the Decline of German Liberalism: A Silesian Case Study, 1898– 1933" (*The Historian*), all in 2002. He is currently working on a book based on his dissertation, "The Price of Exclusion: Ethnic Preoccupation and the Decline of German Liber- alism 1898–1933," which examines the long-term effects of ethnic (*völkisch*) nationalism on the dissolution of the German liberal parties in Imperial and Weimar Germany.

Christof Morrissey is a Ph.D. candidate at the University of Virginia, where he is currently completing his dissertation, "National Socialism and Dissent among the Ethnic Germans of Slovakia and Croatia, 1938–1945." His publications include "Das Institut für Heimatforschung in Käsmark (Slowakei) 1941–1944," in *Südostforschung im Schatten des Dritten Reiches: Institutionen—Inhalte—Personen* (2004) and "Die Karpatendeutschen aus der Slowakei, kollektive Erinnerung und Integration in der Bundesrepub- lik Deutschland, 1945-1975" (forthcoming). His research interests include National Socialism and the German minorities, interethnic relations in Southeastern Europe, and the history of ethnic German generations.

Alexander Pinwinkler received his Ph.D. in Modern History (*Wilhelm Wink- ler (1884–1984)—eine Biographie. Zur Geschichte der Statistik und Demographie in Österreich und Deutschland*) from the University of Salzburg in 2001. Since 2001, he has been a contributor to the DFG-Schwerpunktprogramm

Ursprünge, Arten und Folgen des Konstrukts "Bevölkerung" vor, im und nach dem "Dritten Reich" (Demography in the German Reich and Federal Republic of Germany).

Jan M. Piskorski is Professor of European History at the University of Szczecin in Poland, and is the chairman of the publishing house of the Poznań Society for the Advancement of the Arts and Sciences. He has been a visiting professor at the universities of Mainz and Halle. Among his most recent publications are *"Deutsche Ostforschung" und "polnische Westforschung" im Spannungsfeld von Wissenschaft und Politik. Disziplinen im Vergleich* (2002, co-edited with Jörg Hackmann and Rudolf Jaworski) and *Historiographical Approaches to Medieval Colonization of East Central Europe: A Comparative Analysis Against the Background of Other European Inter-ethnic Colonization Processes in the Middle Ages* (2002).

Karl Heinz Roth, M.D. and Ph.D., is a collaborator with the Bremen-based foundation Stiftung für Sozialgeschichte des 20. Jahrhunderts. He is the co-editor of the review *Zeitschrift Sozial.Geschichte—Zeitschrift für historische Analyse des 20. und 21. Jahrhunderts.* He has published several books and articles on the social, economic, and scientific history of the twentieth century.

Eric J. Schmaltz received his Ph.D. in History at the University of Nebraska-Lincoln (UNL) in 2002. He has taught a number of courses at UNL and has also worked for the Germans from Russia Heritage Collection at the North Dakota State University Libraries. Specializing in ethnic and nationality studies, he has contributed articles to publications such as *Journal of Genocide Research, Holocaust and Genocide Studies,* and *Nationalities Papers.* North Dakota State University Libraries will soon publish his monograph, *An Expanded Bibliography and Reference Guide for the Former Soviet Union's Germans: Issues of Ethnic Autonomy, Group Repression, Cultural Assimilation and Mass Emigration in the Twentieth Century and Beyond,* the most extensive English-language bibliography to appear on the topic.

Samuel D. Sinner is an archivist at the University of Nebraska-Lincoln (UNL) Special Collections Archives. He received his Ph.D. in Modern Languages and Literatures from UNL in 2002. A librarian and archivist for several years, he is also the author of historical essays, literary anthologies, and translations. His most recent monograph is the dual-language volume *The Open Wound: The Genocide of German Ethnic Minorities in Russia and the Soviet Union, 1915–1949 and Beyond/Der Genozid an Russlanddeutschen 1915–1949* (2000). His works on Russian ethnic literature and genocide studies, as well as a number of collections of his creative fiction and poetry, will appear in Russia, Germany, Great Britain, and the United States.

Michael Wedekind received his Ph.D. in 1996. His dissertation, *German Occupation and Annexationist Policy in Northern Italy 1943–1945,* was published in 2003. He has done post-doctoral studies at the University of Münster with a DFG research project on Italian and German nationalism in late nineteenth-century Tyrol. He has been a guest professor at the universities of Trento and Bucharest, and is the author of several studies on nationalism in the Habsburg Empire and its successor states, as well as on the National Socialist occupation regime in Italy. He is the co-author and co-editor of a study (2002) on mountaineering as a social practice of European bourgeoisies in the nineteenth and twentieth centuries that won the Italian Premio ITAS in 2001. He is currently directing a research project on European bourgeoisies at the University of Trento.

SUBJECT INDEX

✦ ✦ ✦

Weimar Republic, vii, ix, x, xv, 2, 6, 8,
30–32, 86–87, 217, 222, 239–240, 253
West German Research Society (Westdeutsche Forschungsgemeinschaft,
WFG), xii, 31, 41, 143, 177, 179–180, 191
West Prussian Historical Society, 87–88
Westforscher/Westforschung, xiii–xv, 175–
183, 185–189, 191–193, 261
Working Group of West German Research
on Region and People (Arbeitsgemeinschaft für westdeutsche Landes- und
Volksforschung, AWLV), 177, 191
World War I, xiv, 3, 7, 32, 54, 72, 87, 112,
118, 123, 156, 160, 177, 184, 204, 217,
250–251, 261–262

World War II, xii, xiv, 29, 33, 37, 43, 52, 54,
57, 74, 77, 88, 139–140, 157–160, 167,
175, 177, 179, 207–208, 214, 248, 251,
265–266

Young Conservatives, 31–32
Yugoslavian Institute of Statistics and
Geography, Belgrade, 148

Zeitschrift für Ostforschung, 89, 96
Zentrum für Niederlande Studien, 183

Names Index

✦ ✦ ✦